150 Leading Cases

Conflict of Laws

Dr Charles Wild
BSc (Lond), LLM, PhD (Sheff), Head of the Centre for International Law, University of Hertfordshire

Old Bailey Press

OLD BAILEY PRESS
at Holborn College, Woolwich Road,
Charlton, London, SE7 8LN

First edition 2003

ISBN 1 85836 420 5

British Library Cataloguing-in-Publication

A catalogue record for this book is available from the British Library.

Printed and bound in Great Britain

Contents

Acknowledgements

Extracts from judgments and decisions of the European Court of Justice and the European Court of Human Rights have been reproduced, free of charge, with the kind permission of the European Court of Justice, the European Court of Human Rights and European Law Centre. Particular thanks are extended to Lloyd's Law Reports, published by Informa Professional, a trading division of Informa UK Limited, Informa House, 30–32 Mortimer Street, London, W1W 7RE (Web: www.informalaw.com) for their kind permission to reproduce extracts from the Lloyd's Law Reports.

The publishers and author would like to thank the Incorporated Council of Law Reporting for England and Wales for kind permission to reproduce extracts from the Weekly Law Reports, and Butterworths for their kind permission to reproduce extracts from the All England Law Reports.

Preface

Old Bailey Press casebooks are intended as companion volumes to the textbooks but they also comprise invaluable reference tools in themselves. Their aim is to supplement and enhance a student's understanding and interpretation of a particular area of law and provide essential background reading. Companion Revision WorkBooks and Statutes are also published.

The *Conflict of Laws* casebook is designed for use by undergraduates who are studying the Conflict of Laws or Private International Law (to give the subject its other common name) in their course. It will also be useful to students on other courses who have chosen to study the Conflict of Laws.

This text includes the most relevant cases relating to the Contracts (Applicable Law) Act 1990 (the Rome Convention) as well as the Private International Law (Miscellaneous Provisions) Act 1995.

The Brussels Convention of 1968 (superseded in March 2002 by EU Council Regulation 44/2001) continues to have a profound influence on the law in this area. Many of the newer cases included relate to the Convention and a mastery of the Convention (and Regulation) is essential to an understanding of this subject. Other aspects of this casebook have been expanded for this edition. These include: domicile, marriage, divorce and habitual residence, as well as a more detailed examination of the area of forum non conveniens.

This edition does not include materials not available to the author on or before June 2003.

Table of Cases

Cases in bold type are the leading cases. Page numbers in bold indicate the main references to them.

1 Introduction

The purpose of this book

What are casebooks for? Many students, I believe, would give the wrong answer to this question, so it will be wise to begin by setting out the intended purpose of this book.

This book is intended to deepen the student-reader's understanding of the law, already obtained from reading a textbook or attending lectures on the subject. The law is far more than a dry catalogue of rules contained in a textbook which can be learnt by heart. It is a living system that is applied in a wide variety of factual situations: the subtleties of the application of those rules cannot be understod unless perceived in the concrete complexity of a decided case. Thus observing the operation of the law by reading some of the leading cases is most important for the student.

This casebook contains a selection of the leading cases on the subject. Reference to this book should save students a lot of time that would otherwise by spent in the law library searching for the report of a particular case.

However, it is most important to stress that it is not a substitute for the law library. There are two good reasons for this: this is simply one person's selection of the leading cases on the subject. It is not the final word on what is important in the conflict of laws. And no good student would allow his knowledge of the conflict of laws to be limited by one person's view of which the most important cases are. This casebook may save time that would otherwise by spent searching for obscure reports in the law library, but the good student will use that time saved by reading other cases not included here, hopefully stimulated by what he has read.

The second reason why this book is not a substitute for the law library lies in the fact that the law is constantly developing and the judges are continually deciding cases and delivering fresh judgements that will change the law. Thus the student who relies upon this book exclusively will have an out of date understanding of the law. This would be a pity, especially since examiners tend to have the most recent developments in the law in mind when they set examination papers.

Using this book

This book is designed to be used in conjunction with the Old Bailey Press textbook on the conflict of laws. Thus, in general, each chapter of the casebook relates closely to a chapter in the textbook. Thus referring from the textbook to the casebook and vice versa should be straightforward and frequent.

Ideally, the book should be used in this manner: the relevant pages of the textbook should be read; and then the student should read the relevant cases in the casebook. Thereafter, the student will have a far better knowledge of the law, but will also have a range of questions prompted by reading the cases. Some of these may be able to be answered by consulting the textbook again, but the more advanced or novel problems will require the student to read further cases or learned articles referred to in either textbook or the casebook.

It should be noted, however, that students without the *Conflict of Laws* textbook at their side will still find much useful material in this casebook.

2 Preliminary Topics

The proof of foreign law

Lazard Brothers & Co v *Midland Bank Ltd* [1933] AC 289 House of Lords (Lords Buckmaster, Blanesburgh, Warrington, Russell and Wright)

- *Foreign law is a question of fact to be proved by expert evidence*

Facts

Since before the Russian revolution in 1917, Lazard Brothers were owed money by the Banque Industrielle de Moscou (the Moscow Bank), a Russian bank. In 1930 Lazard Brothers obtained a default judgment against the bank. They could not enforce this judgment in Russia so they sought to attach the debts owed by the Midland Bank to the Moscow Bank. However, various decrees made by the Government of Russia between 1917 and 1921 purported to nationalise and liquidate all banks in Russia; and the question was whether the Moscow Bank had been liquidated at the time the default judgment was obtained. If it did not exist at that time, the default judgment was null and void and had to be set aside.

Held

Whether the Moscow Bank existed as a juristic person or not was a matter for Soviet law; and that was a question of fact to be proved by qualified experts in the foreign law.

Lord Wright:

> 'The Industrial Bank was a corporation established by an Act of the Tsar; but the governing authority in Russia, as recognised in the English Courts, is now and has been since October, 1917, the Soviet State. Soviet law is accordingly the governing law from the same date in virtue of the recognition de facto in 1921 and de jure in 1924 by this country of the Soviet State as the sovereign power in Russia. The effect of such recognition is retroactive and dates back to the original establishment of Soviet rule which was in the 1917 October Revolution, as was held by the Court of Appeal in *Aksionairnoye Obschestvo A M Luther* v *James Sagor & Co* [1921] 3 KB 532. The question, therefore, is whether by Soviet law the Industrial Bank was at the date of the issue of the writ in this action, that is on October 27, 1930, an existing juristic person. What the Russian Soviet law is in that respect is a question of fact, of which the English Court cannot take judicial cognizance, even though the foreign law has already been proved before it in another case. The court must act upon the evidence before it in the actual case. The recent enactment, s102 of the Supreme Court of Judicature (Consolidation) Act 1925, which provides that this question of fact must be decided by the judge alone instead of by the jury, if there be a jury, expressly treats the question as depending on the evidence given with respect to the foreign law. No earlier decision of the Court can relieve the judge of the duty of deciding the question on the actual evidence given in the particular case. On what evidence of the foreign law a Court can act has been often discussed. The evidence it is clear must be that of qualified experts in the foreign law. If the law is contained in a code or written form, the question is not as to the language of the written law, but what the law is as shown by its exposition, interpretation and adjudication: so in effect it was laid down by Coleridge J in *Baron De Bode's*

Case (1845) 8 QB 208, 266; in the *Sussex Peerage Case* (1844) 11 Cl & F 85, 116, Lord Denman stated his opinion to the same effect as he had done in *Baron De Bode's Case*. He said that if there be a conflict of evidence of the experts, "you (the judge) must decide as well as you can on the conflicting testimony, but you must take the evidence from the witnesses." Hence the Court is not entitled to construe a foreign code itself: it has not "organs to know and to deal with the text of that law" (as was said by Lord Brougham in the *Sussex Peerage Case*). The text of the foreign law if put in evidence by the experts may be considered, if at all, only as part of the evidence and as a help to decide between conflicting expert testimony.

Hence in the present case it is necessary to consider the testimony of the two principal legal witnesses in the matter in order to ascertain the Soviet law. The one is Mr Samuel Dobrin, who had been a member of the Russian Bar in Tsarist days, but remained in Russia till 1925, practising as a lawyer in Soviet Russia, and since then acting in this country as legal adviser on Soviet law to various Soviet institutions; he was called by the respondents. The other is Mr S L Konkevitch, called by the appellants, who also had practised as a barrister in the Tsarist Courts, but had remained in Russia till 1919 practising in Soviet law, and as legal adviser to Soviet institutions. The respondents also called Mr Alexander Hoelfern, who had practised as a lawyer in Russia in Tsarist times, but had left Russia in December 1918. I do not attach the same weight to his evidence, because, though his qualifications and standing as a Tsarist lawyer are very high, he has not had, in my judgment, the same practical experience in regard to Soviet law.'

Comment

Note that today, if the foreign law had already been proved before the English courts in another case, the court might be able to take notice of that in terms of s4 of the Civil Evidence Act 1972. Note further that the modern counterpart to s102 of the Supreme Court of Judicature (Consolidation) Act 1925 is s69(5) of the Supreme Court Act 1981.

The exclusion of foreign law

Attorney-General of New Zealand v *Ortiz* [1982] 3 All ER 432 Court of Appeal (Lord Denning MR, Ackner and O'Connor LJJ)

• *English courts will not enforce foreign public laws*

Facts

A Maori tribesman found an ancient Maori carving and sold it to a dealer in primitive works of art for NZ $6,000. The dealer exported the carving from New Zealand in contravention of s12(2) of the Historic Articles Act 1962, which provided that historic articles exported from New Zealand without permission 'shall be forefeited to Her Majesty'. The dealer sold the carving to Ortiz for US $65,000. The Attorney-General of New Zealand brought an action in England claiming delivery up of the carving and damages for its detention. The defence was that the New Zealand statute was a foreign penal, revenue or public law.

Held

The defendant's appeal was allowed. The courts would not enforce foreign public laws.

Lord Denning MR:

> 'This suit by a foreign state to enforce its laws is to be distinguished altogether from a suit between private firms or individuals which raises a question as to whether a contract has been broken by one or the other or whether a wrong has been done by one to the other. In such a suit our courts will often recognise the existence of the laws of a foreign state. We will recognise the foreign law so much that we will refuse to enforce a contract which is in breach of the laws of

the foreign state: see the prohibition case of *Foster* v *Driscoll* [1929] 1 KB 470, and the jute case of *Regazzoni* v *Sethia* [1958] AC 301.

This present case is different. It is a suit by a foreign state brought in the English courts here to enforce its laws. No one has ever doubted that our courts will not entertain a suit brought by a foreign sovereign, directly or indirectly, to enforce the penal or revenue laws of that foreign state. We do not sit to collect taxes for another country or to inflict punishments for it. Now the question arises whether this rule extends to "other public laws". Dicey & Morris say it does. I agree with them. The term "other public laws" is very uncertain. But so are the terms "penal" and "revenue". The meaning of "penal" was discussed in *Huntington* v *Attrill* [1893] AC 150 and *Loucks* v *Standard Oil Co of New York* (1918) 224 NY 99. The meaning of "'revenue" was discussed in *Government of India* v *Taylor* [1955] AC 491. But what are "other public laws?" I think they are laws, which are eiusdem generis with "penal" or "revenue" laws.

Then what is the genus? Or, in English, what is the general concept which embraces "penal" and "revenue" laws and others like them? It is to be found, I think, by going back to the classification of acts taken in international law. One class comprises those acts which are done by a sovereign "jure imperii", that is, by virtue of his sovereign authority. The others are those which are done by him "jure gestionis", that is, which obtain their validity by virtue of his performance of them. The application of this distinction to our present problem was well drawn by Dr F A Mann 28 years ago in an article "Prerogative Rights of Foreign States and the Conflict of Laws".

Applied to our present problem the class of laws which will be enforced are those laws which are an exercise by the sovereign government of its sovereign authority over property within its territory or over its subjects wherever they may be. But other laws will not be enforced. By international law every sovereign state has no sovereignty beyond its own frontiers. The courts of other countries will not allow it to go beyond the bounds. They will not enforce any of its laws which purport to exercise sovereignty beyond the limits of its authority.

If this be right, we come to the question: what is meant by the "exercise of sovereign authority?" It is a term which we will have to grapple with, sooner or later. It comes much into the cases on sovereign immunity and into the State Immunity Act 1978: see ss3(3)(c) and 14(2)(a). It was much discussed recently in *I Congress del Partido* [1981] 2 All ER 1064 and by Hazel Fox "State Immunity: The House of Lords' Decision in *I Congreso de Partido*" in the Law Quarterly Review. It can provoke much difference of opinion as is shown by the differences amongst the Law Lords on the facts of that very case. But, difficult as it is, it must be tackled.

I suggest that the first thing in such a case as the present is to determine which is the relevant act. Then to decide whether it is of a sovereign character or a non-sovereign character. Finally, to ask whether it was exercised within the territory of the sovereign state – which is legitimate – or beyond it – which is illegitimate …

Returning to our present case, I am of the opinion that if any country should have legislation prohibiting the export of works of art, and providing for the automatic forfeiture of them to the state should they be exported, then that falls into the category of "public laws" which will not be enforced by the courts of the country to which it is exported, or any other country, because it is an act done in the exercise of sovereign authority which will not be enforced outside its own territory.'

***Banco de Vizcaya* v *Don Alfonso de Borbon y Austria* [1935] 1 KB 140 King's Bench Division (Lawrence J)**

- *Foreign penal law is unenforceable in this country*

Facts

In 1923 the Banco de Vizcaya, the plaintiff, acting as agent of the then King of Spain, the defendant, had deposited with the Westminster Bank in London certain bonds and shares. In 1931 the government of the Spanish Republic issued a number of decrees declaring the King guilty of high treason and all his property forfeited to the state. Furthermore, Spanish banks having the property of the ex-King on deposit were ordered to deliver the property to the Spanish Treasury. The question for decision was whether the Westminster Bank should deliver the shares and bonds to the original depositor (the Banco de Vizcaya) or to the ex-King.

Held

The Banco de Vizcaya were not asserting their own right at all, but that of the Spanish state; thus a judgment in their favour would involve the execution of a foreign penal law. The plaintiff's claim, therefore, failed.

Lawrence J:

> 'In my judgment, the substance of the right sought to be enforced by the plaintiffs is the delivery to them of the securities in question and the enforcement of this right will directly or indirectly involve the execution of what are undoubtedly and admittedly penal laws of the Spanish Republic. The plaintiffs' whole case is that they are bound by virtue of the decrees to hand over the securities to the Spanish Government in defiance of the mandate of the defendant, and, that being so, it seems to be unarguable that the enforcement of the plaintiffs' right will not directly or indirectly involve the execution of the decrees. It was contended on behalf of the plaintiffs that, though the decrees may be penal, the plaintiffs' claim is not a penal action, because they are not asserting the right of the Spanish Government, but their own contractual right to the securities as against the Westminster Bank. I am unable to accept this contention. The plaintiffs are not asserting their contractual rights as they originally existed, but as altered by the decrees of the Spanish Republic. Nor are they in substance asserting their own rights at all, but the rights of the Spanish Republic.
>
> It is true, as is pointed out in *Huntington* v *Attrill* [1893] AC 150, 156, that some actions for penalties are not penal actions within the meaning of the above mentioned international rule – where, for instance, the penalties are not exigible by the State in the interest of the community, but by private persons in their own interest. But in the present case the penalty imposed is seizure by the State for its own benefit of all the defendant's properties, rights, and grounds of action, and this penalty is imposed in terms for high treason, and the only way in which the plaintiffs are able to assert their claim that they are entitled as against the defendant is by virtue of these decrees, and they are compelled to admit that they have no personal right or title to the property in the securities. In the words of Lord Loughborough in *Folliott* v *Ogden* (1789) 1 H Bl 124, 135:
>
> > "The penal laws of foreign countries are strictly local, and affect nothing more than they can reach and can be seized by virtue of their authority; a fugitive who passes hither, comes with all his transitory rights; he may recover money held for his use, stock, obligations and the like; and cannot be affected in this country, by proceedings against him in that which he has left, beyond the limits of which such proceedings do not extend."
>
> These words have frequently been cited with approval, and in my judgment they are directly applicable to the present case. I therefore hold that HM Don Alfonso and not the plaintiffs is entitled to the securities in question.'

Dynamit Actien-Gesellschaft* v *Rio Tinto Co [1918] AC 260 House of Lords (Lords Dunedin, Atkinson, Parker and Sumner)

• *English courts will refuse to enforce contracts that are contrary to public policy – trading with the enemy*

Facts

An English company, Rio Tinto, which owned cupreous ore mines in Spain had agreed before the outbreak of the first World War to sell ore from the mines to a number of German companies. Some of the contracts with the German companies were governed by English law and some were, apparently, governed by German law. A clause in the contracts appeared, on some interpretations, to suspend the contracts in the event of war breaking out.

Held

Irrespective of whether the contracts were governed by English or German law, and irrespective of the true meaning of the clause in question, the outbreak of war had rendered the contracts void.

Lord Sumner:

> 'In the abstract, discharge of a contract by reason of the outbreak of war between the countries to which the parties respectively belong should be effected simply by operation of law independently of their arrangements. The rule sets the public welfare above private bargain. It does so for the safety of the State in the twofold aspect of enhancing the nation's resources and crippling those of the enemy. To hold that the parties may be allowed to make their own arrangements for attaining these ends and to set their private judgment, not untinged by considerations of their future interest, above the prescriptions of the public law would be anomalous. To say that for the purpose of preventing such intercourse the law generally determines stipulations which involve commercial intercourse between enemies, but when the parties have agreed not to hold any such intercourse is content to leave it to them, would indeed be rash. True, there is the criminal law against holding commercial intercourse with the enemy, but the offence is one not always easy to detect. In a matter of national safety the State cannot surely rely on the bare integrity and good faith of persons whose commercial interest may so strongly conflict with their public duty. …
>
> My Lords, in my opinion discharge by operation of law upon the outbreak of war operates upon trading contracts as a class by reason of their common characteristic of international intercourse, and is not prevented by special stipulations between the parties. It is not necessary for present purposes to define the term "trading" or the word "enemy". The class affected is not such contracts as contemplate a continuance of trading during war, but trading contracts as such, which are in being as mutually executory contracts at the outbreak of war, and would in ordinary course and circumstances import commercial intercourse. "War", says Lord Lindley in *Janson's Case* [1902] AC 509, " … prohibits all trading with the enemy except with the Royal licence, and dissolves all contracts which involve such trading." As the present case is one of such executory trading, I think the rule that such contracts are discharged upon the outbreak of war must apply.'

Emery's Investment Trusts, Re, Emery* v *Emery [1959] 1 Ch 410 Chancery Division (Wynn-Parry J)

• *A foreign revenue law will not be directly enforced in England*

Facts

The plaintiff (the husband) was a British subject married to an American citizen (the wife). He bought certain Amercian securities but registered them in the name of his wife and no mention was made of his beneficial interest in them in order to avoid payment of certain American taxes which as an alien he would have been obliged to pay. When the marriage broke down the wife sold the securities and refused the husband any share in the proceeds. He sought inter alia a declaration that he had a fifty per cent interest in the securities or the proceeds of their sale. He failed. The registration of the securities in his wife's name raised a presumption that he intended to benefit the wife absolutely (this is the presumption of advancement); and this presumption could not be rebutted by showing that the purpose of so registering the securities was to evade the payment of the American tax.

Held

Wynn-Parry J:

'I do not propose to traverse the evidence in any detail. It is enough to say that the wife, who was clearly a witness of the truth, was not able to help me very much. The husband, on the other hand, satisfied me by his evidence that his intention was that the beneficial interest should be shared, and there are various indications to support that, such as the retention of control and the payment of the dividends into the joint account. But matters such as the retention of control and the payment into the joint account cannot be decisive when once the equitable presumption of advancement has arisen, and it is necessary for the husband, in his endeavour to rebut that presumption, to assert that the property in question was put into his wife's name in order to avoid the payment on his beneficial interest of tax which would otherwise have been payable, so that, upon the basis that the tax had been United Kingdom tax, it appears to me that *Gascoigne* v *Gascoigne* [1918] 1 KB 223 completely covers the present case.

I, of course, am dealing here not with United Kingdom income tax, but with the Federal tax of the United States of America. There is, however, authority of the Court of Appeal which binds me in *Regazzoni* v *KC Sethia (1944) Ltd* [1956] 2 QB 490. I need refer only to a passage in the judgment of Denning LJ, who said: "It is perfectly true that the courts of this country will not enforce the revenue laws or the criminal laws of another country at the suit of that other country, either directly or indirectly. These courts do not sit to collect taxes for another country or to inflict punishment for it; and this is so even between countries of the Commonwealth, as the House of Lords held in the *Government of India* v *Taylor* [1955] AC 491. These courts will not enforce such laws at the instance of the foreign country. It is quite another matter to say that we will take no notice of them. It seems to me that we should take notice of the laws of a friendly country, even if they are revenue laws or penal laws or political laws, however they may be described, at least, to this extent, that if two people knowingly agree together to break the laws of a friendly country or to procure someone else to break them or to assist in the doing of it, then they cannot ask this court to give its aid to the enforcement of their agreement."

It is unnecessary for me to find in this case – and I do not propose to embark on that task – that there was anything in the nature of an agreement between the husband and the Irving Trust Company improperly to evade the Federal tax laws of the United States. But the principle underlying the passing which I have read from the judgment of Denning LJ, and which was part of the ratio decidendi of his judgment, applies, in my view, to such a case as this where a non-resident alien of the United States has so arranged his affairs that he has avoided payment of the withholding tax which he ought to have paid, and which he would have had to pay if the beneficial interest had been, as it should have been, disclosed to the American authorities.'

Government of India* v *Taylor [1955] AC 491 House of Lords (Viscount Simonds, Lords Morton, Reid, Keith and Somervell)

• *Foreign revenue laws will not be enforced, but they will be recognised*

Facts

The respondents were the liquidators of an English company, the Delhi Electricity Supply and Traction Co Ltd, that was for many years involved in electricity supply and tramway operation in Delhi. The appellants, the Government of India, sought to prove when the company was being liquidated a claim for income tax due under the provisions of Indian income tax law.

Held

A claim by a foreign sovereign to recover taxes due under its own laws was unenforceable in England. Moreover, it made no difference that India was a member of the Commonwealth.

Viscount Simonds:

> 'My Lords, I will admit that I was greatly surprised to hear it suggested that the courts of this country would and should entertain a suit by a foreign State to recover a tax. For at any time since I have had any acquaintance with the law I should have said as Rowlatt J said in the *King of the Hellenes* v *Brostron* (1923) 16 Ll LR 190, 193: "It is perfectly elementary that a foreign government cannot come here – nor will the courts of other countries allow our Government to go there – and sue a person found in that jurisdiction for taxes levied and which he is declared to be liable to in the country to which he belongs." That was in 1923. In 1928 Tomlin J, in *In re Visser, Queen of Holland* v *Drukker* [1928] Ch 877, 884 after referring to the case of *Sydney Municipal Council* v *Bull* [1909] 1 KB 7 in which the same proposition had been unequivocally stated by Grantham J, and saying that he was bound to follow it, added: "My own opinion is that there is a well-recognised rule, which has been enforced for at least 200 years or thereabouts, under which these courts will not collect the taxes of foreign States for the benefit of the sovereigns of those foreign States; and this is one of those actions which these courts will not entertain." My Lords, it is not seemly to weigh the pronouncements of living judges, but it is, I think, permissible to say that the opinions of few, if any, judges of the past command greater respect than those of Lord Tomlin and Rowlatt J, and what appeared to one of them to be a "well-recognised rule" and to the other "elementary" law cannot easily be displaced.
>
> It may well be asked, then, upon what grounds this appeal is founded. I think that counsel relied upon two main grounds, first that Lord Mansfield's proposition, [in *Holman* v *Johnson* (1775) 1 Cowp 341, 343 that "no country ever takes notice of the revenue laws of another"], extended to revenue law a doctrine properly applicable only to penal law and (I think it must be faced) that Lord Mansfield was wrong in so extending it and everyone who has since followed him was wrong: and secondly that, whatever may have been the rule in the past, there ought to be and is a trend towards a mitigation of the rule, particularly as between States which are united by the bonds of federal union or by such looser ties as bind the British Commonwealth of nations.
>
> My Lords, these seem to me frail weapons with which to attack a strong fortress. The suggestion that Lord Mansfield's proposition was too wide was supported partly by the fact that in *Huntington* v *Attrill* [1893] AC 150, 8 TLR 341 the proposition was somewhat more narrowly stated, as it was also in the case of the *Attorney-General for Canada* v *William Schulze & Co* (1901) 9 SLT 4. In those cases the question was of enforcement of a penalty imposed by a foreign State and the observations of the court were directed to that question. This seems to me an inadequate reason for challenging a wider statement in regard to a different subject-matter. Further, upon the assumption which must be made, that the decision in *Huntington* v *Attrill* was correct, it was conceded that it must cover not only a penalty strictly so-called but also any tax which could be regarded as penal or confiscatory. This seems to me to create a difficult task of discrimination, which is not made easier by the test suggested by counsel. "If a tax" he said, "is the sort of tax which is recognised in this country, it is not penal".
>
> I am little disposed to introduce so nice a refinement into a rule which has hitherto been stated in terms that are easy to understand and to apply.
>
> The second branch of the argument for the appellant was directed to showing that in the United States of America there had been in certain States a disposition to relax the rigidity of the rule, and counsel was able to point to certain cases not cited to the Court of

Appeal where the courts of one State had admitted and enforced claims for revenue by another State, notably in the States of Missouri and Kentucky. And reference was made also to the fact that in the 1948 supplement to the well-known "Restatement" some doubt was cast upon the rule (Conflict of Laws, s610). But it was conceded that this was not the trend in all States, the States of New York and of Delaware continuing to apply the old rule. My Lords, I do not think it necessary to occupy your time by an examination of the American cases. I am ever willing to get help from seeing how the law, which is our common heritage, has developed on the other side of the Atlantic, but a development which is not universal, and is in any case confined to relations between State and State within the Union, can have no weight in determining what the law is in this country.

Finally, it was urged that, whatever might be the position as between this country and a foreign country, it was not the same as between different members of the British Commonwealth, including those members which, though within the Commonwealth, do not acknowledge the sovereignty of the Queen. For such a distinction there is no authority and I can see no reason. If such a change is to be made, it is not for the courts to make it. It will be the task of Governments and perhaps of Parliaments. I do not think that it will be an easy task.'

Lord Somervell:

'Tax gathering is an administrative act, though in settling the quantum as well as in the final act of collection judicial process may be involved. Our courts will apply foreign law if it is the proper law of a contract, the subject of a suit. Tax gathering is not a matter of contract but of authority and administration as between the State and those within its jurisdiction. If one considers the initial stages of the process, which may, as the records of your Lordships' House show, be intricate and prolonged, it would be remarkable comity if State B allowed the time of its courts to be expended in assisting in this regard the tax gatherers of State A. Once a judgment has been obtained and it is a question only of its enforcement the factor of time and expense will normally have disappeared. The principle remains. The claim is one for a tax.'

Huntingdon* v *Atrill [1893] AC 150 Privy Council (Lords Halsbury LC, Watson, Bramwell, Hobhouse, Morris and Shand)

- *Foreign penal laws will not be enforced by English courts*

Facts

The appellant had loaned money to a company incorporated in New York. He was not repaid in full. The company was insolvent so there was little point in suing it. Instead he sued one of the directors of the company in New York. Normally, the directors of a company are not liable for its debts, but a New York law provided that the directors would be liable if they signed any certificate or report relating to the affairs of the company which was 'false in any material representation'. The respondent director had, in fact, signed a certificate verifying that the whole capital stock of the company had been paid up in cash; and this was not so. Thus the appellant succeeded before the New York courts and he sought to enforce the judgment of the New York court in Ontario. The case came before the Privy Council on appeal from the courts of Ontario. The question was whether the New York law imposing liability upon the directors for the debts of the company was penal and, therefore, unenforceable in Ontario (or England).

Held

The New York law imposed a liability for the protection of private rights (such as those of the appellant) and not public rights (such as those of the state of New York); as such it was not penal and able to be enforced. In addition it was for the Ontario/English courts, not the courts of New York, to decide whether the statute was penal or not.

Lord Watson:

> 'Their Lordships cannot assent to the proposition that, in considering whether the present action was penal in such sense as to oust their jurisdiction, the Courts of Ontario were bound to pay absolute deference to any interpretation which might have been put upon the Statute of 1875 in the State of New York. They had to construe and apply an international rule, which is a matter of law entirely within the cognizance of the foreign court whose jurisdiction is invoked. Judicial decisions in the State where the cause of action arose are not precedents which must be followed, although the reasoning upon which they are founded must always receive careful consideration, and may be conclusive. The Court appealed to must determine for itself, in the first place the substance of the right sought to be enforced; and, in the second place, whether its enforcement would, either directly or indirectly, involve the execution of the penal law of another State. Were any other principle to guide its decision, a Court might find itself in the position of giving effect in one case and denying effect in another, to suits of the same character, in consequence of the causes of action having arisen in different countries; or in the predicament of being constrained to give effect to laws which were, in its own judgment, strictly penal.
>
> The general law upon this point has been correctly stated by Mr Justice Story in his *Conflict of Laws* and by other text writers; but their Lordships do not think it necessary to quote from these authorities in explanation of the reasons which have induced courts of justice to decline jurisdiction in suits somewhat loosely described as penal, when these have their origin in a foreign country. The rule has its foundation in the well-recognised principle that crimes, including in that term all breaches of public law punishable by pecuniary mulct or otherwise, at the instance of the State Government, or of some one representing the public, are local in this sense, that they are only cognizable and punishable in the country where they were committed. Accordingly no proceeding, even in the shape of a civil suit, which has for its object the enforcement by the State, whether directly or indirectly, of punishment imposed for such breaches by the lex fori, ought to be admitted in the Courts of any other country.'

Lemenda Trading Co Ltd v *African Middle East Petroleum Co Ltd*

[1988] 2 WLR 735 Queen's Bench Division (Phillips J)

• *An agreement may be rendered unenforceable if it is contrary to English public policy as well as against that of a foreign state*

Facts

The defendants, an English company, agreed in a contract governed by English law with the plaintiffs, a Bermuda company, that in return for a commission they (the plaintiffs) would secure the renewal of the defendants' contract for the supply of crude oil with the Quatar national oil company. Such an arrangement was contrary to the public policy of Quatar although it did not infringe any Quatar law. An agreement to procure renewal of such a contract from a British government department or state owned industry would have been contrary to English public policy. The supply contract was duly renewed but the defendants refused to pay any commission.

Held

The commission contract was not enforceable in England.

Phillips J:

> 'The principles underlying the public policy in the present case are essentially principles of morality of general application. The practice of exacting payment for the use of personal influence, particularly when the person to be influenced is likely to be unaware of the pecuniary motive involved, is unattractive whatever the context. Yet it is

questionable whether the moral principles involved are so weighty as to lead an English court to refuse to enforce an agreement regardless of the country of performance and regardless of the attitude of that country to such a practice. The later English decisions were influenced, at least in part, by the effect of the practice in question on good government in England. It is at this stage that, in my judgment, it becomes relevant to consider the law of Qatar. The significant fact in *Kaufman* v *Gerson* [1904] 1 KB 591 was that the contractual adventure was not contrary to French law and the contract was valid and enforceable in France. In the present case Qatar, the country in which the agreement was to be performed with which, in my view, the agreement had the closest connection, has the same public policy as that which prevails in England. Because of that policy, the courts of Qatar would not enforce the agreement.

In my judgment, the English courts should not enforce an English law contract which falls to be performed abroad where (i) it relates to an adventure which is contrary to a head of English public policy which is founded on general principles of morality and (ii) the same public policy applies in the country of performance so that the agreement would not be enforceable under the law of that country. In such a situation international comity combines with English domestic public policy to militate against enforcement.'

Peter Buchanan Ltd and Macharg v *McVey* [1955] AC 516 High Court of Justice of Eire (Kingsmill Moore J)

• *A foreign revenue law will not be indirectly enforced in England*

Facts

The defendant, the owner of a 'one man company' in Scotland had, in order to evade the company's liability for excess profits tax, transferred the company's assets into his own name and removed them to Eire after paying all the company's creditors except the United Kingdom revenue authorities. The liquidator of the Scottish company who was acting 'hand in glove' with the United Kingdom revenue authorities sued in Eire to recover the moneys owed by the defendant to the company with a view to using the sums recovered to pay the company's tax debts. The action failed.

Held

Kingsmill Moore J:

'In deciding cases between private persons in which there is present such a foreign element as would ordinarily induce the application of the principles of a foreign law, courts have always exercised the right to reject such law on the ground that it conflicted with public policy or affronted the accepted morality of the domestic forum. Contracts valid according to what would normally be considered "the proper law" of the contract will not be enforced if in the view of the court they are tainted with immorality of one kind and another. Delicts committed abroad are not actionable here unless they are torts by our law. Slavery, or any other status involving penal or private disabilities, is not recognised. If, then, in disputes between private citizens, it has been considered necessary to reserve an option to reject foreign law as incompatible with the views of the community, it must have been equally, if not more, necessary to reserve a similar option where an attempt was made to enforce the governmental claims (including revenue claims) of a foreign State. But if the courts had contented themselves with an option to refuse such claims, instead of imposing a general rule of exclusion, the task of formulating and applying the principles of selection would have been one not only of difficulty but danger, involving inevitably an incursion into political fields with grave risks of embarrassing the executive in its foreign relations and even of provoking international complications. Neither common morality nor "settled public policy" would have sufficed to cover the area of necessary rejection; for the nature and incidence of governmental and revenue claims are not dictated by any moral principles but are the offspring of political considerations and political necessity. Taxation originally expressed only the will of the despot, enforceable by torture, slavery and death. Though it may be conceded that in modern times it is more often designed to further a benevolent social policy, and that the civil servant has usurped the position of the executioner as the agent of enforcement, yet in essence taxation is still arbitrary and depends for its effectiveness only on the executive power of the State. Nor is modern history without examples of revenue laws used for purposes which would not only affront the strongest feelings of neighbouring communities but would run counter to their political aims and vital interests. Such laws have been used for religious and racial discriminations, for the furtherance of social policies and ideals dangerous to the security of adjacent countries, and for the direct furtherance of economic warfare. So long as these possibilities exist it would be equally unwise for the courts to permit the enforcement of the revenue claims of foreign States or to attempt to discriminate between those claims which they would and those which they would not enforce. Safety lies only in universal rejection. Such a principle appears to me to be fundamental and of supreme importance.

If I am right in attributing such importance to the principle, then it is clear that its enforcement must not depend merely on the form in which the claim is made. It is not a question whether the plaintiff is a foreign State or the representative of a foreign State or its revenue authority. In every case the substance of the claim must be scrutinised, and if it then appears that it is really a suit brought for the purpose of collecting the debts of a foreign revenue it must be rejected. Mr Wilson has pressed upon me the difficulty of deciding such a question of fact and has replied on "ratio ruentis acervi". For the purpose of this case it is sufficient to say that when it appears to the court that the whole object of the suit is to collect tax for a foreign revenue, and that this will be the sole result of a decision in favour of the plaintiff, then a court is entitled to reject the claim by refusing jurisdiction.

If the strict application of the principle were in any way relaxed evasion would be easy and the court would be faced with all the difficulties which the adoption of the rule was designed to avoid.'

Comment

Note first that the judgment of Kingsmill Moore J was approved by Lord Keith in the House of Lords in *Government of India* v *Taylor* [1955] AC 491. And note, secondly, where in similar circumstances the revenue authorities are not the only creditors of the company the Australian courts in *Ayres* v *Evans* (1981) 39 ALR 129 have distinguished *Peter Buchanan* and allowed the liquidator to recover; in these circumstances the gathering of tax is not 'the sole object of the suit'.

Regazzoni v *K C Sethia (1944) Ltd* [1958] AC 301 House of Lords (Viscount Simonds, Lords Reid, Cohen, Keith and Somervell)

• *English courts will not enforce a contract if its performance involves doing an act in a foreign and friendly state which violates the law of that state*

Facts

In a contract governed by English law the respondents agreed to sell and deliver certain jute bags to the appellant. The bags were to be shipped cif from India to Genoa; both parties knew that the bags would then be transhipped to South Africa although the relevant Indian legislation prohibited the export of goods 'destined for any port or place in the Union of South Africa or in respect of which the Chief Customs Officer is satisfied ... although destined for a port or place outside the Union of South Africa are intended to be taken to the Union of South Africa.'

Held

The contract would not be enforced against the respondents.

Lord Reid:

> 'To my mind, the question whether this contract is enforceable by English courts is not, properly speaking, a question of international law. The real question is one of public policy in English law: but in considering this question we must have in mind the background of international law and international relationships often referred to as the comity of nations. This is not a case of a contract being made in good faith but one party thereafter finding that he cannot perform his part of the contract without committing a breach of foreign law in the territory of the foreign country. If this contract is held to be unenforceable, it should, in my opinion, be because from the beginning the contract was tainted so that the courts of this country will not assist either party to enforce it.
>
> I do not wish to express any opinion about a case where parties agree to deal with goods which they both know have already been smuggled out of a foreign country, or about a case where the seller knows that the buyer intends to use the goods for an illegal purpose or to smuggle them into a foreign country. Such cases may raise difficult questions. The crucial fact in this case appears to me to be that both parties knew that the contract could not be performed without the respondents procuring a breach of the law of India within the territory of that country.'

Comment

This is a difficult area and the authorities are not clear or consistent. See *Foster* v *Driscoll* [1929] 1 KB 470.

United States of America v *Inkley*

[1988] 3 WLR 304 Court of Appeal (Purchas LJ and Heilbron J)

• *Foreign penal law will not be enforced by English courts*

Facts

Inkley, a British subject, had been charged with various criminal offences under the laws of the United States. A US district court released him on bail on condition that he entered into an 'appearance bond' for $48,000. He also obtained the leave of the court to return to England for 30 days. He returned to England but did not, thereafter, return to the US to stand trial. The United States obtained a final judgment in the US civil courts against him for the amount of the 'appearance bond' and now sought to enforce this judgment against the defendant in England.

Held

The Court of Appeal held that 'notwithstanding its civil clothing, the purpose of the action ... was the due execution by the USA of a public law process aimed to ensure the attendance of persons accused of crime before the criminal courts.' In reaching this conclusion the Court of Appeal, quite correctly, followed *Huntingdon* v *Attrill* in holding that the court asked to enforce the foreign law (or judgment) had the final word in determining whether a particular action involved the execution of a penal law of another state.

> 'After considering the authorities, *Huntington* v *Attrill* [1893] AC 150 and *Attorney-General of New Zealand* v *Ortiz* [1984] AC 1 and the standard textbooks, *Story's Conflict of Laws,* 5th ed (1857) and *Dicey & Morris, The Conflict of Laws*, 11th ed (1987) the judge (in the court below) came to the conclusion that the proceedings were civil proceedings and enforceable by action in the English courts, although he found the question a nicely balanced one. The defendant challenges this decision and asserts that on the authorities the judge should have come to the conclusion that the substance of this action was the enforcement of a public law remedy in the nature of a penal proceeding and, therefore, would not be enforceable in the English courts.
>
> It is necessary to turn shortly to the authorities and the textbooks. The starting

point is the dictum of Gray J in *Wisconsin* v *Pelican Insurance Co* (1887) 127 US 265 approved by the Privy Council in *Huntington* v *Attrill* [1893] AC 150, 157, per Lord Watson:

> "In delivering the judgment of the bench, Gray J after referring to the text books, and the dictum by Marshall CJ already cited, went on to say: 'The rule that the courts of no country execute the law of another applies not only to prosecutions and sentences for crimes and misdemeanors, *but to all suits in favour of the state* for the recovery of pecuniary penalties for any violation of statutes for the protection of its revenue or other municipal laws, and to all judgments for such penalties'. Their Lordships do not hesitate to accept that exposition of the law, which, in their opinion, discloses the proper test for ascertaining whether an action is penal within the meaning of the rule. A proceeding, in order to come within the scope of the rule, must be in the nature of a suit in favour of the state whose law has been infringed." ...

In *Attorney-General of New Zealand* v *Ortiz* [1984] AC 1 the Court of Appeal recognised *Huntington* v *Attrill* as correctly stating the law; although the House of Lords in dealing with the matter decided the appeal on an alternative ground. However, Ackner LJ said, at p33:

> "*Huntington*'s case makes it clear that the first part of Mr Gray's definition of foreign penal law, namely that it must be part of the criminal code of a foreign country, is not sustainable. The right which it is sought to enforce may be a right which arises under legislation which is essentially designed to regulate commercial activities such as company legislation which may well contain a penal provision. I agree with the judge that it cannot be right simply to categorise the statute sought to be enforced as a whole. The court must pay regard to the particular provision of the foreign law which it is sought to enforce ... In the instant submission, the claim is made by the Attorney-General on behalf of the state. it is not a claim by a private individual. Further, the cause of action does not concern a private right which demands reparation or compensation. It concerns a public right – the preservation of historic articles within New Zealand – which right the state seeks to vindicate."

In *Ortiz*'s case the issue arose out of a statute passed in New Zealand which enabled customs officers to impound an artefact of historic importance being exported without a certificate. The claim was brought in the English courts, the artefact in question having been successfully, if illegally, exported. In these circumstances the Court of Appeal and, on other grounds, the House of Lords held that no action lay in the English courts. This is to be compared with *Huntington's* case where the New York statute, although penal in shape and form, in fact provided a right to be enjoyed by an investor to claim compensation from the directors of a company who had issued a fraudulently inaccurate document. In that case the Privy Council held that the claim arising in New York was in fact enforceable in the courts of Ontario. ...

From these authorities the following propositions seem to emerge which are relevant to the present appeal: (1) the consideration of whether the claim sought to be enforced in the English courts is one which involves the assertion of foreign sovereignty, whether it be penal, revenue or other public law; (2) that regard will be had to the attitude adopted by the courts in the foreign jurisdiction which will always receive serious attention and may on occasions be decisive; (3) that the category of the right of action, ie whether public or private, will depend on the party in whose favour it is created, on the purpose of the law or enactment in the foreign state on which it is based and on the general context of the case as a whole; (4) that the fact that the right, statutory or otherwise, is penal in nature will not deprive a person, who asserts a personal claim depending thereon, from having recourse to the courts of this country; on the other hand, by whatever description it may be known if the purpose of the action is the enforcement of a sanction, power or right at the instance of the state in its sovereign capacity, it will not be entertained; (5) that the fact that in the foreign jurisdiction recourse may be had in a civil forum to enforce the right will not necessarily affect the true nature of the right being enforced in this country.

Applying the above criteria to the facts of this case we have come firmly to the conclusion that the general context and background against which the appearance bond was executed was criminal or penal. ... Notwithstanding its civil clothing, the purpose of the action initiated by the writ issued in this case was the due execution by the United States of America of a public law process aimed to ensure the attendance of persons accused of crime before the criminal courts ... We would, therefore, allow this appeal.'

Characterisation

Cohn, Re [1945] Ch 5 Chancery Division (Uthwatt J)

• *The lex fori does not have the final word in matters relating to characterisation*

Facts

Mrs Cohn and Mrs Oppenheimer, who were mother and daughter, were killed by the same explosion during a German air raid on London. Under Mrs Cohn's will, if Mrs Oppenheimer survived Mrs Cohn, her estate was entitled to certain movable property. It was not, however, possible to determine whether mother or daughter died first. Both Mrs Cohn and Mrs Oppenheimer were German nationals domiciled in Germany. Essential validity of a will of movables is governed by the law of the domicile, viz, German law. Article 20 of the BGB (the German Civil Code) provided that where it could not be proved which of a number of dead persons survived each other, they were to be presumed to have died simultaneously. On the other hand, s184 of the Law of Property Act 1925 provides that where the circumstances render it uncertain which persons died first, 'the younger shall be deemed to have survived the elder'. Thus, if art 20 applied Mrs Oppenheimer's estate was not entitled; but it was if s184 applied.

Held

Matters relating to procedure were governed by the lex fori (English law) but that art 20 related to a matter of substance not procedure and would be applied.

Uthwatt J:

> 'The law of the domicile, namely the law of Germany, is alone relevant in determining the effect of the testamentary dispositions of movables made by Mrs Cohn, the basis on which the movables are to be administered, and the facts which it is necessary to ascertain to administer that estate. If, for instance, under the law of Germany, it was not necessary for the efficacy of the disposition in her favour that Mrs Oppenheimer should survive Mrs Cohn, but was only necessary that she should survive either Mr or Mrs Cohn, no inquiry as to survivorship such as is here being made would have been necessary. The question of survivorship is, in fact, opened up by the provisions of German law as to inheritance and is formally not: "Did or did not Mrs Oppenheimer survive Mrs Cohn?" but "Is the administration of Mrs Cohn's estate to proceed on the footing that Mrs Oppenheimer survived Mrs Cohn or on the footing that she did not?" The purpose to which the inquiry as to survivorship is directed must be kept in mind. The mode of proving any fact bearing on survivorship is determined by the lex fori. The effect of any fact so proved is for the purpose in hand determined by the law of the domicile. The fact proved in this case is that it is impossible to say whether or not Mrs Oppenheimer survived Mrs Cohn. Proof stops there. Section 184 of the Law of Property Act 1925, does not come into the picture at all. It is not part of the law of evidence of the lex

fori, for the section is not directed to helping in the ascertainment of any fact but contains a rule of substantive law directing a certain presumption to be made in all cases affecting the title to property. As a rule of substantive law the section is relevant where title is governed by the law of England. It has no application where title is determined by the law of any other country.

I turn now to consider the law of Germany in relation to the facts proved, unhampered by s184 of the Law of Property Act 1925. In my view, the provision contained in the Article of July 4 1939, is part of the general substantive law of Germany and not part of its law of evidence. Its terms and the place in which the repealed Article dealing with the same general subject-matter was to be found make that clear. That rule of law has to be applied, inter alia, as part of the Law of Inheritances, contained in the German Civil Code. Predicating of Mrs Oppenheimer that she is presumed to have died simultaneously with Mrs Cohn, it is clear that Mrs Oppenheimer was not a person living at the time when the succession to Mrs Cohn's estate opened, and that, accordingly, having regard to Articles 1922 and 1923 of the German Civil Code, the defendants, Mrs Freudenthal and Siegfried Cohn, take Mrs Cohn's movable estate.'

Renvoi

Amin Rasheed Shipping Corporation v *Kuwait Insurance Co* [1984] 1 AC 50 House of Lords (Lords Diplock, Wilberforce, Roskill, Brandon and Brightman)

• *Renvoi has no place in the law of contract*

Facts

See Chapter 5.

Held

Lord Diplock

'One final comment upon what, under English conflict rules, is meant by the "proper law" of a contract may be appropriate. It is the substantive law of the country which the parties have chosen as that by which their mutual legally enforceable rights are to be ascertained, but excluding any renvoi, whether of remission or transmission, that the courts of that country might themselves apply if the matter were litigated before them. For example, if a contract made in England were expressed to be governed by French law, the English court would apply French substantive law to it notwithstanding that a French court applying its own conflict rules might accept a renvoi to English law as the lex loci contractus if the matter were litigated before it. Conversely, assuming that under English conflict rules English law is the proper law of the contract, the fact that the courts of a country which under English conflict rules would be regarded as having jurisdiction over a dispute arising under the contract (in this case Kuwait) would under its own conflict rules have recourse to English law as determinative of the rights and obligations of the parties, would not make the proper law of the contract any the less English law because it was the law that a Kuwaiti court also would apply.'

Annesley, Re, Davidson v *Annesley* [1926] Ch 692 Chancery Division (Russell J)

• *Should English courts take account of foreign choice of law rules?*

Facts

Mrs Sybil Annesley, a British national, had died domiciled in France (in the eyes of English law; under French law she was domiciled in England). In her will she disposed of her movable property in a manner permitted under English law, but not under French law.

Apparently French law as the lex domicilii would apply to the distribution of her estate, but what law would the French court apply to the question? Would they not apply English law as the lex patriae of the deceased?

Held

The French courts would have applied French law to the distribution, thus French law applied.

Russell J:

'I accordingly decide that the domicile of the testatrix at the time of her death was French. French law accordingly applies, but the question remains: what French law? According to French municipal law, the law applicable in the case of a foreigner not legally domiciled in France is the law of that person's nationality, in this case British. But the law of that nationality refers the question back to French law, the law of the domicile; and the question arises, will the French law accept this reference back, or renvoi, and apply French municipal law?

Upon this question arises acute conflict of expert opinion. Two experts took the view that the renvoi would not be accepted, but that a French Court would distribute the movables of the testatrix in accordance with English municipal law. One expert equally strongly took the view that a French Court would accept the renvoi and distribute in accordance with French municipal law. I must come to a conclusion as best I can upon this question of fact upon the evidence after considering and weighing the reasons given by each side in support of their respective views. It is a case rather of views expressed by the experts as to what the French law ought to be, than what it is. Although there is in France no system of case law such as we understand it here – the decisions of higher Courts not being binding upon inferior tribunals – yet I think I must pay some attention to the fact that this question of renvoi has at different times come for consideration before the Cour de Cassation, the highest Court in France, and each time with the same result – namely, the acceptance of the renvoi and the application of the French municipal law.'

Askew, Re [1930] 2 Ch 259 Chancery Division (Maugham J)

- *Validity of marriage and legitimacy of child*

Facts

By an English marriage settlement, it was provided that if John Bertram Askew (a British subject then domiciled in England) should marry again he might, by deed or will, appoint his part for the benefit of any child of a subsequent marriage. Mr Askew separated from his wife, and acquired a domicile of choice in Germany prior to a German court decree dissolving the marriage. A year later he married Anna Askew in Berlin. However, before the divorce, a daughter named Margaret Askew had been born to Anna Askew in Switzerland and she was acknowledged to be the daughter of John Bertram Askew. In 1913, he purported to revoke part of the above-mentioned trusts by deed poll for the benefit of Margaret Askew. The trustees of the settlement took out a summons for the determination of the question whether the power of appointment had been validly exercised in favour of Margaret Askew by the deed poll of 1913.

Held

The German court would hold that according to German law Margaret Askew was legitimated by the marriage of her parents notwithstanding the fact that her father at the time of her birth was still married to a woman other than her mother. By reason of this legitimation Margaret Askew became issue of the marriage between John Bertram Askew and Anna Askew.

Maugham J:

'There is no doubt that, if German local law were applicable, the subsequent marriage of the parents of the defendant Margaret Askew would effect her legitimation ...

although she was born before the divorce, which was not made absolute until 27 July 1911. The trustees are naturally desirous of the protection of the court in relation to the question whether the power of appointment in question was validly exercised by the deed poll, and for this purpose it is necessary to determine whether the defendant Margaret Askew, though born out of wedlock during the continuance of a previous marriage, is, having regard to her father's domicile, legitimate …

The question of legitimation of a child by the subsequent marriage of its parents in a foreign country (apart from the provisions of the Legitimacy Act 1926, s1, subs2, and s8) appears at first sight to be well settled. Dicey (Rule 137, Case I, in his *Conflict of Laws*) states the result of the decisions thus:

> "If both the law of the father's domicile at the time of the birth of the child and the law of the father's domicile at the date of the subsequent marriage allow for legitimatio per subsequens matrimonium, the child becomes or may become legitimate on the marriage of the parents."

The authorities cited are *Udny* v *Udny* (1869) LR 1 Sc & Div 441; *Re Wright's Trusts* (1856) 2 K & J 595; *Re Grove* (1888) 40 Ch D 216, and they bear out the proposition. Now, John Bertram Askew was admittedly domiciled in Germany both at the date of the birth and at the time of the subsequent marriage. But what is the meaning of the phrase "the law of the father's domicile"? Does it refer to the municipal law or local law of Germany, or does it refer to the whole of the laws applicable in Germany including the views entertained in Germany as to the rules of private international law? There is no doubt that Dicey means the latter (see his Interpretation of Terms, Definition II); but in my opinion it is very doubtful whether the courts who have dealt with the matter did not mean the former. The so-called doctrine of renvoi, which has been so much discussed by jurists of recent years, had not been formulated in earlier days; and those who look at the statement of the foreign law in the earlier cases (see, for example *Re Wright's Trusts* and *Re Grove*) will find that the foreign law as stated was the local or municipal law, and that no evidence was adduced as to the rules of private international law applied in the foreign country. It would seem that rules of private international law, not being founded on custom or statute but being based upon considerations of justice and what is called 'comity' ought to be the same in all countries, though it is now well known (contrary to the belief entertained by Lord Westbury: see *Udny* v *Udny*) that they are not. I am convinced that 60 or 70 years ago it never would have occurred to lawyers who were proving, say, the law of Italy (or France) in relation to the succession to an Englishwoman dying domiciled in Italy (or France) to depose (first) that the Italian (or the French) law gave a son a legitima portio; (secondly) that foreigners domiciled in Italy (or France) were deemed to retain their personal law; (thirdly) that he was informed that according to English law an English testator had a free power of disposition; and (finally) that, accordingly, by an application of Italian (or French) rules of private international law, the son had not (or had) a right to a legitima portio. It is on evidence of this kind that English courts have now to decide cases relating to the succession to movables belonging to British subjects who die domiciled abroad, and other cognate matters. It may be added that there is generally an acute conflict of expert opinion as to the foreign law, which has to be proved afresh in each case. Foreign jurists and foreign courts take from time to time varying views on the subject of renvoi. The result is not always satisfactory. It may, then, be useful to consider the question from the point of view of principle before dealing with the four modern authorities which must, I think, guide me in the matter …

The English judges and the foreign judges do not bow to each other like the officers at Fontenoy. The English court has to decide a matter within its jurisdiction according to English law in the wide sense, and if the matter depends on foreign domicile it is only necessary to prove certain facts as to rights under the foreign law. It is therefore, I think, clear that, when we inquire whether John Doe has acquired rights in Utopia by Utopian law, we must mean by the whole of the laws of Utopia including any views of private international law which may be deemed to give him rights (or subject him to restrictions), though an Englishman settled in that land. A final question may sometimes remain – namely, whether the lex domicilii is one which the English courts can recognise. If it is (as it nearly always is), we have only to ascertain what the lex domicilii in the wider sense is. I will add that I am not aware of any satisfactory definition of the term renvoi; but it will be noted that, if I am right, an English court can never have anything to do with it except so far as foreign experts may expound the doctrine as being part of the lex domicilii …

For the reasons given above I hold that in an English court the lex domicilii in the wide sense must prima facie apply, and, this being a law which the English courts will recognise, the conclusion is that the defendant Margaret is a legitimate child of John Bertram Askew in our courts and that the power of appointment was effectively exercised in her favour.'

Ross, Re, Ross* v *Waterfield [1930] 1 Ch 377 Chancery Division (Luxmoore J)

• *The orthodox view in English law is to adopt the approach of the foreign court*

Facts

Mrs Janet Ross, a British national who had died domiciled in Italy, had in her will excluded her son, Alexander Ross, from her movable estate situated outside Italy in a manner permitted by English law but not Italian law. Since she had died domiciled in Italy, Italian law seemingly applied; but would the Italian courts apply Italian law or would their choice of law rule direct the application of English law?

Held

Whether the son was entitled to a moiety of the estate as legitimo portio must be decided in accordance with the view that Italian courts would take of the English law; and the Italian courts would in these circumstances have applied English law.

Luxmoore J:

> 'In this connection I would like to refer to the dictum of Scrutton LJ in *Casdagli* v *Casdagli* [1918] P 89, 111, where he says:
>
> > "Practical and theoretical difficulties arise from the fact that, while England decides questions of status in the event of conflict of laws by the law of the domicile, many foreign countries now determine those questions by the law of the nationality of the person in question."
>
> Hence it has been argued that if the country of allegiance looks to or sends back the decision to the law of the domicile, and the country of domicile looks to or sends back (renvoyer) the decision to the law of nationality, there is an inextricable circle in "the doctrine of the renvoi" and no result is reached. I do not see that this difficulty is insoluble. If the country of nationality applies the law which the country of domicile would apply to such a case if arising in its Courts, it may well apply its own law to the subject-matter of dispute, being that which the country of domicile would apply, but not that part of it which would remit the matter to the law of domicile, which part would have spent its operation in the first remittance. The knot may be cut in another way, not so logical, if the country of domicile says, "We are ready to apply the law of nationality, but if the country of nationality chooses to remit the matter to us we will apply the same law as we should apply to our own subjects." This dictum, in effect, approves of the decision of such matters in accordance with the law as interpreted and administered by the Courts of the country of domicile.
>
> I have I think now dealt with all the relevant cases. In addition to them my attention has been called to a number of articles by

international jurists. There is an acute conflict between the various authors on the question, and so far as the English writers are concerned, they seem to be fairly equally divided. I should also add that in the course of the argument my attention was called to the report of the American case referred to by Russell J in his judgment in *In re Annesley* [1926] Ch 692, 709 – namely, the case of *In re Tallmadge, In re Chadwick's Will* 181 New York Supplement (215 New York State Reporter), 330. The decision is that of the Surrogates Court, New York County. The judge of that court goes through most of the authorities to which I have referred, and comes to a conclusion opposite to that at which I have arrived. For the reasons I have endeavoured to express in this judgment. I think his decision is not in accordance with the English authorities.

In my opinion the present case must be decided in accordance with the law of Italy, as that law would be expounded in the Italian Courts. If the Italian Court had in fact dealt with the matter there would be no necessity to inquire into the law, and it would be my duty simply to follow the decision. Since there is no decision by the Italian Court, I am bound to ascertain how the Italian Court would decide the case from the evidence of those competent to instruct me. I am glad to say that the Italian lawyers who have been called on both sides are unanimous in this conclusion, that if the case fell to be decided in the Italian Courts, it would be held that the testamentary dispositions of Mrs Janet Anne Ross were valid, and provide for the total disposition of her property in Italy; and that in no circumstances would the Italian Court recognise any right on the part of the plaintiff to any part of her property as legitima portio, as it would have done had Mrs Janet Anne Ross been an Italian national. Dr Giuseppe Pallicia, who gave evidence on behalf of the plaintiff, said that if the present case fell to be decided in Italy, there is no doubt but that the Italian Court would apply the English law applicable to Mrs Janet Anne Ross as a British subject, without any reference to the fact that she was domiciled in Italy; and the most he would say in favour of the plaintiff's claim was that, if the Court in England should hold that he was entitled, notwithstanding his mother's testamentary dispositions, to the legitima portio, he would have been entitled to if she were in fact an Italian national; the Italian Courts would recognise that decision and enforce it, unless it was against public policy. His answer to the question whether such a decision would be against public policy was a little ambiguous, but I think he really expressed the view that the sounder opinion is that the answer would be in the affirmative. On the other hand, both Dr Adrian Dingli and Dr Ferdinando Bosi are unanimous in the view that the Italian Courts would determine the case on the footing that the English law applicable is that part of the law which would be applicable to an English national domiciled in England; and that if the English Court decided the case in any other manner, the Italian Court would refuse to follow such a decision and dispose of the case as if it came before the Italian Court untrammelled by any English decisions. I accept their evidence on the Italian law.'

United Railways of Havana and Regla Warehouses Ltd, Re [1960] 1 All ER 214 Court of Appeal (Jenkins, Romer and Willmer LJJ)

- *Renvoi has no place in the law of contract*

Facts

An English company owned a railway undertaking in Cuba. It raised loan capital in the United States through the sale of its rolling stock to a Pennsylvania bank and its lease back by the bank to the company.

Held

The Court of Appeal held that the law of Pennsylvania and not that of Cuba was the proper law of the contract.

Jenkins LJ:

> 'While accepting the respondents' contention that the proper law of the trust agreement and of the lease was not the law of Cuba we are not prepared, as at present advised, to accept their alternative suggestion that had the proper law been Cuban the relevant law to apply would nevertheless, on the evidence of Dr Gorrin and by virtue of the renvoi doctrine, have been that of Pennsylvania. This view does seem to have been accepted by the judge and receives some support from the judgment of the Privy Council, delivered by Lord Wright. in *Vita Food Products Inc* v *Unus Shipping Co* [1939] AC 277. This passage from the judgment of the Judicial Committee has, however, by no means escaped criticism (see, for example, Dicey; and an article in vol 56 of the Law Quarterly Review (1940), pp333–335, by Mr Morris and Dr Cheshire). Had it been necessary to decide the point on the present appeal (which it is not), we should have been disposed to hold that the principle of renvoi finds no place in the field of contract; and accordingly that if the parties to the lease here in question ought to be treated as having accepted Cuban law as the proper law of the contract, such law was the domestic law of Cuba and not the rules of the conflict of laws administered by the Cuban courts.'

Substance and procedure

Arab Monetary Fund* v *Hashim and Others [1991] 2 WLR 729 House of Lords (Lords Bridge, Templeman, Griffiths, Ackner and Lowry)

• *Bodies corporate that would not be recognised under English law may be recognised if they are granted juridical personality by the law of a foreign state recognised by the United Kingdom*

Facts

The Arab Monetary Fund was a body created by an agreement between 20 Arab states and Palestine. The agreement conferred on the fund 'independent juridical personality'. A decree of the United Arab Emirates established the fund as an 'independent juridical personality' in the UAE and, in particular, in Abu Dhabi (where the fund had its headquarters). The fund brought proceedings in England to recover sums allegedly stolen from it by its former director-general, Dr Hashim. He raised the defence (based upon *J H Rayner* v *Department of Trade and Industry* [1989] 3 WLR 969 (HL) where it had been held that an international treaty had no effect in English law unless specifically incorporated by legislation) that since the fund had been established by treaty under international law it had no status under English law in the absence of English legislation, and so could not sue.

Held

The comity of nations required that the courts of the UK should recognise a corporate body created by the law of a foreign state (like the UAE) recognised by the Crown. Thus, since on a true construction of the UAE decree corporate personality was established not just under international law but under the law of the UAE, the fund was entitled to sue.

Lord Templeman:

> 'As early as 1728 in an action begun by the Dutch West India Company, the defendants argued unsuccessfully in this House:
>
> > "... that no recognisance in England could be given to this generalis privilegiata Societas Belgica ad Indos Occidentales negotians, for that the law of England does not take notice of any foreign corporation, nor can any foreign corporation in their corporate name and capacity maintain any action at common law in this kingdom, and that therefore the recognisance was void in law": *Henriques* v *Dutch West India Co* (1728) 2 Ld Raym 1532, 1534–1535.

In that case judgment was recovered by the

Dutch company by producing in evidence the proper instrument whereby according to the law of Holland they were effectually created a corporation there. In the present case the federal decree with the articles of agreement annexed suffices to prove incorporation of the fund in the UAE.

In *Lazard Brothers & Co* v *Midland Bank Ltd* [1933] AC 289, 297, Lord Wright said:

> "English courts have long since recognised as juristic persons corporations established by foreign law in virtue of the fact of their creation and continuance under and by that law. Such recognition is said to be by the comity of nations."

In *Gasque* v *Inland Revenue Commissioners* [1940] 2 KB 80, Macnaghten J held that a limited company was capable of having a domicile. Its domicile is the place of its registration and that domicile clings to it throughout its existence. In the present case the domicile and residence of the fund were clearly in the UAE at the headquarters of the fund from which the fund operated. …

The courts of the United Kingdom can therefore recognise the fund as a legal personality created by the law of the UAE.

It was submitted on behalf of the respondent banks that the fund was created a legal personality not only by the UAE but also by the other 20 states who were parties to the AMF agreement. Therefore, it is said, there are 21 legal personalities and it is not clear whether Dr Hashim embezzled the money of the UAE fund or the money of a fund established by some other Arab state. My Lords, though the fund was incorporated by 21 states and has multiple incorporation and multiple nationality there is only one fund with its head office in Abu Dhabi, one board of governors, one executive board of directors and one director-general. The domicile and residence of the fund are in the UAE and nowhere else. Dr Hashim was appointed by the board of governors of the fund as director-general of the fund and stole the money belonging to the fund. It was argued that the fund as incorporated in Iraq, for example, might be different from the fund as incorporated in the UAE and that the Iraqi fund might even sue the UAE fund. But there is only one fund to which each of the member states accorded legal personality. No one can bring an action to recover the money of the fund in any part of the world except the one duly authorised director-general. The articles of agreement which were annexed to the federal decree of the UAE and which thus became part of the law of the UAE are no different from the memorandum and articles of a limited liability company established under the law of England.

It is beyond dispute that if the fund had been incorporated in the UAE and nowhere else, the fund would have been recognised in this country as a legal personality. If the fund has been incorporated not only in the UAE but also in a number of friendly foreign states recognised by the government of this country, it still has legal personality and is capable of suing in this country. …

In 1978 (see *The British Yearbook of International Law 1978*, pp346–348) the advice of Her Majesty's Government was sought with regard to the status of

> "… banks and other financial entities set up by a group of foreign sovereign states by a treaty (to which the United Kingdom is not a party), empowering them, expressly or by implication, to engage in banking, financial or other trading activities in member and non-member states and conferring on them, by virtue of the treaty, any related agreements and any necessary implementing legislation, legal personality in one or more states outside the United Kingdom, and, in particular, under the law of one or more member states or the state wherein the entity concerned has its seat or permanent location."

The reply from the Foreign and Commonwealth Office was:

> "In these circumstances, and on the assumption that the entity concerned enjoys, under its constitutive instrument or instruments and under the law of one or more member states or the state wherein it has its seat or permanent location, legal personality and capacity to engage in transactions of the type concerned gov-

erned by the law of a non-member state, the Foreign and Commonwealth Office, as the branch of the executive responsible for the conduct of foreign relations, would be willing officially to acknowledge that the entity concerned enjoyed such legal personality and capacity, and to state this."

It seems to me that it would be unthinkable for the courts of the United Kingdom applying the principles of comity to reach any other conclusion. It will be observed that the reply of the Foreign and Commonwealth Office stipulates that the international organisation for which recognition is sought must have acquired legal personality and capacity under the laws of one or more member states or the state wherein it has its seat or permanent location. This requirement is necessary because the courts of the United Kingdom cannot enforce treaty rights but they can recognise legal entities created by the laws of one or more sovereign states. A treaty cannot create a corporation but a sovereign state which is party to a treaty can, in pursuance of its obligations accepted under the treaty, create a corporation which will be recognised in the United Kingdom. A member state can create a corporation by signing and ratifying the treaty if in that member state a treaty is self-executing and becomes part of domestic law on signature and ratification. Another member state, such as the UAE, can only create legal personality by the legislative process which was adopted in the case of the AMF agreement. In the present case the fund was given legal personality and capacity by the law of the state wherein it has its seat or permanent location. There is every reason why the fund should be recognised as a legal personality by the courts of the United Kingdom and no reason whatsoever why recognition should be withheld …'

D'Almeida Araujo Lda v *Sir Frederick Becker & Co Ltd* [1953] 2 All ER 288 Queen's Bench Division (Pilcher J)

• *Remoteness of damage is a question of substance, governed by the proper law of the contract – the measure of damages is a question of procedure, governed by the lex fori*

Facts

On 20 March 1947 the plaintiffs, (a firm of merchants carrying on business in Lisbon) agreed to sell to the defendants (an English company carrying on business as merchants in the City of London) 500 tons of palm oil at 14.20 escudos a kilo fob Angora. Payment was to be by way of credit established by 24 March. The proper law of the contract was Portuguese. On the same date the plaintiffs contracted with Mourao for the purchase of 500 tons of palm oil, which was intended to fulfil their contract with the defendants. Payment was to be by credit and opened by 24 March. The contract provided that in the event of breach the party in default should pay to the other as indemnity for the damages an amount corresponding to 5 per cent of the total value of the contract. At the same time, the defendants had agreed to resell the palm oil. However, the sub-purchasers failed to open the appropriate credit, which meant that the defendants were unable to open the credit in favour of the plaintiffs. The plaintiffs were ready to complete the sale up until 12 April. On 14 April the plaintiffs advertised the palm oil for sale in a Lisbon newspaper against immediate opening credit, but were unable to sell it.

The failure of the defendants to open the credit meant that the plaintiffs were unable to open the credit in favour of Mourao. Consequently, they were bound to pay an indemnity for breach. The plaintiffs claimed damages for the defendants' breach of contract under two heads: (1) loss of profit which they would have made on the resale; and (2) the indemnity which they were obliged to pay to Mourao for breach of contract.

Held

Under Portuguese law it was possible to recover unforeseeable damages. However, as per English law, the plaintiff was under a duty to mitigate his damage. Assuming that the costs of the indemnity could have been recovered under Portuguese law apart from this duty, his Lordship held that the plaintiffs could reasonably have mitigated their damage by reselling the palm oil on the Lisbon Produce Exchange. He therefore awarded nominal damages.

Pilcher J:

> 'While it was common ground between the parties that the substantive contract between them was governed by Portuguese law, the plaintiffs contended that the damages which they were entitled to recover in the particular circumstances of the case were also to be determined in accordance with the principles of Portuguese law. The defendants, on the contrary, submitted that even in a case where the substantive contract was governed by foreign law, procedural or remedial questions, which included the question of damages, ought to be determined according to the lex fori, in this case, the law of England. Subject to the question of the obligation of an innocent party to mitigate the damages, to which I will refer in a moment, the question of the proper law to be applied in regard to the damages in this case has importance, because the plaintiffs are seeking to recover from the defendants the £3,500 as one head of damage – that being, of course, the sum which they had to pay to Mourao for failing to carry out their contract with him.
>
> The loss sustained by the plaintiffs in paying that sum was clearly not a loss which was foreseeable by the defendants at the time when they negotiated this contract with the plaintiffs, and it is clear that under English law this sum of £3,500 would be irrecoverable by the plaintiffs from the defendants. It was argued by Mr Mocatta, on behalf of the plaintiffs, that they would, under Portuguese law, have been entitled to include this sum in their damages if damages were assessed on the principles of Portuguese law While I feel no certainty that the plaintiffs' right to recover damages in this case will turn out in the end to be any different whether the principles of English or Portuguese law are applied, it is none the less desirable that I should state my view on the point ...
>
> I was referred to a number of textbooks on the particular point whether in a foreign contract which has to be determined by the lex loci contractus the issue of damages is, in the words of some of the textbook writers, "a procedural or remedial matter" such as falls to be determined in accordance with the lex fori, or whether, on the other hand, it is part of the substantive contract between the parties and so to be determined in accordance with the lex loci contractus. I propose to read certain passages from the textbooks, because there is very little authority on this particular topic in English law. [Pilcher J proceeded to read passages in *Cheshire's Private International Law* (4th ed) at pp659–60] ...
>
> That passage from Professor Cheshire's book seems to me to be very closely reasoned and to offer considerable help in deciding this problem which is not an easy one. The conclusion at which he arrives would seem to be that questions of remoteness of damage should be governed by the proper law of the contract, whereas the quantification of damage, which according to the proper law is not too remote, should be governed by the lex fori.'

Despina R, The [1979] AC 685 House of Lords (Lords Wilberforce, Diplock, Salmon, Russell and Keith)

- *English courts can give judgment in a foreign currency in tort claims, and this would usually be the currency in which the plaintiff conducted his business*

Facts

Here two Greek vessels, the Despina R and the Eleftherotria collided off Shanghai. An agreement was reached between the owners that the owners of the Despina R would pay the owners of the Eleftherotria 85 per cent of the loss and damage caused to them by the collision. The matter was thereafter treated as a tort claim based upon negligence. The repair of the Eleftherotria took place partly in Shanghai, partly in Yokohama and partly in Los Angeles, and expenses were incurred in renmimbi yuan, yen, and dollars as well as a small sum in sterling; and these were met by paying out of a dollar account. In what currency should the owners of the Eleftherotria seek judgment against the owners of the Despina R, the currency (the 'expenditure currency') in which the various losses were sustained (yuan, yen, dollars and pounds etc), or the currency in which the losses were sustained, ie dollars ('the plaintiff's currency') or, perhaps, in sterling?

Held

In tort claims it was fairer to give judgment in the currency in which the loss was sustained rather than either of the other alternatives; and where the plaintiff proved he conducted his business in a particular currency and it was reasonably foreseeable that he would use that currency to acquire the other currencies to met the expenditure occasioned by the defendant's tort, then judgment should be given in that currency.

Lord Wilberforce:

> 'My Lords, I do not think that there can now be any doubt that, given the ability of an English court (and of arbitrators sitting in this country) to give judgment or to make an award in a foreign currency, to give a judgment in the currency in which the loss was sustained produces a juster result than one which fixed the plaintiff with a sum in sterling taken at the date of the breach or of the loss. I need not expand upon this because the point has been clearly made both in *Miliangos* v *George Frank (Textiles) Ltd* [1976] AC 443, and in cases which have followed it, as well as in commentators who, prior to Miliangos, advocated abandonment of the breach-date-sterling rule. To fix such a plaintiff with sterling commits him to the risk of changes in the value of a currency with which he has no connection: to award him a sum in the currency of the expenditure or loss, or that in which he bears the expenditure or loss, gives him exactly what he has lost and commits him only to the risk of changes in the value of that currency, or those currencies, which are either his currency or those which he has chosen to use.
>
> I shall consider the objections against the use of that currency or those currencies, but first it is necessary to decide between the expenditure currency and the plaintiff's currency …
>
> My Lords, in my opinion, this question can be solved by applying the normal principles, which govern the assessment of damages in cases of tort (I shall deal with contract cases in the second appeal). These are the principles of restitutio in integrum and that of the reasonable foreseeability of the damage sustained. It appears to me that a plaintiff, who normally conducts his business through a particular currency, and who, when other currencies are immediately involved, uses his own currency to obtain those currencies, can reasonably say that the loss he sustains is to be measured not by the immediate currencies in which the loss first emerges but by the amount of his own currency, which in the normal course of operation, he uses to obtain those currencies. This is the currency in which his loss is felt, and is the currency which it is reasonably foreseeable he will have to spend.
>
> There are some objections to this, but I think they can be answered. First, it is said that to use the method of finding the loss in the plaintiff's currency would involve the court or arbitrators in complicated inquiries. I am not convinced of this. The plaintiff has to prove his loss: if he wishes to present his claim in his own currency, the burden is on him to show to the satisfaction of the tribunal that his operations are conducted in that currency and that in fact it was his cur-

rency that was used, in a normal manner, to meet the expenditure for which he claims or that his loss can only be appropriately measured in that currency (this would apply in the case of a total loss of a vessel which cannot be dealt with by the "expenditure" method). The same answer can be given to the objection that some companies, particularly large multi-national companies, maintain accounts and operate in several currencies. Here again it is for the plaintiff to satisfy the court or arbitrators that the use of the particular currency was in the course of normal operations of that company and was reasonably foreseeable. Then it is said that this method produces inequality between plaintiffs. Two claimants who suffer a similar loss may come out with different sums according to the currency in which they trade. But if the losses of both plaintiffs are suffered at the same time, the amounts awarded to each of them should be equivalent even if awarded in different currencies: if at different times, this might justify difference in treatment. If it happened that the currencies of the two plaintiffs relatively changed in value before the date of judgment, that would be a risk which each plaintiff would have to accept. Each would still receive, for himself, compensation for *his* loss.

Finally it is said (and this argument would apply equally if the expenditure currency were taken) that uncertainty will take the place of certainty under the present rule. Undoubtedly the present (sterling-breach-date) rule produces certainty – but it is often simpler to produce an unjust rule than a just one. The question is whether, in order to produce a just, or juster, rule, too high a price has to be paid in terms of certainty.

I do not think so. I do not see any reason why legal advisers, or insurers, should not be able from their knowledge of the circumstances to assess the extent of probable liability. The most difficult step is to assess the quantum of each head of damage. Once this is done, it should not be difficult, on the basis of information which the plaintiff must provide, to agree or disagree with his claim for the relevant currency. … To say that this produces a measure of uncertainty may be true, but this is an uncertainty which arises in the nature of things from the variety of human experience. To resolve it is part of the normal process of adjudication. To attempt to confine this within a rigid formula would be likely to produce injustices which the courts and arbitrators would have to put themselves to much trouble to avoid.'

Doetsch, Re [1896] 2 Ch 836
Chancery Division (Romer J)

• *A rule of foreign law to the effect that the defendant's liability is conditional on other persons being sued first is procedural and will be ignored in English proceedings*

Facts

Sundheim & Doetsch (a Spanish firm) was indebted to Matheson & Co (a firm carrying on business in London). One of the partners in the Spanish firm died and Matheson & Co brought an action against the executors of his will for the recovery of their debt. The executors pleaded that by Spanish law they were not liable for the debts of the firm until the property of the firm was exhausted.

Held

The objection raised by the executors failed. The matter was procedural and as such did not bind an English court. The proper order and priority of distribution of assets is always a matter for the lex fori.

Romer J:

'It is admitted that the plaintiffs are creditors of the firm of Sundheim & Doetsch. As such creditors they ask for the usual administration of the estate of Mr Doetsch, who is dead – that is to say, they ask to have the separate assets of Mr Doetsch applied in payment of the joint debts after first satisfying the separate creditors. Objection is taken to that relief on the ground that the firm is a

Spanish firm, and that by Spanish law the estate of one partner who dies cannot be reached by joint creditors of the firm until the estate of the firm has been proceeded against or is exhausted, or there is a proved insufficiency of the joint estate.

The objection fails, and for this reason. In the first place, it is clear that according to English law, as a matter of procedure and to avoid circuity of action, a creditor of a partnership of which one member is dead is entitled as a creditor to share in the administration of the estate of that deceased partner after the separate debts are paid, without first proving that the surviving partner is insolvent and without being obliged first to have recourse to the joint assets. Now, from the admissions before me – and there is no other evidence – it appears to me that the Spanish law only differs from the English law in a matter of procedure. The Spanish courts require that a joint creditor shall before he seeks to reach the estate of a deceased partner first proceed against and exhaust or prove the insolvency of the joint estate. In my opinion, that is a matter of procedure. It is clear that the Spanish firm was not a corporation. On the contrary, the admissions show that the deceased partner's estate can be reached after proper procedure has been taken to exhaust or prove the insolvency of the joint estate; and certainly it cannot, I think, be successfully contended that the plaintiffs are to be considered as having contracted in any way not to take such proceedings as are before me. Now, that being so, there is nothing to prevent the plaintiffs from asking for the relief which they claim. The procedure of the Spanish courts does not bind the courts here; nor does the Spanish law at all affect the right of a creditor here to avail himself of the benefits given by the English courts in administering estates here. For that *Bullock* v *Caird* (1875) LR 10 QB 276 is a sufficient authority. Speaking generally, English assets have to be distributed according to the English law – according to priorities recognised by courts in this country – according to the rules of procedure and course of distribution adopted here. That general proposition was pointed out, amongst other places, in *Thurburn* v *Steward* (1871) LR 3 PC 478 by Lord Cairns, who says: "The proper order and priority of distribution of assets is always a matter for the lex fori, and the country where the distribution takes place always claims to itself the right to regulate the course of distribution."

For these reasons it appears to me that the objection fails. I need only add, that in my opinion the contract between the parties on which the plaintiffs' rights turn is to be governed by the lex loci contractus – that is to say, by the English law.'

Halcyon Isle, The [1981] AC 221 Privy Council (Lords Diplock, Salmon, Elwyn-Jones, Scarman and Lane)

- *The priority of various forms of security and other claims are procedural and for the lex fori to determine*

Facts

Bankers Trust International Ltd obtained a mortgage over a British registered vessel, The Halcyon Isle, to secure a loan to the vessel's owners, in 1973. In 1974 various repairs were carried out to The Halcyon Isle in New York but the repairers were not paid. Under these circumstances under the law of New York, the repairers (known as 'necessaries men') obtained that special form of security known as a maritime lien to secure their claim to payment. Under English law (as well as the law of Singapore) the necessaries man did not obtain a maritime lien. (A maritime lien is a remarkable form of security; the secured creditor does not have to have possession of the vessel in question and the lien was effective whether later creditors had notice of the lien or not; it was enforced by an action in rem against the vessel). A maritime lien would take priority over a mortgage. In late 1974 both the mortgagees and the repairers commenced actions in rem against The Halcyon Isle in Singapore: the vessel was arrested and sold. But the proceeds of the sale were insufficient to satisfy all the claims; and the question arose whether the repairers or the mortgagees had priority.

Held (Lords Salmon and Scarman dissenting)
In such in rem proceedings the order of priority of claims and the recognition of a right to enforce a maritime lien were to be determined by the lex fori.

Lord Diplock:

'At first sight, the answer to the question posed by this appeal seems simple. The priorities as between claimants to a limited fund which is being distributed by a court of law are matters of procedure which under English rules of conflict of laws are governed by the lex fori; so English law is the only relevant law by which the priorities as between the mortgagees and the necessaries men are to be determined; and in English law mortgagees take priority over necessaries men.

In the case of a ship, however, the classification of claims against her former owners for the purpose of determining priorities to participate in the proceeds of her sale may raise a further problem of conflict of laws, since claims may have arisen as a result of events that occurred not only on the high seas but also within the territorial jurisdictions of a number of different foreign states. So the lex causae of one claim may differ from the lex causae of another, even though the events which gave rise to the claim in each of those foreign states are similar in all respects, except their geographical location; the leges causarum of various claims, of which under English conflict rules the "proper law" is that of different states, may assign different legal consequences to similar events. So the court distributing the limited fund may be faced, as in the instant case, with the problem of classifying the foreign claims arising under differing foreign systems of law in order to assign each of them to the appropriate class in the order of priorities under the lex fori of the distributing court.

The choice would appear to lie between (1) on the one hand classifying by reference to the events on which each claim was founded and giving to it the priority to which it would be entitled under the lex fori if those events had occurred within the territorial jurisdiction of the distributing court; or (2) on the other hand applying a complicated kind of partial renvoi by (i) first ascertaining in respect of each foreign claim the legal consequences, *other than those relating to priorities in the distribution of a limited fund*, that would be attributed under its own lex causae to the events on which the claim is founded; and (ii) then giving to the foreign claim the priority accorded under the lex fori to claims arising from events, however dissimilar, which would have given rise to the same or analogous legal consequences if they had occurred within the territorial jurisdiction of the distributing court.

To omit the dissection of the lex causae of the claim that the second choice prescribes and to say instead that if under the lex causae the relevant events would give rise to a maritime lien, the English court must give to those courts all the legal consequences of a maritime lien under English law, would, in their Lordships' view, be too simplistic an approach to the questions of conflicts of law that are involved.

Even apart from the merit of simplicity, the choice in favour of the first alternative, classification by reference to events, appears to their Lordships to be preferable in principle. In distributing a limited fund that is insufficient to pay in full all creditors of a debtor whose claims against him have already been quantified and proved, the court is not any longer concerned with enforcing against the debtor himself the individual creditors' original rights against him. It is primarily concerned in doing even-handed justice between competing creditors whose respective claims to be a creditor may have arisen under a whole variety of different and, it may be, conflicting systems of national law. It may be plausibly suggested that the moral and rational justification of the general conflicts of law rule, applied by English courts to claims arising out of foreign contracts, that the contract should be given the same legal consequences as would be accorded to it under its "proper law", is that the legitimate expectations of the parties to the contract as to their rights against one another, which will result from entering into and carrying out the contract, ought not to be defeated by any change of the forum in which such rights have to be enforced. Rights of priority over other creditors of the defaulting party to such a contract, in a judicial distribution of a fund which is insufficient to satisfy all the creditors in full, are not, however, rights of the parties to the contract against one another. They are rights as between one party to the contract against strangers to the contract, the other creditors, who have done nothing to arouse any legitimate expectations in that party as to the priority to which he will be entitled in the distribution of such a fund. Every such creditor whose claim is based on contract or quasi-contract must have known that in so far as the legal consequences of his claim under its own lex causae included rights to priority over other classes of creditors in the distribution of a limited fund resulting from an action in rem against a ship, that particular part of the lex causae would be compelled to yield to the lex fori of any foreign court in which the action in rem might be brought.'

Miliangos* v *George Frank (Textiles) Ltd [1976] AC 443 House of Lords (Lords Wilberforce, Simon, Cross, Edmund-Davies and Fraser)

• *English courts can give judgment for breach of contract in a foreign currency*

Facts

Here the respondent, a Swiss, sold a quantity of polyester yarn to the appellant, an English company. The proper law of the contract was Swiss law and the price, which was to be paid (within thirty days of invoice) to a Swiss bank, was in Swiss francs. The bills of exchange accepted by the appellant were dishonoured; and in due course the seller sued the purchaser in England for payment. Since sterling had depreciated sharply against the Swiss franc since the cause of action arose, the seller sought judgment in Swiss francs rather than in sterling, calculated according to the rate of exchange prevailing when the contract was breached. But such a judgment would be contrary to the decision of the House of Lords in *Re United Railways of the Havana and Regla Warehouses* [1961] AC 1007.

Held

The currency instability which had overtaken the pound (and other currencies) since the latter decision justified a departure from that decision, thus (Lord Simon dissenting) an English court could give judgment in a foreign currency, where the proper law of the contract in question was not English law and the money of account was not sterling but the currency in which the judgment was sought (or possibly some other foreign currency). When the court authorised enforcement of the judgment conversion into sterling would have to take place but the rate of exchange would be that prevailing when enforcement was authorised.

Lord Wilberforce:

> 'First, I do not for myself think it doubtful that, in a case such as the present, justice demands that the creditor should not suffer from fluctuations in the value of sterling. His contract has nothing to do with sterling: he has bargained for his own currency and only his own currency. The substance of the debtor's obligations depends upon the proper law of the contract (here Swiss law): and though English law (lex fori) prevails as regards procedural matters, it must surely be wrong in principle to allow procedure to affect, detrimentally, the substance of the creditor's rights. Courts are bound by their own procedural law and must obey it, if imperative, though to do so may seem unjust. But if means exist for giving effect to the substance of a foreign obligation, con-

formably with the rules of private international law, procedure should not unnecessarily stand in the way.

There is, unfortunately, as Lord Radcliffe pointed out in the *Havana Railways* case, a good deal of confusion in English cases as to what the creditor's rights are. Appeal has been made to the principle of nominalism, so as to say that the creditor must take the pound sterling as he finds it. Lord Denning said so in the *Havana Railways* case (pp1069–1070) and I can safely and firmly disagree with him in that because he has himself, since then, come to hold another view. The creditor has no concern with pounds sterling: for him what matters is that a Swiss franc for good or ill should remain a Swiss franc. This is substantially the reasoning of Holmes J in the important judgment of the US Supreme Court in *Deutsche Bank Filiale Nurnberg* v *Humphrey* (1926) 272 US 517. Another argument is that the "breach date" makes for certainty whereas to choose a later date makes the claim depend on currency fluctuations. But this is only a partial truth. The only certainty achieved is certainty in the sterling amount – but that is not in point since sterling does not enter into the bargain. The relevant certainty which the rule ought to achieve is that which gives the creditor neither more nor less than he bargained for. He bargained for 415,522.45 Swiss francs; whatever this means in (unstipulated) foreign currencies, whichever way the exchange into those currencies may go, he should get 415,522.45 Swiss francs or as nearly as can be brought about. That such a solution, if practicable, is just, and adherence to the "breach date" in such a case unjust in the circumstances of today, adds greatly to the strength of the argument for revising the rule or, putting it more technically, it adds strength to the case for awarding delivery in specie rather than giving damages.

Secondly, and I must deal with this point more briefly than historically it deserves, objections based on authority against making an order in specie for the payment or delivery of foreign money, are not, on examination, found to rest on any solid principle or indeed on more than the court's discretion. Your Lordships were referred to a number of early cases dealing with claims expressed or which the courts thought should or could have been expressed, in terms of foreign money. ... The most respectful adherent to tradition and legal history can find nothing decisive here. The fons et origo of the modern self-imposed limitation is clearly the judgment of Sir Nathaniel Lindley MR in *Manners* v *Pearson & Son* [1898] 1 Ch 581, 586–587. I shall not cite from this at length. I think it is clear that he is saying no more than that for enforcement purposes conversion into sterling must be made and he leaves open the question whether before the Debtors Act 1869 an order could have been made in Chancery for a foreign currency (in that case Mexican dollars). He continues that no necessity for conversion arises until the court orders payment and says that it does not follow that the sum to be inserted in the order is the (sterling) equivalent at that time, for there may be damages or interest as well. So I think that he leaves open the whole question of specific orders: and since his time, no real re-examination of the practicability of them has been made. In *Beswick* v *Beswick* [1968] AC 58 this House laid down that in a suitable case specific performance may be ordered of an agreement to pay a sum of money of the United Kingdom. Lord Pearce (p89) quoted from *Hart* v *Hart* (1881) 18 Ch D 670, 685 the words:

> "... when an agreement for valuable consideration ... has been partially performed, the court ought to do its utmost to carry out that agreement by a decree for specific performance."

If this is so as regards money of this country, I can see no reason why it should not be so as regards foreign money: indeed, the latter seems to have a more "specific" character than the former.

These considerations and the circumstances I have set forth, when related to the arguments which moved their Lordships in the *Havana Railways* case [1961] AC 1007, lead me to the conclusion that, if these circumstances had been shown to exist in 1961, some at least of their Lordships, assuming always that the interests of justice in the particular case so required, would have been led, as one of them very notably has been led, to take a different view.

This bring me to the declaration made by this House in 1966. Under it, the House affirmed its power to depart from a previous decision when it appears right to do so, recognising that too rigid adherence to precedent might lead to injustice in a particular case and unduly restrict the proper development of the law. My Lords, on the assumption that to depart from the *Havana Railways* case would not involve undue practical difficulties, that a new and more satisfactory rule is capable of being stated, I am of opinion that the present case falls within the terms of the declaration. To change the rule would, for the reasons already explained, avoid injustice in the present case. To change it would enable the law to keep in step with commercial needs and with the majority of other countries facing similar problems. The latter proposition is well vouched by Dr F A Mann's work, *The Legal Aspect of Money*, 3rd ed (1971) Chapter X …

My Lords, in conclusion I would say that, difficult as this whole matter undoubtedly is, if once a clear conclusion is reached as to what the law ought now to be, declaration of it by this House is appropriate. The law on this topic is judge-made: it has been built up over the years from case to case. It is entirely within this House's duty, in the course of administering justice, to give the law a new direction in a particular case where, on principle and in reason, it appears right to do so. I cannot accept the suggestion that because a rule is long established only legislation can change it – that may be so when the rule is so deeply entrenched that it has infected the whole legal system, or the choice of a new rule involves more far-reaching research than courts can carry out.'

Services Europe Atlantique Sud of Paris* v *Stockholms Rederiaktiebolag Svea of Stockholm [1979] AC 685 House of Lords (Lords Wilberforce, Diplock, Salmon, Russell and Keith)

• *In contract cases the court will give judgment in the currency that best expresses the plaintiff's loss, unless the contract provided otherwise*

Facts

This case concerned a cargo of onions that were shipped aboard the Folias from Spain to Brazil. The onions were damaged when they arrived because the vessel's refrigeration had broken down; and the Brazilian cargo receivers recovered damages, assessed in Brazilian cruzeiros, from the charterers, a French firm, which obtained the cruzeiros to settle this claim by selling French francs. The charterers (the respondents) now sought to recover these damages from the Swedish shipowners (the appellants) basing their claim on breach of the charterparty. The proper law of the charterparty was English although the hire was to be paid in dollars. The owners admitted liability but argued that the damages should be paid in cruzeiros (which had depreciated by more than 50 per cent against the French franc since the payment to the cargo receivers) rather than in francs, sterling or dollars.

Held

The parties had not agreed that damages for breach were to be paid in any particular currency, thus judgment should be given in the currency that best expressed the party's loss; and since the charterers had used francs in order to purchase the necessary cruzeiros, French francs were the currency that best expressed their loss.

Lord Wilberforce:

> 'The present case is concerned with a charterparty for carriage by sea, the parties to which are Swedish and French. It was in the

contemplation of the parties that delivery of the goods carried might be made in any of a number of countries with a currency different from that of either of the parties. Loss might be suffered, through non-delivery or incomplete delivery, or delivery of damaged or unsuitable goods, in any of those countries, and if any such loss were to fall upon the charterer, he in turn might have a claim against the shipowners. Although the proper law of the contract was accepted to be English by virtue of a London arbitration clause, neither of the parties to the contract, nor the contract itself, nor the claim which arose against the charterers, nor that by his charterers against the owners, had any connection with sterling, so that prima facie this would be a case for giving judgment in a foreign currency. This is not disputed in the present appeal, and the only question is which is the appropriate currency in which to measure the loss.

Prima facie, there is much to be said in favour of measuring the loss in cruzeiros: the argument for this was powerfully stated by Robert Goff J. The initial liability of the charterers was measured in that currency by the difference between the value of sound goods arrived at the port of discharge and the damaged value at that port. To require or admit a further conversion can be said to introduce an unnecessary complication brought about by an act of the charterers' choice. I am unable in the end to accept this argument. The essential question is what was the loss suffered by the respondents. I do not find this to be identical with that suffered by the cargo receivers: the charterers' claim against the owners is not one for indemnity in respect of expenditure sustained but is one for damages for breach of contract. Robert Goff J makes this plain in his judgment [1979] QB 491, 498:

> "... the charterers' claim [as formulated] was a claim for damages, on the basis that [they] incurred a personal liability to the receivers under the bills of lading which they were compelled to discharge; ..."

I think it must follow from this that their loss, which they claim as damages, was the discharge of the receivers' claim, together with the legal and other expenses they incurred. They discharged all these by providing francs – until they provided the francs to meet the receivers' claim they suffered no loss. Then secondly was this loss the kind of loss which, under the contract, they were entitled to recover against the owners? The answer to this is provided by the arbitrators' finding that it was reasonable to contemplate that the charterers, being a French corporation and having their place of business in Paris, would have to use French francs to purchase other currencies to settle cargo claims arising under the bills of lading. So in my opinion the charterers' recoverable loss was, according to normal principle, the sum of French francs which they paid.'

3 A Special Connecting Factor: Domicile

The domicile of dependence

Beaumont, Re [1893] 3 Ch 490
Chancery Division (Stirling J)

• *The change in the domicile of a fatherless infant which may follow from a change of domicile on the part of the mother should not to be regarded as the necessary consequence of a change of the mother's domicile*

Facts

Mrs B, a widow with several infant children, all of whom had a Scotch domicile, married again in Scotland in November 1834. In January 1835 Mr N, her second husband, went to reside permanently in England, and shortly afterwards Mrs N and all her children, except CB, joined him in England and acquired an English domicile. CB remained in Scotland, with an aunt, with whom she had lived since her father's death in 1821. CB attained 21 in May 1840, and she died in Scotland in April 1841.

Held

Stirling J:

> 'In *Potinger* v *Wightman* (1817) 3 Mer 67 it was held that where the widow of a person domiciled in Guernsey brought her children to England after her husband's death, and herself gained a domicile in England, the domicile of the children became English likewise. In his judgment, Sir W Grant says this:
>
> > "Here the question is, whether, after the death of the father, children remaining under the care of the mother, follow the domicile which she may acquire, or retain that which their father had at his death, until they are capable of gaining one by acts of their own. The weight of authority is certainly in favour of the former proposition. It has the sanction both of Voet and Bynkershoek; the former however qualifying it by a condition that the domicile shall not have been changed for the fraudulent purpose of obtaining an advantage by altering the rule of succession. Pothier, whose authority is equal to that of either, maintains the proposition as thus qualified. There is an introductory chapter to his *Treatise on the Custom of Orleans*, in which he considers several points that are common to all the customs of France, and, among others, the law of domicile. He holds in opposition to the opinion of some jurists, that a tutor cannot change the domicile of his pupil, but he considers it as clear that the domicile of the surviving mother is also the domicile of the children, provided it be not with a fraudulent view to their succession that she shifts the place of her abode. And he says, that such fraud would be presumed, if no reasonable motive could be assigned for the change."
>
> That decision was treated as binding by the House of Lords in the case of *Johnstone* v *Beattie* (1843) 10 Cl & Fin 42. The Lord Chancellor (Lord Lyndhurst) in that case said:
>
> > "The case of *Potinger* v *Wightman* appears to have been well argued and well considered, and must be held conclusive as to the mother's power to change the domicile – which is a novel point in the law of England – unless there is some opposite decision."...

In the present case, Catherine Beaumont's domicile of origin was Scotch. Her residence was in Scotland from her birth to her death, the only exception being the occasional temporary visits to her mother in England referred to in the evidence. She lived nine months after attaining twenty-one, and still remained in Scotland. Under these circumstances she retained her domicile of origin, unless the law be that the domicile of an infant whose father is dead necessarily follows that of the mother. Even so, the continued residence of Catherine Beaumont in Scotland after she attained twenty-one would be evidence of an intention on her part to reside there permanently; but without further information as to the facts, I am not quite satisfied that the case ought to be decided on that ground. There is a considerable weight of authority for the proposition that where the mother of infant children remarries, their domicile ceases to follow hers: if that be so, then the domicile of Catherine Beaumont remained Scotch. I think, however, that the better view is that the change in the domicile of an infant which, as is shewn by the decision in *Potinger* v *Wightman*, may follow from a change of domicile on the part of the mother, is not to be regarded as the necessary consequence of a change of the mother's domicile, but as the result of the exercise by her of a power vested in her for the welfare of the infants, which in their interest she may abstain from exercising, even when she changes her own domicile. I agree with the remark of Mr Dicey (*Dicey on Domicile*):

> "It is reasonable to hold, that the fiction which assigns to a woman on marriage the domicile of her husband should not be extended, so as necessarily to give to step-children the domicile of their stepfather; but it is less easy to see why it should be held, that a widow, on remarriage, loses all control over the domicile of her infant children, born during her first marriage."

In the present case, I think the mother abstained from exercising this power. Catherine Beaumont was not left in Scotland for any temporary purpose, such as education; upon the evidence her home was there with her aunt, not in England with her mother. In my opinion, therefore, her domicile was Scotch.'

IRC v *Duchess of Portland* [1982] Ch 314 Chancery Division (Nourse J)

• *At common law married women took the domicile of their husbands but this rule has been abolished by s1 of the Domicile and Matrimonial Proceedings Act 1973*

Facts

The Duchess of Portland was born in Quebec and had a domicile of origin there. However, she married the Duke of Portland, who was always domiciled in England, in 1948 and thereby acquired a domicile of dependency in England. She maintained strong links with Canada: she kept a house there and made regular and lengthy visits (usually during the summer) to it. She retained her Canadian citizenship. Her husband had agreed to retire with her to Canada. It was necessary to determine for tax purposes where she was domiciled after 1 January 1974. Did she retain her husband's domicile, or had she acquired a domicile of choice in Quebec after her annual visit in 1974?

Held

That the Duchess of Portland had not since the coming into force of the Act ceased to reside in England, thus in terms of s1(2) the domicile of dependence persisted as a domicile of choice; ie she was domiciled in England.

Nourse J:

> 'Immediately before January 1, 1974, the taxpayer had her husband's English domicile by dependency. She was therefore to be treated as retaining that domicile as a domicile of choice unless and until it was changed by acquisition or revival of another domicile. Before the commissioners the tax-

payer put her case in three different ways, but on this appeal she has claimed only that her English domicile of dependency was changed by the revival of her Quebec domicile of origin when she went to Canada for her annual visit in July 1974.

I will now attempt some general observations on s1(2) of the Act of 1973. First, it is a deeming provision. Secondly, that which is deemed in a case where the domicile of dependency is not the same as the domicile of origin is the retention of the domicile of dependency as a domicile of choice. I think that that must mean that the effect of the subsection is to reimpose the domicile of dependency as a domicile of choice. The concept of an imposed domicile of choice is not one which it is very easy to grasp, but the force of the subsection requires me to do the best I can. It requires me to treat the taxpayer as if she had acquired an English domicile of choice, even though the facts found by the commissioners tell me that that would have been an impossibility in the real world. In my judgment it necessarily follows that the question whether, after January 1, 1974, the taxpayer abandoned her deemed English domicile of choice must be determined by reference to the test appropriate to the abandonment of a domicile of choice and not by reference to the more lenient test appropriate to the abandonment of one of dependency.

There can no longer be any doubt as to the test appropriate to the abandonment of a domicile of choice. The leading case on the subject is *Udny* v *Udny* (1869) LR 1 Sc & Div 441. The law is stated with accuracy and concision in rule 13(1) in *Dicey and Morris, The Conflict of Laws*, 10th ed (1980), vol 1, p 128, which is in these terms:

> "A person abandons a domicile of choice in a country by ceasing to reside there and by ceasing to intend to reside there permanently or indefinitely, and not otherwise."

There are therefore two requirements which, with deference to certain arguments which have been advanced on behalf of the taxpayer, must be kept entirely separate. …

Although s1(2) effects a change of domicile, it is important to bear in mind that the change is not necessarily dependent on a change either of intention or of residence. I have already touched on this point in relation to the taxpayer's intention in the present case. I can take the example of a woman with a foreign domicile of origin married to a domiciled Englishman who left her husband and returned to live in her country of origin with the intention of pemanent or indefinite residence there before January 1, 1974. Consistently with the rule which would have applied if the husband had died before January 1, 1974 (see *In re Scullard, decd* [1957] Ch 107), the wife's domicile of dependency would have changed by revival of her domicile of origin on January 1, 1974, without the need for any further act on her part. Accordingly, s1(2) of the Act of 1973 requires you first to look at the state of affairs prevailing on January 1, 1974, to see whether there has been any automatic change on that date. If there has not, you are required to look at events after that date in order to see whether any change has occurred subsequently.

I now return to the material facts of the present case. I start with the fact that the taxpayer has ever since 1948 returned to Quebec for some 10 to 12 weeks in each year to visit her parents, when they were alive, and other relatives, and generally to maintain her links with Canada. In 1956 she made an additional visit to look after her mother who was then ill. For the past 14 years or so she has owned, maintained at her own expense and kept ready for her occupation at all times the family house in Metis Beach at which she and her husband had stayed for the previous eight years. But since 1948 she has otherwise lived with her husband in England. There has been no significant change in the pattern of her life between 1948 and 1978, the latter being the last of the years of assessment with which the revenue claim in this case is concerned. On those facts it appears clear to me that since 1948 the taxpayer has been physically present in this country as an inhabitant of it. Her physical presence in Quebec has been for periods of limited duration and for the purpose of maintaining her links with the country to which it is her intention ultimately to return. That is not enough to have made her an inhabitant of Quebec. In my judgment it is clear that she was resident in England on January 1, 1974, and that that residence was not displaced when she went to Canada in July 1974 or at any other time during the material period. …

My conclusion is that the taxpayer did not cease to reside in this country either in July 1974 or at any other material time and that means that she did not abandon the English domicile of choice which was imposed on her by s1(2) of the Act of 1973.'

The domicile of choice

Drevon v *Drevon* (1834) 34 LJ Ch 129 Court of Chancery (Kindersley V-C)

- *Domicile – English or French?*

Facts

Upon a question whether the domicile of a testator who was a native of France, was English or French, the principal evidence indicated, in support of the English domicile, that he came to England when he was 18; that he carried on a business in London for more than 20 years; that he always resided in England, with occasional visits to his native country; that he married an Englishwoman according to the English rites; that he took leases of his business premises in England for 21 years; that he voted at an election; that he served the office of headborough; that he consulted a lawyer as to obtaining letters of naturalisation; that his children were registered and baptised in England according to the English form; that he made an English will which would have been inoperative in France; and that he repeatedly expressed his intention of making England his home, and becoming an Englishman. And in support of the French domicile: that he purchased a piece of land in his native village, and often said he should build a house there and return to live in France; that he paid a visit every year to France; that he placed his children at school in France; and by his will appointed his brother, who resided in France, one of the executors and guardians of his children.

Held

On the balance of evidence, that the testator's domicile was English.

Kindersley V-C:

'Now, in every case upon the subject of domicile, the first question which presents itself to the mind is, what is meant by "domicile"? What is meant by change of domicile? What is the abandonment of the domicile of origin and the adoption of a new domicile? All that is based upon the question, what is domicile? I shall not, of course, think it necessary on this occasion to go through all the various definitions of "domicile" which have been given or attempted from the celebrated writers on Roman law down to the latest period. It has been observed over and over again that no one has succeeded in giving a definition of "domicile" that will, in the first place, comport with all the decisions which have been come to, or will, in the next place, assist in relieving the Court from the difficulty of defining it. But, whatever is the definition, if you could give one, of domicile, what are the acts, which are sufficient to constitute a change of domicile? It leaves you much in the same difficulty even as you are in as to its definition. I think the Court has been under the necessity of doing this in all cases, taking all the acts of every kind, more or less important, throughout the man's life upon which you can have evidence, taking not only his acts, but his declarations valeant quantum, and then judging whether the testator did or did not mean to give up his domicile of origin and adopt a new one. I may say with regard to the evidence of acts, there is no one circumstance that has ever been brought to the attention of the Court in any of the cases, as to which I think it may not be truly said that in some of the cases that occur, that act or that circumstance which has been treated as of very great importance, in other cases that same act or circumstance has been treated as of very little importance. For example, the first act generally brought forward, and, of course, which is brought forward and relied upon in this case, is length of residence. Length of residence has in many cases, both by English and by foreign jurists, been considered a very important ingredient in the question, and in other cases it has been considered as of little importance, that is, as compared with and brought into connexion and contact with other circumstances, of which evidence is given in the case. I think, with regard to that point, the true conclusion is this, not that any one act or any one circumstance is necessarily per se of vast importance and other circumstances of little importance, but it is a question what is the relative importance of the different acts, whether some acts tending one way are of greater weight than those tending the other as to the animus manendi or the animus revertendi, or the animus as to changing domicile. I think this also maybe said, there is no act, no circumstance in a man's life, however trivial it may be in itself, which ought to be left out of consideration in trying the question whether there was an intention to change the domicile. A trivial act might possibly be of more weight with regard to determining this question than an act, which was of more importance to a man in his lifetime. I think the tendency of the decisions in our Courts of late years, that is, for some time past, has been this, upon the question of the abandonment of the domicile of origin and the adoption of a new domicile, to be less and less disposed to give weight to circumstances and acts which formerly were considered to be of considerable importance … having considered the matter, I think the domicile is English, and therefore the certificate is right.'

Furse (decd), Re, Furse* v *IRC [1980] 3 All ER 838 Chancery Division (Fox J)

• *Effect of a vague and indefinite contingency on an individual's intention to reside in a state*

Facts

The testator was born in Rhode Island with a domicile of origin in Rhode Island in 1883. While still a young child, however, he was brought to England by his father where he was educated and where he remained until he took up employment in New York at the age of 24 (in 1907). He married and remained in New York until 1923, save for a period of war service in the British Army during the First World War. In 1923 he moved with his wife to England and bought a farm here. Although he and his wife considered returning to New York or buying a farm elsewhere in the United States from time to time during the 1940s and 1950s, the testator then decided not to return to the United States as long as he was capable of leading an active life on the farm. When he died the liability of his estate for estate duty depended upon whether he died domiciled in New York or England.

Held

That the testator's intention to remain in England unless he was incapable of leading an active life on the farm, was an intention to remain in England save on a vague and indefinite contingency; thus he had acquired a domicile of choice in England before his death.

Fox J:

> 'In *Inland Revenue Commissioners* v *Bullock* [1976] 1 WLR 1178 both the requirements referred to by Buckley LJ were satisfied. The contingency was a wholly clear and well-defined contingency, namely whether the propositus survived his wife; and there was a substantial possibility that the contingency might occur, having

regard to the respective ages of the propositus and his wife.

The present case, it seems to me, is very different. The fundamental difference in outlook between Group Captain Bullock and the testator was that, while Group Captain Bullock had every wish to leave England, the testator was entirely happy here.

Counsel for the plaintiff says that there are two possible ways of interpreting the testator's expressed intention. First, he wanted to remain in England to the end of his days unless his physical decline was such as to prevent him going on with his usual life at West Hoathly. Second, he did not want to remain here to the end of his days. He wanted to return to the United States but, nevertheless, felt that, while he had a farm and staff and could manage, he should continue to discharge his responsibilities as a farmer.

The latter, counsel for the plaintiff submits, is correct. I do not agree with that. It seems to me that, from the manner in which he expressed his intentions, the testator's hope was that he could go on living his accustomed and very pleasant life at West Hoathly to the end of his days. It was his good fortune to achieve that. The only circumstance on the happening of which he expressed any intention of leaving England was if he was no longer able to live an active physical life on the farm. Apart from that, he intended to remain in England all his life.

But that contingency is altogether indefinite. It has no precision at all. A man's idea of an active physical life is likely to contract with the years. At the age of 80, after 40 years in England, the testator was still living at West Hoathly and, although he had been ill, he had no firm plans at all for leaving England.

The testator's expressed intention, it seems to me, depended entirely on his own assessment of whether an ill-defined event had occurred. I think it really amounted to no more than saying, "I will leave England when I feel I want to leave England". That is substantially the same as Buckley LJ's example of the man who says he will leave "when I've had enough of it".

In a significant piece of evidence Mr Besemer said that the testator always wanted to stay in England a bit longer. That, I think, is only a variant of James LJ's example of the man who expects to reach the horizon. At the end he finds himself no nearer.

If one looks at the other limb of Buckley LJ's formulation, namely, "is there a sufficiently substantial possibility of the contingency happening to justify regarding the intention to return as a real determination to do so on the contingency occurring rather than a vague hope or aspiration", that does not arise unless the court concludes that the contingency itself is sufficiently clear to be identified. But it seems to me that the vagueness of the notion, coupled with the fact that the testator's mode of life was wholly congenial to him, is such that one must be left in the greatest doubt whether, in the end, it had any reality in the testator's mind at all. The possibility of leaving West Hoathly was not, indeed, even a hope or an aspiration. As I interpret his outlook, it was something that the testator cannot have wished for.

Having regard to the way in which the testator expressed his intentions, one cannot, I think, conclude that there was a substantial possibility of the contingency happening. One does not really know with any certainty what the contingency was. The testator himself was the only interpreter.

In *Re Fuld (deceased) (No 3)* [1968] P 675 at 684–685 Scarman J, after referring to the need in establishing the existence of a domicile of choice to show that the propositus intended to reside indefinitely in the country in question, said:

> "If a man intends to return to the land of his birth upon a clearly foreseen and reasonably anticipated contingency, eg the end of his job, the intention required by law is lacking; but, if he has in mind only a vague possibility, such as making a fortune (a modern example might be winning a football pool) or some sentiment about dying in the land of his fathers, such a state of mind is consistent with the intention required by law."

I do not think that the testator can be described as having in mind any clearly foreseen contingency. The contingency which he expressed was vague and permitted of almost infinite adjustment to meet his own wishes.

It is said on behalf of the plaintiff that the testator's intention was simply to return to the United States on his retirement from farming. The case is thus similar to a man returning to his native country at the end of his job. I think that is unreal. Farming was not really the testator's job; rather it was an agreeable adjunct to his mode of life. He was not employed by anybody and there was a manager to run the farm. His intention was not expressed in terms of retirement from farming, but of having to give up an active physical life which he enjoyed.

The examination of the nature of the contingency on which a propositus expresses an intention to leave his place of residence is, of course, only an aid in ascertaining intention. One cannot, I think, apply tests of certainty too mechanically or in too refined a way. The question in the end is whether, on the balance of probabilities, the testator intended to end his days here. …

It seems to me that the intention of the testator was indeed to continue to reside in England for an unlimited period. His intention was to continue to live here for the rest of his life, save on the contingency which he expressed. That contingency is so vague that I do not think it can be regarded as imposing any clear limitation on the period of his residence. I do not believe that he was ever prepared to face up to such a limitation. The contingency is of the sort which Simon P in *Qureshi* v *Qureshi* [1971] 1 All ER 325 at 340, [1972] Fam 173 at 193 described as 'open-ended'. One comes back at the last, it seems to me, to the fact that the testator was determined to live in England for a quite unlimited period. …

The authorities emphasise, of course, that a man cannot acquire a domicile of choice in a country if his intention is merely to reside there for a limited time, or for some temporary or special purpose (see, for example, *Inland Revenue Commissioners* v *Bullock* [1976] 3 All ER 353, [1976] 1 WLR 1178 at 1184). I do not see how the testator's residence in England can, by the time of his death, be described as for some temporary or special purpose. Nor, for the reasons which I have given, was it for a limited time. "By domicile", said Lord Cranworth in *Whicker* v *Hume* (1858) 7 HL Cas 124 at 160, [1843–60] All ER Rep 450 at 458, "we mean home, the permanent home." I think that, when the testator died in his 81st year, still in England and still with no arrangements made for leaving England, one could not realistically regard his permanent home as other than in England. He intended to live out his days here, save on a contingency so vaguely expressed that I do not think, against the history of his life, it could be regarded for practical purposes as limiting that intention.

In the circumstances I will declare the testator died domiciled in England.'

IRC v *Bullock* [1976] 1 WLR 1178 Court of Appeal (Buckley, Roskill and Goff LJJ)

• *A real determination even if contingent to settle elsewhere than in the place of residence prevents the acquisition of a domicile of choice, but a vague aspiration to change one's residence does not prevent the acquisition of a domicile of choice*

Facts

Here Group Captain Bullock's domicile was in issue for income tax purposes. Bullock had a domicile of origin in Nova Scotia (he was born there in 1910). However, he had come to England in 1932 to join the RAF and had served in the RAF until 1959. He had married an English woman who did not want to live anywhere but England. Although Bullock had clearly established a matrimonial home in England, he had maintained a firm intention to return to Canada should he survive his wife. Was this sufficient to prevent him obtaining a domicile in England?

Held

That Group Captain Bullock had not established a domicile of choice in England; his intention to return to Canada if he survived his wife was not a vague aspiration but a real determination.

Buckley LJ:

> 'I must accordingly consider whether on the facts of this case it has been shown that the taxpayer had the intention of establishing a "permanent home" in England within the meaning of that expression appropriate to the law of domicile. It is clear in my judgment that the intention does not have to be shown to have been immutable. It would be rarely that a man could be shown to have set up his home in a new country with the intention that his decision to live there and make his home there should be irrevocable. On the other hand, the intention must not be to make a home in the new country merely for a limited time or for some temporary or special purpose. …
>
> In the present case the commissioners, adopting the language of Lord Chelmsford in the passage from *Moorhouse* v *Lord*, 10 HL Cas 272, 285, 286, which I have already cited, expressed the view that the taxpayer had in contemplation some event, that was his wife's change of mind or prior death, upon the happening of which his residence in England would cease. They therefore concluded that he had not acquired a domicile of choice in England. The judge on the other hand was very much impressed by the fact that the taxpayer had established his matrimonial home in England and that there was no foreseeable prospect of that matrimonial home ever being established elsewhere. He clearly regarded this as the decisive factor in deciding that the taxpayer had acquired a domicile of choice in England.
>
> For the purpose of determining the true nature and quality of the taxpayer's intention it is clearly necessary to take into account all relevant circumstances. Domicile is distinct from citizenship. The fact that the taxpayer chose to retain his Canadian citizenship and not to acquire United Kingdom citizenship would not be inconsistent with his having acquired a domicile in the United Kingdom, but his adherence to his Canadian citizenship is, in my opinion, one of the circumstances properly to be taken into consideration in deciding whether he acquired a United Kingdom domicile. The declaration as to domicile contained in the taxpayer's will is also a matter to be taken into account, although the weight to be attributed to it must depend on the surrounding circumstances. …
>
> No doubt, if a man who has made his home in a country other than his domicile of origin has expressed an intention to return to his domicile of origin or to remove to some third country upon an event or condition of an indefinite kind; for example, "if I make a fortune" or "when I've had enough of it", it might be hard, if not impossible, to conclude that he retained any real intention of so returning or removing. Such a man, in the graphic language of James LR in *Doucet* v *Geoghegan* (1878) 9 Ch D 441, 457, is like a man who expects to reach the horizon; he finds it at least no nearer than it was at the beginning of his journey. In *Aikman* v *Aikman* (1861) 4 LT 374, 376, Lord Campbell LC said that a mere intention to return to a man's native country on a doubtful contingency would not prevent residence in a foreign country putting an end to his domicile of origin.
>
> In the present case it seems to me impossible not to hold that the taxpayer has always maintained a firm intention to return to Canada in the event of his surviving his wife. Whether that event will or will not occur is of course doubtful. That is the characteristic of a contingency. But there is no doubt about the nature of the contingency, nor will there eventually be any doubt whether the contingency has or has not occurred. There is nothing embryonic, vague or uncertain about the taxpayer's intention in this respect. Suppose a man to establish his home in a foreign country with the intention of returning to his country of origin when or if he survives the age of 60; or with the intention of returning to his country of origin when he retires; or of doing so if and when he inherits a particu-

lar family title. I apprehend that in neither the first nor the second case could it be contended that he had adopted a permanent home in the foreign country, notwithstanding that the event upon which he proposed to return to his country of origin was one which might never occur. His intention would have been limited to making a temporary home there. The occurrence of the contingency of the man inheriting a family title might well be more uncertain than his surviving the age of 60 or living to retirement; but, if there were a real likelihood of the contingency occurring, I can see no reason why that man should more readily be treated as having an intention of making a permanent home in the foreign country than the other two examples.

The contingency of the taxpayer surviving his wife seems to me no more remote or unreal than this. *Anderson* v *Laneuville* (1854) 9 Moo PCC 325, must be read in the context of the facts of that case, and Dr Lushington's statement, at p334, that it could never be said that residing in a country until the death of an individual is a residence merely for a temporary purpose, cannot in my opinion be taken as an enunciation of a rule of universal application. The question can perhaps be formulated in this way where the contingency is not itself of a doubtful or indefinite character: is there a sufficiently substantial possibility of the contingency happening to justify regarding the intention to return as a real determination to do so upon the contingency occurring rather than a vague hope or aspiration? In the present case in my opinion that question should be answered affirmatively. I feel that that conclusion is reinforced by the consideration that the taxpayer's decision to live in this country, although no doubt it has been his own free choice reached in consequence of a wish to comply with his wife's wishes, has been induced by his wife's unwillingness to live in Canada. In these circumstances I feel myself unable to agree with the conclusion reached by the judge. I would allow this appeal.'

Jopp* v *Wood (1865) 4 De GJ & Sm 616 Chancery Court (Turner and Knight Bruce LJJ)

- *Domicile can only be changed animo et facto – residence alone, although decisive as to the factum, is an equivocal act as to the animus*

Facts

A domiciled Scotchman (John Smith) went to India and resided there for the purposes of his private business, but always retaining the wish and intention of returning finally to Scotland. After his death a dispute arose in relation to funds between Elisabeth Smith (the English executrix) and the Crown as to their liability to legacy duty. This was a question which depended for its solution upon the further question of whether the domicile of the children was Anglo-Indian or Scotch, which again depended upon the question of whether the domicile of John Smith was Anglo-Indian or Scotch.

Held

That he never lost nor intended to lose his original Scotch domicile. The acquisition of a new domicile involves the abandonment of the previous domicile, and to effect the change the animus of abandonment must be shown.

Turner LJ:

> 'The point principally relied upon by the Appellant in support of his contention that there was a change of domicile from Scotland to India was the long continued residence of the testator in the latter country.
>
> But nothing is better settled with reference to the law of domicile than that the doimicil can be changed only animo et facto, and although residence may be decisive as to the factum, it cannot, when looked at with reference to the animus, be regarded otherwise than as an equivocal act. The mere fact of a man residing in a place different from that in which he has been before domiciled, even although his residence there may be long and continuous, does not of

necessity show that he has elected that place as his permanent and abiding home. He may have taken up and continued his residence there for some special purpose, or he may have elected to make the place his temporary home. But domicile, although in some of the cases spoken of as "home," imports an abiding and permanent home, and not a mere temporary one ...

In considering cases of this description it must be borne in mind that the acquisition of a new domicile involves an abandonment of the previous domicile; and in order, therefore, to effect the change the animus of abandonment, or, as Lord Cranworth has strongly expressed it (*Whicker* v *Hume* 7 HL Cas 124, 159; *Moorhouse* v *Lord* 10 HL Cas 272, 283), the intention "exuere patriam" must be shown. Whether this intention of abandonment may not be inferred from a long and continuous residence alone, in a case in which there may be no other circumstances indicative of the intention, is a question which in this case it is unnecessary to decide and on which therefore I give no opinion. Such a case can very rarely, if ever occur ...

It appears by that evidence that Mr Smith was the only son of a Scotch laird, and the proprietor of a considerable estate: that he went to India in 1805, when a minor, and he did not attain his majority till 1807: that upon the death of his father in 1814 he became entitled to the surplus proceeds of the sale of the paternal estate, which was then heavily incumbered: that the estate however remained unsold; but that immediately upon the death of his father he wrote a letter to his mother, indicating strongly his intention of ultimately returning to Scotland: that in 1819 he came over to that country, and during his residence there took an active part in the management and conduct of the estate; and that from the time of his return to India after this visit till the time of his death he kept up a constant correspondence with the agents of the estate, in the course of which he constantly referred to his return, directed different parts of his estate to be planted, and mentioned his intention of building upon it: that he remitted money to be applied in paying off the charges upon the estate, and actually purchased an adjoining property; and that he caused himself to be put upon the roll of freeholders of his county.

These are facts which, in my judgment, conclusively show that Mr Smith, so far from having abandoned his domicile in Scotland, which, it is to be observed, was his domicile of origin, and therefore not so readily to be considered as abandoned as an acquired domicile, desired at all times to retain it.'

Plummer* v *IRC [1988] 1 WLR 292 Chancery Division (Hoffmann J)

• *The requirement of residence – what happens when there is more than one residence?*

Facts

Elizabeth Plummer's domicile was in issue for income tax purposes. She had been born in England of English parents in 1965, but in 1980 her mother and younger sister had moved permanently to Guernsey and her father, who worked in London, spent the weekends and holidays in Guernsey as well. Elizabeth Plummer remained in England first as a schoolgirl and then as a student at London University. However, whenever possible she went to Guernsey for weekends and holidays and formed a strong attachment to the island intending to settle there permanently once her education was complete. She had a Guernsey bank account, a Guernsey driver's licence and a Guernsey passport. She seemed to be resident in both Guernsey and England. But where was she domiciled: England or Guernsey?

Held

Although it was possible for a person to acquire a new domicile of choice in a new country (ie Guernsey) without ceasing to be resident in their domicile of origin (ie England), that person had to establish that their residence in the new country was their chief residence.

Hoffmann J:

> 'The commissioners began by framing the question for themselves as whether the taxpayer had become an "inhabitant" of Guernsey for all or part of the relevant period. ...
>
> Speaking for myself, while I find the contrast between an inhabitant and a person casually present useful to describe the minimum quality of residence which must be taken up in a new country before a domicile there can be acquired, the concept of being an inhabitant seems to me less illuminating in cases of dual or multiple residence such as the present.
>
> Clearer guidance is to be found in a well-known passage in the speech of Lord Westbury in *Udny* v *Udny* (1869) LR 1 Sc & Div 441, 458:
>
>> "Domicile of choice is a conclusion or inference which the law derives from the fact of a man fixing voluntarily his sole or chief residence in a particular place, with an intention of continuing to reside there for an unlimited time."
>
> I infer from this sentence, which was quoted by the commissioners, that a person who retains a residence in his domicile of origin can acquire a domicile of choice in a new country only if the residence established in that country is his chief residence. The commissioners therefore asked themselves whether the taxpayer had made her grandmother's house in Guernsey : "her chief place of residence". They regarded this question, in my judgment rightly, as being the same as whether "in the sense in which the term is used in this context" the taxpayer had become an inhabitant of Guernsey.
>
> Mr McGregor submitted that a person whose presence in a new country is sufficient to amount to residence may, notwithstanding that his chief residence remains in his domicile of origin, acquire a domicile of choice by evincing an intention to continue to reside permanently in the new country. I think that this submission is inconsistent with the passage which I have quoted from Lord Westbury and which has always been treated as an authoritative statement of the circumstances in which a domicile of choice may be acquired. On the other hand, I agree with Mr McGregor that rule 13(1) of *Dicey and Morris*, p147, if read literally, appears to go too far. This says:
>
>> "A person abandons a domicile of choice in a country by ceasing to reside there and by ceasing to intend to reside there permanently or indefinitely, and not otherwise."
>
> These words might suggest that a domicile of choice, and presumably a fortiori a domicile of origin, cannot be lost unless the person in question has ceased altogether to reside there. I do not think that the rule was framed with dual residence in mind. At any rate, it seems to me that *Udny* v *Udny* shows that loss of a domicile of origin or choice is not inconsistent with retention of a place of residence in that country if the chief residence has been established elsewhere. Although the commissioners cited rule 13(1), I do not think that they applied it literally to the circumstances of this case. Notwithstanding that the taxpayer's continued presence in England amounted, as Mr McGregor conceded, to residence in this country, the commissioners made it clear that they would have found that she had acquired a residence for the purposes of the law of domicile in Guernsey if they were satisfied that she had established her chief residence there. ...
>
> If the taxpayer had in 1980 broken altogether with England and settled in Guernsey like her mother and sister and then, even after a relatively short interval, returned to England for study, the quality of her presence here might have been such as to prevent a revival of her domicile of origin. But the fact is that she has not yet settled in Guernsey, and the reasons why she has been unable to do so are in my view irrelevant. When there is no competing place of continuing residence, settlement may be established by presence for a very short time; even for a single day. But as Nourse J

pointed out in *Inland Revenue Commissioners* v *Duchess of Portland* [1982] Ch 314, 319, an inference of settlement from a short stay is difficult to draw when the person in question divides his physical presence between two countries at a time. To treat the house in Guernsey as her chief residence simply because it is the sole residence of her mother and sister would in my view be attributing to her a kind of quasi-dependent domicile for which there is no legal justification. And the fact that the taxpayer may intend to settle in Guernsey after her education and training are completed and then to remain permanently is not sufficient to give her a proleptic domicile of choice.

In my judgment the commissioners reached the right answer, and the appeal is therefore dismissed.'

Qureshi* v *Qureshi [1972] Fam 173 Probate, Divorce and Admiralty Division (Sir Jocelyn Simon P)

• *Domicile of husband – the effect on recognition of talaq*

Facts

The husband, who was born in what later became part of India, moved to Pakistan and acquired Pakistani nationality in 1957. In 1958 he came to England in order to qualify as a Fellow of the Royal College of Surgeons, intending to return to Pakistan thereafter. He retained his intention to return to Pakistan. In March 1966 the wife, who was then an Indian citizen and domiciled in India, married the husband at a register office in England. The marriage was unhappy and the parties separated in June 1966. In April 1967 the husband sent to the wife a written talaq, at the same time sending a copy to the Head of Chancery at the Pakistan High Commission (H) in London. H issued a notice to the parties requesting them to attend, each with a representative, so that the Arbitration Council could be constituted. H declared that reconciliation was impossible and later drew up a document stating that the divorce had become absolute 90 days after he had received the copy of the talaq. A few days later the husband ceased making payments under the maintenance order. The wife lodged a complaint for the arrears. The husband prayed for a declaration that the marriage had been dissolved.

Held

That on the facts the husband was domiciled in Pakistan and thus the validity of the divorce fell to be tested by Pakistani law.

Sir Jocelyn Simon P:

'*Domicile*

It is common ground that, if the husband is domiciled in England, talaq will not be accorded recognition by an English court. The situation which would obtain if he were domiciled in India was not exhaustively explored. The main domiciliary situations for the husband claimed by the parties respectively were a domicile in Pakistan by the husband and a domicile in England by the wife; though the wife was also content to allege alternatively merely that the husband had lost any domicile he had acquired in Pakistan. It was expressly disclaimed that the wife had assumed any domicile independently of the husband at any time since the marriage. The domicile of the parties might also have some bearing on the jurisdiction of the court. It is therefore the first issue to be determined.

It was only faintly controverted that in 1957 the husband abandoned his domicile of origin in India and acquired a domicile of choice in Pakistan. The most significant event, in my view, was the change of nationality … The evidence in favour of the abandonment of the domicile of origin in India, and the acquisition of a domicile of choice in Pakistan, seems to me to be overwhelming.

The wife, however, claims that the husband has abandoned his domicile of choice in Pakistan. The legal background of the argument on her behalf rests on three propositions, all of which I accept as correct. First, a domicile of choice is less retentive, and therefore more easily abandoned, than a domicile of origin. Secondly, a person may change his domicile without any intention to do so – indeed, without being conscious of doing so ... Thirdly, given the necessary fact of a physical departure from the country of domicile of choice, for its abandonment the animus that must be shown is not necessarily non revertendi; it is sufficient that the residence in the new country is sine animo revertendi; and in this connection there may be a "withering away" of an intention to return to the country of the domicile of choice ...

I therefore propose to refer only to the matters on which the parties placed particular reliance and to those which struck me as being particularly significant. For the wife it was principally urged, first, that the husband had spent less than a year out of his 35 in Pakistan; secondly, that English social customs were obviously congenial to him; thirdly, that he had held, and could hope to continue to hold, responsible and remunerative posts under the National Health Service in this country (resignation from which would involve financial sacrifice), whereas his prospects in Pakistan were less favourable and were deteriorating with the effluxion of time; fourthly, that the letters that the husband wrote before marriage are inconsistent with an intention to return to Pakistan; and, fifthly, that he had told her that he intended to remain in England.

I do not accept that the husband ever declared or evinced to the wife an intention to make this country his permanent home or not to return to Pakistan: this seems to me inconsistent with her evidence before the magistrates, some passages from which I have cited ...

Although I believed the husband when he told me in evidence that he intended to return to Pakistan after having another attempt to qualify as FRCS (whether or not he does in fact qualify), this evidence might not have sufficed alone, on the ground of his knowledgeable self-interest in the matter. The statement in the passport that his domicile was in Pakistan must similarly be received with caution, since it must have been based on a statement of the husband's at a time when his domicile was to his knowledge a matter of legal significance ...

He retained his Pakistani citizenship throughout: and there is no evidence that he ever contemplated applying for British nationality. In 1962 the husband took out in London an endowment policy of insurance with a Pakistani company, in Pakistani currency, the sum assured being payable in Pakistan; and in 1967 he raised money on it to buy land in Karachi for construction of a house (though this was after the purported pronouncement of talaq). ...

I was satisfied that the husband at all times during his residence in this country intended to return to Pakistan; and that he had never lost his Pakistani domicile of choice. I made an interim finding to this effect (reserving my reasons), so as to define the compass of the ensuing argument.'

Comment

Once the domicile of the husband had been determined the judge then focused on the validity of the talaq.

'There can be no doubt that the law of the domicile is prima facie the proper law for determining the efficacy of a purported divorce to bring about a change of status by dissolving a marriage ...

In my view, therefore, the fact that there has been no judicial intervention or even presence is irrelevant if the purported divorce is effective by the law of the domicile to terminate the marriage in question, and it should be recognised as such, unless the result would be offensive to the conscience of the English court.

My conclusions, that the talaq was valid according to the law of the domicile and that there is no rule of English law which precludes its recognition by reason of its non-forensic character, make it unnecessary for me to consider an argument advanced to the effect that the office of the High Commissioner for Pakistan is to be accorded extra-territorial status and considered as part of Pakistan, so that the talaq was pronounced, or the arbitration council sat, in Pakistan.'

Scullard, Re [1956] 3 All ER 898 Chancery Division (Danckwerts J)

• *Effect of husband's death on a wife's ability to acquire a domicile of choice*

Facts

The testatrix married in 1893. In 1908 she left her husband and never returned to him. In 1947 she went to Guernsey and expressed the intention of spending the rest of her days there. All her possessions were moved there. She died in March 1955, in hospital in Guernsey. The testatrix's husband, who died some six weeks before her, had an English domicile up to the date of his death, and in the interval between his death and hers the testatrix had been too ill to evince any intention in respect of her domicile. The question arose as to the domicile of the testatrix.

Held

In the circumstances, the testatrix had an intention to acquire a domicile of choice in Guernsey, and that intention was effective in law.

Danckwerts J:

'The difficulty arises in this way. So long as she was married to her husband, even though she was separated from him as completely as possible short of judicial separation, she could not form an effective intention to change her domicile from that of her husband.

It is argued by Mr Dillon, on behalf of the defendant who wishes to establish that the testatrix's domicile was English, that as she did not express any intention during the short period after her husband's death she could not have acquired a domicile in Guernsey, and, therefore, her domicile remains that of her husband, namely, in England.

I have been referred to two cases. One is the decision of Stirling J in *In re Cooke's Trusts* (1887) 56 LJ Ch 637, which was decided in 1887 ... Held, that she was, at her death, domiciled in New South Wales, and the disposition made by her will was valid. ... There is, however, the case of *In re Wallach* [1950] 1 All ER 199, which was before Hodson J in the Probate Division ... Held, a widow retains her late husband's last domicile until she changes it, and, therefore, the intestate's domicile was English. ...

The whole matter, to some extent, is rather unreal, because, generally speaking, the question of domicile in its legal effects is not present to the mind of women in that position. All that they are thinking about is where they are going to spend the rest of their days, and where their permanent home is going to be.

In the present case the evidence is really stronger in some respects – though it is supported by a rather unsatisfactory affidavit – in this way: there are perfectly good reasons of a legal nature why the wife may have been advised in the present case to change her domicile deliberately from England to Guernsey because of the effect it might have with regard to death duty on her death. In those circumstances I cannot see why an intention which, as I found on the evidence, the wife was plainly shown to have in her mind during her lifetime – namely, to make her permanent home in Guernsey – but which cannot be effective in law until her husband was dead, should not be effective in law in accordance with her intention when she survives him. I have come to the conclusion in the present case that the intention which the testatrix had in fact formed during her lifetime was only prevented by a rule of law relating to the domicile of a wife from being effective in law; and I do not see why it should not be assumed that her intention continued after the death of her husband, and why one should come to the conclusion that some new overt act was required when all previous evidence is consistent with there having been no different intention during her life. Accordingly, in the present case I have come to the conclusion that the testatrix had an intention to acquire a domicile of choice in Guernsey and that that intention was effective in law.'

White et al* v *Tennant et al (1888) 31 WVa 790 Supreme Court of Appeals of West Virginia (Snyder, Johnson, P Green and Woods JJ)

• *Can an individual acquire a new domicile if he has the intention of residing in another state for an indefinite time, but is only present for a few hours before returning to the former state to spend the night with a neighbour?*

Facts

The family lived in West Virginia but Mr and Mrs White decided that they would go and live at the other end of their estate in a house on the Pennsylvania side. They packed all their belongings and made the journey across the state line to the house in Pennsylvania. Unfortunately, when they arrived they found the house in very poor condition. Mrs White refused to spend one night in the house until it was cleaned up and made habitable. Consequently, the family left all their possessions but returned to West Virginia. Mr White fell very ill and died before ever returning to Pennsylvania. The case came before the courts to decide where Mr White was domiciled at the time of his death.

Held

Mr White was domiciled in Pennsylvania at the time of his death. He had taken the decision to move to Pennsylvania; arrived in Pennsylvania in order to become an inhabitant of it; and had the intention of residing there indefinitely. Mr White had simply returned to West Virginia on a temporary basis, with no intention of moving back there again permanently. This was sufficient to satisfy the requirements.

Snyder J:

'The sole question presented for our determination is whether the said Michael White, at the time of his death, in May 1885, had his legal domicile in this state or in the state of Pennsylvania. It is admitted to be the settled law that the law of the state in which the decedent had his domicile at the time of his death will control the succession and distribution of his personal estate. Before referring to the facts proved in this cause, we shall endeavor to determine what in law is meant by "domicile". Dr Wharton says: " 'Domicile' is a residence acquired as a final abode. To constitute it there must be (1) residence, actual or inchoate; (2) the non-existence of any intention to make a domicile elsewhere" ... Two things must concur to establish domicile – the fact of residence, and the intention of remaining. These two must exist, or must have existed, in combination. There must have been an actual residence. The character of the residence is of no importance; and, if domicile has once existed, mere temporary absence will not destroy it, however long continued. *Munro* v *Munro* 7 Clark & F 842. The original domicile continues until it is fairly changed for another. It is a legal maxim that every person must have a domicile somewhere; and he can have but one at a time for the same purpose ... A change of domicile does not depend so much upon the intention to remain in the new place for a definite or an indefinite period, as upon its being without an intention to return. An intention to return, however, at a remote or indefinite period, to the former place of actual residence, will not control, if the other facts which constitute domicile all give the new residence the character of a permanent home or place of abode. The intention and actual fact of residence must concur, where such residence is not in its nature temporary ... Where a person removes from one state to another and establishes a fixed residence in the latter, it will become his domicile, although there may be a floating intention to return to his former place of abode at some future period ...

According to the authorities hereinbefore cited, if it is shown that a person has entirely abandoned his former domicile in one state with the intention of making his home at a fixed place in another state, with no intention of returning to his former domicile, and then establishes a residence in the new place for any period of time, however brief, that will be in law a change of domicile, and the latter will remain his domicile until changed in like "manner". The facts in this case conclusively prove that Michael White, the decedent, abandoned his residence in West Virginia with the intention and purpose not only of not returning to it, but for the expressed purpose of making a fixed place in the state of Pennsylvania his home for an indefinite time. This fact is shown by all the circumstances, as well as by his declarations and acts. He had sold his residence in West Virginia, and surrendered its possession to the purchaser, and thereby made it impossible for him to return to it and make it his home. He rented a dwelling in Pennsylvania, for which he had no use except to live in, and make it his home. In addition to all this, he had moved a part of his household goods into this house, and then, on the 2nd of April, 1885, he, with his family and the remainder of his goods and stock, finally left his former home, and the state of West Virginia, and moved into the state of Pennsylvania, to his house in that state, and there put his goods in the house, and turned his stock loose on the premises. At the time he left his former home on that morning, and while he was on the way to his new home, his declared purpose and intention were to make that his home from that very day, and to occupy it that night. He arrived in Pennsylvania and at his new home with that intention; and it was only after he arrived there, and for reasons not before known, and which had no effect to change his purpose of making that his future home, that he failed to remain there from that time. There was no change in his purpose except that after he arrived at his new home, and unloaded and left his property there, he concluded, on account of the condition of the house and the illness of his wife, that it would be better to go with his wife to remain one night with his relatives, and return the next morning. When he left his former home, without any intention of returning, and in pursuance of that intention did in fact move with his family and effects to his new home with the intention of making it his residence for an indefinite time, it is my opinion that when he and his wife arrived at his new home it became eo instanti his domicile, and that his leaving there, under the circumstances he did, with the intention of returning the next day, did not change the fact. By the concurrence of his intention to make the Pennsylvania house his permanent residence with the fact that he had actually abandoned his former residence, and moved to and put his goods in the new one, made the latter his domicile ... By going from his new home to the house of his relatives to spend the night he certainly did not make the house thus visited his domicile; therefore, unless the Pennsylvania house was, on the evening of 2 April 1885, his domicile, he was in the anomalous position of being without a domicile anywhere, which, as we have seen, is a legal impossibility; and that house having become his domicile, there is nothing in this case to show that he ever did in fact change or intend to change it, or to establish a domicile elsewhere.

It follows, therefore, that that house remained his domicile up to and at the time of his death; and, that house being in the state of Pennsylvania, the laws of that state must control the distribution of his personal estate, notwithstanding the fact that he died in the state of West Virginia.'

The domicile of origin

Bell* v *Kennedy (1868) LR 1 Sc & Div 307 House of Lords (Lords Westbury, Cairns, Cranworth, Chelmsford and Colonsay)

• *A domicile of origin cannot be lost by abandonment – it persists until a new domicile (of choice) is acquired*

Facts

One Mr Bell was born in Jamaica. His parents, although Scots, were domiciled in Jamaica; thus his domicile of origin was Jamaican. At the age of 35 he left Jamaica for good and went to Scotland, looking for an estate to buy and on which to settle down. But the weather was bad and the price of land too high so he became undecided whether to settle in Scotland or in England or in the south of France. At this point his wife died and since in those days her domicile depended upon his it was necessary to determine where he was domiciled at that date.

Held

His domicile of origin in Jamaica persisted.

Lord Westbury:

> 'What appears to me to be the erroneous conclusion at which the Court of Session arrived is in great part due to the circumstance, frequently lost sight of, that the domicile of origin adheres until a new domicile is acquired. In the argument, and in the judgments, we find constantly the phrase used that he had abandoned his native domicile. That domicile appears to have been regarded as if it had been lost by the abandonment of his residence in Jamaica. Now, residence and domicile are two perfectly distinct things. It is necessary in the administration of the law that the idea of domicile should exist, and that the fact of domicile should be ascertained, in order to determine which of two municipal laws may be invoked for the purpose of regulating the rights of parties. We know very well that succession and distribution depend upon the law of the domicile. Domicile, therefore, is an idea of law. It is the relation which the law creates between an individual and a particular locality or country. To every adult person the law ascribes a domicile and that domicile remains his fixed attribute until a new and different attribute usurps its place. Now this case was argued at the Bar on the footing, that as soon as Mr Bell left Jamaica he had a settled and fixed intention of taking up his residence in Scotland. And if, indeed, that had been ascertained as a fact, then you would have had the animus of the party clearly demonstrated, and the factum, which alone would remain to be proved, would in fact be proved, or, at least, would result immediately upon his arrival in Scotland.'
>
> The true inquiry, therefore, is – Had he this settled purpose, the moment he left Jamaica, or in course of the voyage, of taking up a fixed and settled abode in Scotland? Undoubtedly, part of the evidence is the external act of the party; but the only external act we have here is the going down with his wife to Edinburgh, the most natural thing in the world, to visit his wife's relations. We find him residing in Scotland from that time; but with what animus or intention his residence continued there we have yet to ascertain. For although residence may be some small prima facie proof of domicile, it is by no means to be inferred from the fact of residence that domicile results, even although you do not find that the party had any other residence in existence or in contemplation.
>
> I take it that Mr Bell may be more properly described by words which occur in the Digest; that when he left Jamaica he might be described as 'quaerens, quo se conferat, atque ubi constituat domicilium'. Where he was to fix his habitation was to him at that time a thing perfectly unresolved; and, as appears from the letters which your Lordships have heard, that irresolution, that want of settled fixity of purpose, certainly continued down to the time when he actually became the purchaser of Enterkine. But the punctum temporis to which our inquiries are to be directed as to Mr Bell's intention is of an earlier date than that. The question is, had he any settled fixed intention of being permanently resident in Scotland on 28 September 1838? I quite agree with an observation which was made in the Court of Session, that the letters are the best evidence in the case. To those letters your Lordships' attention has been directed, and whether you refer to the language of the wife's letters, or look exclusively at the language of the husband's letters written to his familiar friends or his relatives whom he had left in Jamaica, it is impossible to predicate of him that he was a man who had a fixed and settled purpose to make Scotland his future place of residence, to set up his

tabernacle there, to make it his future home. And unless you are able to shew that with perfect clearness and satisfaction to yourselves, it follows that the domicile of origin continues. And therefore I think we can have no hesitation in answering the question where he was settled on 28 September. It must be answered in this way; he was resident in Scotland, but without the animus manendi, and therefore he still retained his domicile of origin.'

Collier* v *Rivaz (1841) 2 Curt 855 Prerogative Court (Sir Herbert Jenner)

• *Abandonment of domicile and test for acquisition of new domicile – effect of testator's will*

Facts

The testator, Phillip Ryan, died domiciled in Belgium. He left behind him two nieces, Mary Ryan and Mrs Langebear, a widow, who would have been entitled to his personal estate in case he had died intestate. He left property to the amount of about £20,000. In September 1824 he executed a will, of which he appointed Mr V F Rivaz, Mary Ryan and A H Rivaz executors, and his niece Mary Ryan residuary legatee. He also left behind him six codicils, four of which were opposed on the ground that they were not executed according to the forms of the law of Belgium, in which country it was contended that the deceased was domiciled at the time of his death. The main question before the court was whether or not Mr Ryan, the testator, was domiciled in Belgium.

Held

The court pronounced that Mr Ryan had died domiciled in Belgium.

Sir Herbert Jenner:

'He was born at Clonmell in Ireland; in 1762 he entered into the British Navy, in which he continued to serve until 1780. In 1776 he married at Rochester, and his wife died about 1802. The deceased was engaged in business as a dealer in foreign cambrics, and, in consequence of that business, was frequently in the habit of resorting to different places on the Continent for the purposes of that trade, but his principal residence was in this country, where he had a house in Warren Street, Fitzroy Square, – which he sold in 1802. There could then be no doubt that up to this time he had abandoned his original Irish domicile, and had acquired one in England. In 1802 he went to Brussels for the purpose of residing there, as is stated by him in a codicil before the Court, dated the 24th of September 1825; in 1803, the war between England and France being renewed, the deceased was detained as a prisoner; in 1814 he came to England, and remained here for a few months; he afterwards returned to Brussels, and continued to reside there until his death, with occasional excursions on matters of business or pleasure. It also appears that in early life he had adopted his niece, Mary Ryan, and she went to live with him at Brussels, and continued to reside with him until his death.

I cannot think it necessary to go at any length into the facts of the case, because they are all admitted; there is no dispute as to them; the only question is as to the result of them. Now, I cannot but think that all the facts, with respect to the abandonment of the old domicile and the acquisition of a new one, indicate not only an intention to reside at Brussels, and make that place his home, but that the fact and intention concur together, which is all that is necessary to constitute a domicile.

Length of time will not alone do it, intention alone will not do, but the two taken together do constitute a change of domicile. No particular time is required, but when the two circumstances of actual residence and intentional residence concur, there it is, that a change of domicile is effected. In this case I can have no doubt, from the facts, that this was the deceased's selected place of domicile; though from 1803 to 1814 it was a forced residence, yet from that time, 1814, he became habituated to the manners of

Brussels and the inhabitants of Brussels, and preferred to make his continental residence in that place to a return to his original domicile. I am, therefore, of opinion, under the whole circumstances of the case, that the testator must be considered to have been domiciled at Brussels at the time of his death.'

Comment

Despite the fact that the court held that Mr Ryan had died domiciled in Belgium, it nevertheless pronounced in favour of the papers, they being valid instruments by the law of this country (England), in which the deceased was previously domiciled. The court's rather unusual decision is a result of the application of renvoi and is well worth reading. (Refer to Chapter 2 above.)

> 'The question, however, remains to be determined whether these codicils which are opposed are executed in such a form as would entitle them to the sanction of the Court which has to pronounce on the validity of testamentary dispositions in Belgium, in the circumstances under which they have been executed. Because it does not follow that, Mr Ryan being a domiciled subject of Belgium, he is therefore necessarily subject to all the forms which the law of Belgium requires from its own native born subjects. I apprehend there can be no doubt that every nation has a right to say under what circumstances it will permit a disposition, or contracts of whatever nature they may be, to be entered into by persons who are not native born, but who have become subjects from continued residence; that is, foreigners who come to reside under certain circumstances without obtaining from certain authorities those full rights which are necessary to constitute an actual Belgian subject. Every nation has a right to say how far the general law shall apply to its own born subjects and the subject of another country; and the Court, sitting here to determine it, must consider itself sitting in Belgium under the particular circumstances of the case ...
>
> The Court sitting here decides from the evidence of persons skilled in that law, and decides as it would if sitting in Belgium.
>
> Therefore I am of opinion that, notwithstanding the domicile of Mr Ryan must be considered to have been in Belgium, and that he had in point of law abandoned his original domicile, and had acquired animo et facto a domicile in a foreign country, yet that foreign country in which he was so domiciled would uphold his testamentary disposition, if executed according to the forms required by his own country. I am therefore of opinion that I am bound to decree probate of the will and all the codicils.
>
> And I decree the costs of all parties to be paid out of the estate.'

Fuld (decd) (No 3), Re [1968] P 675; [1965] 3 All ER 776 Probate Division (Scarman J)

• *Domicile of origin/choice – effect on validity of will and codicils*

Facts

Peter Fuld was born in Germany in 1921 with a German domicile of origin. In 1939, he came to England as a student. After the outbreak of war in 1939 he was interned in England. In 1940 he was transferred as an internee to Canada. He was released from internment in 1942 and entered the University of Toronto as a law student. He acquired Canadian nationality in 1946 and soon afterwards returned to Europe. From 1946 until his death in 1962 his base was European, not American, though he often visited North America on business. From 1946 onwards he had a house in London. He also spent a lot of time in Germany. In 1959 he entered a clinic for brain surgery, from which he made a temporary recovery. During the last nine months of his life he made a will in England and a codicil in Germany. A second codicil was made in England and two more codicils in Germany. The executors under the will and first codicil challenged the validity of the other three codicils. There were 14 defendants to the action, all beneficiaries under the will and codicils.

Held

Domiciled in Germany. As such the court pronounced in favour of the will and first codicil and against the other three codicils.

Scarman J:

> 'Domicile is "that legal relationship between a person ... and a territory subject to a distinctive legal system which invokes the system as [his] personal law ...": see *Henderson* v *Henderson* [1965] 1 All ER 179. It is a combination of residence and intention ... a word of warning. This branch of the law is adorned by a great number of cases, not all of which is it easy to harmonise. The difficulty arises not from a lack of clarity in judicial thought but from the nature of the subject. Domicile cases require for their decision a detailed analysis and assessment of facts arising within that most subjective of all fields of legal inquiry – a man's mind. Each case takes its tone from the individual propositus whose intentions are being analysed: anglophobia, mental inertia, extravagant habits, vacillation of will – to take four instances at random – have been factors of great weight in the judicial assessment and determination of four leading cases. Naturally enough in so subjective a field different judicial minds concerned with different factual situations have chosen different language to describe the law. For the law is not an abstraction: it lives only in its application, and its concepts derive colour and shape from the facts of the particular case in which they are studied, and to which they are applied. Thus the relationship of law and fact is a two-way one: each affects the other...
>
> In the light of these cases, the law, so far as relevant to my task, may be stated as follows: (1) The domicile of origin adheres – unless displaced by satisfactory evidence of the acquisition and continuance of a domicile of choice; (2) a domicile of choice is acquired only if it be affirmatively shown that the propositus is resident within a territory subject to a distinctive legal system with the intention, formed independently of external pressures, of residing there indefinitely. If a man intends to return to the land of his birth upon a clearly foreseen and reasonably anticipated contingency, eg, the end of his job, the intention required by law is lacking; but, if he has in mind only a vague possibility, such as making a fortune (a modern example might be winning a football pool), or some sentiment about dying in the land of his fathers, such a state of mind is consistent with the intention required by law. But no clear line can be drawn: the ultimate decision in each case is one of fact – of the weight to be attached to the various factors and future contingencies in the contemplation of the propositus, their importance to him, and the probability, in his assessment, of the contingencies he has in contemplation being transformed into actualities. (3) It follows that, though a man has left the territory of his domicile of origin with the intention of never returning, though he be resident in a new territory, yet if his mind be not made up or evidence be lacking or unsatisfactory as to what is his state of mind, his domicile of origin adheres. And, if he has acquired but abandoned a domicile of choice either because he no longer resides in the territory or because he no longer intends to reside there indefinitely, the domicile of origin revives until such time as by a combination of residence and intention he acquires a new domicile of choice.
>
> There remains the question of standard of proof. It is beyond doubt that the burden of proving the abandonment of a domicile of origin and the acquisition of a domicile of choice is upon the party asserting the change But it is not so clear what is the standard of proof: is it to be proved beyond reasonable doubt or upon a balance of probabilities, or does the standard vary according to whether one seeks to establish abandonment of a domicile of origin or merely a switch from one domicile of choice to another? Or is there some other standard? ...
>
> The formula of proof beyond reasonable doubt is not frequently used in probate cases, and I do not propose to give it cur-

rency. It is enough that the authorities emphasise that the conscience of the court must be satisfied by the evidence. The weight to be attached to evidence, the inferences to be drawn, the facts justifying the exclusion of doubt and the expression of satisfaction, will vary according to the nature of the case. Two things are clear – first, that unless the judicial conscience is satisfied by evidence of change, the domicile of origin persists: and secondly, that the acquisition of a domicile of choice is a serious matter not to be lightly inferred from slight indications or casual words ...

I am satisfied that Peter Fuld resided in London from 1946 to November 1961. But London was not his sole residence. He also had a place of residence in Germany. For most of the time, however, and particularly in his later years, he regarded London as his chief place of residence. He did so because of his immediate circumstances, of which the most important was the presence of his mother in Frankfurt. I am not satisfied that he ever made up his mind to settle in England, or, to put it in the language of the authorities to which I have referred, that he ever formed the intention of continuing to reside in England for an unlimited time. It may be, as Mr Parker [counsel for the plaintiffs] has submitted, that he never made up his mind. I think it more likely that his innermost wish was at all times, and more particularly after he had married the German girl Marina, to return to Germany to live in Annastrasse and to play an active part in the management of the family business ...

Thus, though my judgment rests on the negative proposition that those who assert the acquisition of a domicile of choice have failed to prove the intention required by law, I must add that I think in fact Peter Fuld never did acquire such an intention. He may never have made up his mind as to his permanent home, but I believe that, deep down, he never abandoned an intention to return to live in Frankfurt. He was waiting his opportunity when disease, fatal in the event, struck him.

In my opinion, therefore, Peter Fuld was at all material times domiciled in Germany.'

Henderson* v *Henderson [1965] 1 All ER 179 Probate, Divorce and Admiralty Division (Sir Jocelyn Simon P)

• *A domicile of origin is the domicile of dependence at the date of birth and not at the date of majority*

Facts

In December 1962 a wife presented her petition for divorce against her husband. The husband contended that he was at that date domiciled in Scotland. An issue was directed to determine whether the husband was domiciled in England or in Scotland in December 1962. His Lordship found as a fact that the husband's father was domiciled in Scotland at the date of the husband's birth, but acquired a domicile in England by the time the husband attained his majority. The question then arose whether the husband's domicile of origin was Scottish, his domicile of dependence at the date of his birth, or English, his domicile of dependence at the date of his majority.

Held

Sir Jocelyn Simon P:

> 'Domicile is that legal relationship between a person (called the propositus) and a territory subject to a distinctive legal system which invokes the system as the personal law of the propositus and involves the courts of that territorial area in having primary jurisdiction to dissolve his marriage. The relationship arises either, on the one hand, from the propositus being or having been resident in such territorial area with the intention of making it his permanent home or, on the other, from there being or having been such a relationship on the part of some other person on whom the propositus is for this purpose legally dependent. Thus a wife is for this purpose legally dependent on her husband, and a legitimate child on his father. This type of domicile of the child and the wife is termed a domicile of dependence. The domicile that the child derives from the

father is also known as his domicile of origin. Every person capable of acquiring an independent domicile will on independence retain his domicile of dependence, though it may be abandoned at any time thereafter.

Though the principles which govern a change of domicile are well established, they are often difficult of application, and not least if the choice is between a domicile in Scotland and in England ... Many English people to work in Scotland and even more Scotsmen come to work in England. They settle down in a new home near the place where they are working. Intermarriage is frequent. But most people, and not least Scotsmen, retain a pride of ancestry and a sentiment of attachment to the land of their fathers. It is often difficult to determine whether they have settled in their new place of residence with the intention of making it their permanent home; or whether they intend to return at some time to live permanently in their country of origin; or whether, thirdly, the residence is quite indeterminate in character, no clear intention as to ultimate permanent residence being formed.

In order to help resolve such difficulties the law has evolved further rules. First, clear evidence is required to establish a change of domicile. In particular, to displace the domicile of origin in favour of the domicile of choice, the standard of proof goes beyond a mere balance of probabilities. Where residence however long is neutral or colourless or indeterminate in character, it will not give rise to an inference that the domicile of origin has been abandoned. Secondly, on the other hand, a mere "floating intention" to return to the country of origin at some future period is not sufficient for the retention of the domicile of origin if the propositus has settled in some other territory subject to a distinctive system of law with the intention of remaining there for an indefinite time ...

So an intention of the propositus to return to his country of origin on such an indefinite event as when he has made his fortune (*Bruce* v *Bruce* (1790) 2 Bos & P 229; *Doucet* v *Geoghegan* (1878) 9 Ch D 441) or when his mistress dies (*Anderson* v *Laneuville* (1854) 9 Moo PCC 325) will not suffice to prevent the acquisition of a domicile of choice.

Against this background of law I turn to consider the facts of this case.'

His Lordship considered the evidence relating to the husband's father's domicile, found that the husband's father was domiciled in Scotland when the husband was born but was domiciled in England when the husband attained the age of 21, and continued:

'It follows that the husband's domicile of dependence was at birth in Scotland and at the age of 21 in England. Which of these two is to be considered the husband's domicile of origin? The point is of importance owing to the high degree of retentiveness which the law ascribes to the domicile of origin.

In my judgment the domicile of origin of the husband was his domicile of dependence at birth, not at the time when he emerged from dependence ...

Scholarly opinion overwhelmingly concurs in the view that the domicile of origin is the dependent domicile at birth: see, for example, *Dicey's Conflict of Laws*, 7th ed (1957), p94; *Foote's Private International Law*, 5th ed (1925), p79; Cheshire, *Private International Law*, 6th ed (1961), p191; Wolff, *Private International Law*, 2nd ed (1950), p120; Graveson, *The Conflict of Laws*, 4th ed (1960), pp84, 88 et seq; Schmitthoff, *The English Conflict of Laws*, 3rd ed (1954), p89. Indeed Westlake, *Private International Law*, sections 248, 261, 7th ed (1925), at pp344 et seq 356, seems to stand alone in asserting the contrary...

I therefore hold that the husband had a domicile of origin in Scotland, but a domicile (which is to be considered as a domicile of choice) in England when, on his majority in 1953, he became capable of acquiring an independent domicile.'

Ramsay v Liverpool Royal Infirmary [1930] AC 588; 99 LJPC 134 House of Lords (Lords Buckmaster, Dunedin, Macmillan and Thankerton)

• *Acquisition of a domicile of choice – intention as well as residence*

Facts

George Bowie, whose domicile of origin was Scottish, but who had lived the latter part of his life in Liverpool, died in Liverpool on 5 November 1927, leaving a will which was valid by the law of Scotland but was not valid by the law of England. This action was brought by the residuary legatees under the will, against the testator's sole next of kin, for a declaration that the testator's domicile at the date of his death was Scottish.

Held

The residuary legatees had failed to prove that the testator had changed his domicile. Lords Buckmaster, Dunedin, and Macmillan delivered judgment to the same effect. Appeal dismissed.

Lord Thankerton:

'My Lords, the deceased George Bowie died in Liverpool, on 5 November 1927, aged 82 years and unmarried. Originally employed as a commercial traveller in Glasgow, he gave up that employment about 1882, and did no work for the rest of his life. About 1891or 1892 he came to Liverpool, where a brother and sister were already settled, and resided in Liverpool for the remaining thirty-five or thirty-six years of his life. His domicile of origin was Scottish, and the question in the present appeal is whether he still retained that domicile at his death, or was then domiciled in England.

George Bowie left a holograph will, which was made by him in Liverpool on 7 August 1927. That will is valid according to Scottish law and invalid under English law. The appellant, as next of kin, maintains that George Bowie died domiciled in England and that the will is invalid. The respondents are the residuary legatees under the will, and maintain its validity on the ground that George Bowie retained his Scottish domicile.

Admittedly the appellant undertakes the burden of proving that George Bowie acquired an English domicile animo et facto; his long residence established the factum, but there remains the question of the animus. It seems clear on the authorities that mere length of residence by itself is insufficient evidence from which to infer the animus; but the quality of the residence may afford the necessary inference. For instance, the purchase of a house or estate coupled with long residence therein and non-retention of any home in the domicile of origin, might be sufficient to prove the intention to acquire a new domicile. But the long residence of George Bowie in Liverpool is remarkably colourless and suggests little more than inanition.

George Bowie went to Liverpool to live on the bounty of his brother Alexander, and, during his residence there, his means of existence were supplied by that brother and his sister Isabella. He received a legacy of £1,000 from the former and succeeded to the latter's whole estate on her death in 1920. He lived in lodgings until 1914, when he went to live with his sister Isabella, then the only other surviving member of the family, in a leased house, where he lived till his death. With the exception of family ties, he appears to have had few, if indeed any, ties either in Scotland or England.

Apart from residence, the evidence bearing on animus is vague and indecisive. It is not certain whether he knew that his will would be invalid in England, but he named his cousin, a Glasgow writer, as trustee, and he directed that his residuary bequests, of one-fourth each to three Glasgow infirmaries and one Liverpool infirmary, should be given anonymously as from a "Glasgow Man". He told people that he was proud to be a Glasgow man, and received a Glasgow weekly newspaper. With his sister Isabella's estate he became owner of a tenement property in Glasgow, which he desired to sell, but a bad market prevented its sale, and he retained it till his death. There is some evidence of his declining on one or two occasions to move to Glasgow and to visit Glasgow, but until 1912 he was dependent on his brother's bounty, and after 1912 it is probable that his disinclination was owing to the inertness of age and indifferent health. He was buried in Liverpool, but that was alongside of his brother Alexander and three sisters in ground for which Alexander had paid.

I am unable to find in this case sufficient evidence of a definite intention on the part of George Bowie to abandon his domicile of origin and to acquire a new domicile. The law on this subject is well fixed; the difficulty is found in its application to oft varying combinations of circumstances. The present case appears to me to be directly affected by the opinions (a) of Lord Westbury in *Bell* v *Kennedy* (1868) LR 1 SC & Div 307, where he says: "Although residence may be some small prima facie proof of domicile, it is by no means to be inferred from the fact of residence that domicile results, even although you do not find that the party had any other residence in existence or in contemplation"; (b) of Lord Chelmsford in *Udny* v *Udny* (1869) LR 1 SC & Div 441 that "in a competition between a domicile of origin and an alleged subsequently-acquired domicile there may be circumstances to show that however long a residence may have continued no intention of acquiring a domicile may have existed at any one moment during the whole of the continuance of such residence. The question in such a case is not, whether there is evidence of an intention to retain the domicile of origin, but whether it is proved that there was an intention to acquire another domicile"; and (c) of Lord Macnaghten in *Winans* v *A-G* [1904] AC 287 where he states: "Such an intention, I think, is not to be inferred from an attitude of indifference or a disinclination to move increasing with increasing years, least of all from the absence of any manifestation of intention one way or the other." This last opinion appears to apply exactly to the circumstances of George Bowie's residence in Liverpool.

Accordingly, I am of opinion that the appellant has failed to prove the intention on the part of George Bowie to acquire an English domicile, and that the appeal fails.'

Udny v *Udny* (1869) LR 1 Sc & Div 441 House of Lords (Lords Westbury, Hatherley, Chelmsford and Colonsay)

• *The domicile of origin revives and exists whenever there is no other domicile, eg when a domicile of choice or of dependence has been cast off and a new domicile not yet acquired*

Facts

The question raised in this appeal was whether the son of Colonel Udny and Miss Ann Allatt, born out of wedlock, was legitimated by the subsequent marriage of his parents. Although prior to the Legitimation Act 1926 English law did not know the concept of legitimation, Scottish law did. The rule that had been adopted (by both English and Scottish courts) was if the father were domiciled in a country that recognised legitimation by subsequent marriage both at the time of the birth and the time of the marriage, then the legitimation would be recognised but otherwise not. Colonel Udny's domicile of origin had been Scottish, but he had lived for 32 years in London and had probably acquired a domicile of choice in England. However, he got into financial difficulties and left London for France where he lived for some time, occasionally travelling to Scotland and England. During this period he formed a connexion with Miss Allatt and fathered his son; he later married Miss Allatt in Scotland. If he was domiciled in Scotland during these events, the son was legitimated; but if he was domiciled in England the son was illegitimate.

Held

Even if he had acquired a domicile of choice

in England, he had discarded this when he left London and moved to France; thus his domicile of origin in Scotland revived and he was domiciled in Scotland at the relevant time.

Lord Westbury:

> 'The law of England, and of almost all civilised countries, ascribes to each individual at his birth two distinct legal states or conditions; one by virtue of which he becomes the subject of some particular country, binding him by the tie of natural allegiance, and which may be called his political status; another, by virtue of which he has ascribed to him the character of a citizen of some particular country, and as such is possessed of certain municipal rights, and subject to certain obligations, which latter character is the civil status or condition of the individual, and may be quite different from his political status. The political status may depend on different laws in different countries; whereas the civil status is governed universally by one single principle, namely, that of domicile, which is the criterion established by law for the purpose of determining civil status. For it is on this basis that the personal rights of the party, that is to say, the law which determines his majority or minority, his marriage, succession, testacy, or intestacy, must depend. International law depends on rules which, being in great measure derived from the Roman law, are common to the jurisprudence of all civilised nations. It is a settled principle that no man shall be without a domicile, and to secure this result the law attributes to every individual as soon as he is born the domicile of his father, if the child be legitimate, and the domicile of the mother if illegitimate. This has been called the domicile of origin, and is involuntary. Other domiciles, including domicile by operation of law, as on marriage, are domiciles of choice. For as soon as an individual is sui juris it is competent to him to elect and assume another domicile, the continuance of which depends upon his will and act. When another domicile is put on, the domicile of origin is for that purpose relinquished, and remains in abeyance during the continuance of the domicile of choice; but as the domicile of origin is the creature of law, and independent of the will of the party, it would be inconsistent with the principles of which it is by law created and ascribed, to suppose that it is capable of being by the act of the party entirely obliterated and extinguished. It revives and exists whenever there is no other domicile, and it does not require to be regained or reconstituted animo et facto, in the manner which is necessary for the acquisition of a domicile of choice.
>
> Domicile of choice is a conclusion or inference which the law derives from the fact of a man fixing voluntarily his sole or chief residence in a particular place, with an intention of continuing to reside there for an unlimited time. This is a description of the circumstances which create or constitute a domicile, and not a definition of the term. There must be a residence freely chosen, and not prescribed or dictated by any external necessity, such as the duties of office, the demand for creditors, or the relief from illness; and it must be residence fixed not for a limited period or particular purpose, but general and indefinite in its future contemplation. It is true that residence originally temporary, or intended for a limited period, may afterwards become general and unlimited, and in such a case so soon as the change of purpose, or animus manendi, can be inferred the fact of domicile is established.
>
> The domicile of origin may be extinguished by act of law, as, for example, by sentence of death or exile for life, which puts an end to the status civilis of the criminal; but it cannot be destroyed by the will and act of the party.
>
> Domicile of choice, as it is gained animo et facto, so it may be put an end to in the same manner. Expressions are found in some books, and in one or two cases, that the first or existing domicile remains until another is acquired. This is true if applied to the domicile of origin, but cannot be true if such general words were intended (which is not probable) to convey the conclusion that a domicile of choice, though unequivocally relinquished and abandoned, clings,

in despite of his will and acts, to the party, until another domicile has animo et facto been acquired. The cases to which I have referred are, in my opinion, met and controlled by other decisions. A natural-born Englishman may, if he domiciles himself in Holland, acquire and have the status civilis of a Dutchman, which is of course ascribed to him in respect of his settled abode in the land, but if he breaks up his establishment, sells his house and furniture, discharges his servants, and quits Holland, declaring that he will never return to it again, and taking with him his wife and children, for the purpose of travelling in France and Italy in search of another place of residence, is it meant to be said that he carries his Dutch domicile, that is, his Dutch citizenship, at his back, and that it clings to him pertinaciously until he has finally set up his tabernacle in another country? Such a conclusion would be absurd; but there is no absurdity and, on the contrary, much reason, in holding that an acquired domicile may be effectually abandoned by unequivocal intention and act; and that when it is so determined the domicile of origin revives until a new domicile of choice be acquired. According to the dicta in the books and cases referred to, if the Englishman whose case we have been supposing lived for twenty years after he had finally quitted Holland, without acquiring a new domicile, and afterwards died intestate, his personal estate would be administered according to the law of Holland, and not according to that of his native country. This is an irrational consequence of the supposed rule. But when a proposition supposed to be authorised by one or more decisions involves absurd results, there is great reason for believing that no such rule was intended to be laid down.'

Winans v *Attorney-General* [1904] AC 287 House of Lords (The Earl of Halsbury, Lords MacNaughten and Lindley)

• *A domicile of origin once operative is very tenacious and difficult to cast off*

Facts

Winans was an eccentric American millionaire who hated England but who nonetheless spent the last 37 years of his life in England. But he spent that time caring for his health and dreaming to wrest Britain's then predominance in shipping away from her by designing a huge fleet of cigar shaped ships that would dominate the shipping world. He dreamed of returning to the United States to control this fleet from a dock in Maryland. Did he acquire a domicile of choice in England before he died or did he retain his American domicile of origin (the two possibilities were New Jersey or Maryland)?

Held (Lord Lindley dissenting)

That he had not obtained a domicile of choice in England; given Winans's dreams of returning to the United States, proof of a fixed and settled purpose to settle in England had not been made out.

Lord MacNaughten:

> 'Domicile of origin, or as it is sometimes called, perhaps less accurately, "domicile of birth", differs from domicile of choice mainly in this – that its character is more enduring, its hold stronger, and less easily shaken off.
>
> In *Munro* v *Munro* (1840) 7 Cl & F 842; 51 RR 103 Lord Cottenham observed that it was one of the principles adopted, not only by the law of England, but generally by the laws of other countries, "that the domicile of origin must prevail until the party has not only acquired another, but has manifested and carried into execution an intention of abandoning his former domicile and acquiring another as his sole domicile ... Residence alone," he adds, "has no effect

per se, though it may be most important as a ground from which to infer intention." "The law", said Lord Cairns LC in *Bell* v *Kennedy* (1868) LR 1 Sc & Div 307, 310, "is beyond all doubt clear with regard to the domicile of birth that the personal status indicated by that term clings and adheres to the subject of it until an actual change is made by which the personal status of another domicile is acquired." The onus of proving that a domicile has been chosen in substitution for the domicile of origin lies upon those who assert that the domicile of origin has been lost. ...

My Lords, if the authorities I have cited are still law, the question which your Lordships have to consider must, I htink, be this: Has it been proved "with perfect clearness and satisfaction to yourselves" that Mr Winans had at the time of his death formed a "fixed and settled purpose" – "a determination" – "a final and deliberate intention" – to abandon his American domicile and settle in England? ...

My Lords, in the dearth of evidence by written or oral declarations as to Mr Winans' intentions, it seems to me to be important to consider what manner of man Mr Winans was, what were the main objects of his existence, and what sort of a life he lived in this country. I think there is a good deal of force in some observations that were made both by Lord Cranworth and Lord Wensleydale in the case of *Whicker* v *Hume* (1858) 7 HL Cas 124 to the effect that in these days, when the tendency of the educated and leisured classes is to become cosmopolitan – if I may use the word – you must look very narrowly into the nature of a residence suggested as a domicile of choice before you deprive a man of his native domicile.

Mr Winans was a person of considerable ability and of singular tenacity of purpose, self-centred and strangely uncommunicative. He was not interested in many things, but whatever he did he did, as his son says, thoroughly. He became completely absorbed in a scheme when he took it up. At the same time he lived a very retired – almost a secluded – life. He took no part in general or municipal politics. He rarely went into society. He had no intimate friends, if, indeed, he had any friends at all, in this country. There is no evidence that he was interested in any charity or charitable or philanthropic institution in England. Although he was on affectionate terms with his two sons, he never let them into his secrets. "He always worked his business himself," his son says "and never brought us into the business affairs in any way." And although at odd times he mentioned his property in America, he never allowed even his eldest son "to understand much about it." ...

Mr Winans had three objects in life. His first object was his health. He nursed and tended it with wonderful devotion. He took his temperature several times a day. He had regular times for taking his temperature, and regular times for taking his various waters and medicines.

Besides the care of his health, there were two other objects which engrossed his thoughts. The first was the construction of spindle-shaped vessels commonly called cigar ships. This form of vessel was, as Mr Winans asserted, an invention of the Winans family. Many patents were taken out for it both in England and in America. It was claimed that vessels of this type would be able to cross the Atlantic without pitching or rolling. In an application to Congress in the year 1892 Mr Winans represented himself as attached heart and soul to his country, and asked for protection for a long term of years in consideration of the great expenditure which he and his family had incurred in perfecting the invention, and the vast benefits that would result from it to the people of the United States. Mr Winans declared his confident expectation that a fleet of spindle-shaped vessels subsidized by Congress would restore to America the carrying trade which had fallen into the hands of England and other foreign nations, secure to America the command of the sea, and make it impossible for Great Britain to maintain war against the United States. Such a fleet as he described in his application could, he said, "meet war vessels in open sea near the European side and destroy one vessel after another, so that none of them would be able to reach our shores." In the development of his invention Mr Winans stated that he had incurred an expense nearly equal to four millions of dollars.

Mr Winans' confidence in this project remained unshaken to the end of his life, and he kept an office in Beaufort Gardens where a staff of engineers and draftsmen was engaged in working out the problem.

There was another scheme which Mr Winans hoped to develop and work in connection with his fleet of spindle-shaped vessels. In 1859 a property in Baltimore, about 200 acres in extent, called Ferry Bar, was purchased on behalf of the Winans family originally for the purpose of being used, as Mr Winans states in a letter of January 31, 1882, "for the service of the sea-going steamers of the spindle-shaped form."

Of course, to us these schemes of Mr Winans appear wild, visionary, and chimerical. But I have no doubt that to a man like Mr Winans, wholly wrapt up in himself, they were very real. They were the dreams of his life. For forty years he kept them steadily in view. And one was anti-English and the other wholly American. ...

Then it was said that the length of time during which Mr Winans resided in this country leads to the inference that he must have become content to make this country his home. Length of time is of course a very important element in questions of domicile. An unconscious change may come over a man's mind. If the man goes about and mixes in society that is not an improbable result. But in the case of a person like Mr Winans, who kept himself to himself and had little or no intercourse with his fellow men, it seems to me that at the end of any space in time, however long, his mind would probably be in the state it was at the beginning. When he came to this country he was a sojourner and a stranger, and he was, I think, a sojourner and a stranger in it when he died.

On the whole I am unable to come to the conclusion that Mr Winans ever formed a fixed and settled purpose of abandoning his American domicile and settling finally in England. I think up to the very last he had an expectation or hope of returning to America and seeing his grand schemes inaugurated. To take the test proposed by Wickens V-C, "if the question had arisen in a form requiring a deliberate or solemn determination," I have no doubt Mr Winans, who was, as his son says, "entirely American in all his ideas and sympathies," would have answered it in favour of America.

I am therefore of opinion that the Crown has not discharged the onus cast upon it, and I think that the order appealed from ought to be reversed.'

Habitual residence

Cruse* v *Chittum [1974] 2 All ER 940 Family Division (Lane J)

• *Habitual residence means a regular physical presence which must endure for some time – it means something more than ordinary residence and something less than domicile*

Facts

The husband and wife, both domiciled in England, married there in 1950. They lived together in England until 1961 when the wife left. The husband was not in contact with her until August 1964 when he received a letter from her stating: 'I think it is only right to tell you that I have got a divorce so you are a free man now.' He took no steps until 1971 when he wished to marry. His solicitors discovered that the wife had been granted a divorce in Mississippi in July 1963 based on the fact that she was an actual bona fide resident of Harrison County, Mississippi, and had been so for more than a year immediately preceding the filing of the complaint. Section 3 of the Recognition of Divorces and Legal Separations Act 1971 provides that the validity of an overseas divorce shall be recognised if at the date of the institution of the proceedings in the country in which it was obtained either spouse was habitually resident in that country.

Held

Lane J:

'The first question which arises in determining whether or not this court should recognise that decree is what is meant by the phrase "habitually resident in that country". Counsel for the petitioner submits that habitual residence requires an element of intention, an intention to reside in that country. He further submits that "habitual" must indicate a quality of residence rather than a period of residence. He argues that as no period of residence is specified in the 1971 Act, this of itself points to the importance of the quality of residence in order to make it habitual. This submission derives support from the fact that in s5(2) of the Domicile and Matrimonial Proceedings Act 1973, the same phrase "habitually resident" appears, but for the purposes of that subsection is required to be one year's duration. Counsel says further that one may point to characteristics of residency which will not make it habitual but other than habitual. For example the residence must not be temporary or of a secondary nature. He urges that the phrase in the decree of the American court that the residence was "actual" and "bona fide" really defines what is meant by "habitual" in this context, and denotes a regular physical presence which must endure for some time. He further submits that ordinary residence is different from habitual residence in that the latter is something more than the former and is similar to the residence normally required as part of domicile, although in habitual residence there is no need for the element of animus which is necessary in domicile. I accept those submissions.'

Her Ladyship referred to s5 of the 1971 Act and continued:

'I am satisfied that a valid decree of dissolution of the petitioner's marriage was pronounced in the Mississippi court on 17 July 1963, and that sufficient facts are apparent therefrom and from other evidence before me to show that the respondent at the time she instituted the proceedings in that court was habitually resident in the country where the decree was pronounced. I am fortified in my view by the fact that under s5(2) of the Domicile and Matrimonial Proceedings Act 1973 the court has jurisdiction to entertain proceedings for divorce if either party to the marriage has been habitually resident here throughout a period of one year ending with the date when divorce proceedings are begun. It would therefore be somewhat anomalous if habitual residence in a foreign country granting a decree were required to be of more than a year's duration in order that the decree should be recognised here.

These being my conclusions, I grant the declaration sought that the petitioner's marriage was validly dissolved and that the decree may be recognised here.'

4 Jurisdiction in Personam

Traditional rules

Bank of Baroda, The v *The Vysya Bank Ltd* [1994] 2 Lloyd's Rep 87 Queen's Bench Division (Commercial Court) (Mance J)

• *Whether contract between issuing bank and confirming bank made within jurisdiction and/or made by agent residing within jurisdiction – whether court had jurisdiction to grant leave to serve writ out of jurisdiction*

Facts

Vysya was instructed by an Indian importer Aditya Steel Industries to issue a letter of credit in favour of Granada Worldwide Industries Ltd, an Irish company with a London office, in respect of the purchase of about 16,092 tonnes of a pig iron which Aditya had agreed to buy cif shipped from Ventspils in Latvia to Haldia in India. The credit was confirmed by the City of London office of the Bank of Baroda, and that confirmation was notified in writing by notice sent to Granada at its London office. An initial presentation of documents by Granada was apparently rejected for non-conformity on 9 October 1992. However, Vysya agreed to amend the credit and the documents were then negotiated by the Bank of Baroda by payment of $1,742,376.41 under the letter of credit on the same day. The Bank of Baroda despatched the documents to Vysya in India on the next day. Vysya informed the Bank of Baroda that it had mailed reimbursement instructions to Citibank New York and authorised the Bank of Baroda to claim reimbursement. However, Vysya subsequently withdrew that authorisation. The Bank of Baroda issued their writ claiming damages for anticipatory and/or actual breach of the contract between Vysya as issuing bank and the Bank of Baroda as confirming bank. Leave to issue and serve the writ out of the jurisdiction was given pursuant to an affidavit which invoked RSC O.11 r1(1)(d). Vysya applied to set aside the order on the ground that the case did not fall within any of the heads in O.11 and/or that England was not the appropriate forum for its resolution.

Held

The English court had jurisdiction. The contract between the Bank of Baroda and Vysya was made within the jurisdiction. This was also a case where England was the more appropriate forum for the resolution of the case.

Mance J:

> 'First however I will consider as briefly as may be the two other heads of O.11 r1(1)(d) under which Bank of Baroda maintains that jurisdiction existed to grant leave to issue and serve the writ. The first is of some considerable complexity, and concerns the question whether the contract was made within the jurisdiction of the English courts. I have already outlined the parties' respective cases as to the making of the contract. The question is whether Bank of Baroda has made out a "good arguable case" for saying that the contract was concluded by conduct in England …
>
> Bank of Baroda first heard of the present transaction when its City branch was approached direct by Granada in London at the beginning of October, 1992. On Oct 1 1992 Granada faxed to the City branch a photocopy and typed copy of the original

letter of credit. On Oct 5 the City branch reported the approach to the Bombay central office, mentioning that the transaction would yield commission of $14,204, and indicating that it had its approval and asking for head office's. This telex would have been available to be seen first thing on Oct 6. In fact Mr Subramanian says that he did not see it until later that day after he had received the telephone call from Mr Rajaram. He says that he could not have agreed and did not agree in that conversation that the City of London branch should confirm a letter of credit because he could not make operational decisions on behalf of that branch and also because he had not seen the credit's text or received any request in writing from Vysya.

After the conversation he says that he saw the incoming telex from the London branch and endorsed it with the reply "Agree provided Vysya Bank request LMO to add their confirmation". A telex to this effect was sent from the Bombay central office to the City of London office at 17.03 hours Indian time on Oct 6. There may he says have been another short conversation on Oct. 7, 1992 during which Mr Rajaram simply enquired whether there were any difficulties ...

If there was no contract made on the telephone in India, when is the contract likely to have been made? Bank of Baroda says that it was made by conduct when it acted on Vysya's request or requests by communicating or posting its confirmation orally or in writing to Granada in London on Oct 8, 1992. Vysya on the other hand says that communication of acceptance is essential, and that any contract can only have been made when information was received by Vysya in India that Bank of Baroda had confirmed the credit. Since Bank of Baroda's City branch simply acted on the requests received from India by confirming the credit on Oct 8, this leads to the unlikely conclusion that there was no contract until Vysya received from Bank of Baroda on or about Oct 16 the negotiated documents. In my judgment this is a situation where Bank of Baroda has a good arguable case for saying that it was open to it to accept the requests which it received by acting in accordance with them and confirming the credit.

Accordingly, if necessary, I consider that Bank of Baroda has made out a good arguable case for saying that the contract between it and Vysya for the confirmation of the credit was made within the jurisdiction in England. I would add however that I do not regard this as a critical factor in the determination in this case of the most appropriate forum, to which I shall come ...

For the reasons given I have come to the clear conclusion both that the English court has jurisdiction and that this is a case where England is the more appropriate forum for the resolution of this case. I therefore dismiss the defendant's summons.'

Brinkibon Ltd* v *Stahag Stahl [1983] 2 AC 34 House of Lords (Lords Wilberforce, Fraser, Brandon, Russell and Bridge)

- *RSC O.11 r1(1)(d)(i) allows leave to be granted where the contract in question 'was made within the jurisdiction'*

Facts

There had been an exchange of telexes between Brinkibon (in London) and Stahag Stahl (in Vienna) relating to the sale of certain mild steel by Stahag Stahl to Brinkibon. Stahag Stahl sought to withdraw from the contract and Brinkibon sought to sue Stahag Stahl in England. The only head upon which leave to serve outside the jurisdiction was sought was O.11 r1(1)(d)(i), but was the contract made in England?

Held

Leave would be refused. As a general rule where there was instantaneous communication between the parties, the contract was made when and where the acceptance was received, and on the facts this was in Vienna. However, there may be exceptions to this general rule.

Lord Wilberforce:

'The question whether a contract was made within the jurisdiction will often admit of a simple answer: if both parties are in England at the time of making it, or if it is contained in a single document signed by both parties in England, there is no difficulty. But in the case of contracts involving negotiations, where one party is abroad, the answer may be difficult to find. Sophisticated analysis may be required to decide when the last counter-offer was made into a contract by acceptance, or at what point a clear consensus was reached and by virtue of what words spoken or of what conduct. In the case of successive telephone conversations it may indeed be most artificial to ask where the contract was made; if one asked the parties, they might say they did not know – or care. The place of making a contract is usually irrelevant as regards validity, or interpretation, or enforcement. Unfortunately it remains in O.11 as a test for purposes of jurisdiction, and courts have to do their best with it.

In the present case it seems that if there was a contract (a question which can only be decided at the trial), it was preceded by and possibly formed by a number of telephone conversations and telexes between London and Vienna, and there are a number of possible combinations upon which reliance can be placed. At this stage we must take the alternatives which provide reasonable evidence of a contract in order to see if the test is satisfied. There are two: (i) A telex dated 3 May 1979, from the respondents in Vienna, said to amount to a counter-offer, followed by a telex from the appellants in London to the respondents in Vienna dated May 4 1979, said to amount to an acceptance. (ii) The above telex dated May 3 1979, from the respondents followed by action, by way of opening a letter of credit, said to have amounted to an acceptance by conduct.

The first of these alternatives neatly raises the question whether an acceptance by telex sent from London but received in Vienna causes a contract to be made in London, or in Vienna. If the acceptance had been sent by post, or by telegram, then, on existing authorities, it would have been complete when put into the hands of the post office – in London. If on the other hand it had been telephoned, it would have been complete when heard by the offeror – in Vienna. So in which category is a telex communication to be placed? Existing authority of the Court of Appeal decides in favour of the latter category, ie, a telex is to be assimilated to other methods of instanteous communication: see *Entores Ltd* v *Miles Far East Corporation* [1955] 2 QB 327. The appellants ask that this case, which has stood for 30 years, should now be reviewed.

Now such review as is necessary must be made against the background of the law as to the making of contracts. The general rule, it is hardly necessary to state, is that a contract is formed *when* acceptance of an offer is communicated by the offeree to the offeror. And if it is necessary to determine *where* a contract is formed (as to which I have already commented) it appears logical that this should be at the place where acceptance is communicated to the offeror. In the common case of contracts, whether oral or in writing inter praesentes, there is no difficulty; and again logic demands that even where there is not mutual presence at the same place and at the same time, if communication is instantaneous, for example, by telephone or radio communication, the same result should follow.

Then there is the case – very common – of communication at a distance, to meet which the so called "postal rule" has developed. I need not trace its history: it has firmly been in the law at least since *Adams* v *Lindsall* (1818) 1 B & Ald 681. The rationale for it, if left somewhat obscure by Lord Ellenborough CJ, has since been well explained. Mellish LJ in *In re Imperial Land Co of Marseilles (Harris' Case)* (1872) LR 7 Ch App 587, 594 ascribed it to the extraordinary and mischievous consequences which would follow if it were held that an offer might be revoked at any time until the letter accepting it had been actually received: and its foundation in convenience was restated by Thesiger LJ in *Household Fire and Carriage Accident Insurance Co Ltd* v *Grant* (1879) 4 Ex D 216, 223. In these cases too it seems logical to say that the place, as well as the time, of acceptance should be *where* (as *when*) the acceptance is put into the charge of the post office.

In this situation, with a general rule covering instantaneous communication inter praesentes, or at a distance, with an exception applying to non-instantaneous communication at a distance, how should communications by telex be categorised? In *Entores Ltd* v *Miles Far East Corporation* [1955] 2 QB 327 the Court of Appeal classified them with instantaneous communications. Their ruling, which has passed into the textbooks, including *Williston on Contracts*, 3rd ed (1957), appears not to have caused either adverse comment, or any difficulty to businessmen. I would accept it as a general rule. Where the condition of simultaneity is met, and where it appears to be within the mutual intention of the parties that contractual exchanges should take place in this way, I think it a sound rule, but not necessarily a universal rule.

Since 1955 the use of telex communication has been greatly expanded, and there are many variants on it. The senders and recipients may not be the principals to the contemplated contract. They may be servants or agents with limited authority. The message may not reach, or be intended to reach, the designated recipient immediately: messages may be sent out of office hours, or at night, with the intention, or upon the assumption, that they will be read at a later time. There may be some error or default at the recipient's end which prevents receipt at the time contemplated and believed in by the sender. The message may have been sent and/or received through machines operated by third persons. And many other variations may occur. No universal rule can cover all such cases: they must be resolved by reference to the intentions of the parties, by sound business practice and in some cases by a judgment where the risks should lie: see *Household Fire and Carriage Accident Insurance Co Ltd* v *Grant*, 4 Ex D 216, 227 per Baggallay LJ and *Henthorn* v *Fraser* [1892] 2 Ch 27 per Lord Herschell.

The present case is, as *Entores Ltd* v *Miles Far East Corporation* [1955] 2 QB 327 itself, the simple case of instantaneous communication between principals, and, in accordance with the general rule, involves that the contract (if any) was made when and where the acceptance was received. This was on May 3 1979, in Vienna.'

Fehmarn, The [1958] 1 WLR 159; [1958] 1 All ER 333 Court of Appeal (Denning, Hodson and Morris LJJ)

• *Effect of contractual term on jurisdiction of English courts – disputes referred to another jurisdiction*

Facts

Russian shippers loaded a cargo of turpentine on a German ship at Ventspils, a Russian port in the Baltic. The bill of lading provided (inter alia) that the shipowners were bound to make the ship seaworthy before and at the beginning of the voyage; and that all disputes should be judged in the USSR. The ship sailed to London and the Russian shippers sold the turpentine to English buyers, who became holders of the bill of lading.

After the turpentine was unloaded in England the English importers complained to the German shipowners of short delivery and contamination. The English importers brought an action against the German shipowners in the Admiralty Division of the High Court, claiming damages. The German owners moved to set aside the writ on the ground that the English courts had no jurisdiction, or alternatively that the parties had agreed that all disputes should be adjudged in the courts of Russia and not in this country.

Held

Lord Denning:

'As to the first point, it is not now suggested that the Court of Admiralty has not jurisdiction. By s1(1)(g) of the Administration of Justice Act 1956 (following previous statutes), it is plain that the Court of Admiralty in England has jurisdiction to deal with such a claim as this.

Then the next question is whether the action ought to be stayed because of the provision in the bill of lading that all disputes are to be judged by the Russian courts. I do not regard this provision as equal to an arbitration clause, but I do say that the English courts are in charge of their own proceedings: and one of the rules they apply is that a stipulation that all disputes should be judged by the tribunals of a particular country is not absolutely binding. It is a matter to which the courts of this country will pay much regard and to which they will normally give effect, but it is subject to the overriding principle that no one by his private stipulation can oust these courts of their jurisdiction in a matter that properly belongs to them.

I would ask myself therefore: Is this dispute a matter which properly belongs to the courts of this country? Here are English importers who, when they take delivery of the goods in England, find them contaminated. The goods are surveyed by surveyors on both sides, with the result that the English importers make a claim against the German shipowners. The vessel is a frequent visitor to this country. In order to be sure that their claim, if substantiated, is paid by the shipowners, the English importers are entitled by the procedure of our courts of Admiralty to arrest the ship whenever she comes here in order to have security for their claim. There seems to me to be no doubt that such a dispute is one that properly belongs for its determination to the courts of this country. But still the question remains: Ought these courts in their discretion to stay this action?

It has been said by Mr Roche that this contract is governed by Russian law and should be judged by the Russian courts, who know that law. And the dispute may involve evidence from witnesses in Russia about the condition of the goods on shipment. Then why, says Mr Roche, should it not be judged in Russia as the condition says?

I do not regard the choice of law in the contract as decisive. I prefer to look to see with what country is the dispute most closely concerned. Here the Russian element in the dispute seems to me to be comparatively small. The dispute is between the German owners of the ship and the English importers. It depends on evidence here as to the condition of the goods when they arrived here in London and on evidence of the ship, which is a frequent visitor to London. The correspondence leaves in my mind, just as it did in the judge's mind, the impression that the German owners did not object to the dispute being decided in this country but wished to avoid the giving of security.

I think the dispute is more closely connected with England than Russia, and I agree with the judge that sufficient reason has been shown why the proceedings should continue in these courts and should not be stayed. I would therefore dismiss the appeal.

Appeal dismissed.'

Gan Insurance Co Ltd v *Tai Ping Insurance Co Ltd* [1999] 2 All ER (Comm) 54 Court of Appeal (Beldam, Brooke and Mummery LJJ)

- *Reinsurance contract – query whether England was the appropriate forum – effect of applicable law*

Facts

Under Taiwanese law an insured has a more limited duty of disclosure than under English law. The appellant, a Taiwanese insurance company which had issued an 'erection all risks' policy governed by Taiwanese law, reinsured the risk with the respondent on the Lloyd's insurance market through brokers in London. It later claimed under the policy. The respondent sought a declaration of non-liability in the English courts inter alia because of lack of disclosure of material facts by the appellant. The respondent applied for service of the writ to be set aside on the basis that

Taiwan was the more appropriate forum. The question of the law governing the contract was material to the court's exercise of its discretion to allow service out of the jurisdiction. The appellant argued that the original policy of insurance was governed by Taiwanese law; that the reinsurance slip included a reference to 'Slip Policy NMA 1779 following original'; and that this and other references to the original insurance policy must be interpreted as meaning that the choice of Taiwanese law in the original policy was incorporated into the reinsurance policy.

Held

Policies issued in the Lloyd's insurance market were entered into between brokers and underwriters on the basis that they were governed by English law. This implied choice of English law would be respected unless a clear choice of a different law could be identified. Since English law governed the contract and the issue of the respondent's liability on the contract was principally a matter of law, with little factual evidence being required from Taiwan, England was clearly the appropriate forum.

Beldam LJ:

> 'At the hearing of Tai Ping's summons to set aside service, Cresswell J set out the principles governing leave to serve out of the jurisdiction and relevant to the exercise of his discretion in deciding whether to set service aside, including the principle on which he should decide whether an English court was the convenient forum to decide Gan's claim. I propose at this point only to summarise the principles he set out in his judgment. They were:
>
> (1) that Gan had to establish a good arguable case that its claims were within one of the sub-paragraphs of Ord. 11, r.1(1);
>
> (2) that it had to demonstrate that there was a serious issue to be tried on the merits of the claim;
>
> (3) that the English courts were the convenient forum;
>
> (4) that it was a proper case in which the court should exercise its discretion to grant leave; and
>
> (5) the fundamental principle is that the court will choose the forum in which the case can be tried most suitably in the interests of all the parties and to serve the ends of justice.
>
> Gan were required to show not merely that the English court was an appropriate forum for the trial of the action but that it was clearly the appropriate forum taking into account the nature of the dispute, the legal and practical issues involved, availability of witnesses and expense. The aim is to achieve substantial justice for all the parties in the appropriate forum ...
>
> The judge's decision that English law was the proper law of the contract obviously had a significant effect on his decision whether to exercise his discretion in favour of Gan and on his decision whether the English courts were the appropriate forum ...
>
> The importance of the choice of law is highlighted by the differences in the rules permitting avoidance of a contract of insurance ... Thus if Taiwanese law applied to the contract of reinsurance, Gan could not avoid the contract on the ground that Tai Ping had misrepresented the extent of the fire protection available to the building insured unless it had submitted written enquiries which had been untruthfully answered ...
>
> In presenting his argument for Tai Ping, Mr Lockey identified as of fundamental importance the judge's conclusion that English law and not Taiwanese law was the proper law of the contract of reinsurance ... He submitted that even if the parties had not made an express or real choice nevertheless the contract of reinsurance was most closely connected with Taiwan. The judge had placed too much reliance on the fact that the policy of reinsurance was a Lloyds policy effected using an English form ...
>
> The judge considered these submissions in detail. He concluded that if any factual evidence was required from Taiwan it was likely to be within relatively narrow limits and even if Tai Ping's arguments proved to be correct he did not consider that the extent

of the evidence needed from overseas would be significant. He said:

> "In all the circumstances I conclude that the plaintiffs have shown not merely that England is the appropriate forum for the trial of the action(s) but that it is clearly the appropriate forum."

Attractively though Mr Lockey's submissions were presented, he did not persuade me that the judge had made any error in the exercise of his discretion which would entitle this court to review the decision he reached. Accordingly I would dismiss this appeal.'

Comment

For further discussion on the choice of law issue refer to Chapter 5.

Maharanee Seethadevi Gaekwar of Baroda* v *Wildenstein [1972] 2 QB 283 Court of Appeal (Lord Denning, Edmund-Davies and Stephenson LJJ)

• *The common law rules are very liberal and straightforward: if a defendant is served with a writ (claim form) in England the court has jurisdiction*

Facts

The Maharanee had bought a painting believing it to be La Poesie by François Boucher from Wildenstein in Paris for £32,920. In fact the painting was by one of Boucher's followers and was only worth £750! The plaintiff was an Indian princess resident in France (but with connections with England and Ireland) and the defendant was an international art dealer resident in France (but with many international links, including some with England). Although the dispute was obviously essentially French (in that both the parties were resident in France and all the crucial events had taken place in France), the defendant was served with a writ when he paid a fleeting visit to England to attend the Ascot races. The defendant applied to have the plaintiff's actions set aside on the ground that it was frivolous and vexatious and an abuse of the process of the court.

Held

That if the defendant was properly served with a writ within the jurisdiction, then, notwithstanding that he was served on a fleeting visit to England, there was no presumption that the proceedings were oppressive. He failed to satisfy the court that the proceedings were oppressive and the action was not stayed.

Lord Denning:

> 'In this case the writ has been properly served on the defendant in this country. This makes the case very different from those in which the defendant is in a foreign country and the plaintiff has to seek leave to serve him out of the jurisdiction. It is also different from those cases in which the plaintiff has already started an action in another country, and the question is whether he should be allowed to start another action in this country on the same subject matter. In this case the plaintiff has validly invoked the jurisdiction of our courts in this, the one and only action she has brought.'

Edmund Davies LJ:

> 'The nature of the contract, the circumstances in which it was made, the supranational nature of the dispute to which it has given rise, the identity and internationally peripatetic habits of the parties, and the service of the writ in this action on the defendant at Ascot on 20 June 1970, are all matters already dealt with by Lord Denning MR, and call for no further treatment by me. But one thing should be made clear: unless the plaintiff knows full well that she has no cause of action (and that is not suggested), she did no wrong in taking out a High Court writ in the first place (foreigner though she is) and serving it here at the first available opportunity upon the defendant (foreigner though *he* also is). Both in taking it out and serving it (albeit when the defendant was only fleetingly on British soil) she was doing no more than our law permits, even

though it may have ruined his day at the races. Some might regard her action as bad form; none can legitimately condemn it as an abuse of legal process: see *Colt Industries Inc* v *Sarlie* [1966] 1 WLR 440. But there are clear indications that Bridge J [in the court below] thought otherwise, and that this notion coloured his approach to the whole case and, as I respectfully think, led him astray.

There are branches of our law in which the forum conveniens is a factor generally of decisive importance. One example is the case of administration of estates and trusts: see *Ewing* v *Orr Ewing* (1885) 10 App Cas 453, 505 per Lord Selborne. Another is the case where proceedings in respect of the same subject matter have already been instituted in another jurisdiction. Again, in determining whether leave to serve a writ out of the jurisdiction should be granted, Lord Simonds reasserted in *Tyne Improvement Commissioners* v *Armement Anversois S/A (The Brabo)* [1949] AC 326, 350, which was cited to us by Mr Wilmers, that, as Pearson J said in *Société Générale de Paris* v *Dreyfus Brothers* (1885) 29 Ch D 239, 242–243:

> "... it ought always to be considered a very serious question ... whether this court ought to put a foreigner, who owes no allegiance here, to the inconvenience and annoyance of being brought to contest his rights in this country ..."

But such a consideration, while still relevant, is of itself by no means decisive of the problem involved in the present case. Scott LJ said in *St Pierre* v *South American Stores (Gath & Chaves) Ltd* [1936] 1 KB 382, 398:

> "A mere balance of convenience is not a sufficient ground for depriving a plaintiff of the advantages of prosecuting his action in an English court if it is otherwise properly brought. The right of access to the King's court must not be lightly refused."'

Comment

What is said in this case about the exercise of a discretion to stay an action properly commenced in England should be read subject to the introduction of the principle of forum conveniens into English law: see *Spiliada Maritime Corporation* v *Cansulex Ltd*, below.

Seaconsar Far East Ltd v *Bank Markazi Jomhouri Islami Iran*

[1993] 3 WLR 756 House of Lords (Lords Templeman, Griffith, Goff, Browne-Wilkinson and Mustill)

- *Even where a case falls within one of the heads under O.11 r1(1) the court still has a discretion whether to grant leave to serve the writ outside the jurisdiction*

Facts

The plaintiffs had agreed to sell a quantity of artillery shells to the Iranian Ministry of Defence. Payment was to be made by way of letter of credit and the defendant bank opened a letter of credit in favour of the plaintiffs. Several deliveries of shells were made but when the plaintiffs twice presented shipping documents at the designated London bank for payment, they were not paid. Thus the plaintiffs brought proceedings in London against the defendant bank for breach of contract and sought leave to serve the writ outside the jurisdiction in terms of r1(1)(d)(i) or (ii) (alleging that the contract was made within the jurisdiction or made through an agent trading within the jurisdiction), or (e) (breach of the contract within the jurisdiction (through failure to pay in London)). However, Bank Markazi resisted the grant of leave on the ground that, while the case fell within O.11 r1(1), the plaintiff had not established 'a sufficiently strong case on the merits' to justify leave to serve outside the jurisdiction.

Held

That, while it was still necessary for the plaintiffs to show that their case fell within one or more of the paras or sub-paras of O.11 r1(1) (and that the standard of proof of this was that of the 'good arguable case'), on the merits all that the plaintiffs had to show was that there was a substantial question of law or fact, ie, a serious issue, to be tried between the parties. That on the facts Seaconsar had shown this and leave was granted to serve outside the jurisdiction.

Lord Goff:

> 'In argument before the Appellate Committee, attention was concentrated upon the question of the strength of the case on the merits which a plaintiff has to establish in order to justify the grant of leave to serve proceedings out of the jurisdiction under O.11. …
>
> I start, as I must, with the relevant provisions of O.11. Order 11 r1(1) provides that, subject to certain specified exceptions, "service of a writ out of the jurisdiction is permissible with the leave of the court if in the action begun by the writ," and there follows a list of 20 specified circumstances, set out in paragraphs lettered (a) to (t) respectively, in which service out of the jurisdiction is permissible. These lettered paragraphs cover a wide range of circumstances. The paragraphs most commonly invoked are (d) and (e), concerned with contractual claims; indeed many of the decided cases are concerned with one or other or both of these two paragraphs. But the problem which has arisen in the present case is not confined to these two paragraphs and may, in theory at least, arise under others. For this reason alone, it is essential not to consider the problem only in relation to the facts of the present case, or to paragraphs (d) and (e), but also in relation to other fact-situations and other paragraphs of r1(1). I myself have found this exercise both helpful and revealing, especially as it so happens that paragraphs (d) and (e) are, for present purposes, more complicated in their effect than most, if not all, of the other paragraphs of the rule. …
>
> Under many paragraphs, once the plaintiff's claim is shown to have been made under a certain statutory provision, the jurisdiction of the court is established; and a separate question will arise as to the merits of the plaintiff's claim: see, eg paragraphs (q), (r) and (s). Another obvious example is to be found in paragraph (a), concerned with relief sought against a person domiciled within the jurisdiction. There, once the plaintiff has established, to the standard required by r4(2), that the defendant is domiciled within the jurisdiction, jurisdiction under paragraph (a) is established and a separate question will arise as to the merits of his claim. Paragraph (d), the other paragraph concerned with contractual claims, and one which is relevant in the present case, is more complex. It provides:
>
> > "(d) the claim is brought to enforce, rescind, dissolve, annul or otherwise affect a contract, or to recover damages or obtain other relief in respect of the breach of a contract, being (in either case) and contract which – (i) was made within the jurisdiction, or (ii) was made by or through an agent trading or residing within the jurisdiction on behalf of a principal trading or residing out of the jurisdiction, or (iii) is by its terms, or by implication, governed by English law, or (iv) contains a term to the effect that the High Court shall have jurisdiction to hear and determine any action in respect of the contract; …"
>
> As I read the paragraph, however, and having regard to the view formed in *Korner*'s *Case* [1951] AC 869, I am of the opinion that what has to be sufficiently shown by the plaintiff for the purpose of establishing jurisdiction is, in the case of, for example, sub-paragraph (i), not merely that, if the contract existed, it was made within the jurisdiction, but that (1) there was a contract, and (2) such contract was made within the jurisdiction. Likewise, under sub-paragraphs (ii), (iii) and (iv), the existence of the relevant contract has to be sufficiently proved. But, once that is done, there arises a separate question as to the merits of the plaintiff's claim relative to that contract. That question was however not addressed by their Lordships in *Korner*'s *Case*, with the exception of Lord Tucker, who expressed the opinion, at p889 (with reference to claims founded on a tort under paragraph (ee), now paragraph (f)), that a lesser

burden will fall on the plaintiff with regard to the merits of his claim, viz whether the affidavits disclose a case which appears to merit consideration at the trial – a test consistent with the approach of Lord Davey in the *Badische Anilin Case*, 90 LT 733, and indeed with that of Lord Goddard CJ in *Malik* in so far as he was not concerned with the question of jurisdiction under r1(1).

This approach is consistent with r4(1)(d) of O.11, concerned with applications made under r1(1)(c). Moreover, support for this approach is to be derived from the development of the requirement of forum conveniens as an element in the exercise of the court's discretion under O.11. It has been consistently stated, at least since the judgment of Pearson J in the *Dreyfus* case, 29 Ch D 239, that it is a serious question whether the jurisdiction under O.11 ought to be invoked, to put a person outside the jurisdiction to the "inconvenience and annoyance of being brought to contest his rights in this country:" pp242–243. It is, of course, true to say that any inconvenience involved has been much reduced by modern methods of communication; but the point of principle remains. This is however very largely met by the application in this context of the principle of forum conveniens (as to which see *Spiliada Maritime Corporation* v *Cansulex Ltd* [1987] AC 460, 481–482). The effect of this development is that, given that jurisdiction is established under one of the paragraphs of r1(1) and that proper regard is paid to the principle of forum conveniens, it is difficult to see why the fact that the writ is to be served out of the jurisdiction should have any particular impact upon the standard of proof required in respect of the existence of the cause of action. On this point, I find myself in respectful disagreement with the opinion expressed by Lloyd LJ to the contrary in the Court of Appeal [1993] 1 Lloyd's Rep 236, 242. I prefer the approach of Stuart-Smith LJ when, at p248, he commended his preferred view as consonant with common sense and policy, and continued:

> "It seems to me to be wholly inappropriate once the question[s] of jurisdiction and forum [conveniens] are established for there to be prolonged debate and consideration of the merits of the plaintiffs' claim at the interlocutory stage."

It has been suggested that, since both the assessment of the merits of the plaintiff's claim and the principle of forum conveniens fall to be considered as elements in the exercise of the court's discretion, these should be regarded as interrelated in the sense that "the more conspicuous the presence of one element the less insistent the demands of justice that the other should also be conspicuous:" see *Société Commerciale de Réassurance* v *Eras International Ltd* [1992] 1 Lloyd's Rep 570, 588, per Mustill LJ. This approach originated in the speech of Lord Oaksey in *Korner's Case*, at pp881–882, to the effect that the strength of the evidence in that case as to forum conveniens was such that only the slightest evidence was required of there having been a breach of contract within the jurisdiction. Lord Oaksey's speech also provided the inspiration for an expression of opinion by Parker LJ to the effect that, if there is overwhelming evidence that England is the appropriate forum, it will be enough that, on the merits, the plaintiff's case is worthy of serious consideration: see *Overseas Union Insurance Ltd* v *Incorporated General Insurance Ltd* [1992] 1 Lloyd's Rep 439, 448, and see also *Banque Parisbas* v *Cargill International SA* [1991] 2 Lloyd's Rep 19, 25. I must however express my respectful disagreement with this approach. Suppose that, for example, the plaintiff's case is very strong on the merits. If so, I cannot see that a case particularly strong on the merits can compensate for a weak case on forum conveniens. Likewise, in my opinion, a very strong connection with the English forum cannot justify a weak case on the merits, if a stronger case on the merits would otherwise be required. In truth, as I see it, the two elements are separate and distinct. The invocation of the principle of forum conveniens springs from the often expressed anxiety that great care should be taken in bringing before the English court a foreigner who owes no allegiance here. But if jurisdiction is established under r1(1), and it is also established that England is the forum conveniens, I can see no good reason why any particular degree of cogency should be required in relation to the merits of the plaintiff's case. …

Once it is recognised that, so far as the merits of the plaintiff's claim are concerned, no more is required than that the evidence should disclose that there is a serious issue to be tried, it is difficult to see how this matter, although it falls within the ambit of the court's discretion, has not in practice to be established in any event. This is because it is very difficult to conceive how a judge could, in the proper exercise of his discretion, give leave where there was no serious issue to be tried. Accordingly, a judge faced with a question of leave to serve proceedings out of the jurisdiction under O.11 will in practice have to consider both (1) whether jurisdiction has been sufficiently established, on the criterion of the good arguable case laid down in *Korner's Case*, under one of the paragraphs of r(1), and (2) whether there is a serious issue to be tried, so as to enable him to exercise his discretion to grant leave, before he goes on to consider the exercise of that discretion, with particular reference to the issue of forum conveniens.'

Comment

Remember that where there is some other more appropriate forum, then leave will generally not be granted on forum conveniens grounds. (See **Forum conveniens** below.)

Union International Insurance Co Ltd* v *Jubilee Insurance Co Ltd [1991] 1 WLR 415 Queen's Bench Division (Phillips J)

• *Does the agent referred in O.11 r1(1)(d)(ii) have to be the agent of the plaintiff or the defendant?*

Facts

The plaintiff – a Bermudian insurance company trading and residing outside of England – had through its agents (a firm of London insurance brokers) entered into a contract with the defendant, a Kenyan insurance company. Could the court grant leave to serve the Kenyan company outside England? The plaintiff argued that its agent traded and resided in England, while it traded and resided outside the jurisdiction; thus the requirements of the RSC O.11 r1(1)(d)(ii) were satisfied.

Held

That in order to give a sensible interpretation to the rule words were to be implied into it restricting the agent to being the agent of the *defendant*.

Phillips J:

'The basis of jurisdiction asserted by the plaintiffs

The plaintiffs obtained leave ex parte from Morland J to serve out of the jurisdiction on 13 August 1990 pursuant to O.11 r1(1)(d)(ii). This provides:

"(1) … service of a writ out of the jurisdiction is permissible with the leave of the court if in the action begun by the writ – … (d) the claim is brought to enforce, rescind, dissolve, annul or otherwise affect a contract, or to recover damages or obtain other relief in respect of the breach of a contract, being (in either case) a contract which – … (ii) was made by or through an agent trading or residing within the jurisdiction on behalf of a principal trading or residing out of the jurisdiction …"

The plaintiffs submit that they fall fairly and squarely within the terms of this rule in that it is common ground that they trade and reside out of the jurisdiction and that they made the contract through an agent, Lowndes Lambert, trading and residing within the jurisdiction.

The defendants submit (i) on its true interpretation the rule applies only where the principal trading or residing out of the jurisdiction is the defendant, not where that principal is the plaintiff; alternatively (ii) the court should, as a matter of discretion, only exercise jurisdiction under the rule where the principal out of the jurisdiction is the defendant. ...

Careful consideration of other provisions of O.11 r1(1) demonstrates, it seems to me, the need to imply additional words by way of restriction in order to give sensible effect to those provisions. In my judgment similar additional words must be implied to give sensible effect to O.11 r1(1)(d). I can best demonstrate this conclusion by adding in brackets to the words as they stand the additional words that I consider must be implied:

> "(1) ... service of a writ out of the jurisdiction is permissible with the leave of the court if in the action begun by the writ – (a) relief is sought against a person domiciled within the jurisdiction [and the defendant to be served is that person] ... (c) the claim is brought against a person duly served within or out of the jurisdiction and a person out of the jurisdiction is a necessary or proper party thereto [and the defendant to be served is that person] (d) the claim is brought to enforce, rescind, dissolve, annul or otherwise affect a contract, or to recover damages or obtain other relief in respect of the breach of a contract, being (in either case) a contract which – ... (ii) was made by or through an agent trading or residing within the jurisdiction on behalf of a principal trading or residing out of the jurisdiction [and the defendant to be served is that principal]."

In the case of each sub-rule it seems to me obvious that those who drafted the sub-rule only intended that leave should be permissible to serve the person expressly referred to in that sub-rule.

On the basis of this interpretation I rule that the facts of this case do not fall within the jurisdiction of the court under O.11 r1(1)(d)(ii).'

The Convention rules

Cases decided before the European Court on the meaning of particular parts of art 5 Brussels Convention (art 5 EU Council Regulation 44/2001)

Barclays Bank plc v *Glasgow City Council; Kleinwort Benson* v *Glasgow City Council* [1992] 3 WLR 827 Queen's Bench Division (Hirst J)

• *'Matters relating to contract' in art 5(1) does not include claims for restitution arising out of a void contract, nor is such a claim within art 5(3)*

Facts

The plaintiff banks had conducted interest rate swop transactions on behalf of various local authorities including the Glasgow City Council. These swop transactions had, after extensive litigation, been held ultra vires and void (see *Hazell* v *Hammersmith and Fulham London Borough Council* [1992] AC 1 (HL); [1991] 2 WLR 372). The banks were now seeking recovery of sums paid under these agreements by way of claims for restitution (instituted in England) against the English and Scottish local authorities involved. The Glasgow City Council contested the jurisdiction of the English court; the banks responded that there was special jurisdiction under art 5(1), alternatively under art 5(3), or, finally, under art 6(1) of Schedule 4 of the Civil Jurisdiction and Judgments Act 1982. (Since the question here raised was not whether one EC state or another EC state had jurisdiction but whether one part of the UK (Scotland) or another part of the UK (England) had jurisdiction the Brussels Convention proper did not apply; the governing law was to be found in Schedule 4 of the Act. The banks failed in all these contentions and the action in England was stayed; the Glasgow City Council had to be sued in Scotland where it was domiciled.

Held

1. Article 5(1) created special jurisdiction 'in matters relating to contract' in the courts for the place of performance of the obligation in question. But, since the House of Lords had already said that the contracts were void, there was no contract and reliance could not be placed upon art 5(1).
2. The words of art 5(3) presupposed that there had to be a 'harmful event' which suggested that it was quite inappropriate to seek to apply art 5(3) to restitutionary claims.
3. Article 6(1) provides that a person domiciled in a part of the UK '*may*' be sued in the court where his co-defendant is domiciled and the Glasgow City Council was co-defendant with several English local authorities. But the European Court has laid down that before there is art 6(1) jurisdiction there must be such a connection between the claims against the various defendants that it was desirable to rule on them together to avoid the risk of 'irreconcilable judgments' (*Kalfelis* v *Schroder, Munchmeyer, Hengst & Co* [1989] ECR 5565). This was not the case here since the court was satisfied these disputes involving very large sums of money would, unless settled, be determined in the House of Lords which would settle the matter for both the English and the Scottish courts.

Hirst J:

> '*Article 5(1): the rival submissions*
> The decision on this paragraph turns on the proper construction of the crucial words "in matters relating to a contract", it not being disputed that the place of performance of the obligation in question (if it exists) was England. Mr Tecks submitted that the European Court of Justice authorities, cited below, show that the crucial words refer to obligations which have their basis in contract or in a closely similar nexus such as that existing between an association and its members, so that the matters in question must be contractual or closely akin to contractual. In the present case, he submitted, the House of Lords has now conclusively ruled that there is not and never was a contract, and it is thus apparent on the plain words of art 5(1) itself that these restitutionary claims cannot possibly be properly classified as matters relating to a contract. This principle, he submitted, is further exemplified by the line of the Court of Justice authority which shows that the jurisdiction of the court may be invoked under this Article where there is a dispute between the parties as to whether a contract in fact exists, but only if that dispute is real and genuine.
>
> Mr Beazley submitted: (i) the Court of Justice authorities have laid down that the wording of the Schedule is to be given an independent interpretation and is not to be construed in accordance with national law; (ii) There is a general overriding principle that the Schedule must be interpreted by reference principally to the system and objectives of the Convention on Jurisdiction and the Enforcement of Judgments in Civil and Commercial Matters signed at Brussels on 27 September 1968 in order to ensure that it is fully effective; in order to strengthen in the Community the legal protection of persons therein established; and in order to contribute to the proper administration of justice within the Community by preventing parallel proceedings before the courts of different Contracting States, and avoiding conflict between decisions which might result from permitting such parallel proceedings to continue. (iii) So far as art 5(1) itself is concerned, he submitted that it is clearly established by Court of Justice decisions that it reflects the close links created by the contract between the parties thereto, and the need to resolve all difficulties which may arise in connection with the contract in the same court in a country which has a close connection with the case, ie the court in the country where the obligation in question has to be performed. (iv) Although the claims in these actions are not made for the performance of the obligations under the contracts or as a result of their breach, they do concern matters relating to a contract, since the court is determining the consequences of the nullity of the contracts, particularly with

regard to the contractual matters of total failure of consideration and payments under a mistake.

In support of his interpretation of art 5(1) Mr Beazley relied on the following additional points. (a) The provision of art 10(1)(e) in the Convention on the Law applicable to Contractual Obligations 1980 ("the Rome Convention"), enacted into English law by the Contracts (Applicable Law) Act 1990, that the law applicable to a contract shall govern, inter alia, "the consequences of nullity of the contract", supports the view that on the proper independent interpretation of art 5(1) the consequences of nullity must be treated as within the scope of the phrase "matters relating to a contract". (b) In English law the choice of law rules governing claims for restitution are influenced by the claim being connected with a contract, having regard to the English conflict of laws rule that the proper law of the obligation to restore a benefit, if the obligation arises in connection with a contract, is the proper law of the contract: *Dicey & Morris, The Conflict of Laws* 11th ed (1987), p1350, r203. (c) Quasi-contractual claims, at least where there is a contract involved, should probably fall per se under art 5(1): see the opinion of the editors of *Dicey & Morris*, at p341, to this effect, and the decision of the Scottish courts that a statutory claim to contribution falls within the Article in *Engdiv Ltd* v *G Percy Trentham Ltd*, 1990 SLT 617, 621. (d) In the case of a claim for the return of moneys paid under an ineffective contract, there is no artificiality in deducing an implied promise to pay, even though the old theory that restitution was based on the concept of such an implied promise is now largely discredited. …

Analysis and conclusions

The House of Lords having held that the swap transactions were void ab initio, the suggestion that the restitutionary claims in these actions are in matters relating to a contract seems to me to be placing a very severe strain indeed on the language of art 5(1). I can find nothing either in the *Peters Case* [1983] ECR 987 or in the *Arcado Case* [1988] ECR 1539 to support such a conclusion. Mr Beazley relied particularly on the *Peters Case*, which he submitted shows that there does not have to be an actual contract in order to bring the case within art 5(1); but the relationship in that case between the association and its members was a consensual relationship which was manifestly very closely akin to an actual contract and in no way comparable, in my judgment, to the position here where there is no contract. …

In my judgment, when dealing with the Rome Convention in relation to persons of United Kingdom domicile under Schedule 4, as in the present case, the court can and should likewise take into account substantive derogations from the Rome Convention in the law of the United Kingdom, especially one so directly apposite as that presently in question. Furthermore, looking at the question of the wider European context, I am not satisfied that art 10(1)(e) of the Rome Convention is a good guide to the interpretation of the crucial words in art 5(1) of Schedule 4. It was no doubt proper and necessary for the Rome Convention to stipulate a proper law applicable to the consequences of nullity of the contract in order to embody a comprehensive conflicts of law code; but it by no means follows that the consequences of nullity are matters relating to a contract, since ex hypothesi no contract existed; nor is art 10(1)(e) comparable with art 10(1)(c) (which is the sub-paragraph cited in the *Arcado Case* [1988] ECR 1539) or indeed with sub-paragraphs (a), (b) and (d) of art 10(1), since in all these instances there is a contract in existence.

So far as Mr Beazley's other points are concerned: (a) I do not accept that the English choice of law rule is relevant, since we are not here dealing with a choice of law problem. (b) I do not accept that quasi-contractual claims, even where a contract is involved, are properly to be treated as falling per se within art 5(1), having regard both to the general considerations I have already advanced in my analysis of the cases such as *Peters* [1983] ECR 987, and also because it is difficult to locate a place of performance for a quasi-contractual obligation. It is noteworthy that the text book writers are not unanimous on this point: see *Kaye, Civil Jurisdiction and Enforcement of Foreign Judgments,* (1987), p490, where the author doubts whether actions in quasi-contract on the ground of unjust enrichment fall within art 5(1), and cites in the footnote German and French authorities expressing conflicting views. (c) I do not think the *Engdiv* case, 1990 SLT 617 assists Mr Beazley, since both the pursuers seeking contribution and the defenders resisting it were parties to the building contract at issue in the case, so that it was difficult to resist the submission that the claim for contribution in that case was in a matter relating to a contract. (d) I do not think Mr Beazley can draw any comfort from the old implied contract theory in restitution cases, since as he himself recognises that theory is now discredited.

For all these reasons, I have come to the conclusion, and I hold, that the banks have failed to bring themselves within art 5(1).'

Comment

Note that the court was not persuaded by the argument that because art 10(1)(e) of the Rome Convention, the applicable law, governs 'the consequences of nullity of the contract', it followed that the consequence of nullity were included 'in matters relating to contract' under Schedule 4 of the Civil Jurisdiction and Judgments Act 1982. Moreover, the UK Government has derogated from art 10(1)(e) of the Rome Convention and this fact was taken account of by Hirst J in reaching his conclusion. Although it is believed that Hirst J's judgment reproduced here is sound, the Court of Appeal when seised with the same case ([1994] 2 WLR 466) found the interpretation of art 5(1) and (3) perplexing and referred the question to the European Court.

Effer SpA v *Hans-Joachim Kantner*
Case 38/81 [1982] ECR 825
European Court of Justice

• *A national court may have jurisdiction under art 5(1) even where the existence of the contract in question is disputed*

Facts

This was a dispute between a patent agent (Kantner), a domiciled German, and an Italian firm, Effer SpA. Kantner had carried out various patent investigations in Germany in order to ensure that a crane manufactured by Effer could be distributed in Germany. He had not been paid. However, it was not clear whether Kantner had contracted with Effer or Hykra, a now insolvent firm that had distributed Effer's cranes in Germany. Could Kantner in reliance upon art 5(1) sue in Germany?

Held

A plaintiff may invoke the jurisdiction of the courts of the place of performance under art 5(1) 'even when the existence of the contract on which the claim is based is in dispute between the parties' (at 835–6).

Judgment of the ECJ:

> 'It is established that the wording of art 5(1) of the Convention does not resolve this question unequivocally. 'Whilst the German version of that provision contains the words "Vertrag oder Ansprüche aus einem Vertrag", the French and Italian versions contain the expressions "en matière contractuelle" and "in materia contrattuale" respectively. Under these circumstances, in view of the lack of uniformity between the different language versions of the provision in question, it is advisable, in order to arrive at the interpretation requested by the national court, to have regard both to the context of art 5(1) and to the purpose of the Convention.
>
> It is clear from the provisions of the Convention, and in particular from the preamble thereto, that its essential aim is to

strengthen in the Community the legal protection of persons therein established. For that purpose, the Convention provides a collection of rules which are designed inter alia to avoid the occurrence, in civil and commercial matters, of concurrent litigation in two or more Member States and which, in the interests of legal certainty and for the benefit of the parties, confer jurisdiction upon the national court territorially best qualified to determine a dispute.

It follows from the provisions of the Convention, and in particular from those in s7 of Title II, that, in the cases provided for in art 5(1) of the Convention, the national court's jurisdiction to determine questions relating to a contract includes the power to consider the existence of the constituent parts of the contract itself, since that is indispensable in order to enable the national court in which proceedings are brought to examine whether it has jurisdiction under the Convention. If that were not the case, art 5(1) of the Convention would be in danger of being deprived of its legal effect, since it would be accepted that, in order to defeat the rule contained in that provision it is sufficient for one of the parties to claim that the contract does not exist. On the contrary, respect for the aims and spirit of the Convention demands that that provision should be construed as meaning that the court called upon to decide a dispute arising out of a contract may examine, of its own motion even, the essential preconditions for its jurisdiction, having regard to conclusive and relevant evidence adduced by the party concerned, establishing the existence or the inexistence of the contract. This interpretation is, moreover, in accordance with that given in the judgment of 14 December 1977 in Case 73/77 (*Sanders* v *Van der Putte* [1977] ECR 2383) concerning the jurisdiction of the courts of the State where the immovable property is situated in matters relating to tenancies of immovable property (art 16(1) of the Convention). In that case the Court held that such jurisdiction applies even if there is a dispute as to the "existence" of a lease.

It is therefore necessary to reply to the question put by the Bundesgerichtshof that the plaintiff may invoke the jurisdiction of the courts of the place of performance in accordance with art 5(1) of the Convention of 27 September 1968 on Jurisdiction and the Enforcement of Judgments in Civil and Commercial Matters even when the existence of the contract on which the claim is based is in dispute between the parties.'

Ets A de Bloos Sprl* v *Société en Commandite par Actions Bouyer [1976] ECR 1497 European Court of Justice

• *The 'obligation in question' is not any obligation under the contract, but the obligation which forms the basis of the plaintiff's claim*

Facts

Bouyer, a French firm, had by agreement granted to De Bloos, a Belgian firm, the exclusive right to distribute the 'Bouyer' products in Belgium, Luxembourg and Zaire. A dispute arose and De Bloos sought from the Belgian courts a declaration that the agreement had been dissolved through the grantor's wrongful conduct and damages. Bouyer contended that the Belgian courts did not have jurisdiction as it was not domiciled in Belgium; De Bloos, however, relied upon art 5(1). The matter was referred to the European Court for a preliminary ruling.

Held

The word 'obligation' in art 5(1) refers to the legal obligation forming the basis of the legal proceedings and, in the instant case, that was the grantor's obligation not to supply the products to anyone other than the grantee in the agreed territory.

Judgment of the ECJ:

'Under art 5(1) of the Convention, a person domiciled in a Contracting State may, in another Contracting State, be sued:

"in matters relating to a contract, in the

courts for the place of performance of the obligation in question."

As stated in its preamble, the Convention is intended to determine the international jurisdiction of the courts of the Contracting States, to facilitate the recognition and to introduce an expeditious procedure for securing the enforcement of judgments.

These objectives imply the need to avoid, so far as possible, creating a situation in which a number of courts have jurisdiction in respect of one and the same contract.

Because of this, art 5(1) of the Convention cannot be interpreted as referring to any obligations whatsoever arising under the contract in question.

On the contrary, the word "obligation" in the Article refers to the contractual obligation forming the basis of the legal proceedings.

This interpretation is, moreover, clearly confirmed by the Italian and German versions of the Article.

It follows that for the purposes of determining the place of performance within the meaning of art 5, quoted above, the obligation to be taken into account is that which corresponds to the contractual right on which the plaintiff's action is based.

In a case where the plaintiff asserts the right to be paid damages or seeks a dissolution of the contract on the ground of the wrongful conduct of the other party, the obligation referred to in art 5(1) is still that which arises under the contract and the non-performance of which is relied upon to support such claims.

For these reasons, the answer to the first question must be that, in disputes in which the grantee of an exclusive sales concession charges the grantor with having infringed the exclusive concession, the word "obligation" contained in art 5(1) of the Convention of 27 September 1968 on jurisdiction and the enforcement of Judgments in Civil and Commercial Matters refers to the obligation forming the basis of the legal proceedings, namely the contractual obligation of the grantor which corresponds to the contractual right relied upon by the grantee in support of the application.

In disputes concerning the consequences of the infringment by the grantor of a contract conferring an exclusive concession, such as the payment of damages or the dissolution of the contract, the obligation to which reference must be made for the puposes of applying art 5(1) of the Convention is that which the contract imposes on the grantor and the non-performance of which is relied upon by the grantee in support of the application for damages or for the dissolution of the contract.

In the case of actions for the payment of compensation by way of damages, it is for the national court to ascertain whether, under the law applicable to the contract, an independent contractual obligation or an obligation replacing the unperformed contractual obligation is involved.'

Handelskwekerij G J Bier BV v ***Mines de Potasse d'Alsace SA*** Case 21/76 [1976] ECR 1735 European Court of Justice

• *Clarifying the meaning of 'where the harmful event occurred' for the purposes of art 5(3)*

Facts

Here Mines de Potasse, a French firm, discharged chlorides into the Rhine in France, and this discharge allegedly caused damage to Bier, a Dutch firm of nurserymen that relied on Rhine water to irrigate its plants. Bier sued in the Netherlands, but, unless art 5(3) applied and the 'harmful event' included the damage caused in the Netherlands, the Dutch courts did not have jurisdiction over the French firm.

Held (on a preliminary ruling by the European Court)

'Where the place of the happening of the event which may give rise to liability in tort, delict or quasi-delict and the place where that event results in damage are not identical, the expression "place where the harmful event occurred" in art 5(3) ... must be understood as being intended to cover both the place where the damage occurred and the place of the event giving rise to it' (at 1748) and the defendant may be sued at the plaintiff's option in the courts of either place.

Judgment of the ECJ:

> 'Article 5 of the Convention provides: "A person domiciled in a Contracting State may, in another Contracting State, be sued: ... (3) in matters relating to tort, delict or quasi-delict, in the courts for the place where the harmful event occurred"
>
> That provision must be interpreted in the context of the scheme of conferment of jurisdiction which forms the subject-matter of Title II of the Convention.
>
> That scheme is based on a general rule, laid down by art 2, that the courts of the State in which the defendant is domiciled shall have jurisdiction.
>
> However, art 5 makes provision in a number of cases for a special jurisdiction, which the plaintiff may opt to choose.
>
> This freedom of choice was introduced having regard to the existence, in certain clearly defined situations, of a particularly close connecting factor between a dispute and the court which may be called upon to hear it, with a view to the efficacious conduct of the proceedings.
>
> Thus in matters of tort, delict or quasi-delict art 5(3) allows the plaintiff to bring his case before the courts for "the place where the harmful event occurred".
>
> In the context of the Convention, the meaning of that expression is unclear when the place of the event which is at the origin of the damage is situated in a State other than the one in which the place where the damage occurred is situated, as is the case inter alia with atmospheric or water pollution beyond the frontiers of a State.
>
> The form of words "place where the harmful event occurred", used in all the language versions of the Convention, leaves open the question whether, in the situation described, it is necessary, in determining jurisdiction, to choose as the connecting factor the place of the event giving rise to the damage, or the place where the damage occurred, or to accept that the plaintiff has an option between the one and the other of those two connecting factors.
>
> As regards this, it is well to point out that the place of the event giving rise to the damage no less than the place where the damage occurred can, depending on the case, constitute a significant connecting factor from the point of view of jurisdiction.
>
> Liability in tort, delict or quasi-delict can only arise provided that a causal connexion can be established between the damage and the event in which that damage originates.
>
> Taking into account the close connexion between the component parts of every sort of liability, it does not appear appropriate to opt for one of the two connecting factors mentioned to the exclusion of the other, since each of them can, depending on the circumstances, be particularly helpful from the point of view of the evidence and of the conduct of the proceedings.
>
> To exclude on option appears all the more undesirable in that, by its comprehensive form of words. Article 5(3) of the Convention covers a wide diversity of kinds of liability.
>
> Thus the meaning of the expression "place where the harmful event occurred" in art 5(3) must be established in such a way as to acknowledge that the plaintiff has an option to commence proceedings either at the place where the damage occurred or the place of the event giving rise to it.
>
> This conclusion is supported by the consideration, first, that to decide in favour only of the place of the event giving rise to the damage would, in an appreciable number of cases, cause confusion between the heads of jurisdiction laid down by arts 2 and 5(3) of the Convention, so that the latter provision would, to that extent, lose its effectiveness.
>
> Secondly, a decision in favour only of the place where the damage occurred would, in cases where the place of the event giving rise to the damage does not coincide with the domicile of the person liable, have the effect of excluding a helpful connecting factor with the jurisdiction of a court particularly near to the cause of the damage.

Moreover, it appears from a comparison of the national legislative provisions and national case-law on the distribution of jurisdiction – both as regards internal relationships, as between courts for different areas, and in international relationships – that, albeit by differing legal techniques, a place is found for both of the two connecting factors here considered and that in several States they are accepted concurrently.

In these circumstances, the interpretation stated above has the advantage of avoiding any upheaval in the solutions worked out in the various national systems of law, since it looks to unification, in conformity with art 5(3) of the Convention, by way of a systematization of solutions which, as to their principle, have already been established in most of the States concerned.

Thus it should be answered that where the place of the happening of the event which may give rise to liability in tort, delict or quasidelict and the place where that event results in damage are not identical, the expression "place where the harmful event occurred", in art 5(3) of the Convention, must be understood as being intended to cover both the place where the damage occurred and the place of the event giving rise to it.

The result is that the defendant may be sued, at the option of the plaintiff, either in the courts for the place where the damage occurred or in the courts for the place of the event which gives rise to and is at the origin of that damage.'

Industrie Tessili Italiana Como v *Dunlop AG* [1976] ECR 1473 European Court of Justice

• *The words 'the place of performance of the obligation' in art 5(1) should be interpreted according to the law governing the obligation determined according to the conflict rules of the lex fori*

Facts

A dispute arose between the Italian seller (Tessili) and the German purchaser (Dunlop) of 310 women's ski suits as to the quality of the suits. Dunlop sued in the German courts (specifically the Hanau Regional Court) arguing that, although Tessili was not domiciled in Germany, the German courts had jurisdiction under art 5(1) since the 'place of performance of the obligation in question' was in Germany. Tessili contested that the 'place of performance' was in Germany. So the question which arose was how was it to be determined where the 'place of performance' was? This question was referred to the European Court for a preliminary ruling.

Held

The 'place of performance of the obligation in question' is to be 'determined in accordance with the law which governs the obligation in question according to the rules of conflict of laws of the court before which the matter is brought' (at 1486).

Judgment of the ECJ:

> '*The question raised by the national court*
> Article 5 of the Convention provides: "A person domiciled in a Contracting State may, in another Contracting State, be sued: (1) in matters relating to a contract in the courts for the place of performance of the obligation in question". This provision must be interpreted within the framework of the system of conferment of jurisdiction under Title II of the Convention. In accordance with art 2 the basis of this system is the general conferment of jurisdiction on the court of the defendant's domicile. Article 5 however provides for a number of cases of special jurisdiction at the option of the plaintiff.
>
> This freedom of choice was introduced in view of the existence in certain well-defined cases of a particularly close relationship between a dispute and the court which may be most conveniently called upon to take cognizance of the matter. Thus in the case of an action relating to contractual obligations art 5(1) allows a plaintiff to bring the matter

before the court for the place "of performance" of the obligation in question. It is for the court before which the matter is brought to establish under the Convention whether the place of performance is situate within its territorial jurisdiction. For this purpose it must determine in accordance with its own rules of conflict of laws what is the law applicable to the legal relationship in question and define in accordance with that law the place of performance of the contractual obligation in question.

Having regard to the differences obtaining between national laws of contract and to the absence at this stage of legal development of any unification in the substantive law applicable, it does not appear possible to give any more substantial guide to the interpretation of the reference made by art 5(1) to the 'place of performance' of contractual obligations. This is all the more true since the determination of the place of performance of obligations depends on the contractual context to which these obligations belong. In these circumstances the reference in the Convention to the place of performance of contractual obligations cannot be understood otherwise than by reference to the substantive law applicable under the rules of the conflict of laws of the court before which the matter is brought.'

Comment

It may be doubted whether this finding is consistent with the court's earlier finding in *LTU* v *Eurocontrol* [1976] ECR 1541 that in interpreting phrases from the Brussels Convention (in the *Eurocontrol* case the phrase 'civil and commercial matters' in art 1) 'reference must not be made to the law of one of the States concerned but, first, to the objectives and scheme of the Convention and, secondly, to the general principles which stem from the corpus of the national legal systems' (at 1552).

In *Kalfelis* v *Schroder, Munchmeyer, Hengst, & Co and Others* (see judgment below) the European Court laid down that the definition of 'matters relating to tort delict or quasi-delict' in art 5(3) was an autonomous concept to be interpreted by reference principally to the system and objectives of the Convention rather than the national laws of the Contracting States.

Ivenel* v *Schwab Case 133/81 [1982] ECR 1891 European Court of Justice

• *Article 5(1) Brussels Convention – contract of employment – interpretation of article*

Facts

The ECJ considered several questions referred to it by the Supreme Court of France under the Protocol to the Brussels Convention on Jurisdiction and Enforcement of Judgments 1968. The case concerned the interpretation of art 5(1) of this Convention. Here a contract had been agreed between a German company and a Frenchman to employ the latter as a commercial traveller. His work was to be in France. The question involved whether the contract was one which could be classified by the French court as one of employment.

Held

It was a contract of employment and, applying French private international law as the law of obligation, the obligation related to the whole of the contract of employment and not merely to the particular requirement of the contract in dispute, which in this case was the payment. In a case such as the present, the law would normally be that of the place of performance of the work in pursuance to the contract of employment: therefore, here it was France.

Judgment of the ECJ:

> 'It must be observed that, as the Court of Justice has already stated, in particular in its judgment of 6 October 1976 in Case 12/76 *Tessili* [1976] ECR 1473, the "place of performance" within the meaning of art 5 (1) of the Convention is to be determined in accordance with the law which governs the obligation in question according to the conflict rules of the court before which the matter is brought.

The question raised by the national court concerns the obligation to be taken into account for the purposes of that definition when the claim before the court is based on different obligations under a single contract for representation which has been classified by the courts concerned with the substance of the case as a contract of employment. In its judgment of 6 October 1976 in Case 14/76 *de Bloos* [1976] ECR 1497 the Court has already stated that the obligation to be taken into account for the purposes of art 5(1) of the Convention in the case of a claim based on a contract granting an exclusive sales concession between two commercial undertakings is that which forms the basis of the legal proceedings. The problem raised by this case is whether the same criterion must be applied to cases of the kind described by the national court.

It is appropriate to examine that problem in the light of the objectives of the convention and the general scheme of its provisions.

Adoption of the special rules of jurisdiction as contained in arts 5 and 6 of the Convention is justified inter alia by the fact that there must be a close connecting factor between the dispute and the court with jurisdiction to resolve it. The report drawn up by the committee of experts (Official Journal 1979, c59, p1) which drafted the text of the Convention stresses that connection by stating inter alia that the court for the place of performance of the obligation will be useful in proceedings for the recovery of fees since the creditor will have a choice between the courts of the state where the defendant is ordinarily resident by virtue of the general provisions contained in art 2 of the Convention and the courts of another state within whose jurisdiction the services were provided, particularly where, according to the appropriate law, the obligation to pay must be performed where the services were provided.

The above-mentioned report also refers to the reasons why those drafting the Convention did not consider it appropriate to insert into the Convention a provision giving exclusive jurisdiction in contracts of employment. According to the report it is desirable as far as possible for disputes to be brought before the courts of the state whose law governs the contract, whereas at the time the Convention was being drafted work was in progress to harmonise the application of the rules of employment law in the Member States of the Community. The report concludes that at present the existing provisions of the Convention, such as art 2 stipulating the forum for the place where the defendant is ordinarily resident and art 5(1) the forum for the place of performance of the obligation, are likely to satisfy the relevant interests …

It follows from the foregoing account that in the matter of contracts art 5(1) of the Convention is particularly concerned to attribute jurisdiction to the court of the country which has a close connection with the case; that in the case of a contract of employment the connection lies particularly in the law applicable to the contract; and that according to the trend in the conflict rules in regard to this matter that law is determined by the obligation characterising the contract in question and is normally the obligation to carry out work …

It follows from the foregoing considerations, taken as a whole, that the obligation to be taken into account for the purposes of the application of art 5(1) of the Convention in the case of claims based on different obligations arising under a contract of employment as a representative binding a worker to an undertaking is the obligation which characterizes the contract …'

Kalfelis* v *Schroder, Munchmeyer, Hengst & Co and Others Case 189/87 [1989] ECR 5565 European Court of Justice

• *Clarifying the meaning of 'matters relating to tort, delict or quasi-delict' – arts 5 and 6*

Facts

This was a dispute which arose in the German

courts between a German plaintiff and various defendants over dealings in silver and silver futures. Some of the defendants were domiciled in Germany and some of the defendants were domiciled in Luxembourg. The plaintiff relied upon art 6 to establish the German courts' jurisdiction over the non-Germany domiciled defendants. The plaintiff's claim was based in contract, delict and quasi-delict.

Held

The European Court of Justice (Fifth Chamber) ruled:

1. For the application of art 6(1) of the Convention there must exist a connection between the various claims made by one applicant against different defendants such that it was desirable to rule upon them together in order to avoid solutions which might be irreconcilable if the cases were ruled upon separately.
2. (a) The definition of 'matters relating to tort, delict or quasi-delict' in art 5(3) of the Convention was to be regarded as an autonomous concept including any action which sought to call in question liability of a defendant and which was not connected with 'matters relating to a contract' under art 5(1).
   (b) A court which had jurisdiction pursuant to art 5(3) to deal with part of an action based upon tort did not have jurisdiction to deal with other elements of the same claim which were based on non-tortious grounds.

Judgment of the ECJ:

'*Second question*

With regard to the first branch of the question it was necessary to note that the definition of 'matters relating to tort, delict or quasi-delict' was a criterion for the definition of the scope of one of the rules of special jurisdiction available to an applicant.

As the Court had ruled in connection with the definition of 'matters relating to a contract' in art 5(1), taking into consideration the objective and the general scheme of the Convention it was important not to interpret that definition as a simple reference to the national law of one or other of the states concerned.

It was therefore necessary to regard the definition of 'matters relating to tort, delict or quasi-delict' as an autonomous concept which it was necessary to interpret, for the purposes of applying the Convention, by reference principally to the system and objectives of that Convention in order to ensure its full effect.

With a view to ensuring that a uniform solution was adopted in all member states, it had to be accepted that the definition of 'matters relating to tort, delict or quasi-delict' included any action which sought to call in question the liability of a defendant and which did not involve 'matters relating to a contract' under art 5(1) thereof.

Since arts 5 and 6 of the Convention constituted derogations to the general principle of jurisdiction laid down in art 2, they were to be interpreted strictly.

It was therefore necessary to accept that a court which had jurisdiction under art 5(3) to deal with the part of a claim based upon tort, was not necessarily competent to deal with other elements of the same claim which were based on non-tortious liability.

Although it was true that there might be some inconvenience where the different parts of one case were to be ruled upon by different courts, it was necessary to observe, on one hand, that it was always possible for the applicant to bring the whole of his claim before the courts of the defendant's domicile and, on the other hand, that art 22 of the Convention, under certain conditions, enabled the court first seised to deal with the whole dispute, if the claims brought before different courts were connected.'

Shevill v Presse Alliance SA [1992] 2 WLR 1 Court of Appeal (Purchas, Taylor and Beldam LJJ)

• *Clarifying the meaning of the 'place where the harmful event occurred' for the purposes of libel (tort)*

Facts

An article had been published in the French newspaper *France Soir* alleging that a certain firm of Bureaux de Change operators including their employees were involved in the laundering of drug money. An English domiciled employee of the firm (along with the firm) sued the French domiciled owners of the newspaper for libel in England. But did the English court have jurisdiction? After all, only 250 copies of the offending paper had been sold in England (but it was only in respect of those copies that the plaintiff was suing).

Held

That where a libel had been published in England, that publication constitutes a harmful event for the purposes of art 5(3). This was not so because English law assumes special damage on the publication of a libel (that was an idiosyncratic rule of English law) but because the cause of action for libel arose when and where the publishee receives and reads the publication and that was not an idiosyncratic rule of English law. Any state in which the libel had been published would have art 5(3) jurisdiction even if the harm suffered was minimal (although that might affect the quantum of damages). Considerations of whether England was the appropriate forum were irrelevant.

Purchas LJ:

> '... as regards each of the plaintiffs Mr Tugendhat [for the defendants] submitted that they had for differing reasons not suffered any damage so as to constitute a "harmful event within the jurisdiction". As regards the first plaintiff he submitted that there was no evidence that there was anyone who could possibly have been affected who knew her or who had had access to any copies of the offending newspaper. As regards the second plaintiff, which was merely the holding company of the third plaintiffs, Mr Tugendhat submitted that they had not suffered any damage in England and Wales or anywhere else. Furthermore he submitted that being companies registered in France neither the third nor the fourth plaintiffs could have suffered any damage in England and Wales. These submissions were based upon the necessity of demonstrating for the purposes of art 5(3) that damage had been actually suffered, an approach which was inconsistent with the English law which assumed that damage had been suffered once the libel had been established. This raised a point of some subtlety which lies at the heart of the appellants' case ...
>
> Although Mr Tugendhat conceded that in English law the cause of action in libel only arose when the words of which complaint is made come to the attention of the publishee, he submitted, relying upon the provisions of s3 just cited, that it was not justifiable when applying art 5(3) to have regard to this peculiar aspect of the English law. Therefore art 5(3) should be construed in accordance with European law. This, Mr Tugendhat submitted, embraced the principle of "independent interpretation"...
>
> His argument was based upon the rejection by the European Court of the observations submitted by the United Kingdom as to the effect of art 5(3) in *Netherlands* v *Ruffer* (Case 814/79) [1980] ECR 3807 and the opinion of Mr Advocate General Warner. ...
>
> Mr Tugendhat submitted that in the approach to art 5(3) regard must be had to the peculiar characteristics of the law of libel in England and Wales and adopted the description "artificial and archaic" from the judgment of Diplock LJ in *Slim* v *Daily Telegraph* [1968] 2 QB 157, 171. He submitted that it was not appropriate to approach the "independent" interpretation required by the Convention by importing into that exercise the irrational presumption and assumptions forming part of the English law of libel with which the English courts are only too familiar. He submitted that there must be established as a positive feature some actual harm in order to qualify England as a place where 'the harmful event' occurred. It was not open, he submitted, to the plaintiffs to rely in this particular exercise upon the presumption of damage recognised by the English law.

Mr Tugendhat further submitted that the concept of each publication to the publishee giving rise to a cause of action was equally inapplicable to the occurrence of a "harmful event" within the meaning of art 5(3). Notwithstanding the area of the individual publication the approach of the English courts in fact amalgamated the multiple publications into one cause of action. An analogy was drawn with the interpretation of RSC O.11 in its own wording "a tort committed within the jurisdiction". Mr Tugendhat referred to the cases of *Brunswick* v *Harmer* (1849) 14 QB 169 and *Bata* v *Bata* [1948] WN 366 and to the treatment of these cases in *Duncan and Neill on Defamation,* 2nd ed, p36, paras 8.07 and 8.08.

Mr Tugendhat also relied upon the provisions of art 5(4) in support of his contention that the courts of France were the appropriate forum in which the plaintiffs should bring their respective claims. It was common ground that the French courts recognised a procedure under which victims could claim civil damages in criminal proceedings for libel. It is not necessary for me to consider in detail this process and the remedies available. It is sufficient to acknowledge their existence....

I am unable to accept the submission that the concept in English law that the cause of action arises at the place and at the time when the publishee receives and reads the publication is in any way a concept special to English law. It is not in conflict with the approach of the French courts as a criminal matter arising out of the production of a newspaper with a defamatory Article in it which is clearly distinguishable. That this may give a cause of action in favour either of the state or parties against the newspaper and editors involved is not inconsistent with a different cause of action in tort, delict or quasi-delict arising in favour of a different victim in another jurisdiction. *Bier*'s case [1978] QB 708 establishes the possibility of proceedings in two jurisdictions notwithstanding that there may be a conflict. Article 23 resolves this so far as civil actions in tort, delict or quasi-delict are concerned. In my judgment the concept of the appropriate forum which was so firmly rejected by the Advocate General in *Ruffer*'s case [1980] ECR 3807 applies equally to Mr Tugendhat's submission that the "harmful event" occurred in France. The only idiosyncratic aspect arising from the law in England and Wales is the assumption of damage. I do not recognise this as a jurisdictional point. Whether or not there may be detected a publishee in England who both knew the plaintiff and read and understood the French evening newspaper may well arise in the course of the action and be relevant to the assessment of damages. In my judgment, however, to restrict the exercise of jurisdiction to cases where the existence of such a person is established would not be correct. I do not consider that the cases *Bata* v *Bata* [1948] WN 366 and *Brunswick* v *Harmer*, 14 QB 185 affect this approach. If anything, the judgment of the court delivered by Coleridge J in the latter case supports it.'

Comment

It is interesting to compare this case with the German case of *Re the Unauthorised Publication of Approved Photographs* [1991] ILPr 468. There a photograph of the plaintiff (a German domiciliary) had been published without his consent in a Dutch pornographic magazine. He sued the publisher (a Dutch domiciliary) in Germany but did the German courts have jurisdiction? The German courts held that no harmful event had occurred in Germany even though the Dutch magazine could be bought in Germany. Relying on a provision of German law (art 24 of the Unfair Competition Act) the court held that the publication had to circulate to a significant extent or to be distributed regularly even if only in small numbers before the German courts would have jurisdiction. The court said that if one regarded the German courts as having jurisdiction 'simply on the ground that the publication could be bought in Germany, that would produce the result that this court would have jurisdiction over all injury caused by newspapers and periodicals anywhere in the world, since it is possible eventually to buy any newspaper appearing anywhere in the world in Germany'!

Perhaps these two cases may be reconciled on the ground that in *Shevill* it was clear that *France Soir* circulated regularly in England (although in small numbers).

In *Shevill* on a reference to the ECJ (Case C–68/93 [1995] All ER (EC) 289) the European Court accepted the likelihood of multiple fora having jurisdiction in a libel case and the possibility of forum shopping. The decision has at least the merit of certainty. It is suggested that the use of a 'significant connecting factor' (mooted in the judgment) to tie the harm to one jurisdiction would be an even more unsatisfactory response.

Tesam Distribution Ltd v *Schuh Mode Team GmbH and Commerzbank AG* [1990] ILPr 149 Court of Appeal (O'Connor, Stocker and Nicholls LJJ)

• *Special jurisdiction*

Facts

The plaintiff was an English firm of shoe importers and the defendants were a German firm of shoe suppliers (Schuh Mode Team) and a German Bank (Commerzbank); and the plaintiff's claim alleged that both the defendants had breached a contract for the sale and delivery of certain shoes by failing to deliver the shoes as agreed and failing to accept payment therefor. It was clear that, if there was a contract between the parties, then the shoes were to be delivered in London. Thus the 'obligation in question' (the delivery of the shoes) was to be performed in London. This would plainly mean that under art 5(1) the English courts would have special jurisdiction, and the plaintiff did not need to sue the defendants in Germany.

But, although there had been considerable correspondence between the parties, there was doubt whether there was a binding contract between them. That question is a crucial one for it could surely not be right that a plaintiff could, by simply asserting the existence of a contract, ensure that a court convenient for him had jurisdiction. On the other hand, the plaintiff could hardly be expected to provide conclusive evidence of the contract before the matter went to trial for whether there was a contract or not might be (and was in this case) the most important issue to be decided at trial.

Held

1. that in the exercise of its art 5(1) jurisdiction 'the court may determine the dispute whether a contract was entered into by the parties … the court's jurisdiction … is not dependent upon the court first satisfying itself that the contract does exist. That is the subject matter of the dispute, and that is a subject matter which *Effer* v *Kantner* Case 38/81 [1982] ECR 825 established the court has jurisdiction … [to determine]. If in due course the court finds that no contract was entered into, it will dismiss the claim: but it had jurisdiction to determine that issue.'
2. that it would not be enough for the plaintiff simply to assert the existence of the contract: the court had to be satisfied that there was 'evidence from which the conclusion could properly be drawn that a contract existed and that the place of performance was the country in which the action was brought'.
3. that it was for each Contracting State's national law to determine the burden of proof of facts relevant to its jurisdiction.

In the context of a libel action the 'harmful event' was where the libellous publication was purchased and read.

Zelger v *Salinitri* Case 56/79 [1980] ECR 89 European Court of Justice

• *Interpretation of arts 5 and 17 Brussels Convention*

Facts

The Bundesgerichtshof referred to the European Court of Justice, under art 3 of the Protocol of 03/06/71 on the Interpretation of the Convention of Brussels 27/09/68, a question concerning the interpretation of art 5(1) and art 17 of the Brussels Convention. The Court was asked to interpret these articles in an action for the recovery of a debt brought in a German court by a German against an Italian, in which it was claimed the debt was payable in Germany.

Held

If according to the lex contractus the German court has jurisdiction as the locus solutionis, art 5(1) would permit it to use this jurisdiction. The formal requirements concerning the forum in art 17 only apply in the context of this article. The lex contractus decides the validity of the agreement as to the place of performance.

Judgment of the ECJ:

'The provisions of art 5(1) of the Convention, to the effect that in matters relating to a contract a defendant domiciled in a contracting state may be sued in the courts for the place of performance of the obligation in question, introduce a criterion for jurisdiction, the selection of which is at the option of the plaintiff and which is justified by the existence of a direct link between the dispute and the court called upon to take cognisance of it. By contrast, art 17 of the Convention, which provides for the exclusive jurisdiction of the court designated by the parties in accordance with the prescribed form, puts aside both the rule of general jurisdiction – provided for in art 2 – and the rules of special jurisdiction – provided for in art 5 – and dispenses with any objective connexion between the legal relationship in dispute and the court designated. It thus appears that the jurisdiction of the court for the place of performance and that of the selected court are two distinct concepts and only agreements selecting a court are subject to the requirements of form prescribed by art 17 of the Convention.

If the place of performance of a contractual obligation has been specified by the parties in a clause which is valid according to the national law applicable to the contract, the court for that place has jurisdiction to take cognisance of disputes relating to that obligation under art 5(1) of the Convention, irrespective of whether the formal conditions provided for under art 17 have been observed ...

It is appropriate to point out that art 5(1), which occurs in s2 of Title II of the Convention entitled "special jurisdiction", creates a ground of jurisdiction which is an exception to the general rule of jurisdiction provided for in art 2 of the Convention; the provisions of art 5, which provide that in matters relating to a contract a defendant domiciled in a contracting state may be sued in the courts for the place of performance of the obligation in question, introduce a criterion for jurisdiction, the selection of which is at the option of the plaintiff and which is justified by the existence of a direct link between the dispute and the court called upon to take cognisance of it.

By contrast, art 17, which occurs in section 6 of the Convention entitled "prorogation of jurisdiction" and which provides for the exclusive jurisdiction of the court designated by the parties in accordance with the prescribed form, puts aside both the rule of general jurisdiction - provided for in art 2 – and the rules of special jurisdiction – provided for in art 5 – and dispenses with any objective connexion between the legal relationship in dispute and the court designated. It thus appears that the jurisdiction of the court for the place of performance (provided for in art 5(1)) and that of the selected court (provided for in art 17) are two distinct concepts and only agreements selecting a court are subject to the requirements of form prescribed by art 17 of the Convention.

Consequently, if the parties to the contract are permitted by the law applicable to the contract, subject to any conditions imposed by that law, to specify the place of performance of an obligation without satisfying any special condition of form, an agreement on the place of performance of the obligation is sufficient to found jurisdiction in that place within the meaning of art 5(1) of the Convention.

The answer to the question put by the Bundesgerichtshof must therefore be that if the place of performance of a contractual obligation has been specified by the parties in a clause which is valid according to the national law applicable to the contract, the court for that place has jurisdiction to take cognisance of disputes relating to that obligation under art 5(1) of the Convention of Brussels of 27 September 1968, irrespective of whether the formal conditions provided for under art 17 have been observed …'

Cases dealing with the meaning of particular parts of art 6 Brussels Convention (art 6 EU Council Regulation 44/2001)

Gascoine and Another v *Pyrah and Another* [1994] ILPr 82 Court of Appeal (Hirst, Glidewell and Roch LJJ)

- *Article 6(1) – co-defendants – test of risk of irreconcilable judgments*

Facts

Mr and Mrs Gascoine had engaged Mr Pyrah, who was domiciled in England, to find a horse for use by their daughter for show-jumping. Mr Pyrah found an apparently suitable horse, Othello, in France and was then instructed to obtain a veterinary report on the horse and arrange the sale. Mr Pyrah engaged Dr Cronau, a German-domiciled veterinarian, to inspect the horse which he did. Dr Cronau's written report revealed that Othello's right front navicular bone had a central decalcified area but, it was alleged by Mr Pyrah, Dr Cronau had told him in a subsequent telephone conversation that this was not a serious problem; and the horse was thus bought for £75,000. In fact the defect in the bone was a serious problem and rendered the horse unsuitable for show-jumping; its value was reduced to £3,000.

The Gascoines at first instituted action against Pyrah only in England (where he was domiciled). But when he raised as a defence his conversation with Cronau, they wished to institute action against Cronau as well. Plainly the English courts did not have jurisdiction over Cronau on the basis of art 2, but was there jurisdiction under art 6(1) which provided that 'a person domiciled in a Contracting State [such as the German-domiciled Cronau] may also be sued … where he is one of a number of defendants in the courts for the place where any one of them [ie the English-domiciled Pyrah] is domiciled'. It was plain from *Kalfelis* v *Bankhaus Schroder Munchmeyer Hengst and Co* [1988] ECR 5565 that art 6(1) applied where it was expedient to hear the related claims together to avoid the risk of irreconcilable judgments resulting from separate proceedings that would otherwise happen. It was also for the national court to decide whether there was such a risk. At first instance the judge had concluded that there was no such risk and had refused leave to join Dr Cronau under art 6(1).

Held

The Court of Appeal held that the risk of irreconcilable judgments applied just as much to the risk of inconsistent findings of fact as it did to inconsistent findings of law. In this case the telephone conversation was vital both to Mr Pyrah's defence to the Gascoines' cause of action, and to the Gascoines' cause of action against Dr Cronau; and if that factual issue was differently decided by different courts there was a risk of irreconcilable judgments. Thus under art 6(1) the English courts had jurisdiction over Dr Cronau. As Hirst LJ remarked:

> '… where a potential conflict on this vital issue of fact [the telephone call] has been so clearly demonstrated …, there must be an option, which the plaintiffs are entitled to

exercise under art 6(1) to sue Dr Cronau as well as Mr Pyrah in this court.' (p95)

Comment

The Court of Appeal's judgment is entirely convincing in the circumstances. However, the majority of the court (Glidewell LJ dubitante) stressed that a plaintiff suing two defendants, one of whom fell within art 6(1), had an 'option' whether to sue the defendant in his domiciliary court or under art 6(1); he had 'freedom of choice'. But the more usual approach was that art 6(1) was an exception to the basic rule of domicile (contained in art 2) and thus should be narrowly interpreted. Glidewell LJ may well be right in saying that this 'freedom of choice' argument should not have been 'relied upon so strongly'.

Exclusive jurisdiction: art 16 Brussels Convention (art 22 EU Council Regulation 44/2001)

Hacker v *Europ Relais GmbH* (1992) The Times 9 April; [1992] ILPr 515 European Court of Justice

• *Article 16 does not apply to contracts between travel agents and clients for the use of holiday accommodation*

Facts

Hacker, who was domiciled in Germany, entered into a contract (entitled *Meitvertrag* (tenancy contract)) with Europ Relais, a German firm of travel agents. In the contract the firm undertook that Hacker would have the use of a holiday home in the Netherlands and, for an additional payment, a reservation would be made for Hacker's travel to the holiday home. The holiday home was smaller than advertised as a result of which Hacker incurred extra expenses and returned to Germany earlier than planned. She sued in the German courts for a reduction of the price paid and damages under various heads. But did the German courts have jurisdiction in the light of art 16(1)? Jurisdiction was at first instance denied by the German courts but the matter was thereupon referred to the European Court.

Held

That art 16(1) of the Brussels Convention (as unamended by the San Sebastian Convention), 'must be interpreted as not applying to a contract concluded in a Contracting State whereby a professional travel organiser, which has its registered office in that State, undertakes to procure for a client domiciled in the same State the use for several weeks of holiday accommodation in another Contracting State which it does not own, and to book the travel.'

Comment

1. This conclusion is sensible but it is surprising in the light of *Rosler* v *Rottwinkel* [1986] QB 33 where it had been held that even short term holiday lettings fell within art 16(1). However, the ECJ relied upon the more liberal strand of authority in *Sanders* v *Van der Putte* [1977] ECR 2383. *Rosler* v *Rottwinkel* was not expressly overruled; that is not the European Court's style.
2. Although not dealt with in the judgment of the court, the Advocate General's opinion suggested that where art 16(1) is found to apply, then the claims for ancillary damages and the like fell within art 16(1). This was in order to prevent a multiplicity of proceedings over essentially one dispute.
3. Although decided on the unamended art 16(1) the decision is relevant for the amended Article too because that Article, it will be recalled created an exception to the rigid rule in the case of holiday lettings but only where tenant and landlord were domiciled in the same Contracting State and were natural persons. Thus the amendment will not help the case where the letting is from an artificial person, such as a travel company, but *Hacker* v *Euro Relais* will.

Reichert, Reichert and Kockler v *Dresdner Bank* Case 115/88 [1990] 1 ILPr 105 European Court of Justice

• *A more restrictive interpretation of art 16(1) (art 22(1) EU Council Regulation 44/2001)*

Facts

Mr and Mrs Reichert, who lived in Germany, owned property situated in Antibes in France. They made a gift (duly executed in France) of the bare ownership of this property to their son. However, they owed a great deal of money to the Dresdner Bank which considered that the gift to the son had been made to defraud the bank by preventing the bank from executing against the property for satisfaction of the debt. Now under French law specific provision is made for this sort of case: the action paulienne which allows debtors to contest the validity of acts performed by the creditor in fraud of the debtor's rights. In reliance on the action paulienne the bank sued the Reicherts in France. But did the French courts have jurisdiction? Since the Reicherts were plainly domiciled in Germany, the French courts would only have jurisdiction if art 16(1) applied to grant them exclusive jurisdiction.

Held

On a reference to the European Court the court (apart from confirming that art 16 was to be interpreted according to community concepts) held, first, that art 16(1), since it restricted the parties' choice of court and required litigation in a court which might be the domiciliary court of neither party, should be restrictively interpreted. Secondly, the primary reason for the operation of exclusive jurisdiction under art 16 was that the courts of the Contracting State where the property is situated were in the best position to have a good knowledge of the factual situation affecting the property and apply the rules and customs of that State. Thus, thirdly, art 16(1) should not be interpreted to cover all actions relating to rights in rem in immovable property but only those whose 'aim [is] to determine the extent, scale, ownership or possession of immovable property or the existence of other rights in rem in such property and to safeguard for the holders of such rights the powers attaching to their title. Thus, finally, the action paulienne 'arises from the claim, viz, the creditor's right in personam against his debtor, and has the object of safeguarding the charge which the former may hold on the latter's assets. If the action is successful ... the [fraudulent] disposition ... is void as against the creditor alone. Furthermore, the court is not required to assess facts or to apply rules and customs of the place where the property is situated, which are such as to justify the jurisdiction of a court of the state where the property is situated.' Thus art 16(1) did not apply.

Note that equitable interests do not, it appears, fall with art 16(1): *Webb* v *Webb* Case 294/92 [1994] ILPr 389; [1994] 3 WLR 801 European Court of Justice where Judge Paul Baker QC held that where a plaintiff sought a declaration that certain immovable property situated in France was held on trust for him by the defendant that was not a proceeding in rem and thus art 16 was inapplicable.

Theodorus Engelbertus Sanders v *Ronald Van der Putte* [1977] ECR 2383 European Court of Justice

• *Article 16(1) (art 22(1) EU Council Regulation 44/2001) should be strictly interpreted and does not prevent the domiciliary courts hearing a dispute over the operation of a business affecting immovable property elsewhere*

Facts

Two domiciled Dutchmen, Sanders and Van der Putte, agreed that Sanders would take over the running of a flower shop in Germany rented from a third party by Van der Putte. A dispute arose between the two of them over who should pay the rent of the shop to the third party and whether goodwill was payable. Van der Putte sued Sanders in the Dutch courts, but Sanders took the point that the Dutch courts had no jurisdiction because of the exclusive jurisdiction provisions of art 16(1).

Held

'The concept of "matters relating to tenancies of immovable property" in art 16 ... must not be interpreted as including an agreement to rent under a usufructuary lease a retail business carried on in immovable property rented from a third person by the lessor' (at 2392).

Judgment of the ECJ:

> 'Under the terms of art 2 of the Convention and subject to any other provisions thereof, persons domiciled if a Contracting State shall, whatever their nationality, be sued in the courts of that State.
>
> The Convention admits of exceptions to the general rule by allowing the plaintiff in certain cases to sue the defendant before the court of the State in which the latter is domiciled or before the court of another Contracting State, according to the special provisions in arts 5, 6, 8, 9, 10, 13 and 14 of the Convention.
>
> On the other hand, art 16 of the Convention provides for exclusive jurisdiction, regardless of domicile.
>
> As regards the matters listed under subparagraphs (2), (3), (4) and (5) of that Article it is clear that the courts which are given exclusive jurisdiction are those which are the best placed to deal with the disputes in question.
>
> The same applies to the assignment of exclusive jurisdiction to the courts of the Contracting State in which the property is situated in matters relating to rights in rem in, or tenancies of, immovable property.
>
> In fact, actions concerning rights in rem in immovable property are to be judged according to the rules of the State in which the immovable property is situated since the disputes which arise result frequently in checks, inquiries and expert assessments which must be carried out on the spot, with the result that the assignment of exclusive jurisdiction satisfies the need for the proper administration of justice.
>
> Tenancies of immovable property are generally governed by special rules and it is preferable, in the light of their complexity, that they be applied only by the courts of the States in which they are in force.
>
> The foregoing considerations explain the assignment of exclusive jurisdiction to the courts of the State in which the immovable property is situated in the case of disputes relating to tenancies of immovable property properly so-called, that is to say, in particular, disputes between lessors and tenants as to the existence or interpretation of leases or to compensation for damage caused by the tenant and to giving up possession of the premises.
>
> The same considerations do not apply where the principal aim of the agreement is of a different nature, in particular, where it concerns the operation of a business.
>
> Furthermore, the assignment, in the interests of the proper administration of justice, of exclusive jurisdiction to the courts of one Contracting State in accordance with art 16 of the Convention results in depriving the parties of the choice of the forum which would otherwise be theirs and, in certain cases, results in their being brought before a court which is not that of the domicile of any of them.
>
> Having regard to that consideration the provisions of art 16 must not be given a wider interpretation than is required by their objective.
>
> Therefore, the concept of "matters relating to ... tenancies of immovable property" within the context of art 16 of the Convention must not be interpreted as including an agreement to rent under a usufructuary lease a retail business (verpachting van een winkelbedrijf) carried on in immovable property rented from a third person by the lessor.
>
> In the light of the reply to the first question, the second does not call for an answer.'

Webb* v *Webb Case 294/92 [1994] 3 WLR 801; [1994] ILPr 389 European Court of Justice

• *Equitable interest in land (in France) – whether a right in rem*

Facts

The plaintiff, Webb, had in 1971 provided the funds for the purchase of a flat in the south of France in the name of his son, the defendant, Webb. Father and son had now fallen out and the father sought from the English courts a declaration that his son held the property as trustee for him and that the son should execute such documents as would be required to vest legal ownership of the flat in the father's name. However, the son raised art 16(1) which provided that 'in proceedings which have as their object rights in rem in, or tenancies of, immovable property, the Court of the Contracting State in which the property is situated' had exclusive jurisdiction; ie the son argued that the matter should be heard in France where the property was situated.

The case thus squarely raised the question of whether equitable interests where considered to be rights in rem (and thus within art 16(1)) or whether they operated only in personam and were thus outside art 16(1). The Schlosser Report (para 167(b), p121) and Lasok and Stone, *Conflict of Laws in the European Community* (1987), p237, and many other authorities, considered equitable rights to be rights in rem. After all, it is trite that equitable rights operate against the whole world with the exception of 'equity's darling' the bona fide purchaser for value.

Held

That it is not sufficient for art 16(1) to apply that a right in rem in immovable property to be involved in the action or that the action should have a link with immovable property: the action must be based on a right in rem and not on a right in personam (save for the exceptional case of tenancies). Since the father did not claim in the English proceedings that he enjoyed rights against the property that were enforceable against the whole world (ie rights in rem), but simply a declaration against his son, the action was not in rem and thus not within art 16(1).

Judgment of the ECJ:

> 'By its question the national court asks whether an action for a declaration that a person holds immovable property as trustee and for an order requiring that person to execute such documents as should be required to vest the legal ownership in the plaintiff constitutes an action in rem within the meaning of art 16(1) of the Convention.
>
> The son and the Commission, who consider that the test for applying art 16(1) is the plaintiff's ultimate purpose and that by his action the father is ultimately seeking to secure ownership of the flat, contend that the main proceedings are covered by art 16(1).
>
> That argument cannot be accepted.
>
> Article 16 confers exclusive jurisdiction in the matter of rights in rem in immovable property on the courts of the Contracting State in which the property is situated. In the light of the court's judgment in *Reichert v Dresdner Bank AG* Case C–115/88 [1990] ECR I–27, where the court had to rule on the question whether the exclusive jurisdiction prescribed by that Article applied in respect of an action by a creditor to have a disposition of immovable property declared ineffective as against him on the ground that it was made in fraud of his rights by his debtor, it follows that it is not sufficient, for art 16(1) to apply, that a right in rem in immovable property be involved in the action or that the action have a link with immovable property: the action must be based on a right in rem and not on a right in personam, save in the case of the exception concerning tenancies of immovable property.
>
> The aim of proceedings before the national court is to obtain a declaration that the son holds the flat for the exclusive benefit of the father and that in that capacity he is under a duty to execute the documents necessary to convey the ownership

of the flat to the father. The father does not claim that he already enjoys rights directly relating to the property which are enforceable against the whole world, but seeks only to assert rights as against the son. Consequently, his action is not an action in rem within the meaning of art 16(1) of the Convention but an action in personam.

Nor are considerations relating to the proper administration of justice underlying art 16(1) of the Convention applicable in this case.

As the court has held, the conferring of exclusive jurisdiction in the matter of rights in rem in immovable property on the courts of the state in which the property is situated is justified because actions concerning rights in rem in immovable property often involve disputes frequently necessitating checks, inquiries and expert assessments which must be carried out on the spot: see *Sanders* v *van der Putte* (Case 73/77) [1977] ECR 2383, 2390–2391, para 13.

As the father and the United Kingdom rightly point out, the immovable nature of the property held in trust and its location are irrelevant to the issues to be determined in the main proceedings which would have been the same if the dispute had concerned a flat situated in the United Kingdom or a yacht.

The answer to be given to the question submitted to the court must therefore be that an action for a declaration that a person holds immovable property as trustee and for an order requiring to vest the legal ownership in the plaintiff does not constitute an action in rem within the meaning of art 16(1) of the Convention.'

Comment

The general tendency of the ECJ is to give a narrow rather than a wide meaning to 'proceedings which have as their object right in rem'. Thus, for instance, in *Lieber* v *Gobel* Case C–292/93 [1994] ILPr 590 the ECJ held that a claim for compensation for the use of an immovable, since it can only be made against the person liable and not against the whole world, was not a right in rem.

Prorogation of jurisdiction: arts 17 and 18 Brussels Convention (arts 23 and 24 EU Council Regulation 44/2001)

Elefanten Schuh GmbH v *Pierre Jacqmain* [1981] ECR 1671
European Court of Justice

- *Article 18 prevails over art 17*

Facts

A dispute over a contract of employment arose between a Belgian domiciliary, Pierre Jacqmain, and a German firm, Elefanten Schuh. The contract of employment contained a choice of jurisdiction clause providing that the court at Kleve in Germany had exclusive jurisdiction. However, Jacqmain commenced proceedings in Belgium; and at first Elefanten Schuh did not contest the jurisdiction of the Belgian courts. As the dispute proceeded through the Belgian courts, however, Elefanten Schuh relied upon the jurisdiction clause and art 17 and contested the jurisdiction of the Belgian courts. Jacqmain replied that he relied upon Elefanten Schuh's submission in terms of art 18.

Held (on a preliminary ruling by the European Court)

Article 18 applies even where another court has been chosen by the parties in their contract.

Judgment of the ECJ:

'Question 1 is worded as follows:

"1. (a) Is art 18 of the Convention of 27 September 1968 on Jurisdiction and the Enforcement of Judgments in Civil and Commercial Matters applicable if parties have agreed to confer jurisdiction on a court within the meaning of art 17?

(b) Is the rule on jurisdiction contained in art 18 applicable if the defendant has not only contested jurisdiction but has in addition made submissions on the action itself?

(c) If it is, must jurisdiction then be contested in limine litis?"

Articles 17 and 18 form Section 6 of Title II of the Convention which deals with prorogation of jurisdiction; art 17 concerns jurisdiction by consent and art 18 jurisdiction implied from submission as a result of the defendant's appearance. The first part of the question seeks to determine the relationship between those two types of prorogation.

In the first sentence, art 18 of the convention lays down the rule that a court of a Contracting State before whom a defendant enters an appearance is to have jurisdiction and in the second sentence it provides that that rule is not to apply where appearance was entered solely in order to contest the jurisdiction, or where another court has exclusive jurisdiction by virtue of art 16 of the Convention.

This case envisaged in art 17 is not therefore one of the exceptions which art 18 allows to the rule which it lays down. Moreover neither the general scheme nor the objectives of the Convention provide grounds for the view that the parties to an agreement conferring jurisdiction within the meaning of art 17 are prevented from voluntarily submitting their dispute to a court other than that stipulated in the agreement.

It follows that art 18 of the Convention applies even where the parties have by agreement designated a court which is to have jurisdiction within the meaning of art 17.

The second and third parts of the question envisage the case in which the defendant has appeared before a court within the meaning of art 18 but contests the jurisdiction of that court.

The Hof van Cassatie first asks if art 18 has application where the defendant makes submissions as to the jurisdiction of the court as well as on the substance of the action.

Although differences between the different language versions of art 18 of the Convention appear when it is sought to determine whether, in order to exclude the jurisdiction of the court seised, a defendant must confine himself to contesting that jurisdiction, or whether he may on the contrary still achieve the same purpose by contesting the jurisdiction of the court as well as the substance of the claim, the second interpretation is more in keeping with the objectives and spirit of the Convention. In fact under the law of civil procedure of certain Contracting States a defendant who raises the issue of jurisdiction and no other might be barred from making his submissions as to the substance if the court rejects his plea that it has no jurisdiction. An interpretation of art 18 which enabled such a result to be arrived at would be contrary to the right of the defendant to defend himself in the original proceedings, which is one of the aims of the Convention.

However, the challenge to jurisdiction may have the result attributed to it by art 18 only if the plaintiff and the court seised of the matter are able to ascertain from the time of the defendant's first defence that it is intended to contest the jurisdiction of the court.

The Hof van Cassatie asks in this regard whether jurisdiction must be contested in limine litis. For the purposes of interpreting the Convention that concept is difficult to apply in view of the appreciable differences existing between the legislation of the Contracting States with regard to bringing actions before courts of law, the appearance of defendants and the way in which the parties to an action must formulate their submissions. However, it follows from the aim of art 18 that if the challenge to jurisdiction is not preliminary to any defence as to the substance it may not in any event occur after the making of the submissions which under national procedural law are considered to be the first defence addressed to the court seised.

Therefore the answer to the second and third parts of Question 1 should be that art 18 of the Convention must be interpreted as meaning that the rule on jurisdiction which that provision lays down does not apply where the defendant not only contests the court's jurisdiction but also makes submissions on the substance of the action, provided that, if the challenge to jurisdiction is not preliminary to any defence as to the substance, it does not occur after the making of the submissions which under national procedural law are considered to be the first defence addressed to the court seised.'

Meeth v *Glacetal Sarl* Case 23/78 [1978] ECR 2133 European Court of Justice

• *Article 17 Brussels Convention – split jurisdiction*

Facts

The case concerned a dispute over a contract between a German firm and a French firm which contained a clause conferring jurisdiction on the national courts of the defendant in any action. There was a claim by the French party and a counterclaim by the German party. The European Court was asked to provide clarification as to the interpretation of art 17.

Held

Article 17(1) of this Convention allows a contract to provide for a split jurisdiction. In these circumstances it is for the national court to decide if it can hear both claim and counterclaim.

Judgment of the ECJ:

> 'According to the first paragraph of art 17 "if the parties ... Have agreed that a court or the courts of a contracting state are to have jurisdiction to settle any disputes which have arisen or which may arise in connexion with a particular legal relationship, that court or those courts shall have exclusive jurisdiction."
>
> With regard to an agreement conferring reciprocal jurisdiction in the form in which it appears in the contract whose implementation forms the subject-matter of the dispute, the interpretation of that provision gives rise to difficulty because of the fact that art 17, as it is worded, refers to the choice by the parties to the contract of a single court or the courts of a single state.
>
> That wording, which is based on the most widespread business practice, cannot, however, be interpreted as intending to exclude the right of the parties to agree on two or more courts for the purpose of settling any disputes which may arise.
>
> This interpretation is justified on the ground that art 17 is based on a recognition of the independent will of the parties to a contract in deciding which courts are to have jurisdiction to settle disputes falling within the scope of the Convention, other than those which are expressly excluded pursuant to the second paragraph of art 17.
>
> This applies particularly where the parties have by such an agreement reciprocally conferred jurisdiction on the courts specified in the general rule laid down by art 2 of the Convention.
>
> Although such an agreement coincides with the scope of art 2 it is nevertheless effective in that it excludes, in relations between the parties, other optional attributions of jurisdiction, such as those detailed in arts 5 and 6 of the Convention.
>
> The reply to the first question must accordingly be that the first paragraph of art 17 of the Convention cannot be interpreted as prohibiting an agreement under which the two parties to a contract for sale, who are domiciled in different states, can be sued only in the courts of their respective states.'

Lis alibi pendens and protective measures: arts 21–24 Brussels Convention (arts 27–30 EU Council Regulation 44/2001)

Continental Bank NA v *Akakos Compania Naviera SA and Others* (1993) The Times 26 November Court of Appeal (Stephen Brown P, Steyn and Kennedy LJJ)

• *Valid art 17 (art 23 EU Council Regulation 44/2001) agreement overrides arts 21 and 22 (arts 27 and 28 EU Council Regulation 44/2001) and may even justify an injunction to restrain foreign proceedings*

Facts

The Continental Bank had granted a loan of $56 million to the Akakos Compania NA and others. This loan was guaranteed by members of the Papalios family. The loan agreement contained an exclusive jurisdiction clause in terms of which all disputes arising out of the loan were to be submitted to the English courts. In October 1991 the bank issued a writ in England seeking payment of outstanding interest from the appellants (the borrowers and the guarantors), but in May 1991 the appellant had already commenced action in Athens seeking damages against the bank and a declaration that the guarantors had been released.

Held

The structure and logic of the Brussels Convention showed that if art 17 applied, its provisions took precedence over arts 21 and 22 (which deal with lis alibi pendens and related actions and provide that courts other than the court 'first seised' 'shall' (lis alibi pendens) or 'may' (related actions) decline jurisdiction); thus the English court would not decline jurisdiction in favour of the Greek courts notwithstanding that art 21 required that 'any court other than the court first seised shall decline jurisdiction' once it was clear that the court first seised had jurisdiction. Indeed, in such cases, where there was no other effective remedy, the Convention did not preclude the issue of an injunction to restrain the foreign proceedings.

Steyn LJ:

> 'The complaint in the Greek proceedings was served on the bank in March 1991. Its response was to issue a writ in an English action seeking an injunction to restrain the appellants from continuing the Greek proceedings as they were in breach of an agreement conferring exclusive jurisdiction on English courts to try any dispute Mr Justice Gatehouse had found in favour of the bank.
>
> Miss Dohmann had challenged the judge's construction of the exclusive jurisdiction clause.
>
> However, the issue in the Greek proceedings was inextricably interwoven with the contractual rights and duties of the parties and the language of the jurisdiction clause showed an obligation on the appellants, but not the bank, to submit disputes in connection with the loan facility to England.
>
> It was an undoubted fact that the Greek proceedings had been commenced before the English proceedings and it had been submitted that the Athens court was the court "first seised" within the meaning of arts 21 and 22 of the Brussels Convention and that the same cause of action was involved.
>
> There was no discretionary power in the Convention itself to override the conclusive effect of an exclusive jurisdiction agreement which conformed with art 17. It followed that if art 17 applied, its provisions took precedence over the provisions of arts 21 and 22. The structure and logic of the Convention pointed convincingly to that conclusion. There was nothing in the Convention which was inconsistent with a power vesting in the English court to grant an injunction the objective of which was to secure enforcement of an exclusive jurisdiction agreement.
>
> An injunction was the only effective remedy for the appellants' breach of contract. In the opinion of the court, the continuance of the Greek proceedings amounted to vexatious and oppressive conduct on the part of the appellants. The appeal would be dismissed.'

Comment

This conclusion and the reasoning of the Court of Appeal follows that of Hirst J in *Klockner & Co AG* v *Gatoil Overseas Ltd* [1990] ILPr 53; [1990] 1 Lloyd's Rep 177, although this case was, apparently, not referred to by the court. The European Court, however, has left open whether art 17 prevails over arts 21 and 22 or not: *Overseas Union Insurance Ltd and Others* v *New Hampshire Insurance Company* Case C–351/89 [1991] ILPr 495 (ECJ).

A related issue was explored in *IP Metal* v *Ruote OZ SpA* [1993] 2 Lloyd's Rep 60. Related actions concerning the sale of aluminium had been brought in England (pursuant to an art 17 agreement) (writ served 30

January 1992) and earlier in Italy (writ served 29 January 1992). The English court refused to stay its action (art 22 did not oblige it to stay; it said in 'may' stay when a related action is brought elsewhere) to give the Italian courts a chance to decide whether the art 17 agreement was valid. Notwithstanding the risk of irreconcilable judgments, the court said, it would not be in accord with justice to stay the action when, on its view, the English court had exclusive jurisdiction.

Derby & Co Ltd and Others v *Weldon and Others (No 6)* [1990] 1 WLR 1139 Court of Appeal (Dillon, Taylor and Staughton LJJ)

• *Jurisdiction to grant a Mareva injunction (freezing order) depends on the unlimited jurisdiction of the English court in personam against any person who is properly made a party to proceedings*

Facts

In the course of very complicated litigation the plaintiffs (who were claiming damages for deceit, breach of fiduciary duty and conspiracy to defraud from the defendants) obtained at the interlocutory stage worldwide Mareva injunctions against the assets of some of the defendants. Some of these assets were held in Swiss bank accounts in the joint names of the defendants and the duly appointed receiver of the defendants' assets. Some of those assets (the external assets) had been deposited by the Swiss banks on behalf of the account holders in other banks outside Switzerland. It seemed probable that the Swiss courts would not recognise or enforce the English order against some of the defendants; and there was naturally concern that the external assets might be transferred to Switzerland, reducing the assets against which the English order might bite. Moreover, art 271 of the Swiss Penal Code made it an offence punishable with imprisonment for the receiver to act as receiver in Switzerland.

Held

That the purpose of a Mareva injunction was to prevent a defendant from taking action that would render a subsequent order of the court less effective. This consideration was plainly applicable to the present case; thus the external assets were ordered not to be returned to Switzerland and it was ordered that the defendants should procure that the external assets should be held to the sole order of the receiver.

Dillon LJ:

> 'The jurisdiction of the court to grant a Mareva injunction against a person depends not on territorial jurisdiction of the English court over assets within its jurisdiction, but on the unlimited jurisdiction of the English court in personam against any person, whether an individual or a corporation, who is, under English procedure, properly made a party to proceedings pending before the English court. This is particularly underlined by the judgment of Lord Donaldson of Lymington MR in *Derby & Co Ltd* v *Weldon (Nos 3 and 4)* [1990] Ch 65, 82 and at p86, where he said, in relation to CMI:
>
> > "In this situation I do not understand why the order that the assets vest in the receiver should only take effect it and when the order was recognised by the Luxembourg courts. True it is that CMI is a Luxembourg company, but it is a party to the action and can properly be ordered to deal with its assets in accordance with the orders of this court, regardless of whether the order is recognised and enforced in Luxembourg. The only effect of non-recognition would be to remove one of the potential sanctions for disobedience."
>
> Another potential sanction for disobedience that would remain is that a defendant who disobeyed an order of the court could be barred from defending the proceedings.
>
> In truth the original, somewhat territorial, approach in *Ashtiani* v *Kashi* [1987] QB 888 has been turned the other way round by the introduction of the so-called *Babanaft* proviso in *Babanaft International Co SA* v *Bassatne* [1990] Ch 13. That was revised in

Derby & Co Ltd v *Weldon (Nos 3 and 4)* and as so revised is of course the basic order in the present case. Application to a foreign court to recognise the order or to declare it enforceable is only necessary in so far as the order purports to have effect outside England and Wales and it is sought to affect by the order a person to whom the order is not addressed and who is not in certain categories of person subject to the jurisdiction of this court.

To regard the grant of a Mareva injunction not as a matter of territorial jurisdiction to be exercised court by court throughout the various countries of the world where it may be appropriate but as a matter of unlimited jurisdiction in personam of the English court over persons who have properly been made parties, under English procedure, to proceedings pending before the English court is consistent with the approach of the English court to the appointment of receivers of the British and foreign assets of English companies. The court has always been ready to appoint a receiver over the foreign as well as British assets of an English company, even though it has recognised that in relation to foreign assets the appointment may not prove effective without assistance from a foreign court: *In re Maudslay, Sons & Field; Maudslay* v *Maudslay, Sons & Field* [1990] 1 Ch 602. Moreover where a foreign court of the country where the assets are situate refuses to recognise the receiver appointed by the English court, the English court will, in an appropriate case, do what it can to render the appointment effective by orders in personam against persons who are subject to the jurisdiction of the English court; see the helpful decision of Neville J in *In re Huinac Copper Mines Ltd; Matheson & Co* v *The Company* [1910] WN 218.

Conversely the English court is – international convention apart – unwilling to exercise its powers within this country in support of a receiver appointed by a foreign court, save on very strictly limited traditional principles of international law: see *Schemmer* v *Property Resources Ltd* [1975] Ch 273. Indeed, from the observations of Lord Diplock in *Siskina (Owners of cargo lately laden on board)* v *Distos Compania Naviera SA* [1979] AC 210, it would seem that before the enactment of the Supreme Court Act 1981 there could have been problems of jurisdiction in some cases. But provided that third parties do not invoke the jurisdiction of the English court for the protection of their own rights – as in *British Nylon Spinners Ltd* v *ICI Ltd* [1953] Ch 19 – the foreign court is free to achieve its objectives by making orders in personam against persons who are subject to its jurisdiction.

In my judgment, therefore, the Vice-Chancellor misdirected himself in his deference to the Swiss court. This court is therefore free to exercise its own discretion on the appeal.

My own view, with all respect, is that the Vice-Chancellor also misdirected himself in the weight he attached to the fact that amicable arrangements had been made between the receiver and the defendants in November 1988 which had been supplemented in February 1989. As I read the correspondence in November 1988 between Cameron Markby and Theodore Goddard the receiver from the outset reserved his right to apply to the court for further directions, so that the agreement made was merely an interim arrangement. Moreover Theodore Goddard were obviously well aware of the receiver's obligations to the court as a receiver appointed by the court. Beyond that, in November 1988, immediately after his first appointment, the receiver did not know of art 271, nor of the trickery over the Ralgo and Lagor trusts. In my judgment the court's concern should be to make the best practical order under the circumstances for the preservation of the receivership assets.

The object of a Mareva injunction is stated by Lord Donaldson of Lymington MR in *Derby & Co Ltd* v *Weldon (Nos 3 and 4)* [1990] Ch 65, 76, as being that

> "... within the limits of its powers, no court should permit a defendant to take action designed to ensure that subsequent orders of the court are rendered less effective than would otherwise be the case."

See also at p79. That is in line with the statement by Kerr LJ in giving the judgment in this court in *Ninemia Maritime Corporation* v *Trave Schiffahrtsgesellschaft mbH und Co KG* [1983] 1 WLR 1412, 1422:

> "the test is whether, on the assumption that the plaintiffs have shown at least 'a good arguable case,' the court concludes, on the whole of the evidence then before it, that the refusal of a *Mareva* injunction would involve a real risk that a judgment or award in favour of the plaintiffs would remain unsatisfied."

I see no reason why that should not extend, in principle and in an appropriate case, to ordering the transfer of assets to a jurisdiction in which the order of the English court after the trial of the action will be recognised, from a jurisdiction in which that order will not be recognised and the issues would have to be re-litigated, if – which may not be entirely the present case – the only connection of the latter jurisdiction with the matters in issue in the proceedings is that moneys have been placed in that jurisdiction in order to make them proof against the enforcement, without a full retrial in a foreign court, of any judgment which may be granted to the plaintiffs by the English court in this action or indeed if the only connection with the latter jurisdiction is financial, as a matter of controlling investments.

In these circumstances I would without any hesitation refuse to order the return of the external assets to Switzerland and I would therefore dismiss the cross-appeal.'

Dresser UK Ltd and Others v *Falcongate Freight Management Ltd and Others* [1992] 2 WLR 319 Court of Appeal (Sir Stephen Brown P, Ralph Gibson and Bingham LJJ)

• *It is for the national law to determine when they are seised of a case – generally, the English court is seised when the writ is served*

Facts

This case concerned a dispute between the owners of a consignment of electronic goods lost at sea during a voyage from Scheveningen (in Holland) to Great Yarmouth (in England) and various parties associated with the carriage of those goods. Proceedings had been begun in England (writ issued 15 July 1988 and served 13 July 1989) and in Holland (initiated 21 February 1989), ex parte orders published 19 May 1989, jurisdiction of Dutch courts challenged 15 November 1989). Which was the court first seised?

Held

It was service of the proceedings not issue of the writ which ordinarily activated the litigious process and imposed procedural obligation on the parties. And it was artificial, far-fetched and wrong to hold that the English court was seised of proceedings upon the mere issue of proceedings. In straightforward cases service of proceedings would be the time when an English court was seised, but this was not the invariable rule. For instance, where there had been an actual exercise of jurisdiction (eg the issue of a Mareva injunction (freezing order) or the making of an Anton Piller order (search order)) before the writ was issued then the English court would be siesed before the writ was served.

Bingham LJ:

> 'Authoritative guidance on the meaning of this expression was given by the European Court of Justice in *Zelger* v *Salinitri* (Case 129/83) [1984] ECR 2397, 2408, where it was held that the court first seised
>
> > "is the one before which the requirements for proceedings to become definitively pending are first fulfilled, such requirements to be determined in accordance with the national law of each of the courts concerned."

In the course of its judgement the court pointed out the rules of procedure of the various Contracting States are not identical as regards determining the dates at which courts are seised. Having considered the procedural rules of France, Italy, Luxemburg, the Netherlands, Belgium and Germany, the court accepted that a common concept of lis pendens could not be arrived at by a rapprochement of the various relevant national provisions. The court declined to impose on Contracting States a uniform procedural rule which was not to be found in the Convention. Instead, it defined "first seised" and wisely left it to national courts to apply that definition to their own procedure.

Until the United Kingdom acceded to the Brussels Convention in 1987, no English court had ever had to consider when it was "first seised" of proceedings nor when proceedings were "definitively pending" before it. These are not terms of art, nor terms with any established meaning, in English law. But arts 21 to 23 of the Convention are now part of English law and s3(1) of the Civil Jurisdiction and Judgments Act 1982 requires us to apply the Convention in accordance with principles laid down by the European Court of Justice. We must therefore decide when, under English law, the requirements for the present proceedings to become definitively pending were first fulfilled. Since this question never arose, and never could have arisen, before 1987 one could not expect earlier authority to yield a simple, ready-made answer. We must be wary of adopting and applying any rule developed for a different purpose in different circumstances. In determining the effect of national law for purposes of the Convention we must, I think, have regard to the international purpose which the Convention was made to achieve ...

It is service of proceedings, not issue, which ordinarily activates the litigious process and imposes procedural obligations on the parties. Thus the defendant must acknowledge service within the time limited by O.12 r5. Only if he fails to do so and to give notice of intention to defend may judgment in default be obtained under O.13. Only if he does so may the plaintiff seek summary judgment under O.14. The plaintiff's obligation to serve a statement of claim arises on or after service: O.18 r1. Only a defendant who has acknowledged service and given notice of intention to defend is obliged to serve a defence: O.18 r2. The procedure under O.86 is different, but summary judgment cannot be given without notice to the defendant: O.86 rr1(2), 2(3). Until a defendant has been served, a plaintiff cannot apply for an order that he make an interim payment: O.29 r10(1).

It would of course be wrong to suggest that the court has no jurisdiction to make orders against a person until he has been served. Mareva injunctions, Anton Piller orders and other injunctive orders may be and very regularly are granted and made before service. But they may also be granted and made before issue, a practice authorised by the rules in cases of urgency on terms providing for the issue of proceedings (O.29 rr1(3)), and this practice also is very regularly followed. Where a defendant has not acknowledged service, his right to apply for various orders of this kind is restricted: O.29 rr2(6), 3(5), 4(2).

In *In re Evans* [1893] 1 Ch 252, 264 Lindley LJ considered that a defendant had become a party on service. This is certainly the law in respect of additional defendants (O.15 r8(4); *Ketteman* v *Hansel Properties Ltd* [1987] AC 189) and third parties (O.16 r1(3)). In the analogous field of arbitration, where service out of a court office is for obvious reasons inappropriate, the arbitration is treated as being commenced on notice: Limitation Act 1980, s34(3)...

With genuine respect to the contrary opinions of Hirst J and Hobhouse J, it is in my judgment artificial, far-fetched and wrong to hold that the English court is seised of proceedings, or that proceedings are decisively, conclusively, finally or definitively pending before it, upon mere issue of proceedings, when at that stage (1) the court's involvement has been confined to a ministerial act by a relatively junior administrative officer; (2) the plaintiff has an unfettered choice whether to pursue the action and serve the proceedings, or not, being in breach of no rule or obligation if he chooses to let the writ expire unserved; (3) the plaintiff's claim may be framed in terms of the utmost generality; (4) the defendant is usually unaware of the issue of proceedings and, if unaware, is unable to call on the plaintiff to serve the writ or discontinue the action and unable to rely on the commencement of the action as a lis alibi pendens if proceedings are begun elsewhere; (5) the defendant is not obliged to respond to the plaintiff's claim in any way, and not entitled to do so save by calling on the plaintiff to serve or discontinue; (6) the court cannot exercise any powers which, on appropriate facts, it could not have exercised before issue; (7) the defendant has not become subject to the jurisdiction of the court.

It would be wrong, at this stage in the life of the Convention (in so far as it affects the United Kingdom), to attempt to formulate any rule which will govern all problems which may arise in the future. I am, however, satisfied that the English court became seised of these proceedings, which first became definitively pending before it, when the defendants were served on 13 July 1989. The plaintiffs and the defendants then became bound by the Rules of Court to perform the obligations laid on them respectively or suffer the prescribed consequences of default. The defendants became subject to the court's jurisdiction unless they successfully challenged or resisted it which they were required to do then or not at all. In the ordinary, straightforward case service of proceedings will be the time when the English court becomes seised. I would, however, stress the qualification, because that is not an invariable rule. The most obvious exception is where an actual exercise of jurisdiction (as by the granting of a Mareva injunction or the making of an Anton Piller order or the arrest of a vessel) precedes service: plainly the court is seised of proceedings when it makes an interlocutory order of that kind. Further exceptions and qualifications may well arise in practice, but they do not fall for consideration in this case. I would accordingly answer this important second question in the defendants' favour.'

Ralph Gibson LJ delivered a concurring judgment and the President agreed.

Harrods (Buenos Aires), In re (1991) The Times 11 January Court of Appeal (Dillon, Stocker and Bingham LJJ)

• *Application of art 21 (art 27 EU Council Regulation 44/2001) where other proceedings or potential proceedings are outside the EC*

Facts

Ladenimor SA (a Swiss incorporated company) had petitioned the High Court for a winding up order against Harrods (Buenos Aires). Harrods (BA) was incorporated in England but its business was exclusively carried on in Argentina where its central management and control was exercised. Did the English courts have jurisdiction to stay the winding up petition on the grounds that there was an alternative forum conveniens?

Held

There was such jurisdiction in the English courts; the English court was not precluded by the CCJA from staying or dismissing the petition on the ground of forum conveniens where the defendant was domiciled in England and in another non-EC country.

Dillon LJ stated his decision as follows. The company was incorporated in England, but its business was exclusively carried on in Argentina and its central management and control was exercised there. Both the shareholder companies were incorporated in Switzerland.

By their petition Ladenimor, who asserted that the affairs of the company were being conducted in a manner unfairly prejudicial to them, sought an order under s459 of the 1985 Act that Intercomfinanz purchase Ladenimor's shares in the company, alternatively that the company be wound up compulsorily under the 1986 Act. By the relevant statutory rules the company was a necessary party to the proceedings.

The judge held, inter alia, that the English

court and not the Argentine court was the appropriate forum for the trial of the action. But in their Lordship's court a preliminary issue of importance had been taken on behalf of Ladenimor.

It was submitted that as a result of the 1968 Convention the English court had no jurisdiction to refuse on the ground of forum non conveniens to decide the issues raised by the petition, since for the purposes of the Convention the company was domiciled in England, albeit also domiciled in Argentina.

The Convention was set out in Schedule 1 to the Civil Jurisdiction and Judgments Act 1982, by s2 of which it had the force of law in the United Kingdom. With exceptions presently immaterial, the Convention applied in all civil and commercial matters.

Article 2, which was fundamental to the preliminary issue, provided: 'Subject to the provisions of this Convention, persons domiciled in a Contracting State shall, whatever their nationality, be sued in the courts of that state ...'

His Lordship referred to other Articles, and said that it was particularly to be noted that the doctrine of forum conveniens under English and Scottish law, as elaborated in *The Spiliada* [1987] AC 460, was not a recognised basis for jurisdiction under the Convention where the contest was between the jurisdiction of Contracting States.

It was implicit in s49 of the 1982 Act that the court could not stay, strike out or dismiss any proceedings on the ground of forum non conveniens where to do so would be inconsistent with the Convention, and that covered all cases where the defendant in proceedings in England was domiciled in England and the conflict of jurisdiction was between the English court and the court of another Contracting State.

The question was whether there was a similar prohibition where the conflict of jurisdiction was between the English court and the courts of a Non-Contracting State, no other Contracting State being involved.

In *S & W Berisford plc* v *New Hampshire Insurance Co* [1990] 3 WLR 688, where there was a dispute between an American company based in New York and the defendant company, deemed to be domiciled in the United Kingdom, Mr Justice Hobhouse held that the English court had no jurisdiction to stay the action.

That decision was followed by Mr Justice Potter in *Arkwright Mutual Insurance Co* v *Bryanston Insurance Co Ltd* [1990] 3 WLR 705.

The answer to the question depended on the true construction of the Convention and the starting point was art 220 of the EC Treaty, whose implementation was stated in the preamble to the Convention to be the desire of the contracting parties.

The object of art 220 was to secure the simplification of formalities governing the reciprocal recognition and enforcement of judgments of courts or tribunals among the Member States of the EC.

To achieve that object it was evidently decided that the Contracting States should have a common basis of international jurisdiction in matters falling within the scope of the Convention. But that common basis did not apply worldwide since, under art 4, if a defendant was not domiciled in a Contracting State, the jurisdiction of the courts of each Contracting State was to be determined by the national law.

His Lordship concluded that for the English court to refuse jurisdiction, in a case against a person domiciled in England, on the ground that it was more appropriate for the court of a Non-Contracting State to decide the matter in issue, did not in any way impair the objects of the Convention.

Article 2 did not have the wide mandatory effect which Mr Justice Hobhouse would ascribe to it where the only conflict was between the courts of a single Contracting State and those of a non-contracting one.

Differing from the rulings in *Berisford* and *Arkwright*, his Lordship would therefore hold that the English court had jurisdiction to stay or dismiss the petition on the ground of forum non conveniens.

It was not appropriate for the court to request the European Court of Justice to give a ruling on the issue.

Stocker LJ agreed and Bingham LJ delivered a concurring judgment.

Comment

Note that in reaching this conclusion the Court of Appeal differed from the two thoughtful decisions (of Hobhouse J and Potter J) in *S & W Berisford plc* v *New Hampshire Insurance Co Ltd* [1990] 2 QB 631 and *Arkwright Mutual Insurance Co* v *Bryanston Insurance Co Ltd* [1990] 2 QB 649. This is obviously a crucial issue concerning the way in which the EU Council Regulation 44/2001 affects litigants who are not domiciled in an EC country (other than England) but are subject to the English courts.

Overseas Union Insurance Ltd v *New Hampshire Insurance Co* Case C–351/89 [1992] 2 WLR 586 European Court of Justice

• *Article 21 (art 27 EU Council Regulation 44/2001) applies wherever the defendant is domiciled*

Facts

A complicated dispute had arisen between several insurance companies over a complicated reinsurance arrangement. OUI (and several other companies) brought an action on 6 April 1988 in England seeking a declaration that they were no longer bound by the reinsurance policy. The defendant was the New Hampshire Insurance Company which was a company incorporated in New Hampshire (in the USA) but which carried on business in the USA and in France and in England. However, New Hampshire had already issued proceedings in Paris against the other insurance companies (on 4 June 1987) and OUI (on 9 February 1988). Did art 21 require the English court to decline jurisdiction? The central argument of OUI was that art 21 only applied in art 3 cases (where the defendant is domiciled in another Contracting State) but did not apply to art 4 cases (where the defendant is not domiciled in any Contracting State).

Held

That art 21 must be interpreted as applying irrespective of the domicile of the parties to the two sets of proceedings. Thus there is no role for consideration of forum conveniens at any rate where the two sets of proceedings are both in the courts of Contracting States.

Judgment of the ECJ:

> 'In its first question the national court essentially seeks to establish whether art 21 of the Convention applies irrespective of the domicile of the parties to the two sets of proceedings.
>
> In order to answer that question it should be recalled that art 21 of the Convention provides that:
>
> > "Where proceedings involving the same cause of action and between the same parties are brought in the courts of different Contracting States, any court other than the court first seised shall of its own motion decline jurisdiction in favour of that court.
> >
> > A court which would be required to decline jurisdiction may stay its proceedings if the jurisdiction of the other court is contested."
>
> Thus, the wording of art 21, unlike the wording of other provisions of the Convention, makes no reference to the domicile of the parties to the proceedings. Moreover, art 21 does not draw any distinction between the various heads of jurisdiction provided for in the Convention. In particular, it does not provide for any derogation to cover a case where, in accordance with the provisions of art 4 of the Convention, a court of a Contracting State exercises its jurisdiction by virtue of the law of that State over a defendant who is not domiciled in a Contracting State.
>
> Consequently, it appears from the wording of art 21 that it must be applied both where the jurisdiction of the court is

determined by the Convention itself and where it is derived from the legislation of a Contracting State in accordance with art 4 of the Convention.

The interpretation suggested by the wording is borne out by an examination of the aims of the Convention. In *Dumez France and Tracoba* v *Hessische Landesbank* (Case C–220/88) [1990] ECR 49, the Court held that essentially the aim of the Convention was to promote the recognition and enforcement of judges in States other than those in which they were delivered and that it was therefore indispensable to limit the risk of irreconcilable decisions, which is a reason for withholding recognition or an order for enforcement by virtue of art 27(3) of the Convention.

With regard in particular to art 21, the Court observed in the judgment in *Gubisch*, cited above, that the provision, together with art 22 on related actions, is contained in Section 8 of Title II of the Convention, which is intended, in the interests of the proper administration of justice within the Community, to prevent parallel proceedings before the courts of different Contracting States and to avoid conflicts between decisions which might result therefrom. Those rules are therefore designed to preclude, in so far as possible and from the outset, the possibility of a situation arising such as that referred to in art 27(3), that is to say the non-recognition of a judgment on account of its irreconcilability with a judgment given in proceedings between the same parties in the State in which recognition is sought. It follows that, in order to achieve those aims, art 21 must be interpreted broadly so as to cover, in principle, all situations of lis pendens before courts in Contracting States, irrespective of the parties' domicile.

In view of that conclusion, it is necessary to reject the argument of the appellants in the main proceedings to the effect that the very existence of art 27(3) of the Convention shows that art 21 and 22 cannot prevent irreconcilable judgments from being given in certain cases in different Contracting States. The fact that the Convention makes provision for cases in which such situations might nevertheless arise cannot constitute an argument against an interpretation of arts 21 and 22 which, according to the case law of the Court, have the specific aim of precluding or limiting the risk of irreconcilable judgments and non-recognition.

The answer to the first question submitted by the national court must therefore be that art 21 of the Convention must be interpreted as applying irrespective of the domicile of the parties to the two sets of proceedings.'

Owens Bank Ltd* v *Fulvio Bracco and Another (1994) The Times 3 February European Court of Justice

• *Articles 21, 22 and 23 of the Brussels Convention (arts 27–29 EU Council Regulation 44/2001) are inapplicable to proceedings for the recognition and enforcement of foreign judgments*

Facts

Owens Bank had allegedly loaned a large sum of money to Fulvio Bracco and one of its companies. The loan was not repayed and the bank obtained default judgment against Bracco in St Vincent and the Grenadines (a Caribbean Commonwealth state). The bank now sought to enforce this judgment against Bracco, first, in Italy (July 1989) and then in England (March 1990). Relying on arts 21 and 22 of the Brussels Convention, Bracco argued that the English court should stay its proceedings in favour of the Italian courts. (Bracco also argued that the loan documents had been forged and sought to resist enforcement on the ground of fraud as well; this issue was determined in the House of Lords in *Owens Bank Ltd* v *Bracco and Others* [1992] 2 All ER 193.)

Held

The procedures of the Convention applied only to the recognition and enforcement of the judgments of courts of Contracting States; the

Convention laid down no rules for determining the forum for proceedings for the recognition and reinforcement of judgments given in Non-Contracting States. Thus arts 21, 22 and 23 did not apply to proceedings, or issues arising in proceedings, in Contracting States concerning the recognition and enforcement of judgments given in civil and commercial matters in Non-Contracting States.

Judgment of the ECJ:

'*Enforcement of judgments from Non-Contracting States*

The first and second questions referred to the Court had arisen in proceedings which were intended to pave the way in one of the Contracting States to the execution of a judgment given in a civil and commercial matter in a Non-Contracting State.

In view of the purpose of such proceedings, the House of Lords had asked whether the Brussels Convention, in particular arts 21, 22 or 23, applied to proceedings, or issues arising in proceedings, in Contracting States concerning the recognition and enforcement of judgments given in civil and commercial matters in Non-Contracting States.

Fulvio Bracco and Bracco SpA maintained that such proceedings involved civil and commercial matters as defined in art 1 of the Convention and that consequently they fell within the scope of the Convention.

That view could not be accepted.

First, it followed from the wording of arts 26 and 31 of the Convention, which had to be read in conjunction with art 25, that the procedures envisaged by Title III of the Convention, concerning recognition and enforcement, applied only in the case of decisions given by the courts of a Contracting State.

Articles 26 and 31 referred only to "a judgment given in a Contracting State" while art 25 provided that, for the purposes of the Convention, "judgment" meant any judgement given by a court or tribunal of a Contracting State, whatever the judgment might be called.

Next, with regard to the rules on jurisdiction contained in Title II of the Convention, the Convention was, according to its preamble, intended to implement provisions in art 220 of the EEC Treaty by which the member states of the Community undertook to simplify formalities governing the reciprocal recognition and enforcement of judgments of courts or tribunals.

Moreover, one of the objectives of the Convention was to strengthen in the Community the legal protection of persons therein established while also ensuring the greatest possible degree of legal certainty.

To that end, Title II of the Convention established certain rules of jurisdiction which, after laying down the principle that persons domiciled in a Contracting State were to be sued in the courts of that state, went on to determine restrictively the cases in which that principle was not to apply.

So it was clear that Title II of the Convention laid down no rules, determining the forum for proceedings for the recognition and enforcement of judgments given in Non-Contracting States.

Contrary to the arguments advanced by Fulvio Bracco and Bracco SpA, art 16(5), which provided that in proceedings concerned with the enforcement of judgments the courts of the Contracting State in which the judgment had been or was to be enforced were to have exclusive jurisdiction, had indeed to be read in conjunction with art 25, which applied only to judgments given by a court or tribunal of a Contracting State.

It has therefore to be concluded that the Convention did not apply to proceedings for the enforcement of judgments given in civil and commercial matters in Non-Contracting States.

Issues arising in enforcement proceedings

The essential purpose of a decision given by a court of a Contracting State on an issue arising in proceedings for the enforcement of a judgment given in a Non-Contracting State, even where that issue was tried inter partes, was to determine whether, under the law of the state in which recognition was sought or, as the case might be, under the rules of any agreement applicable to that state's relations with Non-Contracting

States, there existed any ground for refusing recognition and enforcement of the judgment in question.

That decision was not severable from the question of recognition and enforcement.

Furthermore, according to arts 27 and 28 of the Convention, read in conjunction with art 34, the question whether any such ground existed in the case of judgments given in another Contracting State fell to be determined in the proceedings in which recognition and enforcement of those judgments was sought.

There was no reason to consider that the position was any different where the same question arose in proceedings concerning the recognition and enforcement of judgments given in Non-Contracting States.

On the contrary, the principle of legal certainty, which was one of the objectives of the Convention militated against making any distinction between or order for enforcement simpliciter and a decision of a court of a Contracting State on an issue arising in proceedings to enforce a judgment given in a Non-Contracting State.

Last, it was clear from the judgment in Case C–190/89 *Marc Rich and Co AG* v *Società Italiana Impianti PA* (The Times September 20, 1991; [1991] TLR 418; [1991] ECR I–3855) that if, by virtue of its subject-matter, a dispute fell outside the scope of the Convention, the existence of a preliminary issue which the court had to resolve in order to determine the dispute could not, whatever that issue might be, justify application of the Convention.

In view of the answer given to the first and second questions, the third question did not call for a reply.

On those grounds, the European Court (Sixth Chamber) ruled:

The Convention of September 27, 1968 on Jurisdiction and the Enforcement of Judgments in Civil and Commercial Matters, in particular arts 21, 22 and 23, did not apply to proceedings, or issues arising in proceedings, in Contracting States concerning the recognition and enforcement of judgments given in civil and commercial matters in Non-Contracting States.'

***Republic of Haiti and Others* v *Duvalier and Others* [1988] 2 WLR 261 Court of Appeal (Fox, Stocker and Staughton LJJ)**

• *Obligation to make available in aid of the courts of Contracting States provisional and protective measures – art 21*

Facts

In proceedings commenced in France the Republic of Haiti was seeking to recover from the defendant Duvalier (the deposed dictator of Haiti) and certain other persons $120 million of the republic's money embezzled by the defendants. The Republic now issued a writ in England claiming orders restraining the defendants from disposing of certain of their assets (ie a Mareva injunction (freezing order)) and requiring them to disclose information about their assets. But since the defendants were outside the jurisdiction how could the writ be served upon them? Moreover, there were no substantive proceedings contemplated in England; did this not fall foul of *The Siskina*?

Held

Under s25(1) of the Civil Jurisdiction and Judgments Act 1982 the court had jurisdiction where 'proceedings have been or are to be commenced in a Contracting State other than the United Kingdom'; this brought the English proceedings within 0.11 r1(2) which provided that the writ could be served outside the jurisdiction without leave. The court also discussed a number of other issues including the territorial range of Mareva injunctions (freezing orders) and the *Babanaft* proviso.

Staughton LJ:

> '*Service without leave*
> The crucial feature of this case is that the republic does not seek any substantive relief in England. It seeks only information, as to where the assets of the Duvalier family are, and a temporary restraint on dealing with those assets. It is said that these remedies

are sought in aid of the French action; and so in a sense they are. But whether further proceedings will be confined to France, and to the tribunal of Grasse, is at the very least doubtful. To the extent that the information already disclosed, and to be disclosed under the order of Leggatt J, reveals assets in other jurisdictions, there may well be other proceedings of an interim nature and possibly also seeking substantive relief.

Until the Civil Jurisdiction and Judgments Act 1982 came into force, an English court would not have entertained a claim of this limited nature. The republic would not have had a cause of action: see *Siskina (Owners of cargo lately laden on board)* v *Distos Compania Naviera SA* [1979] AC 210. There Lord Diplock said at p256:

> "A right to obtain an interlocutory injunction is not a cause of action. It cannot stand on its own ... the High Court has no power to grant an interlocutory injunction except in protection or assertion of some legal or equitable right which it has jurisdiction to enforce by final judgment ..."

That conclusion is now superseded by s25(1) of the Civil Jurisdiction and Judgments Act 1982:

> "The High Court in England and Wales or Northern Ireland shall have power to grant interim relief where (a) proceedings have been or are to be commenced in a Contracting State other than the United Kingdom ..."

Mr Gee, for the defendants, does not dispute that there can now be English proceedings in which only interim relief is sought, if the requirements of that subsection are met. But he contends that there is no means of effecting service of such proceedings out of the jurisdiction, should that be necessary. If right, this is a curious result, since s25(2) expressly confers a discretion to refuse that relief if:

> "the fact that the court has no jurisdiction apart from this section in relation to the subject-matter of the proceedings ... makes it inexpedient for the court to grant it."

Power to effect service out of the jurisdiction must be found in the Rules of the Supreme Court: see RSC O.6 r7. The primary contention of Mr Strauss, which the judge accepted, is that it is to be found in O.11 r1(2):

> "Service of a writ out of the jurisdiction is permissible without the leave of the court provided that each claim made by the writ is either: (a) a claim which by virtue of the Civil Jurisdiction and Judgments Act 1982 the court has power to hear and determine, made in proceedings to which the following conditions apply (i) no proceedings between the parties concerning the same cause of action are pending in the courts of any other part of the United Kingdom or of any other Convention territory, and (ii) either – the defendant is domiciled in any part of the United Kingdom or in any other Convention territory ..."

Mr Gee submits first that a "claim" must mean a cause of action, and that an application for interim relief only is therefore not a claim which the court can "hear and determine", by reason of the *Siskina* decision. I do not accept that argument. Since the enactment of s25, either a claim for interim relief is itself a cause of action, or there can be proceedings and a claim without a cause of action. Which solution one chooses is merely a matter of semantics; there is no need to make such a sterile choice, and I do not do so. Secondly, Mr Gee submits that condition (i) is not satisfied, because the English proceedings concern the same cause of action as the French proceedings. Curiously, the Supreme Court Rule Committee used the word "concerning" in condition (i), in contrast to the word "involving" in O.6 r7(1)(b) and in art 21 of the Brussels Convention on Jurisdiction and the Enforcement of Judgments in Civil and Commercial Matters 1968. But I cannot see anything in the distinction. The answer to Mr Gee's second argument, so far as English domestic law is concerned, emerges from what I have already said in connection with his first point. Either a claim for interim relief does not involve or concern any cause of action, or it is based on a new and distinct cause of action created by s25. Whichever be right, condition (i) is satisfied because any cause of action with which the English proceedings are concerned or involved is not the same as that with which the French is concerned or involved.

Taking a wider view, I must refer to arts 21 and 24 of the Convention. Article 21 is in Title II, section 8, headed "Lis Pendens – Related Actions." It reads:

> "Where proceedings involving the same cause of action and between the same parties are brought in the courts of different Contracting States, any court other than the court first seised shall of its own motion decline jurisdiction in favour of that court ..."

Article 24 is in section 9, headed "Provisional, including protective, measures:"

> "Application may be made to the courts of a Contracting State for such provisional, including protective, measures as may be available under the law of that state, even if, under this Convention, the courts of another Contracting State have jurisdiction as to the substance of the matter."

It is as plain as can be that O.11 r1(2)(a)(i) was intended to reflect art 21 of the Convention, so that two Contracting States should not simultaneously try a dispute between the same parties involving the same cause of action. It is equally plain that art 24 deals with provisional and protective measures as a different topic, not impinging on art 21: see the decision of the Dutch court in *Joh Verhulst & Zn BV* v *PVBA Thovadec Plastics* [1978] Eur Ct Dig 1-21-B1. Yet if Mr Gee's argument is correct, O.11 r1(2)(a)(i) would prevent the United Kingdom giving full effect to art 24 in England and Wales if a substantive action has already been commenced in another Contracting State between the same parties.

Lord Diplock in the *Siskina* case [1979] AC 210, 260, said:

> "as art 24 of the Convention indicates, this is a field of law in which it has not been considered necessary ... to embark upon a policy of harmonisation."

This is because art 21 expressly refers to "measures ... available under the law of that state," and does not attempt to lay down what those measures must be. However, it seems to me that the Convention requires each Contracting State to make available, in aid of the courts of another Contracting State, such provisional and protective measures as its own domestic law would afford if its courts were trying the substantive action. That would he harmonisation of jurisdiction, although not of remedies.

If that be the right construction of the Convention, I refer to the words of Lord Diplock in another case:

> "It is a principle of construction of United Kingdom statutes, now too well established to call for citation of authority, that the words of a statute passed after the Treaty has been signed and dealing with the subject matter of the international obligation of the United Kingdom, are to be construed, if they are reasonably capable of bearing such a meaning, as intended to carry out the obligation, and not to be inconsistent with it ..."

Applying the same principle to the Rules of the Supreme Court, I would construe O.11 r1(2) as giving effect to the obligation of the United Kingdom in England and Wales to make available in aid of the courts of other Contracting States such provisional and protective measures as our domestic law would afford if our courts were seized of the substantive action.

Accordingly, I agree with the judge that this was a case where service out of the jurisdiction without leave was authorised by RSC O.11 r1(2). It is agreed that the action, begun by writ, ought properly to have been begun by originating summons: see O.5 r3. However, it is also agreed that nothing turns on that point in the present case. Order 11 r9(1) provides that O.11 r1 shall apply to the service out of the jurisdiction of an originating summons; consequently there may be service without leave where O.11 r1(2) would allow a writ to be served without leave. Rule 9(5) provides that r4(1)(b), which requires an affidavit that in the deponent's belief there is a good cause of action, "shall, so far as applicable, apply in relation to an application for the grant of leave under this rule." If, which I have refrained from deciding, that would otherwise be an obstacle to a claim for interim relief only, it does not apply where no grant of leave is necessary ...'

Forum conveniens

Berezovsky v *Forbes Inc (No 1) and Others* [2000] 1 WLR 1004; [2000] 2 All ER 986 House of Lords (Lords Steyn, Nolan, Hoffmann, Hope and Hobhouse)

• *Examining the application of the* Spiliada *test and assessing whether England was the most appropriate jurisdiction*

Facts

A Russian businessman commenced proceedings against the American publishers of a magazine, F, for libel. The proceedings were commenced in England and the claim for damage to reputation restricted to the English jurisdiction. At first instance the court imposed a stay on the proceedings on the basis that Russia was the more suitable forum since the connections that B had with the jurisdiction were not strong. The decision was reversed on appeal, the court finding that B had established the existence of a strong business reputation and a significant connection with the jurisdiction. F appealed, contending that (1) the court had erred in adopting the approach in Cordoba Shipping Co; in preference to the approach in The Spiliada; and (2) that the evidence suggested that either Russia or the United States of America were more suitable venues for the action.

Held

Lord Steyn:

'*Issue (4): Did the Court of Appeal apply the* Spiliada *test correctly?*

In the Court of Appeal counsel for Forbes submitted "that the correct approach is to treat multi-jurisdiction cases like the present as giving rise to a single cause of action and then to ascertain where the global cause of action arose". In aid of this argument he relied by analogy on the experience in the United States with the Uniform Single Publication Act which provides, in effect, that in respect of a single publication only one action for damages is maintainable: see also William L Prosser, "Interstate Publication" (1953) 51 Michigan L Rev 959 and Restatement Second on Torts (1977), s577A. The Uniform Single Publication Act does not assist in selecting the most suitable court for the trial: it merely prevents a multiplicity of suits. There is no support for this argument in English law. It is contrary to the long established principle of English libel law that each publication is a separate tort. Moreover, it is inconsistent with the policy underlying the acceptance by the European Court of Justice in *Shevill* v *Presse Alliance SA* (Case C–68/93) [1995] 2 AC 18, admittedly a Convention case, that separate actions in each relevant jurisdiction are in principle permissible: see also *Shevill* v *Presse Alliance SA* [1996] AC 959 and Reed and Kennedy, "International Torts and Shevill: the Ghost of Forum Shopping Yet to Come" (1996) MCLQ 108. And, as Hirst LJ observed, the single cause of action theory, if adopted by judicial decision in England, would disable a plaintiff from seeking an injunction in more than one jurisdiction. In the context of the multiplicity of state jurisdictions in the United States there is no doubt much good sense in the Uniform Single Publication Act. But the theory underpinning it cannot readily be transplanted to the consideration by English courts of transnational publications. Rightly, the Court of Appeal rejected this submission. In oral argument counsel for Forbes made clear that he was not pursuing such an argument before the House.

On appeal to the House counsel for Forbes approached the matter differently. The English law of libel has three distinctive features, viz. (1) that each communication is a separate libel (*Duke of Brunswick* v *Harmer* (1849) 14 QB 185; *McLean* v *David Syme & Co Ltd* (1970) 92 WN (NSW) 611); (2) that publication takes place where the words are heard or read (*Bata* v *Bata* (1948) WN 366; *Lee* v *Wilson and Mackinnon* (1934) 51 CLR 276); and (3) that it is not necessary for the plaintiff to prove that publication of defamatory words caused him damage because damage is presumed (*Ratcliffe* v *Evans* [1892] 2 QB 524 at 529, per Bowen LJ). The rigour of the application of these rules is mitigated by the requirement that in order to establish jurisdiction a tort committed in the jurisdiction must be a real and substantial one: *Kroch v Rossell* [1937] 1 All ER 725. On the findings of fact of the Court of Appeal, which I have accepted, it is clear that jurisdiction under O.11 r1(1)(f) is established and counsel accepted that this is so. But counsel put forward the global theory on a re-formulated basis. He said that when the court, having been satisfied that it has jurisdiction, has to decide under Order 11 whether England is the most appropriate forum "the correct approach is to treat the entire publication whether by international newspaper circulation, transborder or satellite broadcast or Internet posting as if it gives rise to one cause of action and to ask whether it has been clearly proved that this action is best tried in England". If counsel was simply submitting that in respect of transnational libels the court exercising its discretion must consider the global picture, his proposition would be uncontroversial. Counsel was, however, advancing a more ambitious proposition. He submitted that in respect of transnational libels the principles enunciated by the House in *Spiliada* should be recast to proceed on assumption that there is in truth one cause of action. The result of such a principle, if adopted, will usually be to favour a trial in the home courts of the foreign publisher because the bulk of the publication will have taken place there. Counsel argued that it is artificial for the plaintiffs to confine their claim to publication within the jurisdiction. This argument ignores the rules laid down in *Diamond* v *Sutton* (1866) LR 1 Ex 130 at 132, that a plaintiff who seeks leave to serve out of the jurisdiction in respect of publication within the jurisdiction is guilty of an abuse if he seeks to include in the same action matters occurring elsewhere: see also *Eyre* v *Nationwide News Proprietary Ltd* [1967] NZLR 851. In any event, the new variant of the global theory runs counter to well established principles of libel law. It does not fit into the principles so carefully enunciated in *Spiliada*. The invocation of the global theory in the present case is also not underpinned by considerations of justice. The present case is a relatively simple one. It is not a multi-party case: it is, however, a multi-jurisdictional case. It is also a case in which all the constituent elements of the torts occurred in England. The distribution in England of the defamatory material was significant. And the plaintiffs have reputations in England to protect. In such cases it is not unfair that the foreign publisher should be sued here. Pragmatically, I can also conceive of no advantage in requiring judges to embark on the complicated hypothetical inquiry suggested by counsel. I would reject this argument.

Counsel next put forward a more orthodox argument. He acknowledged that the Court of Appeal invoked the well-known principles laid down in *Spiliada*. Hirst LJ correctly stated that the court must identify the jurisdiction in which the case may be tried most suitably or appropriately for the interests of all the parties and the ends of justice: [1987] AC 460 at 474D and 484E. Hirst LJ [1999] EMLR 278 at 293 also emphasised that in an O.11 case the burden of proof rests upon the plaintiff to establish that the English jurisdiction clearly satisfies this test. So far there can be no criticism of the approach of the Court of Appeal. But counsel submitted that Hirst LJ fell into error by relying on a line of authority which holds that the jurisdiction in which a tort has been committed is prima facie the natural forum for the determination of the dispute. The best example is *The Albaforth* [1984] 2 Lloyd's Rep 91 where the Court of Appeal considered a claim founded on a negligent misstatement in a status report by a bank relating to the credit of a guarantor of a company's obligations under a charter party. The statement was contained in a telex sent by the bank from New York to shipowners in London. At first instance the judge set aside leave to serve out of the jurisdiction. The Court of Appeal allowed the appeal. Ackner LJ (subsequently Lord Ackner) observed (at 94):

> "... the jurisdiction in which a tort has been committed is prima facie the natural forum for the determination of the dispute. England is thus the natural forum for the resolution of this dispute."

Goff LJ (who became Lord Goff of Chieveley) observed (at 96):

> "Now it follows from those decisions that, where it is held that a court has jurisdiction on the basis that an alleged tort has been committed within the jurisdiction of the court, the test which has been satisfied in order to reach that conclusion is one founded on the basis that the court, so having jurisdiction, is the most appropriate court to try the claim where it is manifestly just and reasonable that the defendant should answer for his wrongdoing. This being so, it must usually be difficult in any particular case to resist the conclusion that a court which has jurisdiction on that basis must also be the natural forum for the trial of the action. If the substance of an alleged tort is committed within a certain jurisdiction, it is not easy to imagine what other facts could displace the conclusion that the courts of that jurisdiction are the natural forum."

There is also direct support for this approach before and after *The Albaforth*: see *Distillers Co (Biochemicals) Ltd* v *Thompson* [1971] AC 458, PC at 468E per Lord Pearson; *Metall und Rohstoff AG* v *Donaldson Lufkin & Jenrette Inc* [1990] 1 QB 391, a Court of Appeal decision subsequently overruled in *Lonrho plc* v *Fayed* [1992] 1 AC 448 on other aspects; *Schapira* v *Ahronson* [1999] EMLR 735. The express or implied supposition in all these decided cases is that the substance of the tort arose within the jurisdiction. In other words the test of substantiality as required by *Kroch* v *Rossell* [1937] 1 All ER 725 was in each case satisfied. Counsel for Forbes argued that a prima facie rule that the appropriate jurisdiction is where the tort was committed is inconsistent with *Spiliada*. He said that *Spiliada* admits of no presumptions. The context of the two lines of authority must be borne in mind. In *Spiliada* the House examined the relevant questions at a high level of generality. The leading judgment of Lord Goff of Chieveley is an essay in synthesis: he explored and explained the coherence of legal principles and provided guidance. Lord Goff of Chieveley did not attempt to examine exhaustively the classes of cases which may arise in practice, notably he did not consider the practical problems associated with libels which cross national borders. On the other hand, the line of authority of which *The Albaforth* is an example was concerned with practical problems at a much lower level of generality. Those decisions were concerned with the bread-and-butter issue of the weight of evidence. There is therefore no conflict. Counsel accepted that he could not object to a proposition that the place where in substance the tort arises is a weighty factor pointing to that jurisdiction being the appropriate one. This illustrates the weakness of the argument. The distinction between a prima facie position and treating the same factor as a weighty circumstance pointing in the same direction is a rather fine one. For my part *The Albaforth* line of authority is well established, tried and tested, and unobjectionable in principle. I would hold that Hirst LJ correctly relied on these decisions.

Next counsel for Forbes argued that, in any event, on conventional *Spiliada* principles Russia, or the United States, are more appropriate jurisdictions for the trial of the action. This submission must be approached on the basis that the plaintiffs have significant connections with England and reputations to protect here. It is, of course, true that the background to the case is events which took place in Russia. Counsel for Forbes argued that evidence in support of a defence justification is to be found in Russia. Popplewell J and Hirst LJ concluded that in the absence of a particularised plea of justification no or little weight should be given to this factor. Despite the valiant attempts by counsel for Forbes to argue that there is an evidential basis for a plea of justification, I remain unpersuaded. A full examination of the merits and demerits of the charges and counter-charges must, however, await the trial of the action. It is true that Forbes may also be able to plead qualified privilege on the basis of the law as stated by the House of Lords in *Reynolds* v *Times Newspapers Ltd* [1993] 3 WLR 1010. But the evidence of such a plea would presumably largely be in the United States where the reporters are based and where the documents are. In any event, there is nothing to indicate the contrary. Moreover, there are two substantial indications pointing to Russia not being the appropriate jurisdiction to try the action. The first is that only 19 copies were distributed in Russia. Secondly, and most importantly, on the evidence adduced by Forbes about the judicial system in Russia, it is clear that a judgment in favour of the plaintiffs in Russia will not be seen to redress the damage to the reputations of the plaintiffs in England. Russia cannot therefore realistically be treated as an appropriate forum where the ends of justice can be achieved. In the alternative counsel for Forbes argued that the United States is a more appropriate jurisdiction for the trial of the action. There was a large distribution of the magazine in the United States. It is a jurisdiction where libel actions can be effectively and justly tried. On the other hand, the connections of both plaintiffs with the United States are minimal. They cannot realistically claim to have reputations which need protection in the United States. It is therefore not an appropriate forum.

In agreement with Hirst LJ I am satisfied that England is the most appropriate jurisdiction for the trial of the actions …

I would dismiss both the petition and counter-petitions presently before the House. For reasons which are substantially the same as those given by Hirst LJ in his careful and impressive judgment, I would also dismiss both appeals.

Lord Hoffmann:

'My Lords, the plaintiffs are Russian businessmen who claim that they have been defamed by an article published in an American business magazine and distributed almost entirely in the United States but also in limited numbers in other countries including England. The article is concerned with their activities in Russia. The plaintiffs seek to invoke the extra-territorial jurisdiction of the English court to require the American editor and publishers to answer for the injury which they say has been done to them in this country. Their claim is limited to the effects of publication in England and they say that England is clearly the appropriate forum in which such an action should be tried …

The common law approach to conflicts of jurisdiction was altogether different:

There is, so to speak, a jungle of separate, broadly based, jurisdictions all over the world. In England, for example, jurisdiction is founded on the presence of the defendant within the jurisdiction, and in certain specified (but widely drawn) circumstances on a power to serve the defendant with process outside the jurisdiction. But the potential excesses of common law jurisdictions are generally curtailed by the adoption of the principle of forum non conveniens – a self-denying ordinance under which the court will stay (or dismiss) proceedings in favour of another clearly more appropriate forum.

Counsel nevertheless submitted that English case law showed that even outside the Convention, a plaintiff with a reputation in this country who complained of a libel published in this country by a foreign resident had an unqualified right to bring proceedings against him here. He referred first to the well-known decision in *The Albaforth*

(*Cordoba Shipping Co Ltd* v *National State Bank, Elizabeth, New Jersey*) [1984] 2 Lloyd's Rep 91 which decided that a negligent misrepresentation in a telex sent from the United States but received and acted upon in England was a tort committed within the jurisdiction within the meaning of O.11 r1(1)(h) as it then stood. Ackner LJ, following a dictum of Lord Pearson in *Distillers Co (Biochemicals) Ltd* v *Thompson* [1971] AC 458 at 468, said that "the jurisdiction in which a tort has been committed is prima facie the natural forum for the determination of the dispute". Robert Goff LJ said, at 96:

> "Where it is held that a court has jurisdiction on the basis that an alleged tort has been committed within the jurisdiction of the court, the test which has been satisfied in order to reach that conclusion is one founded on the basis that the court, so having jurisdiction, is the most appropriate court to try the claim, where it is manifestly just and reasonable that the defendant should answer for his wrongdoing. This being so, it must usually be difficult in any particular case to resist the conclusion that a court which has jurisdiction on that basis must also be the natural forum for the trial of the action."

The Albaforth was alluded to by Peter Gibson LJ in *Schapira* v *Ahronson* [1999] EMLR 735, in which the Court of Appeal refused to stay proceedings brought by a British national, long resident in England, against an Israeli newspaper which had a very small circulation in this country. The defendants had accepted service within the jurisdiction. The burden of showing that Israel was clearly the more appropriate forum was therefore upon the defendants. Phillips LJ, at 749, described it as an "uphill task". Peter Gibson LJ said that the fact that the tort had been committed in the jurisdiction was a factor which he said should be taken into account, but he went on to say, at 745:

> "It is common ground that the court must conduct a balancing exercise, weighing the factors which tell in favour of a trial in England against the factors which tell in favour of a foreign trial."

Popplewell J considered these cases and decided that they did not constitute an exception to the general principle, laid down in *Spiliada Maritime Corporation* v *Cansulex Ltd* [1987] AC 460, that the question of whether England was clearly the appropriate forum should be decided on a consideration of all the facts of the case. He referred to *Kroch* v *Rossell* [1937] 1 All ER 725, in which the Court of Appeal set aside an order for service of libel proceedings upon a French and Belgian newspaper, notwithstanding the fact that some copies had been distributed in England, and concluded:

> "I therefore do not accept Mr Price's view that his clients have a right, an unchallengeable right, to bring proceedings here and that it is not open to the defendants to argue on the merits about it."

This conclusion has not been disputed.

The judge then proceeded immediately to hear argument on the merits and gave another ex tempore judgment. A large number of cases were cited to him but he referred to no authority except the general principles stated by Lord Goff of Chieveley in *Spiliada Maritime Corporation* v *Cansulex Ltd* [1987] AC.460. He explained his restraint as follows:

> "Each case depends upon its own particular facts, and one element in a particular case which is absent from another case may in fact be the factor which persuaded the judge to decide the case one way rather than the other."

This seems to me entirely right and in accordance with the wish expressed by Lord Templeman in *Spiliada* (at 465) that "I hope that in future the judge ... will not be referred to other decisions on other facts".

The judge considered the evidence of the plaintiffs' links with this country. He summed it up by saying: "I take the view that the two plaintiffs' connection with this country is tenuous. There is some but it is tenuous." He went on to comment on the article: "[T]here is no English connection in the article at all ... [I]t is wholly connected with matters in Russia." He said that he was satisfied on the expert evidence that substantial justice could be done if the plaintiffs sued in Russia. The same would be true if they sued in the United States, despite differences in the libel laws of the three countries. He said:

> "The argument in favour of the case being tried in Russia is that this is a peculiarly Russian case. It involves nothing but Russia. It involves Russian witnesses, it involves Russian companies, it involves Russian personalities and it involves a period of time with which the Russian courts are more familiar than the English courts or those of the United States, with which they have no connection." ...

I come back to look at the matter as a whole. I do not have to decide whether Russia or America is more appropriate inter se. I merely have to decide whether there is some other forum where substantial justice can be done. This case, to my mind, has almost no connection at all with this country. The fact that the plaintiffs want to bring their action here is, I suppose, a matter that I should properly take into account. If a plaintiff is libelled in this country, prima facie he should be allowed to bring his claim here where the publication is. But that is subject to the various matters to which I have already made reference and, in my judgment, it seems to me unarguable that this case should ... be tried in this country.

The plaintiffs appealed against the exercise of the judge's discretion. The function of an appellate court in such a case was stated by Lord Diplock in *Hadmor Productions Ltd* v *Hamilton* [1983] 1 AC 191 at 220:

> "The function of the appellate court is initially one of review only. It may set aside the judge's exercise of his discretion on the ground that it was based upon a misunderstanding of the law or of the evidence before him ..."

The Court of Appeal [1999] EMLR 278, in a judgment given by Hirst LJ, said that the judge had misunderstood the law. After examining a large number of other cases, Hirst LJ, at 299–300, accepted the submission of Mr Price QC for the appellants that where the English circulation of a foreign publication gives rise to a "substantial complaint", the question of the more appropriate forum is "governed" by *The Albaforth* [1984] 2 Lloyd's Rep 91 and *Schapira* v *Ahronson* [1999] EMLR 735. He concluded:

> "The judge gave careful consideration to these cases in his first judgment, but unfortunately erred in principle in failing to take them into account in his second judgment, thus entitling us to exercise our discretion afresh."

My Lords, there seems to me absolutely no basis for thinking that the judge failed to take those cases into account. He had, as Hirst LJ said, analysed them in his earlier judgment. He had explained why he did not think it necessary to refer to them or any other cases again in his second judgment. He had summarised the gist of them in the passage I have already quoted when he said: "If a plaintiff is libelled in this country, prima facie he should be allowed to bring his claim here where the publication is." All that can be said is that he did not give the factor of publication in England the overwhelming weight that the Court of Appeal thought he should have done. But the fact that an appellate court would have given more weight than the trial judge to one of the many factors to be taken into account in exercising the discretion ("The factors ... are legion" said Lord Templeman in *Spiliada* at 465) is not a ground for interfering with the exercise of his discretion.

Your Lordships were invited to examine a large number of cases, both at first instance and in the Court of Appeal. I have already referred to *Kroch* v *Rossell* [1937] 1 All ER 725, in which the plaintiff proved no reputation in this country. On the other hand, in *Schapira* v *Ahronson* [1999] EMLR 735 the plaintiff had lived here for many years and acquired British nationality. The decision of the Court of Appeal in this case has since been distinguished in *Chadha* v *Dow Jones & Co Inc* [1999] EMLR 724, in which the plaintiff and the defendants were both resident in the United States. The respondents say that that case is likewise distinguishable. So it is. All the cases cited are in some respects similar and in some respects different. But, my Lords, I protest against the whole exercise of comparing the facts of one case with those of another. It is exactly what Lord Templeman in *Spiliada* said should not be done and what the judge rightly refused to do …

If, as I think, the judge did not misdirect himself on the law and the fresh evidence would have made no difference, then the appellate court cannot interfere with his discretion unless it is so perverse as to lead to the conclusion that although he recited the law correctly, he could not have adhered to the principles he was purporting to apply. But without an absolute rule, as in *Shevill* v *Presse Alliance SA* (Case C–68/93) [1995] 2 AC 18, that the courts of this country are obliged to take jurisdiction in every case in which there is publication here of a libel on a plaintiff who is known in this country, I do not see why the judge was not entitled to decide that England was not clearly the most appropriate forum for this action between Russian plaintiffs and an American defendant about activities in Russia.

The respondents say that what makes England the most appropriate forum is that the plaintiffs are claiming damages only for the injury to their English reputations. What better tribunal could there be than an English judge or jury to assess the proper compensation? And they rely on the justification which the European Court of Justice gave in *Shevill* v *Presse Alliance SA* (Case C–68/93), [1995] 2 AC 18, at 62 for the rule of jurisdiction which it laid down:

> "… the courts of each contracting state … in which the victim claims to have suffered injury to his reputation are territorially the best placed to assess the libel committed in that state and to determine the extent of the corresponding damages."

My Lords, there may be cases in which this is a relevant consideration and perhaps even an important one, although the decision in *Shevill* has attracted some adverse comment: see Mr Peter Carter QC in [1992] BYBIL 519. But the notion that Mr Berezovsky, a man of enormous wealth, wants to sue in England in order to secure the most precise determination of the damages appropriate to compensate him for being lowered in the esteem of persons in this country who have heard of him is something which would be taken seriously only by a lawyer. An English award of damages would probably not even be enforceable against the defendants in the United States: see Kyu Ho Youm "The Interaction Between American and Foreign Libel Law" (2000) 49 ICLQ 131. The common sense of the matter is that he wants the verdict of an English court that he has been acquitted of the allegations in the article, for use wherever in the world his business may take him. He does not want to sue in the United States because he considers that *New York Times Co* v *Sullivan*, 376 US 254 (1964) makes it too likely that he will lose. He does not want to sue in Russia for the unusual reason that other people might think it was too likely that he would win. He says that success in the Russian courts would not be adequate to vindicate his reputation because it might be attributed to his corrupt influence over the Russian judiciary.

My Lords, this in itself is enough to show that Mr Berezovsky is not particularly concerned with damages. The defendants were willing to undertake to abide by any order of the Russian court as to damages and to accept the jurisdiction of that court to award damages for injury to the plaintiffs' reputation in England as well as anywhere else. But the plaintiffs required and obtained from Popplewell J a further undertaking by the defendants that they would not "denigrate the integrity competence or justice of the Russian court". The real issue in this case is not about the plaintiffs' reputation in one country rather than another but the general question of whether the defendant's article was actionable defamation. It is this issue which the plaintiffs want tried in England.

That is why I said earlier that I did not think that the fresh evidence directed to showing that the article had had the effect of lowering the plaintiffs in the esteem of various bankers and accountants in London and Manchester would have affected the judge's decision. Whatever the reputation of the plaintiffs in this country, it was a reputation based on their activities in Russia. Once it is appreciated that the real object of this litigation is to show that they were defamed in respect of those activities rather than to calculate the compensation for damage to their reputations in England, the existence of those reputations is no longer a factor of overwhelming importance.

The plaintiffs are forum shoppers in the most literal sense. They have weighed up the advantages to them of the various jurisdictions that might be available and decided that England is the best place in which to vindicate their international reputations. They want English law, English judicial integrity and the international publicity which would attend success in an English libel action …

My Lords, I would not deny that in some respects an English court would be admirably suitable for this purpose. But that does not mean that we should always put ourselves forward as the most appropriate forum in which any foreign publisher who has distributed copies in this country, or whose publications have been downloaded here from the internet, can be required to answer the complaint of any public figure with an international reputation, however little the dispute has to do with England. In *Airbus Industrie GIE* v *Patel* [1999] 1 AC 119 your Lordships' House declined the role of "international policeman" in adjudicating upon jurisdictional disputes between foreign countries. Likewise in this case, the judge was in my view entitled to decide that the English court should not be an international libel tribunal for a dispute between foreigners which had no connection with this country. Speaking for myself, I would have come to the same conclusion. Another judge may have taken a different view but in my opinion it is impossible to say that Popplewell J's decision was erroneous in law.

I would allow the appeal and restore the order of Popplewell J.'

Dubai Electricity Co and Others v *Islamic Republic of Iran Shipping Lines, The Iran Vojdan* [1984] 2 Lloyd's Rep 380 Queen's Bench Division (Commercial Court) (Bingham J)

• *Query whether England was the most appropriate forum (see two-stage test in* MacShannon*) – effect of an exclusive jurisdiction clause*

Facts

The plaintiffs were the consignees and consignors of 61 steel drums of electric cable of a total weight of 837,000 kilos. Those drums were loaded on the defendants' vessel at Hamburg and carried via Bremen and Valencia to Dubai between December 1979 and February 1980. A bill of lading was issued at Hamburg on 28 December 1979. This provided that the contract of carriage, the bill of lading and all disputes would in the option of the carrier to be declared by him on the merchant's request be governed either: (i) by Iranian law with exclusive jurisdiction of the courts in Teheran; or (ii) by German law with exclusive jurisdiction of the courts in Hamburg; or (iii) by English law with exclusive jurisdiction of the courts in London. The vessel encountered rough weather in the Bay of Biscay resulting in some of the drums suffering damage. The vessel arrived at Dubai on 18 February 1980 and the drums were discharged. The goods were rejected and on 13 May 1983 the plaintiffs issued their writ in the proceedings claiming £414,800. The defendants applied to stay the action on the ground that there was an exclusive jurisdiction clause under which any dispute arising between the parties was to be tried in Hamburg. The defendants further contended that the proper law was Iranian law while the plaintiffs argued that it was German law.

Held

The defendants failed to demonstrate that a more appropriate forum than England existed.

Bingham J:

> 'The question which … arises is whether, if there is no exclusive jurisdiction clause, there should be a stay. The relevant principles are those summarized in *MacShannon* v *Rockware Glass Ltd* [1978] AC 795, and I refer also to the helpful distillation of the principles there laid down by Mr Justice Robert Goff (as he than was) in *Trendtex* v *Credit Suisse* [1980] 3 All ER 721, beginning at p733j. It is clear that the burden of proof in this situation rests on the defendant to show that there should in justice be a stay, the burden being on him initially to show that there is another clearly more appropriate forum than that in which the proceedings have been brought. The existence of such a more appropriate forum must be clear since the authorities are emphatic that the court will not, even today, lightly stay an action properly brought against a defendant served within the jurisdiction. The burden is, as I say, on the defendants to prove the existence of that other more appropriate forum.
>
> In approaching this task, it is incumbent on the court to consider all the circumstances and at that point it seems relevant to refer briefly to the issues likely to arise in this case. The first is, or may be, the title of the plaintiffs to sue, although it seems unlikely that that will, in the event, give rise to great doubt or difficulty. The first substantial factual issue which may arise is whether the goods were improperly or inadequately packaged or protected. The second is whether damage was caused to them during handling or loading, either at Hamburg or Bremen. The third is whether the goods were improperly stowed at Hamburg. The fourth is whether the damage which the goods undoubtedly suffered was caused by perils of the sea, namely, by rough weather in the course of the voyage between Bremen and Valencia. The last factual issue, as it appears at present, is whether the goods were damaged during discharge at Dubai …
>
> Reviewing these factors in toto, it appears to me that there is no clear balance one way or the other. There are some factors tending in one direction and some in the other, but I certainly do not conclude, viewing the matters in aggregate, that the defendants show a forum which is clearly more appropriate than the forum in England. This is, after all, the place in which the defendants then admninistered their European business and I can see no great inconvenience or expense or difficulty to them in defending the action here. That conclusion, if correct, makes it, strictly, unnecessary to go further, but I should allude, because the argument has been raised, to the further question which would arise if I concluded that a more appropriate forum had been established by the defendants.
>
> The question would then have to be asked and answered whether action in England afforded the plaintiffs a legitimate personal or juridical advantage. The plaintiffs answer that question "Yes" and do so because, in reliance on cl 2(b) of the bill of lading, they submit that in an English action, the agreement on the exclusive jurisdiction of the courts of Teheran, Hamburg or London, and the agreement on the exclusive application of Iranian, German or English law not having been recognised by this Court, the Hague Rules as enacted in England would apply. That, they contend, would give them a very substantial advantage because, they submit, the English law as to the package limitation provision is extremely advantageous and they rely on the provisional views expressed by the learned editors of *Scrutton on Charterparties*, at p449, which provisions, it is common ground, would not avail them in Hamburg …
>
> I should lastly indicate what my view would be if, contrary to the opinion that I have expressed, there is a valid exclusive jurisdiction clause in this case. The principles are those conveniently summarised by

Lord Justice Brandon (as he then was) in *The El Amria* [1981] 2 Lloyd's Rep 119, at pp123–124. I shall not recite the full text of his judgment on the point, save to draw attention to the fact that in this situation the discretion to stay should be exercised in favour of a stay unless strong cause for not staying is shown and the burden of proving such strong cause is on the plaintiffs. The matters which fall to be considered and which he lists, although not exhaustively, are very much the same matters as I have already considered in the context of there being no exclusive jurisdiction clause. When reviewing the matter then, I concluded that there was nothing which made Germany obviously and clearly a more appropriate forum. Viewing the matter in this context, with the burden of proof on the plaintiffs, I conclude that there is insufficient in it to bring the balance down in their favour, bearing in mind the requirement that they should show strong cause …

If, therefore, I am wrong in my initial decision on the exclusive jurisdiction clause and there is a binding exclusive jurisdiction clause in this case so that the application has to be dealt with on that basis, I would conclude that the plaintiffs do not succeed in overcoming the defendants' prima facie entitlement to a stay. Nonetheless, for reasons which I gave earlier on in concluding that there was no effective and valid exclusive jurisdiction clause, it follows that the application for a stay must be refused.'

MacShannon* v *Rockware Glass Ltd [1978] AC 795 House of Lords (Lords Diplock, Salmon, Fraser, Russell and Keith)

- *Set down a two-stage test which must be satisfied (since replaced by the two-stage test in* Spiliada*)*

Facts

Four Scotsmen living and working in Scotland sustained injuries in industrial accidents in Scotland. All the defendants were English companies having their registered offices in England. The plaintiffs, on the advice of experienced solicitors, issued proceedings in England. The defendant companies applied to stay the actions in England, leaving the plaintiffs to bring their claims in Scotland, the natural forum. They contended that the disadvantage to them of contesting the claims in England was oppressive and that the plaintiffs had shown no reasonable justification for choosing to litigate in England. They further alleged that there had recently been a deliberate policy of bringing, in English courts, proceedings arising out of Scottish industrial accidents where the only connection with England was that the defendants were English companies registered in England. They claimed that their cases should be considered in the light of the cumulative effect of that policy. The plaintiffs relied upon the affidavits of their solicitors which contended that damages might be higher, and the legal process shorter and cheaper, in England. In the first two cases, Goff J refused to stay the actions, and his decision was upheld on appeal. In the other two cases, Griffiths J considered himself bound by the decision of the Court of Appeal. The defendants appealed.

Held

The defendants had shown that the natural forum was Scotland, where they could be tried at substantially less inconvenience and expense, and the plaintiffs had failed to discharge the consequent onus upon them of showing that they would be deprived of some real personal or juridical advantage.

Lord Diplock:

'The progress of the common law is gradual. It is undertaken step by step as what has been stated in a previous precedent to be the law is re-examined and modified so as to bring it into closer accord with the changed conditions in which it falls to be applied today. But this is not to say that the result of proceeding by the latter course of reasoning will necessarily be very different from that which would have been achieved by adopting into English law a concept from some other legal system. Destinations that are very close to one another may be reached by different routes. So there would be nothing surprising in the fact that in rejecting as the appropriate route the importation into English common law of the Scots doctrine of forum non conveniens in favour of the more traditional method of developing this branch of the common law from where the precedent in *St Pierre* [1936] 1 KB 382 had left it in 1936, the majority of the House had nevertheless reached a result which could invite the comment by Lord Simon of Glaisdale [1974] AC 436, 473C: "That would be to admit by the back door a rule that your Lordships consider cannot be welcomed at the front." Whether true or not, this, with respect, is not a valid criticism of the reasoning of the majority, particularly in a case in which the English Court of Admiralty, whose jurisdiction had been invoked in rem, was prima facie a natural and appropriate forum in which to bring the action and was recognised as such by international convention.

As a result of their re-examination of the statement of the law by Scott LJ in *St Pierre* the majority were of opinion that the modification that was called for could be best achieved by giving to the words "oppressive" and "vexatious" what was described by Lords Reid and Wilberforce as a more liberal interpretation. Put bluntly what this comes to is that if Scott LJ's judgment in *St Pierre* is still to be treated as the framework on which the statement of the law is built, the words "oppressive" and "vexatious" are no longer to be understood in their natural meaning, but in some strained and "morally neutral meaning" (per Lord Kilbrandon at p478A). To continue to use these words to express the principle to be applied in determining whether an action brought in England should be stayed can, in my view, lead only to confusion – as I believe it has in the instant cases.

If these expressions are eliminated from Scott LJ's statement of the rule, the gist of the three speeches of Lord Reid, Lord Wilberforce and Lord Kilbrandon, in my opinion, enables the second part of it to be restated thus:

> "(2) In order to justify a stay two conditions must be satisfied, one positive and the other negative: (a) the defendant must satisfy the court that there is another forum to whose jurisdiction he is amenable in which justice can be done between the parties at substantially less inconvenience or expense, and (b) the stay must not deprive the plaintiff of a legitimate personal or juridical advantage which would be available to him if he invoked the jurisdiction of the English court"

omitting the reference to burden of proof which follows these words. If the distinction between this re-statement of the English law and the Scottish doctrine of forum non conveniens might on examination prove to be a fine one, I cannot think that it is any the worse for that …

The advantage must be a real one. The plaintiff's own belief that there is an advantage or, what is more likely to determine where the action is to be brought, the belief of his legal advisers, however genuinely it may be held, is not enough. The advantage that is relied upon as a ground for diverting the action from its natural forum must be shown objectively and on the balance of probability to exist. So long as it was necessary to show "oppressive" or "vexatious" conduct by the plaintiff in the ordinary meaning of those words, the test remained subjective; an unsubstantiated but bona fide belief by the plaintiff or his legal advisers in an advantage to be obtained for him by suing in the English courts might be a sufficient answer to the defendant's application for a stay. Since *The Atlantic Star* [1974] AC 436 this is no longer so.

I would allow all these appeals.'

Comment

This two-stage test was restated in the case of *Spiliada* v *Cansulex* (see below) which now represents the current position of the courts.

Owners of the Atlantic Star v *Owners of the Bona Spes, The Atlantic Star and The Bona Spes* [1974] AC 436 House of Lords (Lords Reid, Wilberforce, Kilbrandon, Morris and Simon)

• *The words 'vexatious' or 'oppressive' were pointers rather than boundary marks (see* St Pierre*) – introduced the notion of a natural forum*

Facts

The court has discretion to stay an action brought by a foreign plaintiff, if oppressive or vexatious to the defendant, giving those words a liberal interpretation. Three vessels collided in the river leading to the port of Antwerp, one belonging to A, a Dutch company, the second to R, another Dutch company, and the third to a Belgian company. The Belgian company and R applied to the Antwerp Commercial Court for appointment of a surveyor. His report appeared to be favourable to A and evidence showed that the Antwerp court usually accepted its surveyor's report. After the surveyor's appointment four sets of proceedings had been begun against A in the Antwerp court by the Belgian company, the owners of the cargo in the Belgian vessel, dependants of certain deceased crew members thereof and the owners of the cargo in R's vessel. On learning that A's vessel was due to call at an English port, R began an action in rem in the Admiralty Court. A entered a conditional appearance and applied for the action to be stayed, offering to provide reasonable security for R's claim in Belgium. Brandon J and the Court of Appeal dismissed the motion. A appealed to the House of Lords.

Held (Lords Morris and Simon dissenting)

The court would exercise its discretion and stay the action because the advantages to R afforded by arrest of the ship were substantially outweighed by the disadvantages to A whom it would be unjust to submit to proceedings in England, considering the delays before the action would be heard, the difficulty of obtaining witnesses, the additional expense of action here and the fact that A had already been exposed to a full inquiry by the Antwerp court's surveyor at R's instigation.

Lord Reid:

> 'It is said that the right of access to the Queen's court must not be lightly refused. In the present case Lord Denning MR said [1973] QB 364, 381G, 382C:
>
> > "No one who comes to these courts asking for justice should come in vain. … This right to come here is not confined to Englishmen. It extends to any friendly foreigner. He can seek the aid of our courts if he desires to do so. You may call this 'forum shopping' if you please, but if the forum is England, it is a good place to shop in, both for the quality of the goods and the speed of service."
>
> My Lords, with all respect, that seems to me to recall the good old days, the passing of which many may regret, when inhabitants of this island felt an innate superiority over those unfortunate enough to belong to other races.
>
> It is a function of this House to try, so far as possible, to keep the development of the common law in line with the policy of Parliament and the movement of public opinion. So I think that the time is ripe for a re- examination of the rather insular doctrine to which I have referred.
>
> The appellants' counsel first referred to the law of Scotland, where for a very long time the plea of forum non conveniens has been recognised as valid. No doubt it is a desirable objective to diminish remaining differences between the laws of the sister countries. But we must proceed with all due caution. That plea is particularly important in connection with the peculiar Scottish method of founding jurisdiction by arrestment ad fundandem jurisdictionem. I cannot foresee all the repercussions of making a fundamental change in English law and I am not at all satisfied that it would be proper for this House to make such a fundamental change or that it is necessary or desirable.

So in my opinion we should seek any change within the existing framework of English law. The existing basis is that the plaintiff must not be acting vexatiously, oppressively or in abuse of the process of the court. Those are flexible words and I think that in future they should be interpreted more liberally.

There was a time when a judgment obtained in one country was of little use in any other. There was a time when it could reasonably be said that our system of administration of justice, though expensive and elaborate, was superior to that in most other countries. But today we must, I think, admit that as a general rule there is no injustice in telling a plaintiff that he should go back to his own courts.

So I would draw some distinction between a case where England is the natural forum for the plaintiff and a case where the plaintiff merely comes here to serve his own ends. In the former the plaintiff should not be "driven from the judgment seat" without very good reason, but in the latter the plaintiff should, I think, be expected to offer some reasonable justification for his choice of forum if the defendant seeks a stay. If both parties are content to proceed here there is no need to object. There have been many recent criticisms of "forum shopping" and I regard it as undesirable.

I think that a key to the solution of the problem may be found in a liberal interpretation of what is oppressive on the part of the plaintiff. The position of the defendant must be put in the scales. In the end it must be left to the discretion of the court in each case where a stay is sought, and the question would be whether the defendants have clearly shown that to allow the case to proceed in England would in a reasonable sense be oppressive looking to all the circumstances including the personal position of the defendant. That appears to me to be a proper development of the existing law …

For the reasons which I have given I would allow this appeal.'

Comment

Lord Morris (dissenting):

'In my view, if the present motion is to be decided according to the principles which have for a long time guided and indeed bound learned judges and the Court of Appeal then I think that this appeal must fail. The proceedings brought in this country by the Dutch owner against the Holland America Line cannot, in my view, be regarded as vexatious or oppressive. They were not instituted in order to harass the defendants. There was no bad faith. There was no improper motive. The owner of the Bona Spes considers that as his vessel when lying moored was run into and sunk by the Atlantic Star he has a good cause of action. Rightly or wrongly he believes that in the advancement or for the protection of his legitimate financial interests his prospects of success are better in this country than in Belgium. It is not our province to decide whether he is right or wrong.

For the reasons which I have given I would dismiss the appeal.'

Spiliada Maritime Corporation* v *Cansulex Ltd [1986] 3 WLR 972 House of Lords (Lords Keith, Templeman, Griffiths, Mackay and Goff)

• *Replaced the two-stage test in* MacShannon – *'conveniens' means 'appropriate' and not 'convenient'*

Facts

A cargo of sulphur was shipped from British Columbia to India on board the Spiliada. Severe corrosion was caused to the vessel, allegedly because the cargo was wet when loaded. The shipowners, Spiliada Maritime Corporation, a Liberian company, decided to sue the shippers, Cansulex Ltd, a British Columbian firm, in England and thus sought leave to serve Cansulex outside the jurisdiction. The bills of lading contained an express choice of English law, so the case plainly fell within RSC O.11 r1(1)(d)(iii); but was this a proper case for the court to exercise its discretion to allow service outside the jurisdiction? At the same time a very similar action for sulphur damage (involving the same shippers but a different vessel, the 'Cambridgeshire') was being litigated in England and the Cambridgeshire action involved many of the same solicitors, counsel and expert witnesses as were involved in the Spiliada action. (This suggested that trial in England of the Spiliada action might be more convenient.) If the shipowners were forced to sue in British Columbia, they would be faced with a defence of limitation in the British Columbian courts but were in time in England.

Held

In an extensive review of the applicable law, that the court should exercise its discretion in the interests of the parties and for the ends of justice. In the circumstances, taking the 'Cambridgeshire factor' into account, and the fact that English law was the proper law of the contract, England was the appropriate forum for the more suitable trial of the action. Leave would, therefore, be granted.

Had leave been refused however, this would only have been done if the shippers had undertaken not to rely upon the limitation defence in British Columbia, since the shipowners had not acted unreasonably in failing to sue there.

Lord Goff:

> '(5) *The fundamental principle*
> In cases where jurisdiction has been founded as of right ie, where in this country the defendant has been served with proceedings within the jurisdiction, the defendant may now apply to the court to exercise its discretion to stay the proceedings on the ground which is usually called forum non conveniens. That principle has for long been recognised in Scots law; but it has only been recognised comparatively recently in this country. In *The Abidin Daver* [1984] AC 398, 411, Lord Diplock stated that, on this point, English law and Scots law may now be regarded as indistinguishable. It is proper therefore to regard the classic statement of Lord Kinnear in *Sim* v *Robinow* (1892) 19 R 665 as expressing the principle now applicable in both jurisdictions. He said, at p668:
>
> "... the plea can never be sustained unless the court is satisfied that there is some other tribunal, having competent jurisdiction, in which the case may be tried more suitably for the interests of all the parties and for the ends of justice."
>
> For earlier statements of the principle, in similar terms, see *Longworth* v *Hope* (1865) 3 Macph 1049, 1053, per Lord President McNeill, and *Clements* v *Macaulay* (1866) 4 Macph 583, 592 per Lord Justice-Clerk Inglis; and for a later statement, also in similar terms, see *Société du Gaz de Paris* v *Société Anonyme de Navigation "Les Armateurs Français"*, 1926 SC (HL) 13, 22, per Lord Sumner.
>
> I feel bound to say that I doubt whether the Latin tag forum non conveniens is apt to describe this principle. For the question is not one of convenience, but of the suitability or appropriateness of the relevant jurisdiction. However the Latin tag (sometimes expressed as forum non conveniens and sometimes as forum conveniens) is so widely used to describe the principle, not only in England and Scotland, but in other Commonwealth jurisdictions and in the United States, that it is probably sensible to retain it. But it is most important not to allow it to mislead us into thinking that the question at issue is one of "mere practical convenience". Such a suggestion was emphatically rejected by Lord Kinnear in *Sim* v *Robinow,* 19 R 665, 668, and by Lord Dunedin, Lord Shaw of Dumferline [sic] and Lord Sumner in the *Société du Gaz* case, 1926 SC (H.L) 13, 18, 19 and 22 respectively. Lord Dunedin, with reference to the expressions forum non competens and forum non conveniens, said, at p18:
>
> "In my view, 'competent' is just as bad a translation for 'competens' as 'convenient' is for 'conveniens'. The proper translation for these Latin words, so far as this plea is concerned is 'appropriate'."
>
> Lord Sumner referred to a phrase used by

Lord Cowan in *Clements* v *Macaulay* (1866) 4 Macph 583, 594 viz "more convenient and preferable for securing the ends of justice," and said at p22:

> "... one cannot think of convenience apart from the convenience of the pursuer or the defender or the court, and the convenience of all these three, as the cases show, is of little, if any, importance. If you read it as 'more convenient, that is to say, preferable, for securing the ends of justice,' I think the true meaning of the doctrine is arrived at. The object, under the words 'forum non conveniens' is to find that forum which is the more suitable for the ends of justice, and is preferable because pursuit of the litigation in that forum is more likely to secure those ends."

In the light of these authoritative statements of the Scottish doctrine, I cannot help thinking that it is wiser to avoid use of the word "convenience" and to refer rather, as Lord Dunedin did, to the appropriate forum.

(6) *How the principle is applied in cases of stay of proceedings ...*
In my opinion, having regard to the authorities (including in particular the Scottish authorities), the law can at present be summarised as follows.

(a) The basic principle is that a stay will only be granted on the ground of forum non conveniens where the court is satisfied that there is some other available forum, having competent jurisdiction, which is the appropriate forum for the trial of the action, ie in which case may be tried more suitably for the interests of all the parties and the ends of justice.

(b) As Lord Kinnear's formulation of the principle indicates, in general the burden of proof rests on the defendant to persuade the court to exercise its discretion to grant a stay (see, eg the *Société du Gaz* case, 1926 SC (HL) 13, 21, per Lord Sumner; and *Anton, Private International Law* (1967) p150). It is however of importance to remember that each party will seek to establish the existence of certain matters which will assist him in persuading the court to exercise its discretion in his favour, and that in respect of any such matter the evidential burden will rest on the party who asserts its existence. Furthermore, if the court is satisfied that there is another available forum which is prima facie the appropriate forum for the trial of the action, the burden will then shift to the plaintiff to show that there are special circumstances by reason of which justice requires that the trial should nevertheless take place in this country (see (f) below).

(c) The question being whether there is some other forum which is the appropriate forum for the trial of the action, it is pertinent to ask whether the fact that the plaintiff has, ex hypothesi, founded jurisdiction as of right in accordance with the law of this country, of itself gives the plaintiff an advantage in the sense that the English court will not lightly disturb jurisdiction so established. ...

In my opinion, the burden resting on the defendant is not just to show that England is not the natural or appropriate forum for the trial, but to establish that there is another available forum which is clearly or distinctly more appropriate than the English forum. In this way, proper regard is paid to the fact that jurisdiction has been founded in England as of right (see *MacShannon*'s case [1978] AC 795, per Lord Salmon); and there is the further advantage that, on a subject where comity is of importance, it appears that there will be a broad consensus among major common law jurisdictions. I may add that if, in any case, the connection of the defendant with the English forum is a fragile one (for example, if he is served with proceedings during a short visit to this country), it should be all the easier for him to prove that there is another clearly more appropriate forum for the trial overseas.

(d) Since the question is whether there exists some other forum which is clearly more appropriate for the trial of the action, the court will look first to see what factors there are which point in the direction of another forum. These are the factors which Lord Diplock described, in *MacShannon*'s case [1978] AC 795, 812, as indicating that justice can be donein the other forum at "substantially less inconvenience or expense." Having regard to the anxiety expressed in your Lordships' House in the *Société du Gaz* case, 1926 SC (HL) 13 concerning the use of the word "convenience" in this context, I respectfully consider that it may be more desirable, now that the English and Scottish principles are regarded as being the same, to adopt the expression used by my noble and learned friend, Lord Keith of Kinkel, in *The Abidin Daver* [1984] AC 398, 415, when he referred to the "natural forum" as being "that with which the action had the most real and substantial connection." So it is for connecting factors in this sense that the court must first look; and these will include not only factors affecting convenience or expense (such as availability of witnesses), but also other factors such as the law governing the relevant transaction (as to which see *Crédit Chimique* v *James Scott Engineering Group Ltd* 1982 SLT 131), and the places where the parties respectively reside or carry on business.

(e) If the court concludes at that stage that there is no other available forum which is clearly more appropriate for the trial of the action, it will ordinarily refuse a stay; see, eg the decision of the Court of Appeal in *European Asian Bank AG* v *Punjab and Sind Bank* [1982] 2 Lloyd's Rep 356. It is difficult to imagine circumstances when, in such a case, a stay may be granted.

(f) If however the court concludes at that stage that there is some other available forum which prima facie is clearly more appropriate for the trial of the action, it will ordinarily grant a stay unless there are circumstances by reason of which justice requires that a stay should nevertheless not be granted. In this inquiry, the court will consider all the circumstances of the case, including circumstances which go beyond those taken into account when considering connecting factors with other jurisdictions. One such factor can be the fact, if established objectively by cogent evidence, that the plaintiff will not obtain justice in the foreign jurisdiction; see the *The Abidin Daver* [1984] AC 398, 411, per Lord Diplock, a passage which now makes plain that, on this inquiry, the burden of proof shifts to the plaintiff. How far other advantages to the plaintiff in proceeding in this country may be relevant in this connection, I shall have to consider at a later stage. …

(9) *Application of the principles to the facts of the present case*

The judge proceeded on the basis that the relevant test was that "if the English court is shown to be distinctly more suitable for the ends of justice, then the case is a proper one for service out of the jurisdiction." The applicable principles are, I believe, as I have stated them to be; and the judge's approach was in accordance with those principles. I am therefore unable to accept the submission made on behalf of Cansulex that there was any material error of principle on the part of the judge. …

However, for the reasons I have given I would allow the appeal with costs here and below, and restore the order of Staughton J.'

Lord Templeman:

'The factors which the court is entitled to take into account in considering whether one forum is more appropriate are legion. The authorities do not, perhaps cannot, give any clear guidance as to how these factors are to be weighed in any particular case. Any dispute over the appropriate forum is complicated by the fact that each party is seeking an advantage and may be influenced by considerations which are not apparent to the judge or considerations which are not relevant for his purpose. In the present case, for example, it is reasonably clear that Cansulex prefer the outcome of the Roseline proceedings in Canada to the outcome of the Cambridgeshire proceedings in England and prefer the limitation period in British Columbia to the limitation period in England. The shipowners and their insurers hold other views. There may be other matters which naturally and inevitably help to produce in a good many cases conflicting evidence and optimistic and gloomy assessments of expense, delay and inconvenience. Domicile and residence and place of incident are not always decisive.

In the result, it seems to me that the solution of disputes about the relative merits of trial in England and trial abroad is pre-eminently a matter for the trial judge. Commercial court judges are very experienced in these matters. In nearly every case evidence is on affidavit by witnesses of acknowledged probity. I hope that in future the judge will be allowed to study the evidence and refresh his memory of the speech of my noble and learned friend Lord Goff of Chieveley in this case in the quiet of his room without expense to the parties; that he will not be referred to other decisions on other facts; and that submissions will be measured in hours and not days. An appeal should be rare and the appellate court should be slow to interfere. I agree with my noble and learned friend Lord Goff of Chieveley that there were no grounds for interference in the present case and that the appeal should be allowed.'

St Pierre and Others v *South American Stores (Gath and Chaves) Ltd and Others* [1936] 1 KB 382 Court of Appeal (Greer, Slesser and Scott LJJ)

• *The defendant must demonstrate that the plaintiff is being oppressive or abusing the process of the English court by suing in England – also that staying proceedings would not cause injustice to the plaintiff*

Facts

The appellants (defendants in the action), two English companies having their head offices in London but carrying on business exclusively in South America, were jointly liable to the respondents (the plaintiffs in the action) for rent in respect of premises occupied by one of them in Chile under a lease drawn up in the Spanish language according to Chilean law and executed by all parties in Paris, by which also all parties elected domicile in Chile. Disputes having arisen between the parties in view of Chilean legislation which the appellants contended prevented them remitting the rent from Chile without official authorisation by the Chilean government, the appellants commenced proceedings in Chile, which were still pending, claiming a declaration that the rent could lawfully be paid in notes of the Banco Central de Chile. The respondents having brought the present action in England claiming payment of the rent in sterling equivalent, the appellants applied under s41 of the Judicature (Consolidation) Act 1925, to have it stayed as being vexatious and oppressive.

Held

1. That the action was a personal action, transitory in its nature, which the English Court could competently entertain notwithstanding that incidentally it related to an immovable out of England.
2. That the legal effect of the clause in the lease by which all parties elected domicile in Chile could not properly be determined upon affidavits.
3. That though some inconvenience might be caused to the appellants by having to call evidence as to Chilean law with regard to the mode in which the rent could be paid, this did not amount to an injustice sufficient to entitle the appellants to a stay of the action.
4. That the fact that an action by the appellants against the respondents was pending in Chile was not in itself a ground entitling the appellants to a stay.

Scott LJ:

The appellants ...base their argument on two quite separate grounds: their first is that the English High Court has no jurisdiction because the plaintiffs' action relates to land situated in Chile. Their second ground, alternative to the first, is that the English High Court is not a forum conveniens; and they make the further submission (if mere considerations of convenience, however strong, do not justify a stay) that the action is, in the circumstances of the case, vexatious and oppressive and an abuse of the process of the Court. Neither their summons nor their notice of appeal to this Court indicates any ground for the argument of oppression beyond the fact that litigation is pending before the Courts in Chile in which the matters raised in the English action are in process of determination in accordance with the law of Chile, by which alone the issues between the parties have to be determined.

The appellants' first ground is a plea in bar. The Court either has or has not jurisdiction. No question of discretion enters in. In my opinion the appellants fail on this ground

Mr Evershed, as an alternative justification for an order staying the English action, contended, in the words of his summons, that the action is in the circumstances disclosed in the appellants' affidavits "vexatious, oppressive and an abuse of the process of the Court." I agree with the assumption that these are conditions to the grant of a stay, but his evidence, in my opinion, falls short of what is necessary. He gave, it is true, several strong reasons for contending that the Chilean Court is a more convenient forum: (1) the contract is in Spanish; (2) the law of the contract is Chilean as to both interpretation and performance; (3) the action is about land in Chile; (4) the respondent companies, though registered in England, carry on all their business in Chile; and (5) Chilean lawyers are so scarce in England that expert evidence for the Court here will be difficult to obtain. But these grounds go only to convenience; they do not come near to establishing the allegations of the summons. He sought to rely on the considerations summed up in the phrase lis alibi pendens, which have in some cases led to a party, who is plaintiff both here and in another jurisdiction in actions against the same defendant and on the same disputes, being put to his election. But here the respondents are not plaintiffs in the Chile action; they are defendants and the appellants are the plaintiffs. In such a case the mere fact that the other action is pending raises no presumption to the effect suggested. The true rule about a stay under s41, so far as relevant to this case, may I think be stated thus: (1) A mere balance of convenience is not a sufficient ground for depriving a plaintiff of the advantages of prosecuting his action in an English Court if it is otherwise properly brought. The right of access to the King's Court must not be lightly refused. (2) In order to justify a stay two conditions must be satisfied, one positive and the other negative: (a) the defendant must satisfy the Court that the continuance of the action would work an injustice because it would be oppressive or vexatious to him or would be an abuse of the process of the Court in some other way; and (b) the stay must not cause an injustice to the plaintiff. On both the burden of proof is on the defendant. These propositions are, I think, consistent with and supported by the following cases: *McHenry* v *Lewis* 22 Ch D 397; *Peruvian Guano Co* v *Bockwoldt* (1883) 23 Ch D 225; *Hyman* v *Helm* (1883) 24 Ch D 531; *Thornton* v *Thornton* 11 PD 176; and *Logan* v *Bank of Scotland (No 2)* [1906] 1 KB 141.

I do not think that the cases upon service out of the jurisdiction, some of which were cited to us, are sufficiently germane, to the principles upon which this appeal turns to call for discussion. Discretion looms larger in that exercise of statutory jurisdiction; under s41 there is little, if any, room for discretion; decisions on questions of degree often look like, but are not instances of, discretion.

The decision of the learned judge in the present case is clearly appealable; none the less I am satisfied it was right. I agree that the appeal must be dismissed with costs.'

Granting an injunction to restrain foreign proceedings

Castanho* v *Brown & Root (UK) Ltd
[1981] AC 557 House of Lords (Lords Wilberforce, Diplock, Keith, Scarman and Bridge)

• *In exercising its discretion the court should balance the advantage to the plaintiff with the disadvantage to the defendant*

Facts

It is an abuse of the process of the court to discontinue an action without leave when the defendant has admitted liability and made interim payments. A Portuguese plaintiff was seriously injured on an American ship in an English port. A writ was issued by English solicitors in 1977, and in 1978 a consent order was made for two substantial interim payments. Meanwhile in February 1979 a Texas firm of attorneys were given power of attorney to prosecute his claim for higher damages in the Texas courts. On 30 April 1979 a defence was delivered on behalf of the second defendants admitting liability. Within 14 days the plaintiff served notice of discontinuance, and commenced a fresh action in a Texan federal court. Parker J struck out the notice of discontinuance as an abuse of the process, and granted an injunction restraining the plaintiff from suing in the USA The Court of Appeal allowed the plaintiff's appeal, provided that the interim payments were repaid.

Held

The appeal was dismissed. The court stated that although the notice of discontinuance was an abuse of process, leave should now be given pursuant to RSC O.21 r3(1). Also that to grant an injunction it had to be shown that the English court was a forum in which justice could be done at less inconvenience and expense. (See the two-stage test in *MacShannon*.)

Lord Scarman:

> 'I turn to consider what criteria should govern the exercise of the court's discretion to impose a stay or grant an injunction. It is unnecessary now to examine the earlier case law. The principle is the same whether the remedy sought is a stay of English proceedings or a restraint upon foreign proceedings. The modern statement of the law is to be found in the majority speeches in *The Atlantic Star* [1974] AC 436 ... In *MacShannon* v *Rockware Glass Ltd* [1978] AC 795, 812 my noble and learned friend, Lord Diplock, interpreted the majority speeches in *The Atlantic Star* [1974] AC 436, as an invitation to drop the use of the words "vexatious" and "oppressive" (an invitation which I gladly accept) and formulated his distillation of principle in words which are now very familiar ...
>
> Transposed into the context of the present case, this formulation means that to justify the grant of an injunction the defendants must show: (a) that the English court is a forum to whose jurisdiction they are amenable in which justice can be done at substantially less inconvenience and expense, and (b) the injunction must not deprive the plaintiff of a legitimate personal or juridical advantage which would be available to him if he invoked the American jurisdiction.
>
> The formula is not, however, to be construed as a statute. No time should be spent in speculating as to what is meant by "legitimate." It, like the whole of the context, is but a guide to solving in the particular circumstances of the case the "critical equation" between advantage to the plaintiff and disadvantage to the defendants. No question arises on (a). I will assume that justice can be done in the English proceedings at substantially less expense to the defendants. The balance of convenience is, however, less heavily tipped against them, Texas being their headquarters. The judge directed himself correctly as to the applicable law, founding himself on the *MacShannon* formulation [1978] AC 795, 812 and dealing with (b) at length. The challenge that is

made to his decision is that, in exercising his discretion to grant the injunction, he wrongly analysed the relevant factors, giving weight to something which he ought not to have taken into account and failing to give weight to something which he ought to have taken into account: see *Birkett* v *James* [1978] AC 297, Lord Diplock at p317 …

Having acknowledged that the prospect of higher damages in America can be a legitimate advantage for a plaintiff, he gives two reasons for considering the advantage to be of little weight in this case. First, he instances a situation in which two plaintiffs "suffering identical personal injuries" sue in England but one sues also in Texas because his defendant has an office and assets there. The judge considers it would be unjust to allow the second plaintiff to recover more in Texas than the first can recover in England. But this example, upon which he heavily relies for his conclusion, is an irrelevancy. The criterion, as was emphasised in *The Atlantic Star* [1974] AC 436, is the critical equation between the advantage to the plaintiff and the disadvantage to the defendant; but not, as the judge assumes, a comparison between different plaintiffs in their separate claims against different defendants …

Secondly, he treats as "the question of real importance" whether the plaintiff is likely to obtain a lower award in England than he would in the country where he lives, ie Portugal. There being no evidence that an English award would be treated as unjustly low in Portugal, he considers the prospects of a higher recovery in Texas to be "of little weight." I reject the reasoning and its relevance. The fact that the plaintiff can sue in Texas defendants who have an office and substantial assets in Texas and that under the law there he has the legitimate personal and juridical advantage of the prospect of a much greater recovery than if he were to sue in England cannot be discarded as of little weight merely because an English award would not be regarded as unjustly low in Portugal. The discretion is not to be exercised upon such a comparison, even if there were (which there was not) any evidence to guide the judge's speculation as to the Portuguese possibilities. The balance is between the English and the American proceedings; the relative elements of plaintiff's advantage and defendant's disadvantage in each have to be weighed. The balance is not to be confused by uncertain legal, social and economic elements arising outside the two sets of litigation.

It is, therefore, open to this House to review the exercise of the judge's discretion. My Lords, upon this aspect of the case I find the judgment of Brandon LJ convincing. He found that to restrain the plaintiff from proceeding in Texas would deprive him of a legitimate personal or juridical advantage: I agree … For the reasons which Brandon LJ gives I agree with his conclusion "that the balance comes down clearly in the plaintiff's favour.'

Société Nationale Industrielle Aerospatiale* v *Lee Kui Jak [1987] 3 WLR 59 Privy Council (Lords Keith, Griffiths, Mackay, Goff and Sir John Megaw)

• *Different principles apply to the restraint of foreign proceedings: an injunction would be granted where justice required that the plaintiff should be restrained*

Facts

A helicopter had crashed in Brunei killing Yong Joon San, a Brunei millionaire. His widow and the administrators of his estate sued the helicopter manufacturer (a French firm, SNIAS) and helicopter operator (a Malaysian Company, Bristows) in Brunei. They also sued SNIAS in Texas (whose courts claimed jurisdiction over SNIAS because the firm sold helicopters in Texas). The Brunei action against the helicopter operator was settled. SNIAS wished to issue a third party notice against the operators, but they, while willing to submit to the Brunei courts, would not submit to the Texas courts (and there was no basis upon which the Texas courts would have jurisdiction over them). SNIAS applied to the Brunei courts for an injunction restraining the proceedings in Texas. The application eventually reached the Privy Council on appeal from the Brunei courts.

Held

Injunctions to restrain foreign proceedings should be exercised according to what justice required. Where the English (or Brunei) courts were the natural forum the court then balanced the injustice to the plaintiff, if he was not allowed to continue with his foreign action, with the injustice to the defendant if the plaintiff was allowed to continue. Thus, while there would be no injustice to the plaintiffs if they had to sue in Brunei, it would be oppressive if SNIAS had to defend the proceedings in Texas and then come to the Brunei courts to seek a contribution from the operator. Thus an injunction would be granted.

Lord Goff:

> 'The law relating to injunctions restraining a party from commencing or pursuing legal proceedings in a foreign jurisdiction has a long history, stretching back at least as far as the early 19th century. From an early stage, certain basic principles emerged which are now beyond dispute. First, the jurisdiction is to be exercised when the "ends of justice" require it: see *Bushby* v *Munday* (1821) 5 Madd 297, 307, per Sir John Leach V-C); *Carron Iron Co* v *Maclaren* (1855) 5 HL Cas 416, 453, per Lord St Leonards (in a dissenting speech, the force of which was however recognised by Lord Brougham, at p 459). This fundamental principle has been reasserted in recent years, notably by Lord Scarman in *Castanho* v *Brown & Root (UK) Ltd* [1981] AC 557 and by Lord Diplock in *British Airways Board* v *Laker Airways Ltd* [1985] AC 58, 81. Second, where the court decides to grant an injunction restraining proceedings in a foreign court, its order is directed not against the foreign court but against the parties so proceeding or threatening to proceed. As Sir John Leach V-C said in *Bushby* v *Munday*, 5 Madd, 297, 307:
>
> > "If a defendant who is ordered by this court to discontinue a proceeding which he has commenced against the plaintiff, in some other Court of Justice, either in this country or abroad, thinks fit to disobey that order, and to prosecute such proceeding, this court does not pretend to any interference with the other court; it acts upon the defendant by punishment for his contempt in his disobedience to the order of the court; ..."
>
> There are, of course, many other statements in the cases to the same effect. Third, it follows that an injunction will only be issued restraining a party who is amenable to the jurisdiction of the court, against whom an injunction will be an effective remedy: see eg *In re North Carolina Estate Co Ltd* (1889) 5 TLR 328, per Chitty, J Fourth, it has been emphasised on many occasions that, since such an order indirectly affects the foreign court, the jurisdiction is one which must be exercised with caution: see eg *Cohen* v *Rothfield* [1919] 1 KB 410, 413, per Scrutton LJ, and, in more recent times, *Castanho* v *Brown & Root (UK) Ltd* [1981] AC 557, 573, per Lord Scarman. All of this is, their Lordships think, uncontroversial; but it has to be recognised that it does not provide very much guidance to judges at first instance who have to decide whether or not to exercise the jurisdiction in any particular case.
>
> The decided cases, stretching back over a hundred years and more, provide however a useful source of experience from which guidance may be drawn. They show, moreover, judges seeking to apply the fundamental principles in certain categories of case, while at the same time never asserting that the jurisdiction is to be confined to those categories. ... Since in these cases the court has been presented with a choice whether to restrain the foreign proceedings or to stay the English proceedings, we find in them the germ of the idea that the same test (ie whether the relevant proceedings are vexatious or oppressive) is applicable in both classes of case, an idea which was to bear

fruit in the statement of principle by Scott LJ in *St Pierre* v *South American Stores (Gath & Chaves) Ltd* [1936] 1 KB 382, 398, in relation to staying proceedings in this country, a statement of principle now overlaid by the adoption in such cases of the Scottish principle of forum non conveniens, which has been gratefully incorporated into English law. …

For all these reasons, their Lordships are of the opinion that the long line of English cases concerned with injunctions restraining foreign proceedings still provides useful guidance on the circumstances in which such injunctions may be granted; though of course the law on the subject is in a continuous state of development. They are further of the opinion that the fact that the Scottish principle of forum non conveniens has now been adopted in England and is applicable in cases of stay of proceedings provides no good reason for departing from those principles. They wish to observe that, in *Spiliada Maritime Corporation* v *Cansulex Ltd* [1986] 3 WLR 972, care was taken to state the principle of forum non conveniens without reference to cases on injunctions: see especially, at p989, per Lord Goff of Chieveley. They cannot help but think that the suggestion in *Castanho* v *Brown & Root (UK) Ltd* [1981] AC 557, 574, that the principle is the same in cases of stay of proceedings and in cases of injunctions finds its origin in the fact that the argument of counsel before the House of Lords appears to have proceeded very substantially upon that assumption. In the opinion of their Lordships, in a case such as the present where a remedy for a particular wrong is available both in the English (or, as here, the Brunei) court and in a foreign court, the English or Brunei court will, generally speaking, only restrain the plaintiff from pursuing proceedings in the foreign court if such pursuit would be vexatious or oppressive. This presupposes that, as a general rule, the English or Brunei court must conclude that it provides the natural forum for the trial of the action; and further, since the court is concerned with the ends of justice, that account must be taken not only of injustice to the defendant if the plaintiff is allowed to pursue the foreign proceedings, but also of injustice to the plaintiff if he is not allowed to do so. So the court will not grant an injunction if, by doing so, it will deprive the plaintiff of advantages in the foreign forum of which it would be unjust to deprive him. Fortunately, however, as the present case shows, that problem can often be overcome by appropriate undertakings given by the defendant, or by granting an injunction upon appropriate terms; just as, in cases of stay of proceedings, the parallel problem of advantages to the plaintiff in the domestic forum which is, prima facie, inappropriate, can likewise often be solved by granting a stay upon terms.

It follows that, through no fault of theirs, the Court of Appeal did not proceed upon the correct principles in considering whether or not to grant an injunction in the present case. It is necessary therefore for their Lordships to consider de novo, upon the applicable principles as stated by them, whether the decision to refuse an injunction should stand. …

It follows that, in their Lordships' opinion, the Court of Appeal, in concluding that Texas had replaced Brunei as the natural forum, took into account matters which they ought not to have taken into account. In the opinion of their Lordships, for reasons which are already apparent, the natural forum for the trial of the action remains, as it always has been, the courts of Brunei.

It is against that background that their Lordships have to consider the crucial question, which is whether in the circumstances of this case an injunction should be granted to restrain the plaintiffs from further proceeding in Texas. The mere fact that the courts of Brunei provide the natural forum for the action is, for reasons already given, not enough of itself to justify the grant of an injunction. An injunction will only be granted to prevent injustice, and, in the context of a case such as the present, that means that the Texas proceedings must be shown in the circumstances to be vexatious or oppressive.

Now it can no longer be suggested that the Texas proceedings are vexatious or oppressive on the ground that the plaintiffs are seeking, in an inappropriate forum, to impose a strict liability or liability for punitive damages which would not be available in the natural forum. These points have been effectively neutralised by the plaintiffs' undertaking that neither of them will be pursued, and by their further undertaking that they will not invoke jury trial which, coupled with the effect of the contingency fee system, might lead to a substantial enhancement of an award of damages. These points have therefore ceased to have such relevance as they might otherwise have had. There remains however a matter to which their Lordships attach great importance; and that is the question of a claim by SNIAS over against Bristow Malaysia. …

Their Lordships are of the opinion that for the plaintiffs to be permitted to proceed in a forum, Texas, other than the natural forum, Brunei, with that consequence, could indeed lead to serious injustice to SNIAS, and that the plaintiffs' conduct in continuing with their proceedings in Texas in these circumstances should properly be described as oppressive. Furthermore, no objection to the grant of an injunction to restrain the plaintiffs from continuing with these proceedings can be made by them on the basis of injustice to them, having regard to the undertakings given by SNIAS. It follows that, in their Lordships' opinion, an injunction should be granted.'

5 Choice of Law in Contract

The common law rules governing choice of law in contract

Amin Rasheed Shipping Corporation v *Kuwait Insurance Co* [1984] 1 AC 50 House of Lords (Lords Diplock, Wilberforce, Roskill, Brandon and Brightman); [1983] 1 WLR 228 Court of Appeal (Sir John Donaldson MR, May and Goff LJJ)

- *Where the parties impliedly choose the law to govern their contract*

Facts
The plaintiff was a Liberian company resident in Dubai who had insured a ship with the defendants, a Kuwaiti insurance company. A claim made by the plaintiff was rejected by the defendants whereupon the plaintiff sued in England. Leave to serve the writ outside the jurisdiction was, of course, required but RSC O.11 r1(1)(d)(iii) leave to be granted if the contract was 'by its terms, or by implication, governed by English law'. Thus was the contract governed by English law?

Held (by Lord Diplock (Lords Roskill, Brandon and Brightman agreeing))
That the intention of the parties, although not expressed in the contract, was that English law should govern their contract.

Lord Wiberforce held that the parties had not chosen English law, either expressly or impliedly, but English law was the system of law with which the contract had the closest and most real connection. Sir John Donaldson MR's weighing of the various factors that led to this conclusion in the Court of Appeal was approved.

Lord Diplock:

> 'My Lords, RSC O.11 r1(1)(f)(iii) [now r1(1)(d)(iii)] states as the test that is relevant to the jurisdiction point in the instant case that the policy "is by its terms, or by implication, governed by English law". English conflict rules accord to the parties to a contract a wide liberty to choose the law by which their contract is to be governed. So the first step in the determination of the jurisdiction point is to examine the policy in order to see whether the parties have, by its express terms or by necessary implication from the language used, evinced a common intention as to the system of law by reference to which their mutual rights and obligations under it are to be ascertained. As Lord Atkin put it in *R* v *International Trustee for the Protection of Bondholders Aktiengesellschaft* [1937] AC 500, 529:
>
> > "The legal principles which are to guide an English court on the question of the proper law of a contract are now well settled. It is the law which the parties intended to apply. Their intention will be ascertained by the intention expressed in the contract if any, which will be conclusive. If no intention be expressed the intention will be presumed by the court from the terms of the contract and the relevant surrounding circumstances."
>
> Lord Atkin goes on to refer to particular facts or conditions that led to a prima facie inference as to the intention of the parties to apply a particular system of law. He gives as examples the lex loci contractus or lex loci solutionis, and concludes:
>
> > "But all these rules but serve to give prima facie indications of intention: they are all capable of being overcome by

> counter indications, however difficult it may be in some cases to find such."

There is no conflict between this and Lord Simond's pithy definition of the "proper law" of the contract to be found in *Bonython v Commonwealth of Australia* [1951] AC 201, 219 which is so often quoted, ie "the system of law by reference to which the contract was made or that with which the transaction has its closest and most real connection". It may be worth while pointing out that the "or" in this quotation is disjunctive, as is apparent from the fact that Lord Simonds goes on immediately to speak of "the consideration of *the latter question*". If it is apparent from the terms of the contract itself that the parties intended it to be interpreted by reference to a particular system of law, their intention will prevail and the latter question as to the system of law with which, in the view of the court, the transaction to which the contract relates would, but for such intention of the parties have had the closest and most real connection, does not arise.

One final comment upon what under English conflict rules is meant by the "proper law" of a contract may be appropriate. It is the substantive law of the country which the parties have chosen as that by which their mutual legally enforceable rights are to be ascertained, but excluding any renvoi, whether of remission or transmission, that the courts of that country might themselves apply if the matter were litigated before them. For example, if a contract made in England were expressed to be governed by French law, the English court would apply French substantive law to it notwithstanding that a French court applying its own conflict rules might accept a renvoi to English law as the lex loci contractus if the matter were litigated before it. Conversely, assuming that under English conflict rules English law is the proper law of the contract the fact that the courts of a country which under English conflict rules would be regarded as having jurisdiction over a dispute arising under the contract (in casu Kuwait) would under its own conflict rules have recourse to English law as determinative of the rights and obligations of the parties, would not make the proper law of the contract any the less English law because it was the law that a Kuwaiti court also would apply.

I can state briefly what Lord Atkin refers to as the relevant surrounding circumstances, at the time the policy was issued before I come to deal with its actual terms; since although the policy contains no express provision choosing English law as the proper law of the contract, nevertheless its provisions taken as a whole, in my opinion, by necessary implication point ineluctably to the conclusion that the intention of the parties was that their mutual rights and obligations under it should be determined in accordance with the English law of marine insurance.

The policy was the second renewal of similar policies on the vessel of which the first was issued on April 29 1977. The assured by 1977 carried out the insurance of its ships through the London office of an English company that was a member of the Rasheed Group. As brokers for this purpose it used J H Minet & Co Ltd, ("Minets") who also acted as re-insurance brokers for the insurers. Premiums were paid to Minets in London, policies were issued by the insurers in Kuwait and sent on by them to Minets who passed them on in London to the English company. Claims, though expressed by the policies to be payable in Kuwait, were in practice settled in running accounts in sterling in London between Minets and the insurers and between Minets and the assured.

I mention, in passing, that in these days of modern methods of communication where international contracts are so frequently negotiated by telex, whether what turns out to be the final offer is accepted in the country where one telex is situated or in the country where the other telex is installed is often a mere matter of chance. In the result the lex loci contractus has lost much of the significance in determining what is the proper law of contract that it had close on 50 years ago when Lord Atkin referred to it in the passage that I have cited. As respects the lex loci solutionis the closeness of the connection of the contract with this varies with the nature of the contract. A contract of insurance is performed by the payment of money, the premiums by the assured, claims by the insurers, and, in the case of marine insurance, very often in what is used as an international rather than a national currency. In the instant case, the course of business between the insurers and the assured established before the policy now sought to be sued upon was entered into, ignoring, as it did, the provision in the previous policies that claims were payable in Kuwait, shows how little weight the parties themselves attached to the lex loci solutions. ...

Turning now to the terms of the policy itself, the adoption of the obsolete language of the Lloyd's SG policy as scheduled to the Marine Insurance Act 1906 makes it impossible to discover what are the legal incidents of the mutal rights and obligations accepted by the insurers and the assured as having been brought into existence by the contract, unless recourse is had not only to the rules for construction of the policy contained in the first schedule, but also to many of the substantive provisions of the Act which is (accurately) described in its long title as: "An Act to codify the law relating to marine insurance." To give some examples: the policy is a valued policy; the legal consequences of this in various circumstances are prescribed by sections 27, 32, 67 and 68. The policy contained two type-written insertions "Warranted Lloyd's class to be maintained throughout the policy period" and "Warranted trading in Arabian Gulf waters only"; the legal consequences of the use of these expressions in a policy of insurance is laid down in sections 33 to 35. On the other hand, the printed words include the so-called memorandum: "NB The ship and freight are warranted free from average under three pounds per cent unless general, or the ship be stranded, sunk or burnt," where "warranted" is used in a different sense; to ascertain the legal effect of the expression in this context recourse must be had to sections 64 to 66 and 76. The legal effect of the sue and labour clause included in the policy is laid down in s78. These are but a few examples of the more esoteric provisions of the policy of which the legal effect is undiscoverable except by reference to the Marine Insurance Act 1906; but the whole of the provisions of the statute are directed to determining what are the mutual rights and obligations of parties to a contract of marine insurance, whether the clauses of the contract are in the obsolete language of the Lloyd's SG policy (which, with the FC & S clause added, is referred to in the Institute War and Strikes Clauses Hull-Time, as "the Standard Form of English Marine Policy"), or whether they are in the up-to-date language of the Institute War and Strike Clauses that were attached to the policy. Except by reference to the English statute and to the judicial exegesis of the code that it enacts it is not possible to interpret the policy or to determine what those legal rights and obligations are. So, applying, as one must in deciding the jurisdiction point, English rules of conflict of laws, the proper law of the contract embodied in the policy is English law.

How then did it come about that two such experienced commercial judges as Robert Goff LJ and Bingham J came to the conclusion that the contract embodied in the policy was not governed by English law? There was evidence, and even in the absence of evidence your Lordships could I think take judicial notice of the fact, that the Standard Form of English Marine Policy together with the appropriate Institute Clauses attached, was widely used on insurance markets in many countries of the world, other than those countries of the Commonwealth that have enacted or inherited statutes of their own in the same terms as the Marine Insurance Act 1906. The widespread use of the form in countries that have not inherited or adopted the English common law led both Bingham J and Robert Goff LJ to conclude that the Standard Form of English Marine Policy and the Institute Clauses had become internationalised; the "lingua franca" and the "common currency" of international insurance were the metaphors that Bingham J used to describe it; while Robert Goff LJ [1983] 1 WLR 228, 249, identified what he described as the basic fallacy in the argument of counsel for the assured as being:

> "… that, although the historical origin of the policy may be English and although English law and practice may provide a useful source of persuasive authority on the construction of the policy wherever it may be used, nevertheless the use of a form which has become an international form of contract provides of itself little connection with English law for the purpose of ascertaining the proper law of the contract."

My Lords, contracts are incapable of existing in a legal vacuum. They are mere pieces of paper devoid of all legal effect unless they were made by reference to some system of private law which defines the obligations assumed by the parties to the contract by their use of particular forms of words and prescribes the remedies enforceable in a court of justice for failure to perform any of those obligations; and this must be so however widespread geographically the use of a contract employing a particular form of words to express the obligations assumed by the parties may be. To speak of English law and practice providing a useful source of persuasive authority on the construction of the policy wherever it may be used, begs the whole question: why is recourse to English law needed at all? The necessity to do so is common ground between the experts on Kuwaiti law on either side; it is because in the absence of an indigenous law of marine insurance in Kuwait English law was the only system of private law by reference to which it was possible for a Kuwaiti court to give a sensible and precise meaning to the language that the parties had chosen to use in the policy. As the authorities that I have cited earlier show, under English conflict rules, which are those your Lordships must apply in determining the jurisdiction point, that makes English law the proper law of the contract.

In agreement with Sir John Donaldson MR and May LJ I would accordingly decide the jurisdiction point in favour of the assured.'

Assunzione, The [1954] P 150 Court of Appeal (Singleton, Birkett and Hodson LJJ)

• *Delivering the proper law of the contract where no express choice of law has been made*

Facts

A charterparty that contained no express choice of law clause had been signed in Paris by the agents of French shippers and Italian shipowners. The charterparty was for the carriage of wheat from France to Italy in the Assunzione, an Italian ship, and the wheat was being shipped as part of an exchange agreement between the French and Italian governments (although the shipowners were unaware of this latter fact). The charterparty was in English with additional clauses in French. A great proportion of the freight and demurrage were payable in lire in Italy. The bills of lading were in French but endorsed by the Italian consignees. Did French law or Italian law govern the contract?

Held

After weighing the various factors, Italian law was the proper law of the contract.

Singleton LJ:

> 'Without doubt there are features in this case which appear to point one way, and others which appear to point in another direction. When there are a number of circumstances which have to be considered in deciding which system of law applies, a presumption or inference arising from one alone becomes of less importance. In such a case an inference which might be properly drawn may cancel another inference which would be drawn if it stood by itself. When such a position arises all the relevant cir-

cumstances must be borne in mind, and the tribunal must find, if it can, how a just and reasonable person would have regarded the problem. No good purpose is served by saying that the French charterers would never have agreed to the application of Italian law, or by saying that the Italian shipowners would never have agreed to the application of French law, for that would have meant that there would have been no contract; and there is a contract.

I can summarise the facts relied upon fairly shortly. The charterers, who were also shippers under the bills of lading, were a French organisation; the contract was entered into by a charterparty which was made in France, after discussions to which I have referred, and the bills of lading were issued in France. The language of the charterparty is English, but no one contends that English law is to be applied. Some support is given to the argument of counsel for the plaintiffs by the bills of lading which are in French, and which contain the particular terms which I have mentioned. Sir Robert relies, too, upon the exchange agreement; upon the fact that in making arrangements for the carriage of the wheat from Dunkirk to an Italian port the charterers were acting in pursuance of what had been agreed between two government departments. I do not see, in the circumstances of this case, that great help is given by that fact, if it be a fact. …

With regard to the circumstances which support the defendants' contention that Italian law should be applied, I mention these: the ship was an Italian ship owned by two Italians in partnership, and a ship wearing the Italian flag; the owners were Italians, the master was an Italian; the contract was for carriage from a French port to an Italian port; the cargo was to be delivered at an Italian port. It is right to say that loading was at a French port and discharging at an Italian port, and one may appear to cancel the other, but there are further considerations; the charterpartey provided that freight and demurrage should be paid in Italian currency. I have read clause 16 of the charterparty; I bear in mind that 80 per cent of the freight had to be paid in Italy before the ship arrived at an Italian port, and the balance had to be paid at the discharging port. Clause 7 as to demurrage payable in Italian lire, too, is of importance on this part of the case. The next point is that the bills of lading were indorsed by Italian consignees before the arrival of the ship at Venice. The judge thought that that must have been in the contemplation of the parties as the bills of lading were made out to order, by which it must be assumed that indorsement was contemplated.

I would point out that it is seldom, if ever, that there will be one of the elements or tests, and nothing else. If there is one alone, it may be that it would be right to apply the test as to the place of the contract; it may be that if the only one which there is was the flag, that would be the proper test. Willmer J said:

> "Giving the best consideration I can to the various authorities to which I have been referred, it seems to me that both parties, in putting forward their respective contentions, have stated their case too high. It is undoubtedly the fact that the place where a contract is made is a point of very great importance in considering any contract, whether it be a contract of affreightment or any other kind of contract. It is equally clear, I think, that the nationality of the ship concerned (and by that I mean the real nationality of the ship) is a matter which is obviously of considerable importance in considering the proper law governing a contract of affreightment. But it seems to me that it is putting it too high to say that the place where the contract is entered into is the fact which promotes the 'primary inference', which was the expression used by Sir Robert Aske in his argument on behalf of the plaintiffs. Equally, I doubt whether it is possible to say in these days that the flag of the ship, or, indeed, the nationality of the ship, raises anything in the nature of a presumption."

It may be that in the words the judge used in the last line he overlooked the tests stated both by Lord Wright and by Lord Atkin in the passages that I have read: that you must come down on the side of the flag if there is nothing pointing in an opposite direction. It is a position which can seldom arise. If a contract of affreightment is made in one country for shipment of goods in a ship wearing a flag of another country, different considerations arise at once; there is the place where the contract was made; and a different flag, a flag of a country other than that in which the contract was made. Those are matters for consideration, and so are the terms of the contract. Although I believe it to be impossible to state any rule of general application, I feel that matters of very considerable importance are the form of, and place of, payment. In this case payment had to be made in Italian lire, and in Italy. In the circumstances of this case I regard it as a very important feature, coupled as it is with the facts that the ship was an Italian ship and that the destination was an Italian port.

There are two other authorities of recent date to which we were referred, one a decision of Langton J, in which he put forward convenience as a test, and the other a decision of the President in the year 1936 in which he placed emphasis upon a decision according to business efficacy. It seems to me that both those decisions are completely in line with the general proposition which I have sought to state, and which is taken from the words of Lord Atkin and of Lord Wright: one must look at all the circumstances and seek to find what just and reasonable persons ought to have intended if they had thought about the matter at the time when they made the contract. If they had thought that they were likely to have a dispute, I hope it may be said that just and reasonable persons would like the dispute determined in the most convenient way and in accordance with business efficacy.

Applying the rule which I have stated, and weighing all the facts to which attention was directed, I am satisfied that the scale comes down in favour of the application of Italian law, and that the decision of Willmer J was right. In my opinion, the appeal should be dismissed.'

Bodley Head Limited, The* v *Alec Flegon (trading as Flegon Press) and Another [1972] FSR 21 Chancery Division (Brightman J)

- *Whether an author had by Russian law capacity to contract*

Facts

In an action for infringement of copyright, a British publishing company (The Bodley Head Limited) sought an interlocutory injunction to restrain a first defendant (F) from publishing in English a novel entitled *August 14,* which had been written by the Russian writer Alexander Solzhenitsyn. The Bodley Head Limited claimed to derive title from the author through H, a Swiss lawyer in whose favour the author had executed in January 1970 a power of attorney. In June 1971 H assigned, amongst others, UK publishing rights in the novel to a German publishing house, L. In July 1971 the plaintiffs acquired English translation, publication and serialisation rights for the United Kingdom from L, on condition that there should be no published English translation before August 1972.

Held

Held that the plaintiffs were entitled to the interlocutory relief sought.

Brightman J:

> 'If one assumes first publication by YMCA-Press and accepts as valid the power of attorney, the agreement between Dr Heeb and Luchterhand and the agreement between Luchterhand and The Bodley Head, it is plain that the Bodley Head is entitled to the copyright which it claims and is entitled to interlocutory relief against Mr Flegon. It is, however, submitted on behalf of Mr Flegon that The Bodley Head, in reality, has no copyright at all on three separate grounds. First, it is asserted that the publication by YMCA-Press in France was not a first publication, because the novel had already been published, so it is said, clandestinely in Russia; this clandestine system

is known as "samizdat". Secondly, it is submitted that the court ought not to lend its assistance to a person who is putting forward claims which are based on acts which he knows to be unlawful according to the law of a foreign country with which such acts are connected. Thirdly, it is submitted that under Russian law the author had no capacity to enter into the arrangement with Dr Heeb and therefore the agreement with Luchterhand and the agreement between Luchterhand and The Bodley Head have no validity…

So far as capacity to contract is concerned, the defendant relies on the evidence of Prof Kiralfy … In my judgment, this submission of the defendant also fails. There is no evidence that a Russian citizen cannot appoint an agent. Indeed, Prof Kiralfy says the contrary; I read from his opinion: "Article 64 of the Russian Civil Code recognises a written authorisation similar to our power of attorney as giving the agent the right to perform civil law transactions for his principal".

My understanding of Prof Kiralfy's opinion is that the power of attorney would be void under Russian law, not because the author lacks the capacity to appoint an agent, but because it is unlawful for a Russian citizen to trade abroad on his own account; In Russia there is a State monopoly of foreign trade under article 14 of the Russian Constitution; the carrying on of business by a Russian author would also offend article 9 of the Constitution. There appear from Prof Kiralfy's evidence to be other possible grounds of illegality.

In the result, it appears to me that any invalidity of the power of attorney under Russian law would not stem from the author's lack of capacity to contract under Russian law, but from the illegality attached to unauthorised foreign trading.

Further, I do not accept that the contract of agency was made in Russia. The power of attorney is expressed to be subject to Swiss law. The engrossment was delivered by Dr Heeb to the author's intermediary, ie to his agent, in Switzerland, and the signed document was later handed by the author's intermediary to Dr Heeb in Switzerland. Plainly neither the author nor Dr Heeb intended that Dr Heeb should perform any acts in Russia in reliance on that authority. On analysis, I am of the view that the agency was constituted in Switzerland and was intended to be governed by Swiss law and that the agency contract has no relevant connection with Russia. I have not been referred to any reported case which prevents me from holding that, in such circumstances, the author's capacity should be tested by Swiss law. There is no evidence of the author's incapacity under that law.

I fail to discern any legal or other merits in the defence advanced by Mr Flegon. In my view, the plaintiff is clearly entitled to the interim relief which is sought.'

Boissevain* v *Weil [1950] AC 327 House of Lords (Lords Simonds, Normand, Morton, Macdermott and Radcliffe)

• *An overriding statute cannot be ignored when giving effect to the proper law of the contract*

Facts

A British subject (Mrs Dora Weil) involuntarily resident in enemy-occupied territory in 1944 borrowed foreign currency (320,000 francs) from a Dutch subject (Laurens Boissevain) also resident in enemy-occupied territory, agreeing to repay it in England in sterling after the war as soon as English law permitted. The site of this transaction was the Principality of Monaco in which French francs were legal currency. Mrs Weil had taken up residence on the south coast of France approximately 20 years before the trial, though at all times she retained her British citizenship. At the outbreak of war in 1939 she was ordinarily resident in Monte Carlo. Laurens Boissevain (a Dutch subject with a domicile in Holland) had lived in France on business before the war and in 1941 had relocated to the Principality of Monaco.

Held

The sum was irrecoverable as a debt, the transaction being a borrowing of foreign currency contrary to reg 2 of the Defence Finance Regulations 1939, to which no exception could be implied in the case of British subjects for the time being in enemy territory.

Lord Radcliffe:

> 'It will be convenient at this point to set out in full the contents of reg 2(1) as it stood in June, 1944. It ran as follows:
>
> > "(1) Except with permission granted by or on behalf of the Treasury, no person other than an authorized dealer shall buy or borrow any foreign currency or any gold from, or lend or sell any foreign currency or any gold to, any person …"
>
> This regulation the Court of Appeal have unanimously held to apply to the transactions which are here in question and to produce the result that the appellant cannot recover the sterling debt arising from the loan agreement.
>
> My Lords, it would seem to follow that if the appellant is to succeed he must displace the conclusion that reg 2 applies to his case. That is a simple issue, even if its solution gives rise to some difficulty …
>
> The particular qualification for which the appellant's counsel contended amounted to asking your Lordships to introduce an implied exception for British subjects who found themselves for the time being in enemy territory or territory which the enemy has overrun or occupied. I am ready to assume that Monaco could be so characterized at the material date. But I mean no disrespect to all that was urged on behalf of the appellant in support of this exception if I say that I can see no indication that would warrant your Lordships in putting such a construction on this regulation. If we did, we should be making a new regulation, not interpreting an existing one. Nor, stated as a general exception in favour of British subjects behind the enemy line, does it commend itself to me as a very probable feature of war-time legislation. Finally, the circumstance that the repayment in London was not to take place until the law permitted appears to me irrelevant, since it is the actual obtaining of the loan that the law forbids.
>
> There is only one further matter that I wish to notice before I conclude. Fully as I agree with the Court of Appeal's view that reg 2 prohibited this borrowing and therefore renders the appellant's claim for repayment unmaintainable, I do not find it possible to base my view either on the circumstance that this transaction was an exchange of francs for sterling, or on the fact, if it be a fact, that the proper law of this contract was the law of England. Indeed, it seems to me an unmaintainable proposition that if a British subject who is within the ban carries out such a transaction in foreign currency as the regulation describes, he commits or does not commit an offence according to whether the proper law of the transaction is English or foreign These Defence Regulations were concerned with prohibiting certain acts, under the sanction of severe penalties and their interpretation cannot be assisted by considering in what circumstances the rules of private international law would uphold or reject contracts arising from those acts. I think that both the sterling element and the proper law factor are really irrelevant. I think so because I can find no warrant in the regulation itself for the assumption that it was specially designed for the support or the defence of sterling. Other regulations are, no doubt, directed specifically to this and, appropriately, base their provisions on distinctions between persons resident inside and persons resident outside the United Kingdom or the sterling area, as the case may be, and payments made to such persons. But reg 2 says nothing of this.
>
> Decision of the Court of Appeal affirmed.'

Comment

This decision should be considered in relation to art 7(2) of the Rome Convention.

Dubai Electricity Co and Others* v *Islamic Republic of Iran Shipping Lines, The Iran Vojdan [1984] 2 Lloyd's Rep 380 Queen's Bench Division (Commercial Court) (Bingham J)

• *A floating applicable law is not usually valid – there must be at the outset an applicable law of a contract*

Facts

See Chapter 4.

Held

When applying either German law or Iranian law as the applicable law of the contract, the court held that there was no valid exclusive jurisdiction clause in the contract.

Bingham J:

> 'The antecedent question which therefore falls to be determined in considering whether there is a valid exclusive jurisdiction clause or not is, what is the proper law which I should apply in seeking to determine that question? Two candidates have been advanced, the first being German law this being the candidate favoured by the plaintiffs, and the second candidate being Iranian law, that being the candidate favoured by the defendants.
>
> The plaintiffs contend that German law should apply as being the system of law with which the transaction has its closest and most real connection on the grounds that that is the country from which the goods were shipped, the country where the goods were loaded and the country in which the bill of lading was issued and, as it seems fair to infer, the contract of carriage was made. In seeking to rely on Iranian law, the defendants draw attention to the fact that the defendants are not a mere one-ship company flying a flag of convenience but a national shipping line running an established liner service. Accordingly, they submit that the flag of the vessel is an important consideration and my attention has particularly been drawn to the observations of the Court of Appeal in *Coast Lines Ltd* v *Hudig & Veder Chartering NV* [1972] 1 Lloyd's Rep 53; [1972] 2 QB 34. Both parties have drawn my attention to different passages in the judgments in that case…
>
> The choice between German law and Iranian law on the present facts is not, in my judgment, an easy one, but, being obliged to make a decision, it is my opinion that the system of law with which the transaction has its closest and most real connection is German law, and in reaching that conclusion I do not overlook the submissions made by Mr Gaisman [counsel for the defendants] that the flag of the vessel is of very much greater weight in the present case than it would be in many of the cases which come before the Courts.
>
> Approaching the matter, therefore, initially on the basis that the proper law is German, I apply myself to the evidence of German law which is before me bearing on the validity and effect of the exclusive jurisdiction clause on which the defendants rely…
>
> In the light of that evidence, the defendants emphasised and contended that the clause in question was voidable and not void; it was not invalid per se but remained an effective clause of the contract until it was challenged. Reliance was accordingly placed by analogy on the decision of *Mackender* v *Feldia AG* [1966] 2 Lloyd's Rep 449; [1967] 2 QB 590.
>
> The plaintiffs contended that, while it was quite true that the clause would not be invalidated unless the point was taken, it was nonetheless clear on the two opinions which were before the Court that a German Court would hold the clause to be invalid if the point were taken. It was further emphasised that the language used by Dr Umlauf in his affidavit was the language of offer and acceptance and it appears to me that the way in which his opinion is expressed reflects a Continental doctrine that a party is not bound by that of which he has been given inadequate actual notice. The effect therefore is, if the point is taken, that the Court will, on the authority cited, declare the

clause to be of no effect. It is, of course, true, as I understand, that this is a point which the German Court would not take of its own motion in the way that an English Court might take a point on illegality. Nonetheless, if the point were taken, the clause would be rejected and, in my judgment, the plaintiffs are accordingly correct in submitting, on the authority before me, that the clause is to be treated as invalid. It is true, as the defendants contend, that if the plaintiffs were to issue their proceedings in Germany, in all probability those proceedings would go ahead, because the plaintiffs could not be heard to challenge, or raise a procedural objection to, an action which they had themselves begun. Nonetheless, that does not appear to me to be a compelling consideration, it being, as I understand the evidence, the law in Germany that a clause intended to be incorporated in a contract in this manner is not to be given contractual effect …

If, therefore, I am right in my initial conclusion that the proper law of this contract is German law, it appears to me that, applying that law, the clause in question is to be regarded as invalid.

I must, however, proceed to review the matter on the alternative assumption that Iranian and not German law is the proper law. I have no evidence whatever of Iranian law and I therefore proceed on the assumption that it is the same as English law. As a matter of English law, it is, I think, clear and not disputed that this clause in the bill of lading is bad insofar as it envisages what may be called a "floating proper law." … The proper law is something so fundamental to questions relating to the formation, validity, interpretation and performance of a contract that it must in my judgment, be built into the fabric of the contract from the start and cannot float in an indeterminate way until finally determined at the option of one party. As I say, it is, as I understand, common ground that as a matter of English law effect cannot be given to that part of this clause. That is, however, the limit of the common ground …

I find this, as I feel bound to say, an extremely unattractive clause, introducing maximum complexity and difficulty into what could and should be a simple matter. It is nonetheless the duty of the Court to give a sensible meaning so far as possible to what the parties have agreed and not readily to reject the text of an agreement between the parties as unintelligible. If the clause had confined itself to conferring three options for the choice of jurisdiction on the carrier alone that would seem to me a clause to which effect could properly and without difficulty be given. Moreover, it would seem to me that the plaintiff could well protect himself against abortive proceedings, if that were the effect of the clause, by requesting an exercise of the option before issuing proceedings in one jurisdiction or another. I very much doubt if there is any obligation on the merchant to request the exercise of the option. I do not, however, construing this clause as a whole, think that the choice of jurisdiction can be excised from each of these sub-clauses and given independent effect if the choice of law falls. They are intimately connected with the choice of law options and are not expressed in the clause as separate options. I think, as a matter of construction, that it is artificial and unreal to give effect to the ancillary provision while rejecting the main provision to which it is, as I think, parasitic. Accordingly, I reach the conclusion that this must be treated as a case in which there is no exclusive jurisdiction, applying the principles of English law on the assumption that that is the same as Iranian law.'

Euro-Diam Ltd v *Bathurst* [1987] 2 WLR 1368 Queen's Bench Division (Staughton J)

- *Even if the contract does not involve the performance of an act in a foreign and friendly state which is contrary to that state's law, it may nonetheless be tainted by illegality*

Facts

An English firm of diamond wholesalers had insured certain diamonds against theft anywhere in the world with the defendant, a Lloyd's underwriter. The plaintiff sent the diamonds to Verena GmbH, a West German firm of diamond merchants on a 'sale or return' basis. The diamonds were stolen in Germany and a claim was made. The proper law of the insurance contract was English law, both the parties were English and the premium, as well as any claim, was to be paid in England. However, in order to evade the payment of the German turnover equalisation tax by Verena, a false invoice that undervalued the diamonds had been sent to Verena. This was an offence under West German law. Did this offence taint the contract and render it unenforceable?

Held

That a contract could be tainted with illegality and thus unenforceable (even if it did not require the performance of any act illegal were it was to be performed) if the plaintiff needed to prove illegal conduct in order to establish his claim or if his claim was closely connected with the proceeds of crime so that the conscience of the court was offended. In the present case this was not the case.

Staughton J:

'In *Mackender* v *Feldia AG* [1967] 2 QB 590, 600–601, there is this passage in the judgment of Diplock LJ:

> "It is said that the adventure insured was 'tainted' with illegality, not under Belgian law but under English law. This is a picturesque metaphor which invites analysis."

For my part, I would with respect substitute the word "demands" for "invites". Another metaphor is to be found in the speech of Lord Diplock in *United City Merchants (Investments) Ltd* v *Royal Bank of Canada* [1983] 1 AC 168, 189 – "tarred with the same brush". "Tainted" in its literal sense means contaminated with something poisonous, or with incipient putrefaction. As a metaphor in the context of a contract and illegality I think it means that, while the contract is not itself illegal, it has a connection with some other illegal transaction which renders it obnoxious.

The contract of insurance was not itself illegal in the present case; neither the making of the contract nor the performance of it, by the payment of premium on the one hand and claims on the other, was illegal by English law. The question is therefore whether it has that degree of connection with illegal acts in Germany which would render it tainted and therefore unenforceable here. One can divide this question into two parts. First, if the acts concerned had been illegal by English law, would the contract of insurance have been enforceable? Secondly, if so do the rules of conflict of laws justify reference to German law, and so produce the same result in this case? ...

So, in my judgment, a claim may be said to be tainted with illegality in English law by virtue of the *Bowmaker* principle [see [1945] KB 65] if the plaintiff needs to plead or prove illegal conduct in order to establish his claim; or by virtue of the *Beresford* principle [see [1938] AC 586] if the claim is so closely connected with the proceeds of crime as to offend the conscience of the court. On the facts of this case, I do not think that either principle would apply, even if the case were concerned only with English law. It would not be within the *Bowmaker* principle because the plaintiffs do not need to plead, or prove, or show in the course of opening their case, any of the illegal acts which I have found to be committed. They do not need to produce or prove the false invoice: see the judgment of Browne J in *Pye Ltd* v *BG Transport Service Ltd* [1966] 2 Lloyd's Rep 300, 309 ... As to the *Beresford* principle, I do not consider that the claim in this case represents the proceeds of crime at all, let alone directly and immediately or proximately. *Geismar* v *Sun Alliance and London Insurance Ltd* [1978] QB 383 is in my judgment distinguishable, for the illegality there went directly to the plaintiff's possession of the goods stolen, whereas here the title of the plaintiffs is not in any way affected by illegality. Nor do I consider that the conscience of the court would be affronted if the plaintiffs were to recover. For acts which were by English law criminal they might be convicted and sentenced. But those acts would have been at most incidental to their claim, if that. Public policy does not require that they be deprived of it. The claim is not tainted with illegality.

In the light of that conclusion, it is not, as will appear later, necessary for me to consider the second question under this head, whether the rules of conflict of laws justify reference to German law. …

From those authorities I conclude that, when an English claim is said to be tainted by foreign illegality, one must first inquire whether, applying the appropriate connecting factor, the transaction from which the taint is said to arise would be enforceable here. If not, one has next to decide whether there is sufficient connection between that transaction and the claim to amount to taint within the *Bowmaker* or *Beresford* principle. If the answer to that second question is yes, the claim is unenforceable here.

One can test those conclusions by reference to the three cases cited. In *Mackender* v *Feldia AG* [1967] 2 QB 590, a contract to smuggle jewellery into Italy would, I suspect, now be regarded as unenforceable in England, because Italy would be the place of performance. That is subject to the exception about foreign revenue law which, as Diplock LJ said, is unsettled and need not be determined in the present case. Was the insurance contract tainted by the intention to smuggle goods? It is not clear what proportion of the goods insured were to be smuggled. For my part, I doubt if that contract was tainted: it was not necessary for the assured to plead or prove their own illegality (*Bowmaker* principle), in order to recover in respect of a theft in Naples; nor did the claim represent the proceeds of crime or, in my opinion, offend the conscience of the court (*Beresford* principle). I certainly do not regard the Court of Appeal as having decided that it was a case of taint. To judge from the observation of Russell LJ in the course of the argument, he at least might well have held that it was not.

In *In re Emery's Investments Trusts* [1959] Ch 410, a contract to register securities in New York in the wrong name in order to evade United States federal taxation would be unenforceable here, since New York would be the place of performance. Wynn-Parry J must have considered that to be the case, as he referred to authority on the recognition of foreign revenue laws. He also held the claim before the court to be tainted, as it plainly was within the *Bowmaker* principle.

In *United City Merchants (Investments) Ltd* v *Royal Bank of Canada* [1983] 1 AC 168, the sale contract would have been unenforceable in part because it was in part an exchange contract, involving the currency of Peru, and was contrary to Peruvian exchange control regulations. The letter of credit contract was tainted within the *Beresford* principle, because to enforce it (as to half of the proceeds) would achieve a criminal objective – not criminal by English law, but by a system of law which the court was bound to take notice of.

Applying my conclusions to the present case, I consider that an English court would not enforce a contract to deceive the German customs authorities in Germany, subject always to the point about foreign revenue law, since Germany would be the place of performance; nor, for that matter, would it enforce a contract by Mr Bonim to reside in Germany without a permit, or to carry on business there without notifying the local authority, for the same reason. So this is indeed a case where German law is potentially relevant thus far. But the second stage of the inquiry is whether there is sufficient connection between the insurance claim and those activities to amount to taint. I have held that there is not. So German law is no obstacle to the success of the plaintiffs' claim.'

Comment

Note in this context *Dimskal Shipping Co SA* v *International Transport Workers' Federation* [1991] 4 All ER 871 (HL). Here the International Transport Workers' Federation was a federation of trade unions based in London that sought to prevent the employment of cheap labour on vessels flying flags of convenience. Dimskal Shipping was a company that owned a vessel, the Evia Luck, that flew the Panamanian flag, and which employed its crew on terms inferior to those approved by the ITWF. Because of this the ITWF threatened to 'black' the vessel while it was in a Swedish port unless Dimskal entered into fresh contracts with the crew (and an agreement with the ITWF) to bring the crew's conditions of employment up to ITWF standards and to pay the ITWF (for the crew) various sums in respect of past wages. In order to avoid the 'blacking' Dimskal entered into these agreements and paid these sums. However, they then sued ITWF in London for a declaration that the various contracts were void for duress and for the return of the sums paid under the void contracts. The proper law of the relevant contracts was English law; and under English law a contract induced by duress was voidable by the innocent party and one form of duress was illegitimate economic pressure (which included the 'blacking' of a ship). However, under the law of Sweden, where the duress was exercised, such pressure was lawful. Could this prevent Dimskal from recovering the sums paid under the contracts to ITWF? On analogy with tort where, in order to recover damages in England, the act complained of had to be actionable both under the law of the place where it was performed and under the law of England (see *Boys* v *Chaplin* [1971] AC 356), it was argued that the fact that the duress was lawful in Sweden, meant that there could be no recovery in England. Lord Goff of Chieveley, in the leading speech, rejected the analogy with tort since, for one thing, an act could amount to duress even if it was not tortious, and for another, the fact that the proper law of the contract was English anchored the matter in English law much more strongly than a foreign tort was anchored. It followed that English law would be used to determine whether the contracts were voidable for duress. Thus the ship owners succeeded. Although Lord Templeman dissented on the ground that the English courts should not concern themselves with acts lawful where they were committed, Lord Goff's speech is convincing. One wonders, however, what the position would be if the proper law of the contract had been Swedish (one may be sure that the ITWF's lawyers have already advised their clients to avoid English law in future). Presumably, the ship owners would not be able to avoid the contracts and would not recover the sums paid. However, one may readily assume that some forms of duress (for instance, a threat of violence) would allow the contract to be voided whatever the proper law for to countenance such forms of duress would be contrary to a fundamental English public policy.

Forsikringsaktiesekapet Vesta v *Butcher* [1986] 2 All ER 488 Queen's Bench Division (Hobhouse J)

• *The intention of the parties may be that the contract, or part of it, is to be interpreted by a law other than the proper law of the contract*

Facts

The plaintiffs, a Norwegian insurance company, had insured the owners of a Norwegian fish farm against loss of fish whatever the cause of the loss. Ninety per cent of this risk had been reinsured with London underwriters. The proper law of the insurance contract was Norwegian law and the proper law of the reinsurance contract was English law. Both the insurance contract and the reinsurance contract required a 24-hour watch to be kept on the fish farm. Breach of the 24-hour watch condition did not, under Norwegian law, allow the insurer to avoid liability unless the breach of the condition had caused the loss. But under English law breach of the condition provided a total defence to the insurer or reinsurer.

A violent storm then caused severe

damage (the loss of 100,000 fish). The 24-hour watch condition had been breached but this had not caused the damage; thus the Norwegian insurance company paid the claim made against it. It now sought to recover under the reinsurance contract, but was met with the defence that the breach of the 24-hour watch condition allowed the reinsurers to avoid liability altogether.

Held

That, although English law was the proper law of the reinsurance contract, in the circumstances, the parties intended that the 24 hour watch clause in the reinsurance contract was to be construed according to Norwegian law.

Hobhouse J:

'In English law the parties are at liberty, subject to certain exceptions, to choose what law shall govern their contract. They can make express provision. If they do not make express provision the court must see if it can infer what their intention was. If it cannot be inferred, then the contract is governed by the system of law with which the transaction has its closest and most real connection. But here again the rationale of what the court is doing is based on the intention of the parties: "The court has to impute an intention or determine for the parties what is the proper law which as just and reasonable persons they ought to and would have intended if they had thought about the question when they made the contract" (see *Mount Albert BC* v *Australasian Temperance and General Mutual Life Assurance Society Ltd* [1937] 4 All ER 206 at 214, [1938] AC 224 at 240 per Lord Wright). For this reason, one of the most important criteria for assessing the proper law is the object of the contract and the inferences from its express terms.

Where a contract such as the present provides that its terms and conditions are to be the same as those of another contract and where its clear commercial purpose is to provide a corresponding cover to that provided by the other contract, then, unless some other powerful consideration is to intervene, the conclusion must be that there is an intention that both contracts are to be governed by the same law. However, there remains something surprising and improbable about the conclusion that the Lloyd's slip and the Lloyd's policy are governed by anything other than English law and the decision of the Court of Appeal in *Citadel Insurance Co* v *Atlantic Union Insurance Co SA* certainly encourages one to question such a conclusion.

I consider that there is a solution to the problem of the choice of law in the present case which does give a satisfactory answer. It is the almost invariable rule that there is only a single proper law of a contract which governs all aspects of the contract. This is conceptually sound as the primary function of the proper law is to give effect to the parties' intention not merely to agree but also to make a legal contract, ie to create a legal relationship. This presupposes a legal system since a legal contract cannot be made without a reference to a legal system which is to give it its legal effect. As Lord Diplock said in *Amin Rasheed Shipping Corp* v *Kuwait Insurance Co, The Al Wahab* [1983] 2 All ER 884 at 891, [1984] AC 50 at 65: " ... contracts are incapable of existing in a legal vacuum. They are mere pieces of paper and void of all legal effect unless they were made by reference to some system of private law ..." In the present case one would prima facie assume that this underlying legal system was English law. But by the same logic the choice of law is a matter for the actual or imputed choice of the parties and it has been recognised for a long time that parties may choose that different parts of the contract should be governed by different laws. ...

In the present case there is an express provision for the terms and conditions of the reinsurance contract and those of the original insurance to be the same and the reinsurance is manifestly to be back-to-back with the original insurance. From this one should infer a contractual intent that the legal effect of the clauses which define and limit the scope of the cover should be the same in the reinsurance and in the original insurance.

When one takes into account that the parties clearly must contemplate that the original insurance is governed by Norwegian law I infer as a matter of English law that the parties intended the construction and effect of the clauses of the Aquacultural wording shall be governed by Norwegian law. Whether one chooses to categorise this conclusion as an application of the English substantive law of construction of an English law contract or as the application of the English choice of law rules does not matter. They are in the present context essentially the same thing. The parties have on the true ascertainment of their contractual intention chosen that that part of the contract shall be governed by Norwegian, not English law. It will be appreciated that it is a corollary of this particular conclusion that it is the law of Norway applicable to domestic contracts of original insurance which the parties intend shall govern, not the Norwegian law which may or may not apply to reinsurance contracts. The reinsurance contract itself is and remains an English law contract but it is one which is made with reference to, and on the terms of, the Norwegian law contract of original insurance. This view of the English law parallels that of Mr Rafen on the first point I discussed under the heading of Norwegian law and which I accepted. It follows from this that the dispute about the Norwegian law applicable to reinsurance contracts is really irrelevant and the plaintiffs could succeed even if that dispute had been decided against them.

I therefore hold as a matter of English law that the proper law of the reinsurance contract is English law subject to the construction and effect of the clauses of the Aquacultural wording being determined in accordance with Norwegian law in the same manner as they are as part of the contract of original insurance. If I had not decided that this hybrid and admittedly somewhat unorthodox conclusion was open to me, I would have been compelled to the conclusion that the whole contract should be governed by Norwegian law, because any other conclusion would be contrary to the manifest intention of the parties to provide the plaintiffs with reinsurance cover in respect of a contract of original insurance on the same terms which is governed by Norwegian law.

I accordingly hold that the plaintiffs are entitled to judgment against the reinsurers.'

The Hollandia [1983] 1 AC 565 House of Lords (Lords Diplock, Keith, Roskill, Brandon and Brightman)

• *Particular statutes from the lex fori may override an express choice of law*

Facts

A road finishing machine had been shipped from Leith in Scotland to Bonaire in the Dutch West Indies aboard a Dutch vessel. It sustained £20,000 damage while being unloaded and the shippers sued the carriers in England. The bill of lading contained an express choice of the law of the Netherlands and that law incorporated the Hague Rules limiting the carrier's liability to £250 per packet. The bill of lading also contained a clause giving the Amsterdam courts exclusive jurisdiction over disputes arising under the contract of carriage.

The English Carriage of Goods by Sea Act 1971 incorporated the Hague/Visby Rules into English law. And the Hague/Visby Rules would in the circumstances allow recovery of £11,000, which is why the plaintiffs sued in England rather than the Netherlands. The carriers, however, sought a stay of the English proceedings because of the exclusive jurisdiction clause. Would the exclusive jurisdiction clause (and the Hague Rules limitation of liability) be enforced?

Held

Article 111(8) of the Hague/Visby Rules which had 'the force of law' in England (s1 of the Carriage of Goods by Sea Act 1971) provided that 'Any clause ... in a contract of carriage relieving the carrier ... from liability ... otherwise than as provided in these Rules, shall be null and void and of no effect'. In the circumstances, the choice of jurisdiction clause fell within art 111(8) and was thus of no effect; thus the action was not stayed.

Condition 2 of the bill of lading:

> 'Law of application and jurisdiction. The law of the Netherlands in which the Hague Rules, as adopted by the Brussels Convention of 25 August 1924, are incorporated – with the exception of art 9 – shall apply to this contract. The maximum liability per package is Dfl 1,250. For goods loaded or discharged at a Belgian port, the rules of art 91 of chapter 2 of the Belgian Commercial Code shall apply.
>
> Whenever the carrier is not the owner or demise charterer of the ocean vessel, the owner or demise charterer of such vessel shall, nevertheless, be entitled to avail himself of every exemption, limitation, condition and liberty herein contained and every right, exemption from liability, defence and immunity of whatsoever nature applicable to the carrier or to which the carrier is entitled hereunder as if this bill of lading had been issued by the said owner or demise charterer in his own name and on his own behalf.
>
> All actions under the present contract of carriage shall be brought before the Court of Amsterdam and no other court shall have jurisdiction with regard to any such action unless the carrier appeals to another jurisdiction or voluntarily submits himself thereto.'

Lord Diplock:

> 'My Lords, like all three members of the Court of Appeal, I have no hesitation in rejecting this narrow construction of art III, paragraph 8, which looks solely to the form of the clause in the contract of carriage and wholly ignores its substance. The only sensible meaning to be given to the description of provisions in contracts of carriage which are rendered "null and void and of no effect" by this rule is one which would embrace every provision in a contract of carriage which, if it were applied, would have the effect of lessening the carrier's liability otherwise than as provided in the Rules. To ascribe to it the narrow meaning for which counsel contended would leave it open to any shipowner to evade the provisions of art III, paragraph 8 by the simple device of inserting in his bills of lading issued in, or for carriage from a port in, any Contracting State a clause in standard form providing as the exclusive forum for resolution of disputes what might aptly be described as a court of convenience, viz, one situated in a country which did not apply the Hague/Visby Rules or, for that matter, a country whose law recognised an unfettered right in a shipowner by the terms of the bill of lading to relieve himself from all liability for loss or damage to the goods caused by his own negligence, fault or breach of contract.
>
> My Lords, unlike the first paragraph of condition 2 a choice of forum clause, such as that appearing in the third paragraph, does not ex facie offend against art III, paragraph 8. It is a provision of the contract of carriage that is subject to a condition subsequent; it comes into operation only upon the occurrence of a future event that may or may not occur, viz: the coming into existence of a dispute between the parties as to their respective legal rights and duties under the contract which they are unable to settle by agreement. There may be some disputes that would bring the choice of forum clause into operation but which would not be concerned at all with negligence fault or failure by the carrier or the ship in the duties and obligations provided by art III; a claim for unpaid freight is an obvious example. So a choice of forum clause which selects as the exclusive forum for the resolution of disputes a court which will not apply the Hague/Visby Rules, even after such clause has come into operation, does not necessarily always have the effect of lessening the liability of the carrier in a way that attracts the application of art III, paragraph 8.
>
> My Lords, it is, in my view, most consistent with the achievement of the purpose of the Act of 1971 that the time at which to ascertain whether a choice of forum clause will have an effect that is proscribed by art III, paragraph 8 should be when the condition subsequent is fulfilled and the carrier

seeks to bring the clause into operation and to rely upon it. If the dispute is about duties and obligations of the carrier or ship that are referred to in that rule and it is established as a fact (either by evidence or as in the instant case by the common agreement of the parties) that the foreign court chosen as the exclusive forum would apply a domestic substantive law which would result in limiting the carrier's liability to a sum lower than that to which he would be entitled if art IV, paragraph 5 of the Hague/Visby Rules applied, then an English court is in my view commanded by the Act of 1971 to treat the choice of forum clause as of no effect.

The rule itself speaks of a proscribed provision in a contract of carriage as a "clause, covenant, or agreement in a contract of carriage" and describes the effect of the rule on the offending provision as being to render it "null and void and of no effect". These pleonastic expressions occurring in an international convention (of which the similarly pleonastic version in the French language is of equal authenticity) are not to be construed as technical terms of legal art. It may well be that if they were to be so construed the most apt to be applied to a choice of forum clause when brought into operation by the occurrence of a particular dispute would be the expression "of no effect," but it is no misuse of ordinary language to describe the clause in its application to the particular dispute as being pro tanto "null" or "void" or both.

As foreshadowed at an earlier point in this speech I must return in a brief postscript to an argument based on certain passages in an article by a distinguished commentator, Dr F A Mann, "Statutes and the Conflict of Laws" which appeared in (1972–73) 46 BYIL 117, and which, it is suggested, supports the view that even a choice of substantive law, which excludes the application of the Hague/Visby Rules, is not prohibited by the Act of 1971 notwithstanding that the bill of lading is issued in and is for carriage from a port in, the United Kingdom. The passages to which our attention was directed by counsel for the carriers I find myself (apparently in respectable academic company) unable to accept. They draw no distinction between the Act of 1924 and the Act of 1971 despite the contrast between the legislative techniques adopted in the two Acts, and the express inclusion in the Hague/Visby Rules of art X (absent from the Hagues Rules), expressly applying the Hague/Visby Rules to every bill of lading falling within the description contained in the article, which article is given the force of law in the United Kingdom by s1(2) of the Act of 1971. The Act of 1971 deliberately abandoned what may conveniently be termed the "clause paramount" technique employed in s3 of the Act of 1924, the Newfoundland counterpart of which provided the occasion for wide-ranging dicta in the opinion of the Privy Council delivered by Lord Wright in *Vita Food Products Inc* v *Unus Shipping Co Ltd* [1939] AC 277. Although the actual decision in that case would have been the same if the relevant Newfoundland statute had been in the terms of the Act of 1971, those dicta have no application to the construction of the latter Act and this has rendered it no longer necessary to embark upon what I have always found to be an unrewarding task of trying to ascertain precisely what those dicta meant.

I would dismiss this appeal.'

Regazzoni v *K C Sethia (1944) Ltd* [1958] AC 301 House of Lords (Viscount Simonds, Lords Reid, Cohen, Keith and Somervell)

• *English courts will not enforce a contract, or award damages for its breach, if its performance would involve the doing of an act in a foreign and friendly state that violates the law of that state*

Facts

See the discussion of and extracts from this case in Chapter 2.

Comment

Note an exception to the above rule created in *Howard* v *Shirlstar Container Transport Ltd* [1990] 3 All ER 366. Here two aircraft had been leased from the defendant company but the lessees had ceased to pay the hire and had taken the aircraft to Nigeria. The plaintiff was a pilot who had undertaken to recover the aircraft from Nigeria. He went to Nigeria, found one of the aircraft, and in difficult circumstances – having been warned by the Nigerian authorities that his life and that of his wireless operator were in danger – flew it to the Ivory Coast. However, the Ivory Coast government seized the aircraft and returned it to Nigeria. The defendant refused to pay the plaintiff the full amount agreed arguing that the contract had been illegally performed in Nigeria since he had taken off without permission from Nigerian air-traffic control. However, Staughton LJ held that, the conscience of the court would not be affronted by allowing the plaintiff to succeed where the plaintiff, as here, had committed the illegal acts in order to escape the danger to his life. Thus the contract was enforced against the defendants. The judge also said that the same result would be reached if the illegalities had been against English law.

Vita Food Products Inc v *Unus Shipping Co Ltd* [1939] AC 277 Privy Council (Lords Atkin, Russell, Macmillan, Wright and Porter)

• *The parties may expressly choose the law to govern their contract*

Facts

Unus Shipping, a Nova Scotian company, owned a vessel, the Hurry On, and agreed with Vita Food Products (a New York company) in bills of lading signed in Newfoundland to carry in the Hurry On a cargo of herrings from Middle Arm (a Newfoundland port) to New York. Through the captain's negligence the vessel ran aground and the cargo was damaged. Vita Foods sued Unus Shipping in the Nova Scotian courts and, on appeal, came before the Privy Council.

The Newfoundland Sale of Goods Act 1932 provided that the Hague Rules (governing the limitation of liability of shipowners for damage to cargo) should apply to every shipment of goods from a Newfoundland port and that every bill of lading issued in Newfoundland should contain an express statement that the Hague rules applied. The bills of lading issued in respect of the herring contained no such statement, but did contain in addition various clauses limiting liability an express choice of English law. (Although the Hague rules were part of English law, they only applied to shipments from United Kingdom ports.) Did the Hague rules apply or did the clauses limiting liability in the bills of lading apply?

Held

That the parties' choice of English law was effective; and this was so even if the bills of lading were illegal under the law of the place where they were issued (Newfoundland).

Lord Wright:

> 'It is now well settled that by English law (and the law of Nova Scotia is the same) the proper law of the contract " is the law which the parties intended to apply". That intention is objectively ascertained, and, if not expressed, will be presumed from the terms of the contract and the relevant surrounding circumstances. But as Lord Atkin, dealing with cases where the intention of the parties is expressed, said in *R* v *International Trustee for, etc, Bondholders AG* [1937] AC 500, 529 (a case which contains the latest enunciation of this principle), "Their intention will be ascertained by the intention expressed in the contract if any, which will be conclusive". It is objected that this is too broadly stated and that some qualifications are necessary. It is true that in questions relating to the conflict of laws rules cannot generally be stated in absolute terms but rather as prima facie presumptions. But

where the English rule that intention is the test applies, and where there is an express statement by the parties of their intention to select the law of the contract, it is difficult to see what qualifications are possible, provided the intention expressed is bona fide and legal, and provided there is no reason for avoiding the choice on the ground of public policy. In the present case, however, it might be said that the choice of English law is not valid for two reasons. It might be said that the transaction, which is one relating to the carriage on a Nova Scotian ship of goods from Newfoundland to New York between residents in these countries, contains nothing to connect it in any way with English law, and therefore that choice could not be seriously taken. Their Lordships reject this argument both on grounds of principle and on the facts. Connection with English law is not as a matter of principle essential. The provision in a contract (eg of sale) for English arbitration imports English law as the law governing the transaction, and those familiar with international business are aware how frequent such a provision is even where the parties are not English and the transactions are carried on completely outside England. Moreover in the present case the 'Hurry On', though on a Canadian register, is subject to the Imperial statute, the Merchant Shipping Act 1894, under which the vessel is registered, and the underwriters are likely to be English. In any case parties may reasonably desire that the familiar principles of English commercial law should apply. The other ground urged is that the choice of English law is inconsistent with the provisions of the bill of lading, that in respect of certain goods the Harter Act or the Canadian Water Carriage of Goods Act of 1910 (now repealed, but in force at the date of the bill of lading) was to apply. It has been explained that the incorporation of these Acts may have only contractual effect, but in any case, though the proper law of the contract is English, English law may incorporate the provisions of the law of another counry or other countries as part of the terms of the contract, and apart from such incorporation other laws may have to be regarded in giving effect to the contract. The proper law of the contract does indeed fix the interpretation and construction of its express terms and supply the relevant background of statutory or implied terms. But that part of the English law which is commonly called the conflict of laws requires, where proper, the application of foreign law: eg English law will not enforce a performance contrary to the law of the place of performance in circumstances like those existing in *Ralli Bros* v *Compania Naviera Sola y Aznar* [1920] 2 KB 287, and the law of the place of performance, though it will not be effective to affect the construction of the contract in regard to its substance (which must be ascertained according to the rule of the proper law, as was held in *Jacobs, Marcus & Co* v *Crédit Lyonnais* (1883–4) 12 QBD 589), will still regulate what were called in that case the incidents and mode of performance in that place. English law will in these and sometimes in other respects import a foreign law, but the contract is still governed by its proper law. The reference to the United States and the Canadian Acts does not on any view supersede English law which is to govern the contract, nor does Newfoundland law, though Newfoundland was the place where the contract was made, apply to oust English law from being the law of the contract, and as such from being the law which defines it nature, obligation and interpretation, though Newfoundland law might apply to the incidents of performance to be done in Newfoundland. There is, in their Lordships' opinion, no ground for refusing to give effect to the express selection of English law as the proper law in the bills of lading. Hence English rules relating to the conflict of laws must be applied to determine how the bills of lading are affected by the failure to comply with s3 of the Act.'

Choice of law in contract under the EC Convention

Arcado Sprl v *Haviland SA* Case 9/87 [1988] ECR 1539 European Court of Justice

• *Proceedings related to a contract for the purposes of art 5(1) Brussels Convention (art 5(1) EU Council Regulation 44/2001) – art 10 Rome Convention governs the consequences of a total/partial failure to comply with the contract*

Facts
The case centred on the alleged wrongful repudiation of a commercial agency contract. A judicial question arose as to whether the proceedings were proceedings related to a contract for the purposes of art 5(1) of the Brussels Convention.

Held
The ECJ held that they did in fact relate to contract. The Court was of the opinion that art 10 of the Rome Convention was descriptive of the incidences of a contract and the claim fell neatly within the described incidences of the contract. In obiter, the Court remarked:

> 'Article 10 governs the consequences of a total or partial failure to comply with the obligations arising under it and consequently the contractual liability of the party responsible for such breach.'

Bank of Baroda, The v *The Vysya Bank Ltd* [1994] 2 Lloyd's Rep 87 Queen's Bench Division (Commercial Court) (Mance J)

• *Letters of credit – governing law of the contract under art 4 of the Rome Convention*

Facts
See Chapter 4.

Held
Under the Rome Convention the letter of credit was governed by English law. The Bank of Baroda made out its case for saying that the Court had jurisdiction to grant leave to issue and serve the writ out of the jurisdiction under the first head of O.11 r1(1)(d).

Mance J:

> 'I shall start with the issue of the governing law which arises under O.11 r1(1)(d)(iii). This is of some general importance, since it involves the application to international letters of credit of the Rome Convention as enacted by the Contracts (Applicable Law) Act 1990. It was common ground before me in view of the wide provisions of s2(1) of the Act and art 3(1) of the Rome Convention that the proper law of the present contract, however it was made, must be determined in accordance with the Convention. So it is necessary to examine the provisions of art 4 ...
>
> The relevant presumption is contained in para 2. It raises the question: what is "the performance which is characteristic of the contract" made between Vysya and Bank of Baroda? Bank of Baroda says that the answer is the addition of its confirmation to the credit and the honouring of the liability accepted thereby. Vysya says that this fails to distinguish the contract between Vysya and Bank of Baroda from the contract between Bank of Baroda as confirming banker and Granada as beneficiary. In Vysya's submission the performance which is characteristic of the contract between Vysya and Bank of Baroda is the former's obligation to pay the latter upon presentation of conforming documents.
>
> There are several different contractual relationships which can be identified in a situation such as the present. Leaving aside the underlying sale contract, there are contracts between (i) the buyer and the issuing bank, (ii) the issuing bank and the confirming bank, (iii) the confirming bank and the

seller and (iv) the issuing bank and the seller. The last two relationships co-exist, giving a beneficiary two banks which he may hold responsible for payment …

For each category of contract, it is the characteristic performance that is in principle the relevant factor in applying the presumption for determining the applicable law, even in situations peculiar to certain contracts, as for example in the contract of guarantee where the characteristic performance is always that of the guarantor, whether in relation to the principal debtor or the creditor …

It follows in the present case, looking at the position of Bank of Baroda in relation to the confirmation given to Granada, that the performance characteristic of Bank of Baroda's contract with Vysya, however made, was the addition and honouring of its confirmation of the credit in favour of Granada. That performance was to be effected through Bank of Baroda's City of London office, viz "a place of business other than [its] principal place of business " and so by the express terms of art 4(2) the presumption is that English law governs the contract between Vysya and Bank of Baroda. For reasons which will further appear below, any wider examination of the circumstances under art 4(5) simply confirms the application of English law.

So far I have focused on the contract between Vysya and Bank of Baroda which is the contract immediately in issue. It is relevant to consider the matter more widely, as the arguments before me did, and in this context to consider the proper laws of other contracts involved in the present situation. Whether one looks at art 4(2) or at art 4(5) of the Rome Convention, the contract of confirmation between Bank of Baroda's City of London branch as confirming bank and Granada as beneficiary was clearly governed by English law. Even if one ignores the clear application of the presumption in art 4(2) to that contract, the reasoning in such cases as *European Bank* v *Punjab Bank* [1981] 2 Lloyd's Rep 651 at pp656–657 per Mr Justice Robert Goff is as relevant when determining the closeness of connection with any country under art 4(5) as it was for the purposes of the similar common law test. A suggestion that English law did not, as between beneficiary and confirming bank, govern a credit confirmed through the London branch of a foreign bank for payment in London would be wholly uncommercial …

In my judgment this is a situation where it would be quite wrong to stop at art. 4(2). The basic principle is that the governing law is that of the country with which the contract is most closely connected (art 4(1)). Article 4(2) is, as stated in Professors Giuliano and Lagarde's report, intended to give "specific form and objectivity" to that concept. In the present case the application of art 4(2) would lead to an irregular and subjective position where the governing law of a letter of credit would vary according to whether one was looking at the position of the confirming or the issuing bank. It is of great importance to both beneficiaries and banks concerned in the issue and operation of international letters of credit that there should be clarity and simplicity in such matters. Article 4(5) provides the answer. The Rome Convention was not intended to confuse legal relationships or to disrupt normal expectations in the way which is implicit in Vysya's submissions. Under art 4(5) the presumptions in art 4(2), (3) and (4) are to be … disregarded if it appears from the circumstances as a whole that the contract is more closely connected with another country.

I accept that the presumptions are to be applied unless there is valid reason, looking at the circumstances as a whole, not to do so. But I note and consider that there is force in the comment in *Dicey and Morris on The Conflict of Laws* (12th ed) at pp1137–1138: Inevitably the solution of individual cases will depend on the facts, but in principle it is submitted that the presumption may be most easily rebutted in those cases where the place of performance differs from the place of business of the party whose performance is characteristic of the contract.

The present situation provides in my judgment a classic demonstration of the need for and appropriateness of art 4(5). I conclude that English law applies to the contract between Vysya and Granada.

The fact that the credit was to be confirmed by Bank of Baroda's City of London branch highlights the need for art 4(5) and its applicability in this case. But I should not be taken as suggesting that the conclusion would be any different if the credit had been an unconfirmed credit to be opened and advised on Vysya's behalf in London through National Westminster or Bank of Baroda's City branch available for negotiation here …

I therefore conclude that the letter of credit was governed by English law as between the beneficiary and each of the banks. On this basis, it would be wholly anomalous if English law were not also to govern the contract between Vysya and Bank of Baroda and in my opinion it does. As between Bank of Baroda and Vysya the application of the presumption arising under art 4(2) accords with good sense and sound policy and there is therefore no reason to depart from it.'

Compagnie d'Armement Maritime SA v *Compagnie Tunisienne de Navigation SA* [1971] AC 572 House of Lords (Viscount Dilhorne, Lords Reid, Morris, Wilberforce and Diplock)

• *Can an express arbitration clause in a contract amount to a decisive choice as to the proper law of the contract?*

Facts

In 1967 the claimants, a Tunisian company, and French shipowners negotiated a contract through brokers in Paris for the transport of specified quantities of crude oil from one Tunisian port to another over a period of nine months. The contract was made in Paris on an English printed form. Freight was payable in French francs in Paris. French law was assumed to prevail in Tunisia and no question arose as between French and Tunisian law. A clause in the contract provided for the settlement of disputes by arbitration in London. There was no other connection between the contract and English law. Disputes arose and the Tunisian company claimed damages for repudiation of the contract. The disputes were referred to arbitration in London. The arbitrators made an interim award holding that French law was the proper law of the contract. This award was upheld by Megaw J but reversed by the Court of Appeal, which held that English law was the proper law because of the arbitration clause.

Held

The appeal was allowed. It was held that the proper law of the contract was French law.

Lord Reid

'Clause 13 reads: "This contract shall be governed by the laws of the flag of the vessel carrying the goods, except in the cases of average or general average when same to be settled according to the York-Antwerp Rules 1950." This clause remains unaltered in the signed contract. The printed form, being for a charterparty, had blanks at the beginning for the insertion of the name of the shipowner's tanker and its flag. These were left blank. Clause 28 provides: "Shipments to be effected in tonnage awned, controlled or chartered by the Compagnie d'Armement Maritime SA of 16,000/ 25,000 tons 10 per cent. more or less at owners' option."

The first question is whether it is possible to give any meaning to clause 13. The printed form, including clause 13, obviously contemplates that there is to be one vessel and one flag and that the law of that flag shall be the proper law. But under clause 28 there could be a variety of vessels with a variety of flags. Which is to be selected as determining the proper law? Even if one could hold that with regard to a dispute concerning a particular voyage the law of the flag of the vessel making that voyage should prevail, that would not provide for the dispute in this case which does not relate to any particular voyage …

Even if it were relevant, it would be useless to ask in this case what the parties in fact intended as to the proper law, because it is found as a fact in the interim award that there was no discussion at any time of the law by which the transaction was to be governed. But clause 13, like any other provision in a contract, must be construed in light of the facts known to both parties at the time when it was agreed. They knew that the appellants owned a number of tankers flying the French flag and it is found in the interim award that it was contemplated by both parties that vessels owned by the appellants would be used "at least primarily" to perform the contract.

If the parties had contemplated that the appellants' vessels would always be used, except in some unforeseen circumstances, I would have held that clause 13 could be held to mean that the contract was to be governed by the law of the flag of those vessels, that is, the law of France. But, in my opinion, this finding is too indefinite to justify such a gloss. "Primarily" might mean "in the first instance" or it might mean "in the majority of cases." The parties must have known that many other tankers not owned by the appellants would be available on this route, and that as the dates of shipment were to be determined by the respondents, vessels other than those belonging to the appellants might well have to be used. In my judgment, clause 13 must in the circumstances be regarded as having failed in its purpose to determine the proper law of the contract.

If that is so, then we are no longer concerned with the parties' intention. In the absence of any positive indication of intention in the contract the law will determine the proper law by deciding with what country or system of law the contract has the closest connection. Here three countries are involved. The contract was negotiated and signed in France and the freight was payable in Paris in French francs. The contract was to be performed in Tunisia. The only connection with England was that any dispute was to be settled by arbitration in London. The contract is in the English language and in English form, but it was not argued, in my view rightly, that any great importance should be given to this.

Until this case reached this House it appears to have been assumed that France and Tunisia could be treated as one country or as having the same system of law. It is stated in the interim award that: "The civil law of Tunisia (which until 1956 was a French colony) is based on the Code Napoléon" and that "neither side contended for any other system of law" than French or English law. On that basis when one comes to weigh the various factors which tell in favour of French or of English law being regarded as the proper law, the fact that Tunisia was to be the place of performance of the contract would be put in the scale for French law. Then it is clear that the balance comes down heavily in favour of French law…

The respondents do not deny that, if we are free to apply the general rule that the proper law is the law of the place with which the contract is most closely associated, then the proper law would be French law. Their case is that that general rule does not apply where there is an arbitration clause requiring disputes to be settled by arbitration in England. They admit that such a clause does not prevent the parties from agreeing that some other law shall be the proper law, but they maintain that if such an agreement cannot be deduced from the terms of the contract, then the arbitration clause is decisive as to the proper law and requires an English court to hold that the proper law is the law of England.

Of course the fact that the parties have agreed that arbitration shall take place in England is an important factor and in many cases it may be the decisive factor. But it would, in my view, be highly anomalous if our law required the mere fact that arbitration is to take place in England to be decisive as to the proper law of the contract. For the reasons given by others of your Lordships I agree that this is not the law of England.'

Definitely Maybe (Touring) Ltd* v *Marek Lieberberg Konzertagentur GmbH [2001] 2 Lloyd's Rep 455 Queen's Bench Division (Commercial Court) (Morison J)

• *Article 4 of the Rome Convention – place of performance*

Facts

The claimants (based in England) provided the services of the pop group Oasis to those who organised live concerts. The defendants (Marek Lieberberg Konzertagentur GmbH) were a German-based company which organised two pop festivals in Germany in June 2000 and contracted with the claimants for live performances by Oasis. There was a rift between the two Gallagher brothers and Noel the lead guitarist did not play in Germany. The defendants contended that Oasis without Noel Gallagher was not really the group contracted for and refused to pay the full price. The claimants issued proceedings in England claiming the balance of the moneys owing. The defendants applied to set aside the service of the writ on the ground that the proper place for these proceedings was Germany and not England. Under the Brussels Convention the normal rule was that a person, including a corporate entity, should be sued in the place where he was domiciled, ie Germany, but the normal rule was displaced if the place of performance of the obligation in question, namely, the duty to pay, was England. The issue for decision was whether the contract was governed by English or German law.

Held

Aside from the location of the claimants and the group and the place of payment there was no other connection between England and the contract for Oasis to perform live in Germany. The centre of the gravity of the dispute was Germany. Furthermore, Germany would provide the more convenient forum for deciding to what extent Oasis without Noel Gallagher was worth anything and if so how much. Appeal dismissed.

Morison J:

'In order to resolve the jurisdiction issue the court must, initially, turn to the Brussels Convention, to which both countries have acceded. Under that Convention, the normal rule is that a person, including, of course, a corporate entity, should be sued in the place where he is domiciled; in other words, Germany. But the normal rule is displaced if the place of performance of the obligation in question, namely the duty to pay, is England. But the place of performance of an obligation such as this may, and in this case does, depend upon which system of law governs the contract. Under German law the place of performance of an obligation to pay is the domicile of the debtor, namely Germany. Under English law the place of performance of the defendant's obligation to pay is England, the place where the money is to be received. Thus, the question as to whether these proceedings can continue in this jurisdiction is dependent upon the answer to the question: what is the governing law of the contract? If the answer is English law, then the proceedings can continue here and the appeal must be allowed. Conversely, if the answer is German law then the appeal must be dismissed and the stay of proceedings in this jurisdiction continued.

The answer to the question comes from a proper interpretation of the Rome Convention adopted by both countries. Article 3 of the Convention gives effect to parties' own choice of law. There is no express or implied choice of law clause in this case and, therefore, one must turn to art 4. Paragraph 1 of that article directs that a contract is governed by the law of the country with which it is most closely connected. Paragraph 2 provides, subject to the provisions of para 5, that the country with the closest connection with the contract is to be determined by identifying the place where the party who effects or is to effect the characteristic performance of the contract is "located" [has its central administration or principal place of business]. Thus, subject to para 5, there are two questions to be answered: which party effects the characteristic performance of the contract, and where is that party located [in the sense used above]? Here, it is common ground that the claimants have the characteristic performance of the contract, in the sense that the substantive obligation under the contract was for Oasis to perform in two concerts in Germany. The claimants are located in England, and hence, by virtue of art 4(2) English law would be the governing law of the contract.

But art 4(2) is expressly made subject to the provisions of para 5 of the same article. Paragraph 5 displaces the presumption in para 2:

> "... if it appears from the circumstances as a whole that the contract is more closely connected with another country."

In such a case, para 5 provides that para 2 shall be disregarded.

The real issue between the parties centres on the relationship between these two paragraphs of art 4. While para 2 looks to the location of the principal performer, para 5 looks more widely to a connection between the contract and a country. If there is a divergence between the location of the principal performer and the place of substantial or characteristic performance, what then? On the one hand, were the presumption to be displaced whenever such divergence existed, the presumption would be of little weight or value. Paragraph 2 must have been inserted to provide a "normal" rule which is simple to apply. Giving wide effect to para 5 will render the presumption of no value and represent a return to the English common law test of ascertaining the proper law, which places much less weight on the location of the performer and much more on the place of performance, and the presumed intention of the parties.

Rather than seeking to find an answer to this issue, I turn to those factors which are said to show a closer connection between the contract and Germany than with England. The contract provided for Oasis to perform live in Germany; that was the place of the characteristic or substantial performance of the contract. The defendants were obliged to make arrangements in Germany to enable the performances to take place (for example, marketing and promotion) and to provide facilities such as security and bits of equipment. Thus, the contract required performance of contractual obligations in Germany by both parties. For what it is worth, the defendant company is German and payment was to be made in DMs and subject to deduction for German tax. Apart from the location of the claimants and the group, and the place of payment, there is no other connection between England and the contract. The centre of gravity of the dispute is, I think, Germany. Therefore, if the test were simply that laid down in para 5, namely, to say with which country was the contract most closely connected, I would have said Germany, rather than England.

But I return to the issue of the relationship between paras 2 and 5 of art 4 and the legal effect of the presumption. There are, I think, two schools of thought. The first is to say that the presumption in para 2, which is expressly made subject to para 5, is weak and will more readily be displaced where the place of performance differs from the place of business of the performer. The second, adopts a narrower view of the "exception" to the presumption in para 5 and gives firm dominance to the presumption ...

I must confess that I have not found this an easy case to decide. To some extent the Court must recognise, I think, a natural tendency to wish to maintain the old, well developed common law position where factors were weighed and attempts were made to ascertain the true intention of the parties. Intention does not appear to exist as a factor any more, save in an art 3 context. Although art 18 of the Rome Convention encourages a uniform interpretation of the Convention, that is less easy to achieve than to say. The importance attached to the location of the principal performer stems from Swiss law. The provisions of art 4 have been the subject of much criticism by academics; it is rightly pointed out that the Giuliano-

Lagarde report (to which reference may be made), does not provide much useful guidance as to the interpretation of art 4 although the authors accept that judges have been left with a measure of discretion or judgment. It may be that the Convention represents a compromise between different positions adopted by different countries during the negotiations of its terms.

It seems to me not to be helpful to characterize art 4 by asking whether there is a one, two or three stage test. Nor am I attracted to the notion that the words of the article should be twisted so as to accord with what is thought to be the intention of the draftsman. With an international convention of this sort, I prefer to stay with the words and apply them as best as possible. On that basis, it seems to me that the presumption in art 4.2 "shall be disregarded" [not rebutted] if it appears from the circumstances as a whole that the contract is more closely connected with Germany rather than England. I accept that it is for the defendant to show that the presumption should be disregarded, by establishing factors which point to Germany I accept that this will be more readily achievable where the place of performance is different from the place of the performer's business. But in carrying out what must be regarded as a comparative exercise, due weight must be given to the factor identified in art 4.2.

Here, the defendants have established to my satisfaction that, overall, the contract between the parties has a closer connection with Germany than with England. Even recognizing the Convention's emphasis on England as the place of the performer's business, having regard to the place of performance by both parties and the other factors referred to above, Germany has more attachment to or connection with the contract than England. Aside from any other consideration, the centre of gravity of the dispute is Germany, which will provide the more convenient forum for deciding to what extent Oasis without Noel Gallagher was worth anything, and, if so, how much.

Thus, in the result, I endorse the decision of Master Foster and dismiss the appeal.'

Gan Insurance Co Ltd v *Tai Ping Insurance Co Ltd* [1999] 2 All ER (Comm) 54 Court of Appeal (Beldam, Brooke and Mummery LJJ)

• *Express selection in a pre-existing or previous course of dealings*

Facts

Tai Ping decided to reinsure part of their risk with Gan Insurance. The reinsurance slip referred to terms 'as original'. The original contract of insurance between Tai Ping and the insured in Taiwan was to be governed by Taiwanese law. Thus, was the reinsurance contract governed by English law?

Held

The relevant law was that of art 3(1) of the Rome Convention as it was a circumstance that could demonstrate an inferred intention; a contract in standard form which was known to be governed by a particular legal system despite the fact that there was no express statement to that effect within it. It pointed to a choice of English law 'demonstrated with reasonable certainty by the terms of the contract or the circumstances of the case.'

Beldam LJ:

> 'In the present case it is clear that Tai Ping's brokers were instructed to present the risk to reinsurers on the basis of the statement of fire protection contained on the drawings. According to brokers this was in response to a specific enquiry by Gan though not apparently in writing. In my view, where by its express terms, the risk presented to underwriters is materially different from that assumed by the reinsured, it cannot reasonably be presumed that underwriters intended to afford back-to-back cover.
>
> In his analysis and conclusions of the proper law of the reinsurance contract, Cresswell J cited s2(1) of the Contracts (Applicable Law) Act 1990 providing for the incorporation into the law of the United Kingdom of the Rome Convention.'

Beldam LJ proceeded to outline the contents of

art 3(1) and art 4(1), (2), (5) of the Convention and continued:

'The judge relied on the example given in the Guiliano-Lagarde Report as a circumstance which could demonstrate an inferred intention, of the case of a contract in a standard form which is known to be governed by a particular system of law even though there is no express statement to this effect, such as a Lloyds policy of marine insurance. The judge said that the reinsurance contract was placed in London on the London market, the terms of the slip and the claims co-operation clause pointed to an implied choice of English law "demonstrated with reasonable certainty by the terms of the contract/the circumstances of the case". He considered that the words "as original" were intended to ensure that the risk undertaken by reinsurers was identical as to period, geographical limits and nature of the risk with the risk undertaken by Tai Ping as direct insurer. He relied on the case of *Pine Top* v *Unione Italiana* [1987] 1 Lloyd's Rep 90, a decision of Gatehouse J, and the observations of Neill LJ in *Forsikringsaktiesekapet Vesta* v *Butcher* [1986] 2 All ER 488.

In my judgment Mr Lockey's [counsel for the appellant] argument involves a departure from the usual course of business on the London reinsurance market which could only be justified if the terms of the reinsurance policy unequivocally pointed to an intention that the proper law should be Taiwanese law. If the terms are construed as a whole, they fall a long way short of demonstrating such an intention. Three descriptive phrases appear in the slip: "as original", "following original" and "as more fully described in the original policy wording". In describing the form of the reinsurance policy the description is "Slip Policy NMA 1779 following original – original wording agreed leading reinsurance underwriter". It is common ground that NMA 1779 is an English non- marine policy form. There is further difficulty in interpreting the words "as original" in the way Mr Lockey suggests because the slip draws a clear distinction between "conditions" which plainly refer to the conditions of the reinsurance: Full Reinsurance clause NMA 416 ... NMA 464 unless war and civil war exclusion clause contained in original policy wording ... and "original conditions": ... all risks as per local standard EAR policy. I do not think it is possible to infer from the terms of the slip that the parties to the reinsurance intended to incorporate all the terms of the EAR policy.

In my view where a contract of reinsurance is made in London between London underwriters and brokers their agreement is based on the well-known duty of disclosure and the right of an insurer to avoid a policy for misrepresentation. Clause 22 of the EAR contract would introduce a term of Taiwanese law in conflict with this basis. On principle, in the absence of express agreement, I would hold that it cannot reasonably be imputed to the parties that they intended clause 22 to apply. At the most, scope for the words "as original" and "in the original policy wording" could be given by its application to the provisions of the EAR policy which defined the extent of the risk insured...

I would therefore reject Mr Lockey's submission that the express terms of the reinsurance policy included a clause making Taiwanese law the proper law of the contract. In my opinion the judge was correct to hold that there was an implied choice of English law "demonstrated with reasonable certainty by the terms of the contract or the circumstances of the case as required by art 3". The judge pointed to the reference to "slip policy NMA 1779", "full reinsurance clause NMA 416", "claims co-operation clause NMA 464, NMA 1685" and the claims co-operation clause itself as demonstrating a choice of clauses commonly found in contracts of reinsurance placed on the London market. Moreover the procedure adopted was to place the business in London using London brokers who presented the risk to reinsurers in the conventional way in concluding a contract of reinsurance governed by English law. In my view the judge was also right to hold that, in the absence of express choice, the applicable law was English law.'

6 Choice of Law in Tort

The common law rules governing the choice of law in tort

Babcock v *Jackson* (1963) 12 NY 2d 473; 191 NE 2d 279 New York Court of Appeals (Desmond CJ, Dye, Burke, Foster, Fuld, Van Hoorhis and Scileppi JJ)

• *In most of the United States the rights and liabilities of the parties with respect to an issue in tort are determined by the law of the country which, with respect to that issue, has the most significant relationship to the occurrence and the parties*

Facts

Miss Georgia Babcock and her friends, Mr and Mrs William Jackson, all residents of Rochester NY left that city in Mr Jackson's automobile, Miss Babcock as guest, for a weekend trip to Canada. Some hours later, as Mr Jackson was driving in the Province of Ontario, he apparently lost control of the car; it went off the highway into an adjacent stone wall, and Miss Babcock was seriously injured. Upon her return to New York she brought an action against William Jackson alleging negligence on his part in operating his automobile. At the time of the accident there was in force in Ontario a statute providing that 'the owner or driver of a motor vehicle, other than a vehicle operated in the business of carrying passengers for compensation, is not liable for any loss or damage resulting from bodily injury to, or the death of, any person being carried in ... the motor vehicle'. Even though no such bar is recognised under New York state's substantive law of torts, the defendant moved to dismiss the complaint on the ground that the law of the place where the accident occurred governs and that Ontario's guest statute bars recovery.

Held (Van Hooris and Scileppi dissenting) Appeal allowed.

Fuld J:

'The question presented is simply drawn. Shall the law of the place of the tort invariably govern the availability of relief for the tort or shall the applicable choice of law rule also reflect a consideration of other factors which are relevant to the purposes served by the enforcement or denial of the remedy?

The traditional choice of law rule, embodied in the original Restatement of Conflict of Laws and until recently unquestioningly followed in this court, has been that the substantive rights and liabilities arising out of a tortious occurrence are determinable by the law of the place of the tort. It had its conceptual foundation in the vested rights doctrine, namely, that a right to recover for a foreign tort owes its creation to the law of the jurisdiction where the injury occurred and depends for its existence and extent solely on such law. Although espoused by such great figures as Holmes J and Professor Beale, the vested rights doctrine has long since been discredited because it fails to take account of underlying policy considerations in evaluating the significance to be ascribed to the circumstance that an act had a foreign situs in determining the rights and liabilities which arise out of that act. "The vice of the vested rights theory", it has been aptly stated, "is that it affects to decide concrete cases upon generalities which do not state the practical considerations involved."

More particularly, as applied to torts, the theory ignores the interest which jurisdictions other than that where the tort occurred may have in the resolution of particular issues. It is for this very reason that, despite the advantages of certainty, ease of application and predictability which it affords, there has in recent years been increasing criticism of the traditional rule by commentators and a judicial trend towards its abandonment or modification. …

The "center of gravity" or "grouping of contacts" doctrine adopted by this court in conflicts cases involving contracts impresses us as likewise affording the appropriate approach for accommodating the competing interests in tort cases with multi-state contacts. Justice, fairness and "the best practical result" may best be achieved by giving controlling effect to the law of the jurisdiction which, because of its relationship or contact with the occurrence or the parties, has the greatest concern with the specific issue raised in the litigation. The merit of such a rule is that "it gives to the place having the most interest in the problem paramount control over the legal issues arising out of a particular factual context" and thereby allows the forum to apply the policy of the jurisdiction most intimately concerned with the outcome of the particular litigation …

Comparison of the relative "contacts" and "interests" of New York and Ontario in this litigation, vis-à-vis the issue here presented, makes it clear that the concern of New York is unquestionably the greater and more direct and that the interest of Ontario is at best minimal. The present action involves injuries sustained by a New York guest as the result of the negligence of a New York host in the operation of an automobile, garaged licensed and undoubtedly insured in New York, in the course of a weekend journey which began and was to end there. In sharp contrast, Ontario's sole relationship with the occurrence is the purely adventitious circumstance that the accident occurred there …

The issue here, however, is not whether the defendant offended against a rule of the road prescribed by Ontario for motorists generally or whether he violated some standard of conduct imposed by that jurisdiction, but rather whether the plaintiff, because she was a guest in the defendant's automobile, is barred from recovering damages for a wrong concededly committed. As to that issue, it is New York, the place where the parties resided, where their guest-host relationship arose and where the trip began and was to end, rather than Ontario, the place of the fortuitous occurrence of the accident, which has the dominant contacts and the superior claim for application of its law. Although the rightness or wrongness of defendant's conduct may depend upon the law of the particular jurisdiction through which the automobile passes, the rights and liabilities of the parties which stem from their guest-host relationship should remain constant and not vary and shift as the automobile proceeds from place to place. Indeed, such a result, we note, accords with "the interests of the host in procuring liability insurance adequate under the applicable law, and the interests of his insurer in reasonable calculation of the premium".

Although the traditional rule has in the past been applied by this court in giving controlling effect to the guest statute of the foreign jurisdiction in which the accident occurred, it is not amiss to point out that the question here posed was neither raised nor considered in those cases and that the question has never been presented in so stark a manner as in the case before us with a statute so unique as Ontario's. Be that as it may, however, reconsideration of the inflexible traditional rule persuades us, as already indicated, that, in failing to take into account essential policy considerations and objectives, its application may lead to unjust and anomalous results. This being so, the rule, formulated as it was by the courts, should be discarded …

The judgment appealed from should be reversed, with costs, and the motion to dismiss the complaint denied.'

Boys* v *Chaplin [1971] AC 356 House of Lords (Lords Hodson, Guest, Donovan, Wilberforce and Pearson)

• *Flexible approach towards the application of the rule of double actionability*

Facts

Both plaintiff and defendant were British servicemen normally resident in England but stationed in Malta. The plaintiff, while a passenger on a motor scooter, had been injured in a motor accident in Malta with a car driven negligently by the defendant. Under art 1088 of the Maltese Civil Code the plaintiff could recover only his actual financial loss, ie he could not recover, as he could under English law, damages for pain and suffering. The plaintiff sued in England but did the second limb of *Phillips* v *Eyre* (1870) LR 6 QB 1 prevent him from recovering damages for pain and suffering?

Held

The plaintiff could recover damages for pain and suffering.

Lord Wilberforce:

> '*The existing English law.* Apart from any revision which this House may be entitled, and think opportune, to make, I have no doubt that this is as stated in Dicey and Morris, *Conflict of Laws,* 8th ed. (1967), Rule 158, adopting with minor verbal adaptations the "general rule" laid down by the Court of Exchequer Chamber in *Phillips* v *Eyre*, LR 6 QB 1. This is as follows:
>
> > "An act done in a foreign country is a tort and actionable as such in England, only if it is both
> > (1) actionable as a tort, according to English law, or in other words, is an act which, if done in England, would be a tort; and
> > (2) not justifiable, according to the law of the foreign country where it was done."
>
> I am aware that different interpretations have been placed by writers of authority upon the central passage in the judgment of Willes J, in which the general rule is contained (LR 6 QB 1 28, 29). Like many judgments given at a time when the relevant part of the law was in course of formation, it is not without its ambiguities, or, as a century of experience perhaps permits us to say, its contradictions. And if it were now necessary to advance the law by reinterpretation, it would be quite legitimate to extract new meanings from words and sentences used. Two of the judgments in the Court of Appeal have done just this, reaching in the process opposite conclusions. I do not embark on this adventure for two reasons: first, because of the variety of interpretation offered us by learned writers no one of which can claim overwhelming support; secondly, and more importantly, because, on the critical points, I do not think there is any doubt what the rule as stated has come to be accepted to mean in those courts which apply the common law. And it is with this judicially accepted meaning and its applications that we are now concerned.
>
> (a) The first part of the rule – "actionable as a tort according to English law." I accept what I believe to be the orthodox judicial view that the first part of the rule is laying down, not a test of jurisdiction, but what we now call a rule of choice of law: is saying, in effect, that actions on foreign torts are brought in English courts in accordance with English law. I would be satisfied to rest this conclusion on the words of the rule itself "if done [committed] in England" which seem clear enough to exclude the "jurisdiction" theory but, since the point is important, I give some citations to support it. …
>
> I am of opinion, therefore, that as regards the first part of this rule, actionability as a tort under and in accordance with English law is required.
>
> (b) The second part of the rule – "not justifiable according to the lex loci delicti". There can hardly be any doubt that when this formulation was made in *Phillips* v *Eyre,* LR 6 QB 1, it was intended to cover the justification by act of indemnity which had occurred in Jamaica – the word "justifi-

cation" is derived from or at least found in *Mostyn* v *Fabrigas* in a similar context (see particularly 1 Cowp 161, 175). It might have been better for English law if the rule had continued to be so understood. But *Machado* v *Fontes* [1897] 2 QB 231 gave the authority of the then Court of Appeal to the proposition that "not justifiable" included not only "actionable" but "liable to criminal penalty", or, putting it another way, that "justifiable" means "innocent". Until the decision of the Court of Appeal in the present case this was undoubtedly still the law. …

It remains for me to consider (and this is the crux of the present case) whether some qualification to this rule is required in certain individual cases. There are two conflicting pressures: the first in favour of certainty and simplicity in the law, the second in favour of flexibility in the interest of individual justice. Developments in the United States of America have reflected this conflict: I now consider them. …

Given the general rule, as stated above, as one which will normally apply to foreign torts, I think that the necessary flexibility can be obtained from that principle which represents at least a common denominator of the United States decisions, namely, through segregation of the relevant issue and consideration whether, in relation to that issue, the relevant foreign rule ought, as a matter of policy or as Westlake said of science, to be applied. For this purpose it is necessary to identify the policy of the rule, to inquire to what situations, with what contacts, it was intended to apply; whether not to apply it, in the circumstances of the instant case, would serve any interest which the rule was devised to meet. This technique appears well adapted to meet cases where the lex delicti either limits or excludes damages for personal injury; it appears even necessary and inevitable. No purely mechanical rule can properly do justice to the great variety of cases where persons come together in a foreign jurisdiction for different purposes with different pre-existing relationships, from the background of different legal systems. It will not be invoked in every case or even, probably, in many cases. The general rule must apply unless clear and satisfying grounds are shown why it should be departed from and what solution, derived from what other rule, should be preferred. If one lesson emerges from the United States decisions it is that case to case decisions do not add up to a system of justice. Even within these limits this procedure may in some instances require a more searching analysis than is needed under the general rule. But unless this is done, or at least possible, we must come back to a system which is purely and simply mechanical."

I find in this approach the solution to the present case. The tort here was committed in Malta; it is actionable in this country. But the law of Malta denies recovery of damages for pain and suffering. Prima facie English law should do the same: if the parties were both Maltese residents it ought surely to do so; if the defendant were a Maltese resident the same result might follow. But in a case such as the present, where neither party is a Maltese resident or citizen, further inquiry is needed rather than an automatic application of the rule. The issue, whether this head of damage should be allowed, requires to be segregated from the rest of the case, negligence or otherwise, related to the parties involved and their circumstances, and tested in relation to the policy of the local rule and of its application to these parties so circumstanced.

So segregated, the issue is whether one British subject, resident in the United Kingdom, should be prevented from recovering, in accordance with English law, against another British subject, similarly situated, damages for pain and suffering which he cannot recover under the rule of the lex delicti. This issue must be stated, and examined, regardless of whether the injured person has or has not also a recoverable claim under a different heading (eg, for expenses actually incurred) under that law. This Maltese law cannot simply be rejected on grounds of public policy, or some general conception of justice. For it is one thing to say or presume that domestic rule is a just rule, but quite another, in a case where a foreign element is involved, to reject a foreign rule on any such general ground. The foreign rule must be evaluated in its application.

The rule limiting damages is the creation of the law of Malta, a place where both plaintiff and defendant were temporarily stationed. Nothing suggests that the Maltese state has any interest in applying this rule to persons resident outside it, or in denying the application of the English rule to these parties. No argument has been suggested why an English court, if free to do so, should renounce its own rule. That rule ought, in my opinion, to apply.'

Comment

Lord Wilberforce's speech is only one of the five concurring speeches delivered in this case. It is difficult, if not impossible, to extract a ratio decidendi from these five speeches with their varying grounds of decision. Fortunately, however, Lord Wilberforce's speech has emerged as the canonical one; and the Court of Appeal has accepted on at least two occasions that it contains a correct statement of the law. (See *Church of Scientology of California* v *Commissioner of the Metropolitan Police* (1976) 120 SJ 690 (discussed by Hodgson J in *Coupland* v *Arabian Gulf Petroleum* [1983] 2 All ER 434 at 443) and *Armagas Ltd* v *Mundogas SA* [1985] 3 All ER 795 at 811.)

Canadian Pacific Railway v *Parent* [1917] AC 195 Privy Council (Viscount Haldane, Lords Dunedin, Parker, Parmoor and Wrenbury)

- *Application of double actionability rule*

Facts

A stockman (Chalifour) travelled with his employer's cattle on the defendants' railway from Manitoba to Quebec. He signed a form exempting the defendants from all liability in respect of death or injury of any person travelling in charge of stock (and thus paying less than the full fare) caused by the negligence of the defendants or their employees. He was killed in a collision in Ontario and his widow and son brought an action in Quebec. Under the law of either Ontario or Manitoba the exemptions clause was valid, but under the law of Quebec the wife and son had an independent right of action that was not affected by any contract entered into by the deceased.

Held

Since the wife and son had no right under the law of Ontario (the lex loci delicti), the double actionability rule was not satisfied and the railway company was thus not bound to compensate them.

Viscount Haldane:

> 'The crucial questions which arise are whether Chalifour, by signing the pass under the circumstances in which he was accepted as a passenger in charge of the cattle at less than the full fare, bound himself to renounce what would otherwise have been his rights, and, if so, whether the respondents were precluded from claiming under the Article in the Quebec Code. If that Article applied, it is not in controversy that the widow and son were proper plaintiffs in this action. [His Lordship held that the exemption clause in the contract of carriage was valid under Canadian railway legislation. In addition, the defendants did enough to enable Chalifour to know what he was about when he signed the form.] …
>
> It follows that, as the statute law of Ontario, the province where the accident occurred which caused Chalifour's death, did not confer on anyone claiming on his account a statutory right to sue, there was, so far as Ontario is concerned, no other right. For in Ontario the principle of the English common law applies, which precludes death from being complained of as an injury. If so, on the general principles which are applied in Canada and this country under the title of private international law, a common law action for damages for tort could not be successfully maintained against

the appellants in Quebec. It is not necessary to consider whether all the language used by the English Court of Appeal in the judgments in *Machado* v *Fontes* [1897] 2 QB 231 was sufficiently precise. The conclusion there reached was that it is not necessary, if the act was wrongful in the country where the action was brought, that it should be susceptible of civil proceedings in the other country, provided it is not an innocent act there. This question does not arise in the present case, where the action was brought, not against the servants of the appellants, who may or may not have been guilty of criminal negligence, but against the appellants themselves. It is clear that the appellants cannot be said to have committed in a corporate capacity any criminal act. The most that can be suggested is that, on the maxim respondeat superior, they might have been civilly responsible for the acts of their servants.

The other point that remains is whether art 1056 of the Quebec Code which has already been quoted conferred a statutory right to sue in the events which happened. Their Lordships answer this question in the negative. The offence or quasi-offence took place not in Quebec but in Ontario. The presumption to be made is that in enacting art 1056 the Quebec Legislature meant, as an Act of the Imperial Parliament would be construed as meaning, to confine the special remedy conferred to cases of offences or quasi-offences committed within its own jurisdiction. There is, in their Lordships' opinion, nothing in the context of the chapter of the Code in which the art occurs which displaces this presumption in its construction. The rule of interpretation is a natural one where law, as in the case of both Quebec and England, owes its origin largely to territorial custom. No doubt the Quebec Legislature could impose many obligations in respect of acts done outside the province on persons domiciled within its jurisdiction, as the railway company may have been by reason of having its head office at Montreal. But in the case of art 1056 there does not appear to exist any sufficient reason for holding that it has intended to do so, and by so doing to place claims for torts committed outside Quebec on a footing differing from that on which the general rule of private international law already referred to would place them.'

***Corcoran* v *Corcoran* [1974] VR 164**
Supreme Court of Victoria (Adam J)

• *Rule of double actionability – flexible application of the second limb of this rule?*

Facts

The plaintiff and defendant were wife and husband, both were resident and domiciled in Victoria. The wife had been injured in a motor accident that resulted when the husband drove negligently in New South Wales. (The car driven by the husband was registered in Victoria). By the law of New South Wales there was interspousal immunity in actions for tort, while this immunity had been abolished in Victoria. Could the wife recover?

Held

That the second limb of *Phillips* v *Eyre* (1870) LR 6 QB 1would be flexibly applied and did not preclude the wife from suing in Victoria.

Adam J:

'The accident occurred in New South Wales. This was the only connexion between the action and New South Wales. It appears that the husband and wife, who were both resident and indeed domiciled in Victoria, were proceeding in a Victorian registered motor car on a visit to New South Wales, and the accident which occasioned her personal injuries occurred beyond the border. By the law of New South Wales a spouse is not entitled to sue the other spouse in tort in respect of personal injuries, save in the one case where the injuries have arisen out of the use of a "registered motor vehicle" within the meaning of that expression in s16B of the Married Persons (Property and Torts) Act 1901–1964 (NSW). ...

The difficulty arises with the second of the requirements or conditions prescribed by *Phillips* v *Eyre* as a condition for maintaining an action on a foreign tort, that is the requirement that the tortious act should be one which was, to use the words of that case, "not justifiable" according to the lex delicti.

Mr Winneke [counsel for the defendants] contended that this second of the requirements or conditions, which I will refer to as the second limb in *Phillips* v *Eyre*, would be satisfied only if it could be shown that this cause of action relied upon by the plaintiff would have been actionable in New South Wales had the action been brought in the courts of that jurisdiction. In other words, his submission was that properly interpreted thepropositions enunciated in *Phillips* v *Eyre* required double actionability between the same parties, actionability according to the lex delecti where the tortious act was committed. Although the words "not justifiable" as used in the rules enumerated in *Phillips* v *Eyre* do not, on their face, compel any such restricted interpretation, Mr Winneke's contention was that the body of authority in favour of his construction, as the preferred one, was much too strong for me at this age and place to disregard. …

Although no doubt the matter will continue to be hotly debated among academic writers, concerned at times more with what the law should be, and may even still be considered open to review by the highest courts (see per Kitto J in *Anderson* v *Eric Anderson Pty Ltd,* at CLR p28), the House of Lords decision in *Boys* v *Chaplin* [1971] AC 356 discourages any such hope. It was conceded by all parties that the present application should be decided by me on the basis that the answer is to be found upon the proper interpretation of the rules formulated by Willes J, in *Phillips* v *Eyre* – the rules which indicate what should properly be taken into consideration in determining the actionability in one court of a claim for damages based on a tort committed within the territorial jurisdiction of another court. …

It seems to me that the justification for reading the requirement in *Phillips* v *Eyre* that the act should not be justifiable according to the lex delicti, as requiring that the act should give rise in the lex delicti to a cause of action of damages there and nothing less, has a theoretical justification only if in the choice of laws the lex delicti should be regarded as dominant, and the "obligation" doctrine adopted. The doctrine that under the principles of private international law in the case of foreign torts the courts of this country are in effect enforcing an obligation arising and having its source under a foreign law, rather than an obligation arising under our law, is one which has in the past commanded interest and influence in the courts of the United States, and I think at an earlier stage may have done so in the English courts, but one thing is clear, at least for me, that is that any notion that in enforcing a claim based on a foreign tort we are, by courtesy or for some other reason, giving effect to an accrued obligation arising in a foreign country, is a doctrine which is now now acceptable. …

With the rejection of the "obligation" doctrine, it is difficult to see why, on principle, actionability in every respect in the foreign country should be insisted upon when the actionability according to the lex fori is of course insisted upon under the first limb in *Phillips* v *Eyre*.

A practical benefit, however, which flows undoubtedly from the rule of double actionability – actionability both under the lex fori and under the lex delicti – is the protection that that affords against the evils and injustices of forum shopping. If civil actionability under the lex delicti is insisted upon as a condition of bringing the action in another country, then clearly a plaintiff can gain no benefit from selecting his own forum because whatever forum he selects can only give effect to an action which is maintainable in the country in which the tortious act was done.

Although I am not persuaded that in strict theory I am bound by authority in this matter, I have concluded, I may say with some reluctance, that the weight of authority favours construing the second limb of *Phillips* v *Eyre* as in itself requiring that the act complained of as an actionable tort in the forum should be one which would give rise to an actionable tort by the lex loci. Not only has this concusion the support of the High Court in *Koop* v *Bebb* (1951) 84 CLR 629, although not essential to that decision, but I consider that it also commands substantial support from the Lords in the case of *Boys* v *Chaplin* [1971] AC 356; [1969] 2 All ER 1085. I have thought it proper in the existing uncertain state of authority for me to accept, as it appeals to me, what was said by Lord Wilberforce in *Boys* v *Chaplin* at (AC) p389:–

> "Assuming that, as the basic rule, we continue to require actionability by the lex fori, subject to some condition as to what the lex delicti requires, we should, in my opinion allow for greater and more intelligible force to the lex delicti than is is included in the concept of unjustifiability as normally understood.

The broad principle should surely be that a person should not be permitted to claim in England in respect of a matter for which civil liability does not exist, or is excluded, under the law of the place where the wrong was committed. ...

I feel persuaded by the force of what Lord Wilberforce has said in the passage cited above and I propose in this last portion of this judgment to indicate why, in my opinion, this is clearly a case where the rules in *Phillips* v *Eyre* are flexible enough to admit of an action in the circumstances of this case although if rigidly applied they would defeat the wife's action.

Shortly, the reasons are that I consider that having due regard to the requirements of certainty and individual justice where, as in the present case, there is a conflict in one respect between the laws of New South Wales and the laws of Victoria, there are strong reasons why that conflict should be resolved in favour of the law of Victoria. I say the conflict here is in one respect only. Were it not for the immunity which a husband has in New South Wales from action by his wife in a suit of tort for personal injuries, (except in the use of a New South Wales registered motor vehicle) there would be no doubt whatever that the conduct of the husband would have been actionable in New South Wales in an action for tort. ...

I might just add this: another thing which has persuaded me to this flexible application of *Phillips* v *Eyre*, is that I see no danger, by allowing this, of encouraging "forum shopping". It is to be recalled that this proceeding is arising in the natural forum of the parties, not any forum chosen at random with a view to benefiting the plaintiff. Other consequences may well arise were such an action as the present to come before what might be called a fortuitous forum. Here we have the natural forum, Victoria, where both the parties reside and where the car itself is registered, the link with New South Wales being entirely fortuitous, New South Wales is not a natural forum. And therefore by allowing this action to proceed in Victoria as maintainable according to Victorian law, I am doing nothing to encourage "forum shopping". Had the case been brought in some State which had no connexion with the parties at all, and in that State the law allowed the action to be brought, whereas in the natural forum the law did not, one might well conclude that the rule in *Phillips* v *Eyre* should apply with all its rigour, namely, that it should require to be shown that the action brought was one which was maintainable and actionable according to the lex delicti.'

Machado* v *Fontes [1897] 2 QB 231 Court of Appeal (Lopes and Rigby LJJ)

- *Under the rule of double actionability it is not necessary that the act should be the subject of civil proceedings in the foreign country*

Facts

The plaintiff brought this action to recover damages from the defendant for an alleged libel upon the plaintiff contained in a pamphlet in the Portuguese language alleged to have been published by the plaintiff in Brazil. The defendant delivered a statement of defence and he afterwards took out a summons for leave to amend his defence by adding the following plea:

> 'Further the defendant will contend that if (contrary to the defendant's contention) the said pamphlet has been published in Brazil, by the Brazilian law the publication of the said pamphlet in Brazil cannot be the ground of legal proceedings against the defendant in Brazil in which damages can be recovered, or (alternatively) cannot be the ground of legal proceedings against the defendant in Brazil in which the plaintiff can recover general damages for any injury to his credit, character, or feelings.'

Held

Appeal allowed.

Lopes LJ:

> 'Now that plea, as it stands, appears to me merely to go to the remedy. It says, in effect, that in this case no action in which damages could be recovered would lie in Brazil, and, assuming that any damages could be recovered in Brazil, they would be special damages only. Mr Walton [counsel for the defendants] contends that is not the meaning of the plea: that the plea is intended to raise a larger question than that, and to say that libel cannot be made the subject of any civil proceedings at all in Brazil, but is only the subject-matter of criminal proceedings; and, for the purposes of what I am about to say, I will assume that to be so.
>
> Now the principle applicable in the present case appears to me to be this: where the words have been published outside the jurisdiction, then, in order to maintain an action here on the ground of a tort committed outside the jurisdiction, the act complained of must be wrongful – I use the word "wrongful" deliberately – both by the law of this country, and also by the law of the country where it was committed; and the first thing we have to consider is whether those conditions are complied with.
>
> In the case of *Phillips* v *Eyre* (1870) LR 6 QB 1 Willes J lays down very distinctly what the requisites are in order to found such an action. He says this:
>
> > "As a general rule, in order to found a suit in England for a wrong alleged to have been committed abroad, two conditions must be fulfilled: First, the wrong must be of such a character that it would have been actionable if committed in England … Secondly, the act must not have been justifiable by the law of the place where it was done."
>
> Then in *The M Moxham* 1 PD 107 James LJ, in the course of his judgment, uses these words:
>
> > "It is settled that if by the law of the foreign country the act is lawful or is excusable, or even if it has been legitimized by a subsequent act of the Legislature, then this Court will take into consideration that state of the law – that is to say, if by the law of the foreign country a particular person is justified, or is excused, or has been justified or excused for the thing done, he will not be answerable here."
>
> Both those cases seem to me to go this length: that, in order to constitute a good defence to an action brought in this country in respect of an act done in a foreign country, the act relied on must be one which is innocent in the country where it was committed. In the present case there can be no doubt that the action lies, for it complies with both of the requirements which are laid down by Willes J. The act was committed abroad, and was actionable here, and not justifiable by the law of the place where it was committed. Both those conditions are complied with; and, therefore, the publication in Brazil is actionable here.
>
> It then follows, directly the right of action is established in this country, that the ordinary incidents of that action and the appropriate remedies ensue.
>
> Therefore, in this case, in my opinion, damages would flow from the wrong committed just as they would in any action brought in respect of a libel published in this country.'

Rigby LJ:

> 'It is not really a matter of any importance what the nature of the remedy for a wrong in a foreign country may be …
>
> I think there is no doubt at all that an action for a libel published abroad is maintainable here, unless it can be shewn to be justified or excused in the country where it was published. James LJ states in *The M Moxham* what the settled law is. Mellish LJ is quite as clear upon that point as James LJ in laying down the general rule; and Baggallay LJ also takes the same view. We start, then, from this: that the act in question is primâ facie actionable here, and the only thing we have to do is to see whether there is any peremptory bar to our jurisdiction arising from the fact that the act we are dealing with is authorised, or innocent or excusable, in the country where it was committed. If we cannot see that, we must act according to our own rules in the damages (if any) which we may choose to give. Here we cannot see it, and this appeal must be allowed with costs.'

Metall und Rohstoff AG* v *Donaldson Lufkin & Jenrette Inc [1990] 1 QB 391 Court of Appeal (Slade, Stocker and Bingham LJJ)

- *Whether a tort was committed within the jurisdiction and the effect of a foreign defence*

Facts

A plaintiff seeking leave to serve a writ out of the jurisdiction was bound by the cause of action pleaded. A tort had to be in substance committed within the jurisdiction: if so it was immaterial that a foreign defence existed. M & R was a Swiss company who traded on the London Metal Exchange through brokers AML. M & R's chief aluminium trader, G, instructed AML to open a number of accounts and with the assistance of certain employees of AML fraudulently traded, exposing M & R to loss. AML, its American parent company ACLI and its American holding company DLJ knew that G was trading fraudulently without M & R's knowledge. M & R obtained judgment against AML for over £50 million but recovered only part of this since AML became insolvent. M & R then started proceedings against ACLI and DLJ and obtained an order to serve the writ out of the jurisdiction. They claimed damages for conspiracy but without alleging that the purpose of the conspiracy was to harm M & R for inducing breach of contract, abuse of the process of the court, accounting as constructive trustees, and procuring breaches of trust. The defendants took out a summons under RSC O.12 r8(1)(c) to have the order for service set aside. The judge set it aside on certain grounds only.

Held

Although the acts alleged against the defendants of inducing or procuring a breach of contract had mainly taken place in New York, it was the breaches by AML in England that caused the plaintiffs substantial damage in England and so the tort was committed within the jurisdiction. It was immaterial that the claim would be statute-barred by the law of New York, and this claim came within O.11 r1(1)(f). The only cause of action available to the plaintiffs was that founded on inducement or procurement of breaches of contract, and London was the appropriate forum for determining that issue, and leave would be granted to serve the writ out of the jurisdiction on that basis.

Slade LJ:

> '*Inducing or procuring breaches of contract: where was the tort (or where were the torts) committed?*
>
> The tort of inducing (or procuring) a breach of contract has in English law three ingredients: (1) intentional acts of inducement or procurement (we take these words to mean the same and shall henceforth speak of inducement only); (2) a breach or breaches of contract caused by that inducement; (3) resulting damage to the innocent party whose contract is broken. It is necessary for

present purposes to consider M & R's case in the light of these ingredients ...

The acts of inducement which M & R allege against DLJ and ACLI as having led to the trading contract breaches took place largely, if not wholly, in New York. There were a series of meetings in New York attended by representatives of AML The inducement then took place. M & R have not pleaded any inducing letters, telexes or telephone calls from New York to London, nor (as we understand the pleading) any acts of inducement in London.

It is not entirely clear from the pleading where or exactly how DLJ and ACLI are said to have induced the compromise agreement breach. It is understandable that M & R do not know. The probability is that the inducement occurred in London.

It seems clear, and M & R plead in paragraphs 18(f) and (h), that AML's first breaches of contract occurred in New York. ASOMA, on behalf of M & R, were there told that AML would not pay the ledger credit due to M & R and would retain M & R's metal warrants. These were plain repudiations of the trading contracts and none the less so because M & R did not accept them. There then followed further breaches when AML in London took the action threatened in New York. These breaches took place in London, and the judge was, in our view, right to treat these as the most significant breaches: until these occurred M & R had suffered little injury; and until then AML could have availed itself of the locus poenitenti which M & R's refusal to accept the earlier repudiations had given. It was the action taken by AML in London in breach of the trading contracts, not the action taken in New York, which really injured M & R.

The compromise agreement breach took place in London. It had no significant New York dimension.

The damage which M & R suffered as a result of the trading contract breaches was, in our view, suffered in London: M & R did not receive the ledger credit payment which should have been made in London, did not receive the warrants which should have been delivered in London and suffered the detrimental closing out of their accounts in London. Similarly, it appears to us that the damage caused to M & R by the compromise agreement breach was suffered in London since security which should have been available to M & R in London was (it is said) wrongly charged in London and paid out of London.

If the acts of inducement alleged are viewed in isolation, the torts alleged here in our judgment, would, be properly regarded as, in substance, torts committed in New York. We do not think the acts inducing the compromise agreement breach would displace that conclusion. But if, as we have concluded, the question is where as a matter of substance the torts were committed, the matter must be looked at more broadly, taking account of the breaches (particularly the effective breaches) induced and the resulting damage. On this approach we conclude that as a matter of substance the torts were committed in London. This is the view which the judge took and we agree with him. It leads to the conclusion that the defendants cannot rely on the rule in *Boys* v *Chaplin* [1971] AC 356 as barring M & R's claim for inducing breaches of contract.

M & R are also able, under this head, to satisfy the requirements of O.11, r1(1)(f). The claim is founded on what is, in English law, a tort. Significant damage has been suffered within the jurisdiction. That is enough. It is not incumbent on M & R also to show that that damage was caused by tortious acts committed by the defendants within the jurisdiction. If it were necessary, we do not think that M & R (save in respect of the compromise agreement breach) could do so.'

Phillips* v *Eyre (1870) LR 6 QB 1 Exchequer Chamber (Kelly CB, Martin, Channell, Pigott, and Cleasby BB, Willes and Brett JJ)

• *As a general rule, an act done in a foreign country is a tort and actionable as such in England, only if it is both (a) actionable as a tort according to English law, and (b) civilly actionable according to the law of the foreign country where it was done*

Facts

This was an action complaining of false imprisonment and other injuries to the plaintiff by the defendant in the island of Jamaica. The defendant was governor of the island at the time that a rebellion broke out on the island, which the governor and others acting under his authority suppressed by force of arms. An Act was subsequently passed by the legislature of the island (receiving royal assent) under which the defendant and all officers and other persons who had acted under his authority, were indemnified in respect of all acts, matters, and things done in order to put an end to the rebellion and all such acts were 'thereby made and declared lawful, and were confirmed'. The defendant pleaded that the grievances complained of were measures used in the suppression of the rebellion, and were reasonably and in good faith considered by the defendant to be proper for the purpose of putting an end to the unrest, and bona fide done in order to put an end to the rebellion, and so were included in the indemnity. A number of objections were levelled at the validity of the Act.

Held

Willes J:

> 'Our courts are said to be more open to admit actions founded upon foreign transactions than those of any other European country; but there are restrictions in respect of locality which exclude some foreign causes of action altogether, namely, those which would be local if they arose in England, such as trespass to land: *Doulson* v *Matthews* (1792) 4 Term Rep 503, and even with respect to those not falling within that description our courts do not undertake universal jurisdiction. As a general rule, in order to found a suit in England for a wrong alleged to have been committed abroad, two conditions must be fulfilled. First, the wrong must be such a character that it would have been actionable if committed in England; therefore, in *The Halley* (1868) LR 2 PC 193, the Judicial Committee pronounced against a suit in the Admiralty founded upon a liability by the law of Belgium for collision caused by the act of a pilot whom the shipowner was compelled by that law to employ, and for whom, therefore, as not being his agent, he was not responsible by English law. Secondly, the act must not have been justifiable by the law of the place where it was done ... As to foreign laws affecting the liability of parties in respect of bygone transactions, the law is clear that, if the foreign law touches only the remedy or procedure for enforcing the obligation, as in the case of an ordinary statute of limitations, such law is no bar to an action in this country; but if the foreign law extinguishes the right it is a bar in this country equally as if the extinguishment had been by a release of the party, or an act of our own legislature ... So that where an obligation by contract to pay a debt or damages is discharged and avoided by the law of the place where it was made, the accessory right of action in every court open to the creditor unquestionably falls to the ground. And by strict parity of reasoning, where an obligation, ex delicto, to pay damages is discharged and avoided by the law of the country where it was made, the accessory right of action is in like manner discharged and avoided. Cases may possibly arise in which distinct and independent rights or liabilities or defences are created by positive and specific laws of this country in respect of foreign transactions: but there is no such law (unless it be the Governor's Act already discussed and disposed of) applicable to the present case.

It may be proper to remark, before quitting this part of the subject, that the colonial Act could not be overruled upon either of these two latter grounds of objection without laying down that no foreign legislation could avail to take away civil liability here in respect of acts done abroad; so that, for instance, if a foreign country after a rebellion or civil war were to pass a general Act of oblivion and indemnity, burying in one grave all legal memory alike of the hostilities, and even the private retaliations which are the sure results of anarchy and violence, it would, if the argument for the plaintiff prevailed, be competent for a municipal court of any other country to condemn and disregard, as naturally unjust or technically ineffectual, the law of a sovereign state, disposing, upon the same constitutional principles as have actuated our own legislature, of matters arising within its territory – a course which to adopt would be an unprecedented and mischievous violation of the comity of nations.

The judgment of the Court of Queen's Bench for the defendant was right, and is affirmed.'

Red Sea Insurance Co Ltd v Bouygues SA and Others [1994] 3 WLR 926 Privy Council (Lords Slynn, Keith, Woolf, Lloyd and Nolan)

• *Tort not actionable under the lex fori –* Boys *v* Chaplin *flexibility applied – lex loci delicti applied as governing law*

Facts

This case concerns a dispute that arose over the construction of the University of Riyadh in Saudi Arabia. The plaintiffs, who may be divided into two groups (Group 1 and Group 2), were involved in various capacities in the construction of the university and had incurred substantial losses in repairing and replacing structural damage which occurred when the buildings were constructed. They sought to recover these losses in an action in the Hong Kong courts under an insurance policy issued by the defendant insurance company (which was incorporated in Hong Kong although it had its head office in Saudi Arabia). The defendant raised various defences, but more significantly, the defendant counterclaimed against the Group 2 plaintiffs, on the ground that it was Group 2's supply of faulty precast concrete units which had caused the losses.

Now, under English law (which applied in Hong Kong), an insurer who has paid a claim made by a policy-holder can recover from the wrongdoer who caused the policy-holder's losses, the amount he has paid. But the insurer brings the policy-holder's tort claim against the wrongdoer; the insurer is 'subrogated' to the policy-holder's tort claim. However, an insurer can only bring such a 'subrogated' claim if he has already paid the policy-holder; and the defendant had not done so. However, the defendant claimed that under the law of Saudi Arabia he could bring a claim directly against the Group 2 plaintiffs in tort without having paid the policy-holder.

The difficulty with this was that the English law approach to choice of law in tort (which was also applied by the Hong Kong courts) required that the alleged wrong should be actionable under both the lex loci delicti commissi (the place where the wrong was committed; in our case Saudi Arabia) and the lex fori (the law of the forum; in our case Hong Kong). And since the Group 1 plaintiffs had not been paid, the defendant's claim was not actionable against the Group 2 plaintiffs in the courts of Hong Kong.

Since *Boys* v *Chaplin* [1971] AC 356 the rule requiring actionability under the lex loci could be applied flexibly so as to allow the court in proper cases to disregard the fact that the wrong complained of was not actionable under the lex loci. However, the rule requiring actionability under the lex fori had never been flexibly applied.

Held

That, notwithstanding the general rule of English law requiring actionability under both the lex fori and lex loci, exceptionally, in an appropriate case, the plaintiff could rely exclusively on the lex loci delicti even if under the lex fori his claim would not be actionable. This exception could apply to the whole claim, not just to particular issues, and, indeed, particular issues could in any event be governed by the law of the country which, with respect to that issue, had the most significant relationship with the occurrence and the parties.

Lord Slynn:

'Their Lordships, having considered all of these opinions, recognise the conflict which exists between, on the one hand, the desirability of a rule which is certain and clear on the basis of which people can act and lawyers advise and, on the other, the desirability of the courts having the power to avoid injustice by introducing an element of flexibility into the rule. They do not consider that the rejection of the doctrine of the proper law of the tort as part of English law is inconsistent with a measure of flexibility being introduced into the rules. They consider that the majority in *Boys* v *Chaplin* [1971] AC 356 recognised the need for such flexibility. They accept that the law of England recognises that a particular issue between the parties to litigation may be governed by the law of the country which, with respect to that issue, has the most significant relationship with the occurrence and with the parties. They agree with the statement of Lord Wilberforce, at pp391–392, which has been set out above as to the extent and application of the exception. They accept, as he did, that the exception will not be successfully invoked in every case or even, probably, in many cases and, at p391H, that:

> "The general rule must apply unless clear and satisfying grounds are shown why it should be departed from and what solution, derived from what other rule, should be preferred."

The books to which reference has been made indicate that many questions may need to be resolved in regard to the application of the exception to the double actionability rule. Only two of those questions need to be answered in the present case. The first is this. In *Boys* v *Chaplin* the application of the exception enabled the plaintiff to rely on the lex fori and to exclude the limited measure of damages imposed by the lex loci delicti. Can the exception be relied on to enable a plaintiff to rely on the lex loci delicti if his claim would not be actionable under the lex fori? There is obviously a difference between a court being able to apply its own law exclusively and it being required to apply exclusively another legal system. This, however, is not necessarily fatal to the contention that only the lex loci delicti be applied since the foreign law can be proved and it is clear that in appropriate cases the lex loci delicti can be applied to give a just result when the lex fori might not do so.

In *Boys* v *Chaplin* it is not suggested that the exception [to the "double actionability" rule] can be relied on only to exclude the lex loci delicti in favour of the lex fori. Their Lordships do not consider that the element of flexibility which exists is so limited ... Whilst recognising that to do so is a departure from the strict rule in *The Halley*, LR 2 PC 193, they consider that in principle the exception can be applied in an appropriate case to enable a plaintiff to rely exclusively on the lex loci delicti. To limit the rule so as to enable an English court only to apply English law would be in conflict with the degree of flexibility envisaged by Lord Wilberforce, though the fact that the forum is being required to apply a foreign law in a situation where its own law gives no remedy will be a factor to be taken into account when the court decides whether to apply the exception.

The second question is this. The present appeal is not based on an isolated issue (as was the case in *Boys* v *Chaplin*). The contention put forward is that the whole case be decided according to the lex loci delicti. Although the cases may be rare where the exception should be applied to the whole case, their Lordships do not consider that to apply the exception to the whole case is in principle necessarily excluded. In their Lordships' view the exception is not limited to specific isolated issues but may apply to the whole claim, for example where all or virtually all of the significant factors are in favour of the lex loci delicti.

It follows that the Court of Appeal was wrong to rule that the "direct" cause of action was unsustainable on the basis of *The Adhiguna Meranti* [1988] 1 Lloyd's Rep 384 (which their Lordships regard as having been wrongly decided) and to uphold the judge's refusal to give leave to amend. It remains to be considered, since clause (2) of the rule is to be applied only in exceptional cases, whether this is a case which satisfies the test, so that the lex loci delicti alone can be relied on and the first limb of the rule be dispensed with.

The appeal in this case is based on a number of factors relied on by the defendant, which need to be considered in the light of what has been said. Thus the policy of insurance was subject to Saudi Arabian law, the project was to be carried out in Saudi Arabia and the property was owned by the government. The main contract, the supply contract, and the HOK +4 consortium's service contract are all subject to the law of Saudi Arabia and were to be performed there. The breaches and the alleged damage occurred in Saudi Arabia. The expense of repairing alleged damaged occurred in Saudi Arabia. The defendant, though incorporated in Hong Kong, had its head office in Saudi Arabia.

In their Lordships' view these are all factors which should have been taken into account by the trial judge in deciding whether leave should have been given for the counterclaim to be amended. It being established that an exception to the general rule of double actionability exists on the lines set out above, they all point to the exception being applied in this case. The arguments in favour of the lex loci delicti are indeed overwhelming.'

Comment

For criticism of this case see Briggs, 'The Halley: Holed but Still Afloat' (1995) 111 LQR 18.

Sayers* v *International Drilling Co NV [1971] 1 WLR 1176 Court of Appeal (Lord Denning, Salmon and Stamp LJJ)

• *Effect of exclusion clause on tortious action – proper law of the tort*

Facts

An English domiciled workman was employed by a Dutch company on an oil rig in Nigerian waters. His contract contained a clause which provided that the benefits that he was entitled to under a company Compensation programme was his exclusive remedy if he were injured or disabled at work. Such a clause was invalid under English law because of s1(3) of the Law Reform (Personal Injuries) Act 1948 which provided that clauses that excluded or limited the liability of an employer 'in respect of personal injuries caused to the person employed ... by the negligence of persons in common employment with him' were void. Dutch law contained similar legislation, but that legislation did not apply to international contracts such as the one signed by the plaintiff. The plaintiff was injured shortly after he arrived at the oil rig. In due course he sued the Dutch company in England and the question whether the Dutch company could raise the exemption clause as a defence was tried as a preliminary issue.

Held

That the proper law of the contract was Dutch law (contra Lord Denning) and thus the exemption was valid and could be relied upon by the company.

Lord Denning:

> 'The issue raises an important question of private international law. On the one hand, the claim by the plaintiff is claim founded on tort. In considering that claim, we must apply the proper law of tort, that is, the law of the country with which the parties and the acts done have the most significant connection. That is how I put it in *Boys* v *Chaplin*

[1968] 2 QB 1, 20. I think it is confirmed by what Lord Wilberforce said in [1971] AC 356, 391–393, in the House of Lords, though he put it with more scholarship and precision than I could hope to do.

On the other hand, the defence by the defendants is a defence based on contract. In considering that defence we must apply the proper law of the contract, that is, the system of law with which the contract has its closest and most real connection: see *Compagnie Tunisienne de Navigation SA* v *Compagnie d'Armement Maritime SA* [1970] 3 WLR 389, 393, 397.

But it is obvious that we cannot apply two systems of law, one for the claim in tort, and the other for the defence in contract. We must apply one system of law by which to decide both claim and defence. To decide it I would ask this question: What is the proper law by which to determine the issues in this case? And I would answer it by saying: it is the system of law with which the issues have the closest connection.

So far as the claim in tort is concerned, the accident took place in the territorial waters of Nigeria. But it took place on an oil drilling rig owned and controlled by a Dutch company and manned by employees of that company. The Nigerians had nothing to do with the rig. So Nigeria is out. The injured man was English, but his fellow employees (who were negligent) may have been English or American or of some other nationality. The only common bond between them was that they were employed by the Dutch company. So Dutch is in. If I were asked to decide the proper law of the tort (apart from contract) I should have said it was Dutch law.

So far as the defence in contract is concerned, the contract with Mr Sayers was negotiated and made in England. It was for the services of Mr Sayers, an Englishman, asking him to go overseas for a spell of work. It was in the English language. His salary was to be paid in the English currency, sterling. He was insured under the English national insurance scheme. He was to come back on leave to his home in England. True it is that the employers were Dutch (who employed personnel of all nationalities), but the contract was administered in London. The records were kept in London, Texas and Holland. If I were asked to decide the proper law of the contract (apart from the tort) I should be inclined to say that it was English.

But seeing that the action is founded on tort and the proper law of the tort is Dutch, I would say that, as between the two systems, English or Dutch, the issue of liability should be determined by Dutch law. In any case, there is a provision in clause 8 of the contract which turns the scale against English law. It runs thus:

> "As the company is a Netherlands Corporation, and as my employment contract hereby applied for will be wholly performable overseas and outside of United Kingdom, the company does not subscribe to or carry workmen's compensation insurance under the laws of United Kingdom. Accordingly, I realise that I shall not be covered by virtue of my proposed employment with the company by workmen's compensation insurance or benefits under the law of United Kingdom … I am satisfied with the provisions and benefits of the said Compensation Program."

Seeing that English law is in terms excluded, I think that the issue of liability has its closest connection with Dutch law; and should be determined by Dutch law. According to that law this exemption clause is valid and effective to bar Mr Sayers' claim in tort. His claim must be limited to the benefits in the Dutch company's Compensation Program.'

Comment

Although Lord Denning, unlike Salmon LJ, recognised the tortious aspects of this case, the approach he then adopted to resolving the question – adopting neither the choice of law rules for contract nor for tort, but seeking the system of law with which the issue of liability has its 'closest connection' – is entirely novel. It has not been followed, and it is unlikely to be followed.

The choice of law under the Private International Law (Miscellaneous Provisions) Act 1995

Edmunds v Simmonds [2001] 1 WLR 1003 Queen's Bench Division (Garland J)

• *Action relating to damages for personal injuries arising out of a road traffic accident whilst on holiday in Spain where both parties were English – appropriate forum and quantification of damages*

Facts

E, an English citizen who had suffered a severe head injury in Spain while travelling as a passenger in a hire car driven by S, sought damages for personal injury from S. The principles governing the determination of liability were the same in both Spanish and English law, but the quantification of damages differed, with the result that Spanish law was likely to produce a substantially lower award. E sought resolution of the case under English law and submitted that since the assessment of damages was a procedural process as opposed to a substantive one, quantification fell to be determined in accordance with the law of the forum, namely the same law as that which was applied to determine liability issues. S maintained that Spanish law was applicable because all issues, including quantification, were subject to the Private International Law (Miscellaneous Provisions) Act 1995, ss11 and 12.

Held

Although heads of damages were matters of substantive law, the quantification of damages was a procedural task and, where a tort had been committed in a foreign country, damages were to be assessed in accordance with the law of the forum. The fact that both parties were English, coupled with the fact that the principal heads of damage had arisen in England, firmly indicated that it was more appropriate to assess damages according to English law.

Garland J:

'Two issues have been ordered to be tried. Firstly, what is the applicable law under the provisions of the 1995 Private International Law (Miscellaneous Provisions) Act: and, secondly, liability.

I will deal first with liability ... I have already referred briefly to the 1995 Act, which, as Mr Grime [counsel for the plaintiff] said, was a fresh start in determining the proper law of torts committed abroad. The relevant parts of s9 are ...

The common law rules were abolished except for claims in defamation preserved by s13.

The Act avoids the Latin with which this aspect of private international law was liberally provided. The general rule in personal injuries is that the applicable law is that of the country in which the events constituting the tort occurred; in this case, Spain. However, s12 allows for the possible displacement of the general rule. The general rule is, s11 ... Subsection (2) does not apply to the instant case, but it does serve to emphasise, to use the forbidden Latin, the lex loci basis of the general rule.

Section 12, which allows for the displacement of the general rule, provides ... Obvious connecting factors are that both the complainant and defendant are English and that the complainant's damages, particularly the major heads, cost of care and loss of future earnings as consequences of the events constituting the tort, arise in England, but Mr Grimes submitted that this was not an entirely domestic matter, as in *Boys* v *Chaplin* [1971] AC 356, which concerned a collision between vehicles driven by members of the British Armed Services in Malta. Here, both vehicles were Spanish, one driver was Spanish, both insurers are Spanish. And even though the complainant's damages all arise in England, the significant connection is with the country whose law would be the applicable law under the general rule, that is Spain.

Mr Grime went on to submit that the distinction between substantive matters of law and purely procedural matters is a pre-1995 concept, which has been replaced in s9 by "issues", so that quantification appears to have been equated with liability. He referred to the article by Professor CG. Morse in "International and Comparative Law Quarterly" for October 1996 at 895 …

Procedural aspects of damages which will be governed by the law of the forum and not by the applicable law, clearly include the question whether damages should be determined by a judge or jury and whether damages may be awarded in the form of periodical payments or must be awarded in a lump sum. At common law it was thought that the quantification or assessment of damages was also a matter for the law of the forum. If this view persists under Part III of the 1995 Act, difficulties will arise if the applicable law recognises a cause of action which is unknown to English domestic law, for the simple reason that there will be no English domestic rules on quantification and assessment for the English court to apply as the lex fori. A possible solution would be to model the English quantification or assesssment on that which obtains in the foreign law so far as that is possible."

Mr Grime relied on the latter part of the passage quoted to suggest that the effect of the Act was that all issues, including quantification, should be governed by ss11 and 12.

Mr Strachan's argument was that once it is determined that the events constituting the tort arose from the defendant's loss of control, the involvement of the lorry is, so far as s12 is concerned, irrelevant, and the tort is indeed a domestic one, save only that the insurers are Spanish. However, insurers of hire cars in tourist areas, a fortiori those who provide fly-drive services, must contemplate that the majority of the hirers will be foreign and that accidents will occur involving not only nationals but other foreigners with the consequent possibility of damages being quantified according to some other system of law.

In my view, Brunning J (sitting as a Deputy Judge of the Queen's Bench Division) in the case of *Hamill* v *Hamill* (unreported, July 24, 2000) was correct in reaching the same conclusion. He considered that the question of the Spanish insurer was not of overwhelming weight for reasons very similar to those which Mr Strachan [counsel for the defendants] advanced and which I accept. Mr Strachan therefore submitted that the factors connecting the tort to this country were very strong and that the insurance point was not of sufficient strength to bring down the scales on the side of s12(1)(a). The ratio of *Boys* v *Chaplin* was, he submitted, still good law, a view taken by the editors of Dicey & Morris when considering s12, at paragraphs 35–102 to 35–104 of Volume 2 and I shall just quote from 35–103:

> "For example, in *Boys* v *Chaplin* the issue in the case was as to the heads of recoverable damage. Given the distribution of the relevant factors in the case (particularly the normal residence of the parties in England, and their temporary presence in Malta as members of the British Armed Forces) it would seem that the particular issue which arose would be substantially more appropriately governed by English law, not least because heads of damage is an issue strongly linked to the country where the claimant normally resides, a link which is rendered even stronger when the defendant resides in the same country. Further, no policy or interest of Malta, the law of which would have been applicable under the general rule, would be infringed if one English resident is required to compensate another English resident according to the heads of damage available in English law."

If we substitute Spain for Malta, I endorse the view expressed by the learned editors.

I find no difficulty in carrying out the comparison required by s12. The connecting factors to Spain are that the collision occurred there and that the car was insured there. Even if quantification is to be regarded as falling within "the applicable law for determining issues", the s12(1)(b) factors appear to me overwhelming. The claimant and the defendant are English, the claimant's damages arise wholly in England and it appears to me that the passage that I have quoted from Dicey & Morris is wholly apt to cover the present situation.

Mr Strachan also drew some comfort from Professor Morse in the passage quoted.

In my judgment, accepting that the insurance point is not one of overwhelming weight, it is substantially more appropriate that damages should be assessed according to English law. Having reached this conclusion, it is not strictly necessary that I should decide the "substantive or procedural" point, but I am not persuaded that the 1995 Act has abrogated the distinction which appears to me to be expressly preserved by s14(3)(b), which provides for questions of procedure to be determined in accordance with the law of the forum. Heads of damage are matters of substantive law. How damages are quantified under those heads, are in my view, matters of procedure. Even if I had not decided the s12 point in the claimant's favour, I would, unless persuaded that Spanish law did not recognise any head of damage recoverable by the claimant, have decided that quantification was purely procedural and should be carried out according to English law in any event. I therefore determine both of the issues ordered to be tried in favour of the claimant for the reasons which I have given.'

Glencore International AG and Others v *Metro Trading International Inc* [2001] 1 Lloyd's Rep 284 Queen's Bench Division (Commercial Court) (Moore-Bick J)

- *Application of s11 Private International Law (Miscellaneous Provisions) Act 1995*

Facts

The defendant (MTI) was engaged in the buying, blending and selling of fuel oil either to vessels as bunker fuel for their own consumption or to traders on the international oil market as cargoes or part cargoes of fuel oil. These activities were carried out in Fujairah itself and in the waters of Fujairah. Parcels of oil received by MTI were generally not kept in segregated tanks. The claimants all entered into agreements at one time or another with MTI under which they delivered oil products to MTI for storage. In February 1998 MTI became insolvent and could not continue its operations. A receiver was appointed. The oil claimants (which included Glencore) all asserted proprietary claims to the oil held by MTI. However, during this time MTI had obtained finance from a number of banks in order to run its business. These banks claimed they were entitled to a first charge over various sums of money due to MTI and over the products remaining in storage.

MTI and the purchasers alleged that questions of the passing of title to oil situated in Fujairah was governed by the law of Fujairah under which property had passed from the oil companies to MTI and from MTI to the purchasers. The oil companies disputed that, relying on the terms of the contracts between themselves and MTI and upon a different understanding of the effect of the law of Fujairah.

Held

The claims being made by the oil claimants against the purchasers were for wrongful interference with goods. By s11 of the Private International Law (Miscellaneous Provisions) Act 1995 the applicable law for determining issues relating to tort was generally the law of the country in which the events constituting the tort occurred. All the relevant acts occurred in Fujairah where the goods were situated at the relevant time. The law of Fujairah governed such claims

Moore-Bick J:

'*Issue C.2 – Whether, as a matter of English conflict of law principles, questions as to whether any claims against the relevant co-defendant are governed by Fujairah law, English law or some other law as the applicable law of the claim.*

The claims being made by the oil claimants

against the purchasers are for wrongful interference with goods; as such they proceed on the footing that property in the oil remained in the oil claimants at the time it was delivered to the purchasers. The rules governing the choice of law for determining issues relating to tort are now contained in Part III of the Private International Law (Miscellaneous Provisions) Act, 1995. By s11 of the Act the applicable law is generally the law of the country in which the events constituting the tort occurred. In the present case all the relevant acts occurred in Fujairah where the goods were situated at the relevant time. However, this general rule is displaced if factors connecting the tort with some other country indicate that it is substantially more appropriate to take as the applicable law the law of that country: see s12.

[It has been] submitted that a comparison between the factors connecting the case with Fujairah and those connecting it with England indicated that it was substantially more appropriate for the applicable law in the present case to be English law. However, the only basis for that submission was the fact that in each case the purchaser agreed to buy the goods on English law terms. As I have already pointed out, there was no direct relationship between the oil claimant and the purchaser in any of these cases and I am quite unable to accept that the mere fact that MTI agreed to sell bunkers on English law terms is sufficient to displace the general rule in s11. The fact that all the events in question occurred in Fujairah where the goods themselves were situated seems to me to provide the strongest possible connection with that country. My answer to the question raised by issue C.2 is that such claims are governed by the law of Fujairah.'

Hulse v *Chambers* [2002] 1 All ER (Comm) 812 Queen's Bench Division (Holland J)

- *The assessment of damages was a procedural matter for the English court, falling within s14(3)(b) Private International Law (Miscellaneous Provisions) Act 1995*

Facts

A preliminary issue arose in an action in negligence brought by H against C, following a road accident in Greece, as to what law should apply to the assessment of damages. C had admitted liability for causing personal injuries to H while driving in a hire car whilst on holiday in Greece. It was common ground that pursuant to s11 Private International Law (Miscellaneous Provisions) Act 1995 the applicable law was Greek law. In accordance with Greek law, a right of action supported the suing of the Greek insurance company which, in any event, had admitted liability to indemnify the defendant. H had prepared a schedule of damages and contended that since the assessment of damages was a procedural matter English law applied. C argued that not only the head of damage but its assessment was the subject of the substantive applicable law.

Held

Determining the preliminary issue in favour of H, that the assessment of damages was subject to the procedural law governing the English court. The assessment of damages was a procedural matter for the English court, falling within s14(3)(b) of the Act. Accordingly, damages would be assessed in accordance with English law irrespective of the provisions of the local law. The assessment of damages was a 'jury question', albeit one that was usually taken over by the judge. To impose a Greek bracket would inevitably take that assessment away from the judge as jury.

Holland J:

> 'In prosecuting the claims the premise has been that substantive issues are governed by Greek law and similarly the premise for the respective admissions of liability has been that such as matters of substance can and have to be justified by Greek law. This focus by both parties reflects the relevant provisions of the Private International (Miscellaneous Provisions) Act 1995 …
>
> Upon the matter first coming before me in July 2000, Mr Saggerson for the claimants pointed out that by virtue of s11 the applicable law was prima facie Greek law; he acknowledged an inability to displace that presumption by way of a s12 application. That stance has remained unaltered notwithstanding two subsequent first instance decisions in each of which there was a ruling in favour of English law on the basis of a s12 displacement in reliance upon markedly similar facts: *Hamill* v *Hamill*, unreported, 24th July 2000 and *Edmunds* v *Simmonds*, unreported, 4th October 2000. I emphasise: before me in the instant case there has been no issue but that Greek law is the applicable law, its status as such flowing from s11 …
>
> At the heart of the respective submissions is the distinction between substantive and procedural law and its significance in the present context. This distinction arises out of necessity: as and when a foreign law is the applicable law for application by an English court there has inevitably to be some limit to its potential ambit – an English court can only function as such and it cannot become for all purposes a court of the jurisdiction from whence came the applicable law. The distinction thus made (and this is common ground) is between substantive law and procedural law: any applicable law provides the former but the latter is invariably the lex fori , that is, the procedural law governing the English Court. This distinction, well established in authority is sensibly perpetuated in the 1995 Act. As to the former the distinction cannot be more clearly or more authoritatively set out than in Dicey & Morris, 13th Edition, 200, Rule 17: "All matters of procedure are governed by the domestic law of the Country to which the Court wherein any legal proceedings are taken belongs (lex fori)." In the commentary the authors add at paragraph 7–004 "The primary object of this Rule is to obviate the inconvenience of conducting the trial of a case containing foreign elements in a manner with which the court is unfamiliar."…
>
> I am entirely satisfied that assessment of the General Damages justified as a head of claim by Greek law as the applicable law, is to be made by reference to English law, as the lex fori. I am satisfied that the preponderance of such guidance as is available is to that effect but I also venture the following analysis. Starting with the machinery for making an assessment of damage, I take it to be beyond dispute that that is a procedural consideration to be governed by the lex fori. In the event for this jurisdiction the original machinery of choice for making the inevitable value judgment was the jury and on my reading of s69 Supreme Court Act 1981 there is still no absolute obstacle to a jury trial of the quantum of general damages. In the event, of course, as pointed out by Lord Woolf MR in *Heil* v *Rankin* [2000] 2 WLR 1173 at 1186 judges have for pragmatic reasons taken over quantum assessment from juries since the 1960's (if not much earlier) so that it is now virtually inconceivable that a jury trial of this issue would be ordered. That said, assessment remains a "jury question" (See Lord Woolf MR at 1186) and subject to the guidance given from time to time by the Court of Appeal (for example in *Heil* v *Rankin*) it must always be such. In essence the procedure dictates the nature of the assessment process and thus its product, quantification. To impose a Greek bracket would inevitably take assessment away from the judge as jury: "do not make your own value judgment, make such as you think on the evidence might be made by a Greek court". We only get to this latter assessment by imposing a foreign procedure on the quantification exercise.'

Johnson v *Coventry Churchill International Ltd* [1992] 3 All ER 14 Queen's Bench Division (J W Kay QC)

• *Dual-actionability test – actionability in England – act committed abroad*

Facts

The defendants were an English employment agency, which recruited English personnel to work abroad world-wide. The plaintiff responded to an advertisement placed by the defendants seeking concrete shutterers for work in West Germany. He was hired under a contract which referred to him as a 'sub-contractor' and provided that he was at all times to work as and where directed by the defendants and their clients, and that the defendants would pay the plaintiff his remuneration. The plaintiff travelled to Stuttgart and two weeks later suffered serious personal injuries while walking across two wooden planks positioned over an eight-foot deep trench on the site. West German law did not provide for an employer to be liable for personal injuries suffered by an employee as the result of the employer's negligence and the plaintiff therefore brought an action in England against the defendants claiming damages for negligence on the ground that the defendants, as his employers, had failed to comply with their duty to provide a safe system of work. The defendants contended amongst other things that the plaintiff's case failed to satisfy the dual-actionability rule. The plaintiff contended that his claim fell within the exception to the dual-actionability rule and that English law should apply because there was a particular issue between the parties, which ought to be governed by the law of the country with the most significant relationship to the occurrence, and the parties.

Held

The plaintiff's case did not satisfy the dual-actionability test because, although the defendants' failure to provide a safe system of work, if it had occurred in England, would have amounted to the tort of negligence and given rise to liability for the personal injuries and loss suffered by the plaintiff, it was not actionable under West German law, which exempted an employer from liability for damages arising out of personal injuries incurred by a worker in the course of his employment save where the injuries resulted from a wilful breach of duty, which excluded negligence. However, the issue whether the defendants were liable as employers to compensate the plaintiff for the injury suffered in the course of his employment as a result of their negligence was an issue which fell within the scope of the exception to the dual-actionability rule under which a wrong allegedly committed in a foreign country was actionable as a tort according to English law in circumstances where justice to the plaintiff dictated that English law should be applied to a particular issue between the parties as the law of the country having the most significant relationship with the occurrence relating to that issue and the parties. On that basis, justice to the plaintiff dictated that the issue should be governed by English law, since the country with the most significant relationship to the occurrence and the parties was England and the defendants, who had taken out insurance to protect their position as employers of English workers abroad, were unlikely to be taken unawares by the consequences of applying English law. Accordingly, the defendants' liability for the personal injuries and loss suffered by the plaintiff having been established, the plaintiff was entitled to judgment.

J W Kay QC:

> 'For these reasons I have come to the conclusion that, if all the matters with which this case is concerned had happened in England, they would amount to the tort of negligence and give rise to liability for the personal injuries and loss suffered by the plaintiff. It is necessary, therefore, to proceed to the second question.
>
> The defendants called before me a West German lawyer, Dr Reischauer ... In the cir-

cumstances of this case, Dr Reischauer concluded that if German law were to be applied the action would be bound to fail because of this exemption. No evidence to the contrary was called and I am satisfied that the defendants have established this to be the position. Initially Mr Brennan [counsel for the plaintiff] sought to distinguish a rule of foreign law that exempted liability that would otherwise arise from a situation where there was no liability at all in the foreign law. However, when his attention was drawn to *McMillan* v *Canadian Northern Rly Co* [1923] AC 120 and *Walpole* v *Canadian Northern Rly Co* [1923] AC 113 he recognised that such an argument could not be sustained.

It follows that the action does not satisfy the dual-actionability test and must therefore fail unless it can be brought within the exception envisaged in *Chaplin* v *Boys* [1969] 2 All ER 1085, [1971] AC 356 …

All these factors lead me to the conclusion that the country with the most significant relationship with the occurrence and the parties is England. I therefore ask myself whether this is not one of that limited number of cases to which Lord Wilberforce referred where the law of England should govern this particular issue. Justice to the plaintiff seems to dictate that it should, but I first consider whether the defendants and others in a similar position would be so disadvantaged by such a decision that I ought still to follow the general rule.

An employer sending employees to work in a foreign country can always protect his position in a number of ways. One is to insure against any liability that may arise. In considering whether the defendants were likely to be taken unawares by the consequences of applying English law to this situation, it cannot be without significance that the defendants had in fact taken out insurance against just such an eventuality. I, of course, accept that the purpose of such a policy is to provide cover if the insured is liable and as such cannot determine liability but it nonetheless establishes that the possibility was not beyond the contemplation of the defendants …

Having considered all these aspects of such a decision, I am of the opinion that justice does require this to be treated as one of those exceptions to the general rule envisaged in *Chaplin* v *Boys* and that English law should be applied to the crucial issue in this case.

For these reasons it follows that the defendants' liability for the injuries, loss and damage suffered by the plaintiff is established on the facts of this case and that the plaintiff is entitled to judgment accordingly. Damages have been agreed in the sum of £75,000 inclusive of interest and that is the sum that I award.'

Roerig* v *Valiant Trawlers Ltd [2002] 1 All ER 961 Court of Appeal (Waller, Simon Brown and Sedley LJJ)

• *Application of s12 Private International Law (Miscellaneous Provisions) Act 1995 (displacement of general rule)*

Facts

V appealed against a decision that Dutch law did not apply to a compensation claim brought against it by R. R, a Dutch woman, brought the claim when her Dutch partner, who was the father of her children, was killed on an English registered trawler owned by V, an English company. V argued that Dutch law should apply to the question of compensation as the matter was 'substantially' more connected with Holland than England and therefore came within s12 Private International Law (Miscellaneous Provisions) Act 1995. Under Dutch law benefits paid to the deceased's defendants were deductible from any compensation. The judge found against V and V appealed, arguing that the relevant factors were that the deceased and his dependants were Dutch and that the trawler had been sailing from a Dutch port.

Held

Appeal dismissed. The factors identified by

V were not sufficient to warrant a finding that Dutch law was 'substantially' more applicable. To do so would be to suggest that whenever a foreigner was injured in England, the law of his country should apply to compensation. Far more would be required to displace the general rule under the Fatal Accidents Act 1976 by which English law, given that both V and its trawler were registered in England, was applicable. In any event, as R had brought the claim under the 1976 Act the English court was required to implement the provisions of that Act, including s4 by which benefits were to be disregarded in calculating compensation. *Boys* v *Chaplin* [1971] AC 356 considered.

7 Jurisdiction and Choice of Law in Property

The distinction between immovables and movables

Berchtold, Re, Berchtold v *Capron* [1923] 1 Ch 192 Chancery Division (Russell J)

• *The doctrine of conversion does not operate in the field of the conflict of laws – an interest in English freehold land, held on trust for sale, is an interest in an immovable*

Facts

Count Richard Berchtold had died domiciled in Hungary, leaving freehold property in Birmingham. By his will this land was left to his trustees to hold on trust for sale; the primary beneficiary of these trusts was his son Count Nicholas, who was also domiciled in Hungary. Count Nicholas died intestate. If the interest in the Birmingham land (which had not yet been sold) was an immovable, then his heirs under English law (as lex situs) were entitled. But if the doctrine of conversion operated to transmute that interest into a movable, then his heirs under Hungarian law (as lex domicilii) were entitled.

Held

That the doctrine of conversion did not operate to convert the interest in the land into a movable.

Russell J:

> 'On behalf of the Countess Szokolyi it was argued that according to English law land directed to be sold and turned into money must be considered to be money; and that on the principle that equity considers done what should be done, the Birmingham freeholds are, in the eye of the law, money. This argument, to be effective, must add the words "for all purposes". That the Birmingham freeholds are to be treated as money for some purposes, no one doubts. Thus the interest of the taker is personal estate. But this equitable doctrine of conversion only arises and comes into play where the question for consideration arises as between real estate and personal estate. It has no relation to the question whether property is movable or immovable. The doctrine of conversion is that real estate is treated as personal estate, or personal estate is treated as real estate; not that immovables are turned into movables, or movables into immovables. As Farwell LJ pointed out in *In re Hoyles* [1911] 1 Ch 179, 187 the fact that a mortgage is regarded as personal estate for certain purposes in questions between our fellow subjects here has no bearing on the question whether such a mortgage should be regarded as a movable or not in questions of international law.
>
> Various authorities were cited in support of Countess Szokolyi's claim which I will now refer to. *Forbes* v *Steven* LR 10 Eq 178 was a decision of Sir William James. The question for decision was whether legacy duty was payable under the will of a domiciled Englishman on his share of the proceeds of partnership real estate in Bombay which was sold after his death. The testator died in 1849. The real estate in question was not sold until 1864, and in 1867 the share of the testator in the proceeds of sale was transferred to the account of his executors. The Inland Revenue claimed that legacy

duty was payable on this share as arising from property impressed by the partnership contract with the character of personal estate and evolving in that character on the testator's legatees. The Vice-Chancellor decided in favour of the claim on the ground that the produce of a partnership asset was personal estate, that the residuary legatees only took it because it was personal estate, and that they must take it subject to the legacy duty imposed on residuary legatees. That case had nothing to do with the question whether the interest in the Bombay real estate (which in equity was personal property) was movable property or immovable property. *In re Stokes* 62 LT 176, 178 was cited as a case in which North J had in effect held that an interest in partnership land or in land agreed to be sold was movable property. The testator, Robert Stokes, was a domiciled Englishman, who was in partnership with his brother, John Stokes, in the business of sheep breeding. The testator was entitled to four-sevenths of the partnership property. Part of the partnership property consisted of a freehold estate in New Zealand called the Milbourne Estate. There was a question whether this was converted under an agreement between the partners, or whether it was converted by being part of the capital of the business. North J held that, upon either view, the estate was subject to a trust for conversion. The testator by his will had disposed of all those, his four equal seventh shares and all other, if any, the estate and interest which he might at the time of his death possess or have power to dispose of in the Milbourne Estate upon certain trusts. North J held that what was disposed of by the words of the will was his interest under his agreement with his brother by virtue of which he was entitled to receive: "not four-sevenths of the estate, or four-sevenths of the proceeds, but a share amounting to four-sevenths of the surplus after making all the deductions that were necessary in respect of expenses and also bringing into hotchpot any advances that either of the brothers had received and which ought to be set against his share". The learned judge then describes that interest as personal estate, as a credit to which the testator was entitled in respect of the estate. In these circumstances North J held that legacy duty was payable in respect of that interest. He followed *Forbes* v *Steven* LR 10 Eq 178, the liability to legacy duty depending not on whether the interest was a movable or immovable but on whether or not it was personal estate. He nowhere decides that the interest was movable property ...'

Comment

The result reached in *Re Berchtold* is certainly logical and sound, but it may not be reconcilable with *Re Piercy* (see below), which Russell J mentioned only to dismiss as giving 'no assistance'.

Piercy, Re, Whitwham v *Piercy* [1895] 1 Ch 83 Chancery Division (North J)

- *Once land is sold, then the proceeds of the sale are movables*

Facts

Here a testator domiciled in England left land in Sardinia (where Italian law applied) to trustees upon trust for sale and conversion and to hold the land before conversion and the proceeds of the sale after conversion on certain trusts for his children and their issue. Italian law, the applicable lex situs of the land, outlawed such 'trust substitutions' and would hold the children absolutely entitled. If the land held on trust for sale could be treated as a movable, however, then English law could be applied as lex domicilii.

Held

Whether the trustees or the children were the heirs of the land under Italian law, the direction in the will that the land be sold was valid under Italian law. Once sold, however, the proceeds of the sale were then movables, and should be held under the trusts declared in the will. Prior to the sale, the rents of the land would go to the children, but they could elect that the rents be applied as if they were income resulting from the proceeds of the sale.

North J:

'The question is, What is the position of matters as regards the real estate in *Sardinia*? It is not necessary for me to decide the question whether, under Italian law, the trustees take "as heirs", or whether the testator's children and brother and sister take "as heirs", because quacunque via the will is good. If the trustees take as heirs, then everything beyond is "trust substitution", which would not be good according to Italian law, but the gift to the heirs would stand. If, on the other hand, as I think, the trustees are not the heirs, but the testator's children and brother and sister are the heirs, then, in my judgment, according to the preponderating weight of opinion, coupled with the evidence derived from what has actually taken place, the trustees have, according to Italian law, a clear power to sell the testator's real estate in *Sardinia* without any interference on the part of the persons beneficially interested in it. Therefore the direction given by the will to the trustees to sell the estate is perfectly good according to Italian law.

Then the next question is, as to the application of the proceeds of sale. With respect to that, in my opinion, the will is perfectly good, because the application of the proceeds is not in any way inconsistent with the Italian law. The Italian law relates to the land: it determines how the land is to go, and regulates the rights of the various persons interested in it. When an absolute sale has taken place, the Italian law still applies to the land in the hands of the then owner or owners; but it has nothing whatever to do with the proceeds of sale, after the land has been placed outside the scope of the will by a disposition which is valid according to Italian law.

Then, as regards the proceeds of sale, is there anything in Italian law which renders it illegal for the testator to do what he has done? The testator has directed that the proceeds of the sale of the land – that is, money to be obtained by the English trustees – is to be received by them, to be invested upon English securities, and then to be held by the trustees upon the trusts declared by an English will in favour of English beneficiaries. No one suggests that there is anything in Italian law forbidding this. It is, indeed, said by one of the Italian advocates that the land is the "patrimony", and that, when the land is sold, the proceeds of sale – the money – is still the "patrimony". What is the law as to that? It depends altogether upon the person to whom the money belongs. No doubt, if the money belongs to an owner who is subject to Italian law, whatever the Italian law forbids as to trusts must be observed, and if any person owning this property is subject to Italian law, and attempts to create a trust which the Italian law forbids, then, according to Italian law, the trust would be void. But when there is an English owner of money arising from the sale of land which belongs to other persons, and is subject in their hands to Italian law, there is nothing in Italian law to make that money itself subject to Italian law; and therefore, in my opinion, the proceeds of sale, when received by the trustees in pursuance of the valid exercise of the power of sale which they have according to the Italian law, pass entirely by the testator's will: because the disposition is good according to English law, and is in no way at variance with Italian law – meaning now by "Italian law" not merely anything which is expressed in the Italian Code, but anything contrary to "good custom" (whatever that may mean) – for the Italian law does not profess to regulate the disposition of English securities passing under the will of an Englishman to English legatees. In my opinion, therefore, the trust for sale being valid, the application of the proceeds of sale directed by the will is valid also.

Then the only question remaining is this. The trust has not yet been entirely executed, and at the present moment a part of the testator's Italian land remains unsold, and is, therefore, subject to the law of *Italy*. The enjoyment of that land in the meantime, until it has been sold, is not in any way affected by the trust for sale, which has not yet been executed. We must look, therefore, to the Italian law to say what is the right to enjoy the land in the meantime, before the sale has actually taken place. I will take first the case of the testator's widow. It seems to me clear that, according to Italian law, she is a "usufructuary", in the sense that the disposition in her favour for life is perfectly good, and that the gift to the testator's children and brother and sister, subject to that usufruct, is a good disposition.

Then comes the question of the "trust substitution"; and as to that, I come to the conclusion upon the evidence that the property is unconverted during that limited period. The Italian law applying, there can be no "trust substitution", and, that being so, the attempt to settle the shares on the children and the brother is not valid. As regards the sister there is no question, because she takes absolutely in any case. As regards the children, to the extent of one moiety of their shares, and the brother as to the whole of his share, there is an attempt to settle. With the exception of the heir-at-law *Robert Charles Piercy* and the brother (who is dead), none of these persons raise any question. According to the Italian law they take absolutely, and the trusts over are ineffectual; but with those two exceptions they all say, "We wish to give effect to the testator's will in this respect; we are desirous that the income of the property until conversion shall, so far as our interests go, be applied in the same way as our shares of the income to arise from the proceeds of the conversion directed by the will will go after the conversion has taken place." There is nothing, in my view, contrary to Italian law in their saying that they wish their shares of the income of the unsold land to be applied in the same way as if they were shares of the income arising from the proceeds of sale after the conversion had taken place. The heir-at-law, however, does not elect or waive any right which he may have, and it is unnecessary for me to decide anything as to his share at present. So long as he lives, and the land remains unsold, he will, of course, be entitled to receive the income of his share, whether the trusts in favour of his children are good or bad, and no question between him and his children, or any other person, can possibly arise. It may be that all the land will be sold during his lifetime, and the question will never arise as between him and his children. But it is possible that he may die while part of the land remains unsold, and the question may then arise between him and his children. Any directions, therefore, which I now give must be without prejudice to any question between *Robert Charles Piercy* on the one hand, and, on the other hand, any person who may claim upon his death to be entitled to his one-eleventh of the income to arise from any part of the Italian property then remaining unsold, until the conversion thereof.'

Jurisdiction in property cases

Hesperides Hotels Ltd v *Muftizade* [1978] 3 WLR 378 House of Lords (Lords Wilberforce, Salmon, Fraser, Keith and Viscount Dilhorne)

• *At common law English courts have no jurisdiction to try trespass to foreign land*

Facts

Two Cypriot companies owned hotels in the northern part of Cyprus that was occupied by Turkish troops in 1974. The Cypriots who controlled the companies left the hotels when the Turkish troops invaded and moved to Limassol in the South. They learnt in 1976 that efforts were being made in London by the unrecognised government of the northern part of the island (the so-called Turkish Federated State of Cyprus) and a travel agent (Aegean Turkish Holidays) to organise holiday tours to the hotels. The companies thus sought from the English courts relief against the representative of the Turkish Federated State of Cyprus (Muftizade) for trespass and conspiracy to trespass to the hotels and (this claim was added later) trespass to the contents of the hotels.

Held

In reliance upon *British South Africa Company* v *Companhia de Mocambique* [1893] AC 602, English courts do not have jurisdiction to try actions for trespass (or conspiracy to trespass) to foreign land, even where the title to the land in not in dispute. However, they did have jurisdiction to try trespass to the contents of the hotels.

Lord Wilberforce:

> 'I shall consider first the question whether the present action is precluded by the rule in the *Mocambique* case [1893] AC 602. The appellants' argument are threefold:
>
> First they contend that the rule established by that case has no application where there is no dispute as to the title to foreign land and (I use their words) "no real dispute over the right to possession of the foreign land". This result, they say, can be reached by a process of interpretation of the decision of this House without departing from it.
>
> Secondly they invite your Lordships to overrule, or depart from, the decision in the *Mocambique* case, at least to the extent necessary to allow the present action to be brought.
>
> Thirdly they argue that the rule has no application to an action based on a conspiracy entered into in England even if the conspiracy is to effect or procure trespass to foreign land.
>
> The rule in the *Mocambique* case can be conveniently stated in the form in which it is generally accepted, viz, in *Dicey & Morris, The Conflict of Laws*, rule 79. I quote from the 9th ed (1973), but it appears as rule 53 in the same form (except for one letter) in the 3rd ed (1922) edited by Professor Dicey himself and Dr Berriedale Keith.
>
> > "Subject to the exceptions hereinafter mentioned, the court has no jurisdiction to entertain an action for (1) the determination of the title to, or the right to the possession of, any immovable situate out of England (foreign land); or (2) the recovery of damages for trespass to such immovable."
>
> The exceptions later mentioned relate to actions in equity (*Penn* v *Lord Baltimore* (1750) 1 Ves Sen 444) and other special cases on which reliance cannot be placed in this appeal.
>
> It will be seen that the rule is in two parts – if either applies, the court has no jurisdiction. The second part refers to the recovery of damages for trespass and if correctly stated must (subject only to the conspiracy point) preclude the action. So the questions are (1) whether this part of the rule is correct in law, (2) whether it should be read subject to an exception for actions where no question as to title arises. My Lords, the answer to the first of these questions cannot, in my opinion, admit of doubt. The history of the rule, which is a long one, was examined in depth in the *Mocambique* case, both in this House [1893] AC 602, and in the Court of Appeal [1892] 2 QB 358. Two of the Lords Justices in the Court of Appeal were prepared to hold that an action in trespass, being in their view an action in personam, could lie against a defendant found in England: Lord Esher MR thought otherwise and his opinion prevailed in this House. In his speech (which I shall not attempt to summarise) Lord Herschell LC traced the development of the rule from *Skinner* v *East India Co* (1666) 6 St Tr 710 to 1893; it was Lord Mansfield who attempted, in two cases decided by himself and referred to in *Mostyn* v *Fabrigas* (1774) 1 Cowp 161, to support the doctrine that actions for trespass against a defendant in England could lie. But this doctrine was decisively rejected *per* Buller J in *Doulson* v *Matthews* (1792) 4 Term Rep 503, 504:
>
> > "It is now too late for us to inquire whether it were wise or politic to make a distinction between transitory and local actions: it is sufficient for the courts that the law has settled the distinction, and that an action quare clausum fregit is local. We may try actions here which are in their nature transitory, though arising out of a transaction abroad, but not such as are in their nature local."
>
> It has not been revived since in any English reported case.

There is no more doubt, in my opinion, as to the second question. It is certainly true that in the *Mocambique* case itself the plaintiff's title was disputed, but the House considered the legitimacy of actions in trespass in the broadest and most general terms. Lord Herschell LC opened his speech in these words at p617:

> "... the principal question raised by this appeal is whether the Supreme Court of Judicature has jurisdiction to try an action to recover damages for a trespass to lands situate in a foreign country"

and the whole of the discussion is in terms as general as this. The rejection of Lord Mansfield's doctrine is inconsistent with any supposed limitation of the rule to a case where title is disputed, for in neither of the cases decided by him was there a dispute as to title. But Lord Herschell (as Buller J before him), recognising this fact (see p624), rejected the admissibility of actions in trespass. There are passages no doubt in the speech which are directed towards the actual facts of the case which the House was considering, in which not only was there a dispute as to title, but the action was brought in order that the title should be determined. In these passages Lord Herschell LC draws attention to the particular, and additional, difficulties which would be involved if the English court were to adjudicate upon title. But in my understanding these are treated as a fortiori cases, and there is nothing in the examination of them which supports a proposition that the rule is limited to them.

The speech of Lord Halsbury follows the same course. He states the question for decision in the same general way as it had been stated by Lord Herschell, at p630, and he deals with it similarly without a single reference, even as regards the case under discussion, to support an argument that the rule applies only when title is disputed.

My Lords, this is not the first time that this supposed limitation of the rule has been contended for. It was raised in *The Tolten* [1946] P 135 and firmly rejected by Somervell LJ at p163, and by Cohen LJ at p169. It is suggested that Scott LJ took a different view, but all he said at pp141–142, was this:

> "I recognise that in a case where the action is brought by a party in possession of land and structures, suing merely for damages for negligence, or even, it may be, for trespass quare clausum fregit, and the plaintiff relies solely on his possession as the foundation for his action, the House of Lords might hereafter distinguish the *Mocambique* case. I do not think, however, that it would be right for this court to attempt that distinction, as I am satisfied that, in regard to common law actions, no such distinction was then in the mind of the House ..."

But, whether or not this House possesses greater powers of distinguishing earlier decisions than does the Court of Appeal – a question which may raise some interesting jurisprudential questions – I hardly find in this passage any encouragement to exercise such powers as we have.

I therefore regard the formulation in *Dicey*, rule 79(2) as correctly stating the law.

Before considering whether we should overrule or depart from the *Mocambique* rule in any respect In must deal with the argument that we have here the distinguishable claim of a conspiracy formed in England. The majority in the Court of Appeal gave short shrift to this argument and I think they were right. In my opinion the answer to this argument is to be found in a passage in the judgment of Scarman LJ [1978] QB 205, 231:

> "But, more significant, the reliance upon the alleged conspiracy as distinct from the alleged trespass which it is intended to effect is wrong in principle. The combination or agreement, which is said to constitute (with overt acts and ensuing damage) the tort of conspiracy, is unlawful only if there be the intention to effect a trespass upon foreign land. Unless that be shown, there is nothing unlawful. And that can be established only if the court is prepared to adjudicate upon the right to possession of the foreign land – which is exactly what the House of Lords said the

English courts may not do: see Lord Herschell LC in the passage already cited."

I gratefully adopt this passage on which I am unable to improve.

The rule being then as I have stated it, should your Lordships accede to the appellants' invitation to restate it, in different terms? There is no doubt that the rule can be criticised. Although Professor Dicey seems to have approved it (3rd ed, pp223–224) the diligence of the appellants' counsel has assembled a massive volume of academic hostility to the rule as illogical and productive of injustice: see inter alia *Dicey & Morris*, 9th ed, pp516–518, 525; *Cheshire's Private International Law*, 3rd ed (1947), p719, 8th ed (1970), p481, 9th ed (1974), p495; *American Law Institute, Restatement of the Law, Second, Conflict of Laws* (1957), ss10, 87; Beale, *The Conflict of Laws* (1935), s614.1; Goodrich, *Conflict of Laws*, 4th ed (1964), s96 and Ehrenzweig, *Conflict of Laws*, (1962), s39.

Although these writers are concerned with the conflict of laws, as to which academic authority is of particular value, rather than with the English law as to jurisdiction which is what now concerns us, the consensus as to where considerations of logic and justice might lead if this matter were tabula rasa is impressive. But there are other factors to be weighed when revision of an old established rule, sanctioned by this House is suggested. ...

On these considerations I have reached the conclusion that the necessary conditions to bring into operation the Practice Direction of 1966 [*Practice Statement (Judicial Precedent)* [1966] 1 WLR 1234] do not exist and that the rule should be maintained in this House. The consequence is that the appellants' action, as regards the hotels themselves, being land situate abroad, cannot be maintained.'

Comment

The result of this case has been overturned by the enactment of s30 of the Civil Jurisdiction and Judgments Act 1982, which reads as follows:

'30. – (1) The jurisdiction of any court in England and Wales or Northern Ireland to entertain proceedings for trespass to, or any other tort affecting, immovable property shall extend to cases in which the property in question is situated outside that part of the United Kingdom unless the proceedings are principally concerned with a question of the title to, or the right to possession of, that property.
(2) Subsection (1) has effect subject to the 1968 Convention and to the provisions set out in Schedule 4.'

Note further that if the matter falls within EU Council Regulation 44/2001, the provisions of art 22(1) apply. See the textbook.

Choice of law and movables

Winkworth* v *Christie Manson and Woods Ltd and Another [1980] 2 WLR 937 Chancery Division (Slade J)

• *Where there has been a change of title of a movable under the lex situs, that change of title will be recognised and enforced in the English courts*

Facts

Certain works of art had been stolen from their owner Winkworth, the plaintiff, in England. They were taken to Italy where they were sold to the second defendant who was in good faith. He returned them to England with a view to sale at Christie's. The plaintiff sought a declaration that he was the owner of the works of art. Under Italian law, which was not fully proved, it appeared that the second defendant, being in good faith, and having complied with the necessary formalities, would have acquired good title. Did Italian law or English law determine who owned the works of art? This question was tried as a preliminary issue.

Held

That Italian law as lex situs at the time of transfer applied and the matter was sent to trial on the contents of the Italian law.

Slade J:

'The general principle relating to the validity of dispositions of personal property, as formulated by Pollock CB and approved by the Court of Exchequer Chamber, to which I shall refer briefly as "the principle of *Cammell* v *Sewell*", has been reaffirmed in many subsequent decisions. I will mention only a few of them. As thus formulated, it was expressly approved by Blackburn J delivering the joint opinion of himself and Bramwell B, Mellor J, Brett J and Cleasby B in *Castrique* v *Imrie* (1870) LR 4 HL 414 when, after quoting the words of Pollock CB he said, at p429: "This, we think, as a general rule, is correct, though no doubt it may be open to exceptions and qualifications."

The general principle has been subsequently stated in very similar terms, for example, by Maugham J in *In re Anziani* [1930] 1 Ch 407, 420. Devlin J in *Bank Voor Handel En Scheepvaart NV* v *Slatford* [1953] 1 QB 248, 257, summarised the present position by saying: "There is little doubt that it is the lex situs which as a general rule governs the transfer of movables when effected contractually."

Faced with these and a number of other 20th century authoritites on the same lines, Mr Mummery, on behalf of the plaintiff, accepted that as a general rule the validity of a transfer of movables is governed by the lex situs and that accordingly the principle of *Cammell* v *Sewell* would have the effect of rendering Italian law the relevant law for the purpose of determining the rights of the second defendant and the vendor in Italy, from whom he purchased, as between themselves and their respective successors in title. He pointed out, however, that the present case is, in contrast, concerned with the respective proprietary rights of the second defendant and the plaintiff. He pointed out the many circumstances which cumulatively give this case a strong association with England, at least if it be regarded solely from the standpoint of his client. At the time of the theft, the goods were situated in England, in the ownership and lawful possession of a person who was domiciled in England. The plaintiff neither knew of nor consented to the removal of the goods from England or anything which made such removal more probable. The goods have now been voluntarily redelivered to England where they or their proceeds of sale still remain. Finally, it is an English court which is now hearing the matter.

Laying emphasis on what may be called these English connecting factors, Mr Mummery advanced two main propositions as possible avenues of escape from the principle of *Cammell* v *Sewell*. Briefly, the first was, that for the purpose of applying this principle to determine the respective rights of the plaintiff and the second defendant in the peculiar circumstances of this case, the lex situs should be treated as being English, rather than Italian law. The second was that if, contrary to his first submission, the application of the principle of *Cammell* v *Sewell* would result in the relevant issue being determined according to Italian law, then the exceptional facts of the case bring it outside this principle.

No authority has been cited the facts of which can be said to be precisely on all fours with the present case, in the sense that all the English connecting factors relied on by Mr Mummery are present. Since, however, I have found three decisions especially illuminating in the context of his two principal submissions, I shall refer to these decisions in some detail.

The first of them is *Cammell* v *Sewell*, 5 H & N 728, itself. In that case a cargo of timber had been shipped on board a [Russian] vessel in Russia by Russian vendors for delivery to English purchasers in England. The vessel was then wrecked off the coast of Norway, but the cargo was safely landed. On learning of the wreck, the English purchasers abandoned their rights to the cargo. The plaintiffs, English underwriters with whom the timber was insured, paid the purchasers as for a total loss, while the purchasers endorsed the relevant bill of lading to them and delivered it to them. Before the underwriters had accepted the abandonment, however, a survey had been held, on the instigation of an agent acting for the ship's master, which had reported that it would be in the interests of the underwriters and all parties concerned that the whole of the cargo should be sold. The timber had been accordingly sold in Norway to a Mr Clausen. An agent of the plaintiff underwriters then brought proceedings in the Norwegian court to set aside the sale, but the proceedings failed. The Norwegian purchaser then shipped the timber to England and sold it to the defendants in the action. The plaintiff underwriters sued these defendants in trover for its value.

The Court of Exchequer found in favour of the defendants. The plaintiff underwriters appealed to the Court of Exchequer Chamber, which dismissed the appeal. Crompton J, delivering the judgment of the majority of the court (Cockburn CJ, Wightman, Williams, Crompton and Keating JJ) said, at pp742–743:

> "If we are to recognise the Norwegian law, and if according to that law the property passed by the sale in Norway to Clausen as an innocent purchaser, we do not think that the subsequent bringing the property to England can alter the position of the parties."

Pausing there, *Cammell* v *Sewell* is thus, in my judgment, clear authority for the following proposition: the mere circumstances that the goods in the present case have been brought back to England, following the sale to the second defendant and that their proceeds are now in England do not entitle the English court to decline to apply Italian law for the purpose of determining the relevant issue if, but for those circumstances, that would be the law applicable. …

No case has been cited to me in which the decision in *Cammell* v *Sewell* has either been ovrerruled or, I think even criticised. It is therefore binding on me except insofar as it can properly be distinguished on its material facts. If therefore my analysis of it is correct, it presents at very least a serious obstacle to the plaintiff in the present case and correspondingly powerful support to the second defendant. …

Accordingly, I think it clear that, if the principle of *Cammell* v *Sewell* applies at all on the facts of the present case, then the lex situs of the relevant disposition cannot be treated as being English rather than Italian. Intolerable uncertainty in the law would result if the court were to permit the introduction of a wholly fictional English situs when applying the principle to any particular case, merely because the case happened to have a number of other English connecting factors.

It therefore follows that, if the plaintiff is to succeed, he must satisfy the court that the second principal submission made on his behalf is correct, namely that the principle of *Cammell* v *Sewell* does not apply to this case, because the particular circumstances bring it within an exception to that principle. …

In these circumstances, there are, in my view, very strong grounds of business convenience for applying the principle of *Cammell* v *Sewell* even in a case such as the present. Maugham J said in *In re Anziani* [1930] 1 Ch 407, 420, with reference to the principle: "Business could not be carried on if that were not so." This was putting the point very strongly. I think, however, that most undesirable uncertainty in the commercial world would result if the choice of the system regulating the validity of a disposition of chattels were to depend not only on the situation of the goods at the time of the disposition, but also on the additional factors suggested on behalf of the plaintiff.

It must be accepted that exclusive reference to the lex situs must cause hardship to a previous owner in some cases, particularly, if his goods have been moved to and sold in a foreign country without his knowledge or consent. …

I thus summarise my conclusions as follows:

(1) The relevant general principle is, in my judgment, clearly and accurately stated in *Cheshire & North's Private International Law*, 10th ed (1979), p527:

"Therefore, it is now established that the proprietary effect of a particularly assignment of movables is governed exclusively by the law of the country where they are situated at the time of the assignment. An owner will be divested of his title to movables if they are taken to a foreign country and there assigned in circumstances sufficient by the local law to pass a valid title to the assignee. The title recognised by the foreign lex situs overrides earlier and inconsistent titles no matter by what law they may have been created."

(2) The rule, however, is not one of universal application; in particular it is not likely to be applied in any of the five exceptional cases already mentioned.

(3) It is not, however, contended that any of these five exceptions applies on the facts of the present case. For the reasons already given, I cannot accept the plaintiff's submission that the court should regard such facts as giving rise to a further exception, based on the grounds that the goods were stolen from the plaintiff in England, then removed to Italy and sold there without the plaintiff's knowledge or consent and have now been returned to England.'

Comment

It is worth considering how many of Slade J's exceptions to the general rule are true exceptions to the predominance of the lex situs.

Assignment of intangible movables

Deutsche Schachtbau-und Tiefbohrgesellschaft mbH and Others v *R'As al-Khaimah National Oil Co, Shell International Petroleum Co Ltd intervening* [1988] 3 WLR 230 House of Lords (Lords Keith, Brandon, Templeman, Oliver and Goff)

• *Involuntary assignment of a debt – English courts will garnish debts situated in England, but only if the risk of the debtor being forced to pay twice (once in England and once in a foreign state) is substantial*

Facts

Deutsche Schachtbau-und Tiefbohrgesellschaft mbH (DST) and the R'As al-Khaimah National Oil Company (RAK) had entered into an oil exploration agreement which provided for disputes to be settled by arbitration in Geneva. A dispute was referred to arbitration and an award was made in favour of DST. DST now sought to enforce this award in England (as it was entitled to in terms of the Arbitration Act 1975). However, RAK now sued DST in the courts of R'As al-Khaimah (in breach of the agreement to submit to arbitration in Geneva) and succeeded in obtaining recission of the contract and damages. (Neither party took any part in the others' proceedings.) RAK's judgment, however, was of little value outside R'As al-Khaimah (and RAK's attempt to enforce its judgment in England failed (see s32(1)(a) of the Civil Jurisdiction and Judgments Act 1982)). DST, on the other hand, sought to garnish a debt, situated in England (a debt is situated generally where it is recoverable and a garnishee order given by the courts where the debt is situated is usually recognised everywhere) owed by Shell International to RAK and to satisfy its award therefrom. A Mareva injunction (freezing order) was granted to prevent Shell from paying the debt. RAK now sued Shell in R'As al-Khaimah and obtained judgment and when the New London, a ship chartered by an associated company of Shell put into R'As al-Khaimah port it was seized and the court announced that it would be held until Shell paid the debt due to RAK. Meanwhile, DST sought to have their garnishment of the debt made absolute.

Held

The garnishee order would not be made absolute: Lord Oliver (Lords Goff, Keith and Brandon concurring) held that there was a real and substantial risk that if forced to pay in England, Shell might also be forced to pay in R'As al-Khaimah. This risk was the result of the failure of the courts of R'As al-Khaimah to recognise the arbitration award and the garnishment of Shell's debt. But that made no difference to the principle that Shell should not be made to run the risk of paying the same debt twice.

Lord Templeman dissented: although there was a real risk that Shell would have to pay twice, the courts should not be influenced by the threats of R'As al-Khaimah or the coercive detention of the New London.

Lord Oliver:

> 'The critical issue was whether there was a real and substantial risk that Shell might, if the garnishee order absolute was to be upheld, be compelled to pay the same debt a second time. As a matter of fact it was beyond doubt that there was some risk.
>
> Whether rightly or wrongly as a matter of the comity of nations, the courts of R'As al-Khaimah quite clearly did not and would not recognise that the debt which was due to the defendants and which the State claimed as due to it was capable of discharge by payment under a garnishee order made in this country.
>
> Whether rightly or wrongly as a matter of internationally recognized maritime law and practice, it had taken and continued to take steps by way of arrest in aid of the judgment which it had obtained against Shell in its own courts. That was not a matter of theory or speculation. The risk had to that extent materialised.
>
> In considering, therefore, whether, as a matter of discretion, the garnishee order should have been made absolute there were two questions which required to be answered.
>
> (1) There being clearly some risk of double jeopardy, did Shell demonstrate a risk of sufficient substantiality to justify withholding the ordinary process of execution of a regularly obtained judgment in favour of DST. The risk could not be regarded as anything other than substantial.
>
> If the risk became translated into actuality it would be as a result of what was clearly an exorbitant claim to jurisdiction which transcended the bounds of what, at any rate in English law, were considered to be generally accepted norms.
>
> The judgment was not one which had any prospect of being recognized or enforced in an English court or in any other court that accepted those principles of private international law which were applied in this country.
>
> (2) Even assuming the substantiality of the risk, did the circumstance that the jeopardy arose from a judgment against Shell obtained only by the exercise of an exorbitant jurisdiction require that it should be ignored or discounted?
>
> The actual existence of proceedings elsewhere for the recovery of the debt sought to be garnished was one of the features which rendered the present case unique.
>
> Were those proceedings such as would, in accordance with the recognized principles of English private international law, be recognised and enforced by the courts of this country, there could be no doubt that the court's discretion should be exercised against the making of a garnishee order absolute.
>
> Did it make any difference that the foreign judgment had been irregularly obtained as a result [of] the exercise of an exorbitant jurisdiction?

Certainly so far as the garnishee was concerned it did not. On the other hand there was a natural reluctance to recognize that the ordinary process of execution of a judgment regularly obtained in this country could be frustrated by the action of the judgment debtor in subjecting the garnishee to pressure in another jurisdiction in a manner which our jurisprudence did not recognize as legitimate.

However, it would not be right to allow a disapprobation of the conduct of the judgment debtor to outweigh the consideration of the injustice likely to be suffered by the garnishee, who was not a party to the dispute.

The fact that the particular foreign legal process was not one which commended itself to our jurisprudence was really immaterial.

It could not simply by virtue of its nonconformity with the accepted norms of private international law, be equated with mere commercial pressure.'

Lord Goff:

'It was not right to balance what were perceived to be flaws in a foreign judgment against the virtues of the English judgment.

It was not to be forgotten that there were many countries in the world which exercised what were, in the eyes of international law, an exorbitant jurisdiction; indeed, in some cases, the jurisdiction exercised by the English courts could be so regarded.

But the mere fact that the exercise of jurisdiction by the foreign court was regarded as exorbitant, or even as very exorbitant, could not of itself affect the exercise of the English court's discretion to make a garnishee order absolute.

The crucial feature was the reality of the risk of the garnishee being required to pay the debt a second time.

It would be inequitable to make a garnishee order absolute and, in the circumstances of the case, it would not be right to maintain the *Mareva* injunction in existence to enable DST to pursue some other method of execution, bearing in mind that an injunction was itself an equitable remedy.'

Macmillan Inc v *Bishopsgate Investment Trust plc and Others (No 3)* (1995) The Times 7 November Court of Appeal (Staughton, Auld and Aldous LJJ)

• *Choses in action – title to shares governed by lex situs*

Facts

The plaintiff (a Delaware company controlled by Robert Maxwell) owned approximately 55.6 per cent of Berlitz, a company incorporated in New York. Maxwell agreed in London with certain investment banks to pledge the Berlitz shares as security for loans to him. The shares were transferred in New York. The plaintiff claimed against the banks for the return of the 10.6 million shares in Berlitz, or compensation.

Held

The issue of law was whether the banks were purchasers for value in good faith without notice and so acquired good title to the shares. The issue as to ownership of shares should be decided by the lex situs. The situs would usually be the place of incorporation, although there could be situations where it was the law of the place where the share register was kept. Staughton LJ stressed that situs and incorporation had the advantage of pointing to one system of law which was unlikely to be transient and which could not be manipulated by a purchaser of shares in order to get priority.

Republica de Guatemala v *Nunez* [1927] 1 KB 669 Court of Appeal (Bankes, Scrutton and Lawrence LJJ)

• *Assignment of money void due to duress and failure to comply with relevant provisions*

Facts

The President of Guatemala deposited £20,000 in a London bank. Shortly before he was deposed by his political opponents he assigned in Guatemala this deposit to his illegitimate son, Nunez. Shortly after being deposed, while in prison in Guatemala, his political opponents forced him to assign the deposit to the Republic of Guatemala. Under English law the assignment to Nunez was valid, but it was formally invalid under Guatemalan law which required such assignments to be made on stamped paper before a notary and also because assignments to minors (such as Nunez) could only take place with the consent of the minor's tutor. Was Nunez or Guatemala entitled to the money?

Held

The assignment to the Republic of Guatemala was void for duress and the assignment to Nunez was void for failure to comply with the various provisions of Guatemalan law mentioned above. Thus the £20,000 went to the creditors of the ex-president.

Scrutton LJ:

'It will be seen, therefore, that if Guatemalan law, being both the law of the domicile of both parties and the lex loci actus, is to be applied, the document was a nullity. If English law, as the law of the situs of the debt assigned, or the lex loci solutionis of the contract to pay, is to be followed, the document was effective. It is to be assumed, however, that in any case it is English law which the English courts enforce: the question is whether English law directs them to ascertain the validity of the assignment by the law of Guatemala, or by the law of England applicable to such documents.

On the question of the law applicable to an assignment of personal property invalid by the law of the country where the transaction takes place, or by the lex domicilii of the parties to the transaction, but valid by the law of the country where the property is, or is deemed to be, situate, the English authorities are scanty and unsatisfactory. Channell J, in *Dulaney* v *Merry* [1901] 1 KB 536, 541, 542, "had not found any clear case of a transfer, good according to the law of the domicile of the owner, and made there, but held bad for not conforming to the law of the country where the goods are situate." Mr Dicey has not found any clear case in reference to individual assignments by gift or sale as to the validity of an assignment good by the lex domicilii of the owner, but bad in the country where the goods are situate. Conversely, I have not been able to find, nor could counsel refer me to, any clear statement of the principles governing the question whether a transaction in personal property, as distinct from land, invalid by the law of the country where the transaction takes place, may be valid by the law of the place where the property is situate. Mr Foote, *Private International Law*, 5th ed, p293, points out that in most of the judgments where general statements are made the transaction took place in the country where the property was, and a conflict between the lex loci actus and the lex loci rei sitae was not dealt with.

There seem to me, however, in this case to be two clear matters which help to a conclusion. First, in cases of personal property, the capacity of the parties to a transaction has always been determined either by the lex domicilii or the law of the place of the transaction; and where, as here, the two laws are the same it is not necessary to decide between them. In *Lee* v *Abdy* 17 QBD 309, an assignment was made in Cape Colony by a man there domiciled to his wife of a policy issued by an English company, and it was assumed for the purposes of the case that such an assignment was invalid by the law of the Colony, husband and wife not being capable of entering into such a transaction. A Divisional Court, composed of Day and Wills JJ, held that, on that assumption, the assignment, though valid by the law of England, could not be enforced against the company in England. Neither judge draws a distinction between the lex domicilii or the lex loci actus. The Court of Appeal, in *Sottomayor* v *de Barros* (1877) 3 PD 1, 5, a case of marriage, laid down in general terms: "It is a well recognised principle of law that the question of personal capacity to enter into any contract is to be decided by the law of domicile"; and Lord Halsbury says, in *Cooper* v *Cooper* (1888) 13 App Cas 88, 99, that "incapacity to contract by reason of minority ... is regulated by the law of domicile." Lord Macnaghten, in the same case (1888) 13 App Cas 108, is more doubtful, treating the question as not finally settled, but with a preponderance of opinion in favour of the lex domicilii. "But," he says, "when the contract is made in the place where the person whose capacity is in question is domiciled there can be no room for dispute. It is difficult to suppose that Mrs Cooper (the infant) could confer capacity on herself by contemplating a different country as the place where the contract was to be fulfilled." Lord Watson, ibid p105, declines to decide the point, as the two laws are the same. The opinion of the Court of Appeal, in *Sottomayor* v *de Barros* (1877) 3 PD 1, 5, in favour of the lex domicilii, was criticised by the same court in *Ogden* v *Ogden* [1908] P 46 and by Sir James Hannen in the later *Sottomayor* case. But most of the authorities seem to agree that capacity to contract depends either on the lex domicilii or the lex loci actus, and here they are the same: see also per Lord Eldon in *Male* v *Roberts* (1799) 3 Esp 163, as to infancy. It seems to me, therefore, that Nunez, being a minor incapable by the law of his domicile or the law of the place where the transaction takes place, of receiving a valid donation, so that a gift to him, without the intervention of a next friend judicially appointed to receive it, would be void and a nullity in Guatemala, cannot claim that he has received a good title to the deposit by such an invalid donation.'

Comment

This judgment indicates the difficulties involved but do not really establish the law clearly. See the textbook for a discussion of this case.

Governmental seizure of property

Williams and Humbert Ltd* v *W & H Trade Marks (Jersey) Ltd [1986] 1 AC 368 House of Lords (Lords Scarman, Bridge, Brandon, Templeman and Mackay)

• *English courts recognise the compulsory acquisition laws of foreign states, without considering the merits of those laws, and acknowledge the changes of title effected by those laws to property situated within the foreign state*

Facts

In 1983 the Spanish government had expropriated all the shares in Rumasa SA, a Spanish company that owned the entire share capital of the holding company of Williams and Humbert Ltd, an English firm of port and sherry shippers. One of the latter's assets used to be the 'Dry Sack' sherry trade mark, but this had earlier been assigned to a Jersey company, W & H Trade Marks (which was controlled, through nominees, by the major shareholders in Rumasa). This did not disrupt Williams and Humbert's business because W & H granted a licence to them to continue to use the trade mark. The licence, however, was liable to be cancelled should the shares of Rumasa be expropriated. After the expropriation Williams and Humbert, now under the control of the Spanish government, sought a declaration that the assignment of the trade mark was null and void.

Held

The action was simply to recover property to which an English company claimed to have been entitled even before the Spanish expropriatory decrees were enacted; thus the action did not constitute an indirect attempt to enforce those decrees.

Lord Templeman:

> '... according to the defence which the appellants now seek to plead, Williams and Humbert as plaintiffs in the trade marks action:
>
> > "are not entitled to the relief sought or any relief by reason of the fact that the proceedings represent an attempt to enforce a foreign law which is penal or which otherwise ought not to be enforced by this court and further, or alternatively, that it would be contrary to public policy to grant the relief sought or any relief."
>
> This pleading could be justified if English law abhorred the compulsory acquisition legislation of every other country, or if international law abhorred the compulsory acquisition legislation of all countries. But in fact compulsory acquisition is universally recognised and practised. As early as 1789 the Declaration of the Rights of Man, more recently repeated in the French Constitutions of 1946 and 1958, provided that no one should be deprived of property "except in case of evident public necessity legally ascertained and on condition of just indemnity". In the United States the Fifth Amendment to the Constitution of 1791 provided that private property should not "be taken for public use, without just compensation". In modern times written constitutions recognise compulsory acquisition in the public interest subject to the payment of compensation; see, for example, the 1949 Basic Law of the German Federal Republic, the 1949 Constitution of India, the 1969 South American Convention on Human Rights, and the written constitutions of the African states which achieved independence from colonial rule. The United Nations and European Conventions recognise compulsory acquisition in the public interest and in accordance with domestic law and international law. In the United Kingdom, the courts are bound to accept and enforce any compulsory acquisition authorised by the United Kingdom parliament and to recognise compulsory acquisitions by other governments subject only to limitations for the safeguarding of human rights.
>
> There is undoubtedly a domestic and international rule which prevents one sovereign state from changing title to property so long as that property is situate in another state. If the British government purported to acquire compulsorily the railway lines from London to Newhaven and the railway lines from Dieppe to Paris, the ownership of the railway lines situate in England would vest in the British government but the ownership of the railway lines in France would remain undisturbed. But this territorial limitation on compulsory acquisition is not relevant to the acquisition of shares in a company incorporated in the acquiring state. If the British government compulsorily acquired all the shares in a company incorporated in England which owned a railway line between Dieppe and Paris, the ownership of that railway line would remain vested in the company, subject to any exercise by a French government of power compulsorily to acquire the railway line. In the present case, the Spanish government acquired all the shares in Rumasa and Jerez. Ownership of the shares in Williams & Humbert was and remained vested in Rumasa. Ownership of any right of action to recover the Dry Sack trade mark and to recover damages was and remained vested in Williams and Humbert.
>
> There is another international rule whereby one state will not enforce the revenue and penal laws of another state. This rule with regard to revenue laws may in the future be modified by international convention or by the laws of the European Economic Community in order to prevent fraudulent practices which damage all states and benefit no state. But at present the international rule with regard to the non-enforcement of revenue and penals laws is absolute. ...
>
> If the principles of English domestic law and international law are applied and if the plaintiffs succeed in establishing liability against any of the appellants in tort, misfeasance or breach of fiduciary duty then an English court will grant the appropriate relief. If the Mateos family had remained in charge of the Rumasa group perhaps no

action would have been brought by any of the companies comprised in the Rumasa group against the appellants. But that consideration is irrelevant to the actions which have now been brought.

In *Aksionairnoye Obschestvo A M Luther* v *James Sagor & Co* [1921] 3 KB 532 the Russian government confiscated a wood factory and stock of wood belonging to the plaintiffs in Russia. The wood was exported to England by the agents of the Russian government and unsuccessfully claimed by the plaintiffs. Bankes LJ said, at p545:

> "The court is asked to ignore the law of the foreign country under which the vendor acquired his title, and to lend its assistance to prevent the purchaser dealing with the goods."

Scrutton LJ refused to entertain an argument that the Soviet legislation was confiscatory and unjust saying, at pp558–559:

> "... it appears a serious breach of international comity, if a state is recognised as a sovereign independent state, to postulate that its legislation is 'contrary to essential principles of justice and morality'.

... Individuals must contribute to the welfare of the state, and at present British citizens who may contribute to the state more than half their income in income tax and super tax, and a large proportion of their capital in death duties can hardly declare a foreign state immoral which considers (though we may think wrongly) that to vest individual property in the state as representing all the citizens is the best form of proprietary right."

Similarly, in *Princess Paley Olga* v *Weisz* [1929] 1 KB 718 the plaintiff unsuccessfully sought to recover heirlooms formerly belonging to her in Russia. Russell LJ said, at p736:

> "The evidence ... clearly establishes a seizure of the property in 1918, either by a section of revolutionaries, whose act was subsequently adopted by the government, or by a usurping power which subsequently became the government. This court will not inquire into the legality of acts done by a foreign government against its own subjects in respect of property situate in its own territory."

Scrutton LJ said, at p725:

> "Our government has recognised the present Russian government as the de jure government of Russia, and our courts are bound to give effect to the laws and acts of that government so far as they relate to property within that jurisdiction when it was affected by those laws and acts."

These authorities illustrate the principle that an English court will recognise the compulsory acquisition law of a foreign state and will recognise the change of title to property which has come under the control of the foreign state and will recognise the consequences of that change of title. The English court will decline to consider the merits of compulsory acquisition. In their pleadings the appellants seek to attack the motives of the Spanish legislators, to allege oppression on the part of the Spanish government and to question the good faith of the Spanish administration in connection with the enactment, terms and implementation of the law of the 29 June 1983. No English judge could properly entertain such an attack launched on a friendly state which will shortly become a fellow member of the European Economic Community. ...

An English court, by English law and international law must recognise that Spanish law and accept its consequences. The consequences are that the management of the three Spanish companies and of their Spanish, English and other subsidiaries have passed to representatives of the Spanish government. The consequences are irrelevant to the trade marks action and the banks' action. ...

My Lords, on principle and authority the appellants' attempt to persuade an English court to ignore the effect and consequences of the Spanish law dated 29 June 1983 is misconceived. Nourse J came to the same conclusion and acceded to an interlocutory application by the plaintiffs in the trade marks action to strike out the appellants' defence so far as it pleaded the Spanish law as a bar to the right of Williams and Humbert to recover its trade mark and struck out the objectionable particulars which impugn the motives, conduct and good faith of the Spanish authorities. The judge also refused the appellants in the banks' action leave to amend their pleadings by including a defence which challenged the effect and consequences of the Spanish law.'

Comment

Note that there are two cases which are not consistent with the proposition that the lex situs governs title to movable property, thus if the property is situated within the territory of the foreign state at the time of the enactment of the expropriatory decree, the change of title will be recognised. These cases, *The Rose Mary* [1953] 1 WLR 202 and *Lorentzen* v *Lydden & Co* [1943] 2 KB 202, are discussed in the textbook.

Intestate succession

Collens (decd), Re, Royal Bank of Canada (London) Ltd v *Krogh and Another* [1986] 2 WLR 919 Chancery Division (Browne-Wilkinson V-C)

• *Intestate succession to immovables is governed by their lex situs, while intestate succession to movables is governed by the law of the deceased's last domicile*

Facts

The deceased died domiciled in Trinidad and Tobago leaving property there, in Barbados and in England (some of which was immovable). $1,000,000 was paid to his widow in full settlement of her claim against the Trinidad and Tobago estate. She now claimed, in reliance upon s46 of the Administration of Estates Act 1925, the statutory legacy of £5,000 from her husband's immovable English estate.

Held

On a true construction of s46(1) the residuary estate that was charged with the payment of the statutory legacy was confined to assets, succession to which was governed by English law; thus a statutory legacy had to be paid out of the proceeds of the sale of the deceased's immovable property in England, notwithstanding the widow having already taken benefits from the Trinidad and Tobago estate.

Browne-Wilkinson V-C:

'These being the relevant facts, I turn shortly to the underlying law. Under the law of the intestate's domicile, namely Trinidad and Tobago, the widow is entitled to one third of the estate absolutely. Subject thereto the children take the estate equally. As to the law of England, it is common ground between counsel that the succession to the English immovable property on the intestacy of the deceased is regulated by the domestic English law of intestacy. That is the rule as stated by *Dicey & Morris, The Conflict of Laws*, 10th ed (1980), vol 2 p612, r98. The comment on the rule that succession to immovables of an intestate is governed by the law of the country where the immovables are situate suggests that although that was the position before 1925 it might be that after 1925 the law was different. However, counsel has not sought to argue that point (I think advisedly) and the argument has proceeded on the basis that the English estate, so far as it consisted of immovable property or the proceeds of sale of immovable property, is regulated by domestic English law.

The question which arises is this. Is the widow entitled to her statutory legacy out of the English immovable estate notwithstanding that she has taken $1 million under the deed of compromise out of the Trinidad and Tobago estate, and would have been entitled to one-third of the rest of the estate under the law of domicile? Can she take both the share of the estate under the law of domicile which regulates the movable property of the deceased and in addition the statutory legacy under the English law of intestacy in relation to the English immovable property? It is common ground between counsel that the deed of compromise does not affect the matter.

The relevant statutory provisions are contained in the Administration of Estates Act 1925, as amended by the Intestates' Estates Act 1952. Section 33 of the Act of 1925 provides that on the death of a person intestate "as to any real or personal estate" the estate is to be held as to the real estate upon trust to sell and as to the personal estate upon trust to sell and convert into money such part thereof as may not consist of money, and then to apply the globular mixed fund of realty and personalty to pay debts and testamentary expenses and other matters. Then s33(4) provides:

> "The residue of the said money and any investments for the time being representing the same, including (but without prejudice to the trust for sale) any part of the estate of the deceased which may be retained unsold and is not required for the administration purposes aforesaid, is in this Act referred to as 'the residuary estate of the intestate'."

The right to the statutory legacy arises under s46, as amended. Section 46 is headed: "Succession to real and personal estate on intestacy". Subsection (1), so far as relevant, provides that if the intestate leaves a wife and issue, the surviving husband or wife shall take the personal chattels absolutely:

> "… and, in addition, the residuary estate of the intestate (other than the personal chattels) shall stand charged with the payment of a fixed net sum of £5,000, free of death duties and costs, to the surviving husband or wife with interest thereon from the date of the death … until paid or appropriated, and, subject to providing for that sum and the interest thereon, the residuary estate … shall be held *(a)* as to one half upon trust for the surviving husband or wife during his or her life, and, subject to such life interest, on the statutory trusts for the issue of the intestate, and *(b)* as to the other half, on the statutory trusts for the issue of the intestate."

I should mention s49, as amended, which provides for a hotchpot in cases of partial intestacy. It provides that where any person dies leaving a will disposing of a part of the property, the Act shall have effect as regards the part of the property not disposed of by the will, subject to provisions contained in the will and subject to the modification that the statutory legacy is to be reduced pro tanto by the amount of the benefits taken by the surviving husband or wife under the will. But that provision for hotchpot does not in terms provide for any hotchpot when there is a total intestacy. Accordingly if the English immovable property is liable to pay the statutory legacy under s46 of the Act, the widow will be entitled to £5,000 plus interest from the date of death notwithstanding the fact that she has had $1 million out of the Trinidad and Tobago estate.

Mr Ham for the widow submitted that, in dealing with the residuary estate of the intestate in circumstances where part of the estate is in England and part outside England, as a matter of construction s46 of the Act applies only to such part of the estate as is subject to English law. From that it would follow that the charge for the statutory legacy in s46(1) attaches solely to the proceeds of sale of the English immovable property. There is no question, says Mr Ham, of any charge on any part of the estate not devolving under English law. Accordingly, says Mr Ham, that charge on the proceeds of sale of the English immovable property has to be satisfied and the widow is entitled to £5,000 out of the English estate. He points out that in s49 of the Act there are express hotchpot provisions affecting interests taken under a will in a partial intestacy; there is accordingly no room for an implied hotchpot, there being no express provision dealing with a case of total intestacy. He relies on two cases in other jurisdictions. First, the decision in the Irish courts, *In re Rea, decd* [1902] IR 451 and secondly the decision in Australia, *In re Ralston* [1906] VLR 689.

Mr Simmonds, for some of the children of the first marriage, submits that s46 of the Act does not operate in that way at all. He says that as a matter of construction of the words used (as opposed to the application of the section, when construed, to the circumstances of a particular case) "the residuary estate of the intestate" means all the property of the intestate of whatever nature and wherever situated, and under whatever law such estate devolves. Mr Simmonds accepts that the provisions of s46 will not in fact regulate the devolution of any part of the estate other than the English immovable estate; but that does not alter its construction, since, says Mr Simmonds, the words "residuary estate of the intestate" include all of the assets, including assets outside the United Kingdom. Therefore, he says, on the true construction of s46 it is the whole estate that is charged with the payment of the statutory legacy, and that charge has been satisfied by the payment of considerably more than the statutory legacy out of the part of the estate situate outside England. Therefore, submits Mr Simmonds, the immovable estate in England is not subject to any charge for the £5,000 statutory legacy. It is no part of his case that there is here any form of implied hotchpot requiring the widow to bring in her benefits under the Trinidad and Tobago intestacy against her benefits under the English intestacy.

I would very much like to reach the view urged upon me by Mr Simmonds. In my judgment it is unjust that because the estate is spread around the world the widow takes not only one-third under Trinidad and Tobago law but in addition the further capital sum under English law. However, in my judgment it is not possible on the construction of the Act of 1925 to hold in favour of the children. The truth of the matter is that the draftsman of the Act of 1925 did not have in mind circumstances such as arise in the present case and one has to do one's best on the basis of the words he has used.

I find it difficult to construe sections 33 and 46 of the Act together so as to provide a consistent code regulating the position where an intestate dies leaving some assets inside, and some outside, England. Section 33 makes it clear that it is dealing with any real or personal estate as to which the testator died intestate. I was for a time persuaded to the view that those words were limited to the real or personal estate the succession to which was regulated by English law; but Mr Simmonds has convinced me that that cannot be the right construction since the provisions for administration in s33 apply not only to assets which pass by way of succession under English law but also to assets which fall to be administered under English law, the ultimate succession to which is regulated by some other system of law. Accordingly the phrase "any real or personal estate" must include movable property in England the succession to which is regulated in the present case by the law of Trinidad and Tobago.

In those circumstances when one comes to the definition of "the residuary estate of the intestate" in s33(4) of the Act as being the net proceeds of sale of such "real or personal estate", in my judgment such "residuary estate of the intestate" must include assets which do not fall for purposes of succession to be regulated by English law. This adds some force to Mr Simmonds' submission that when the Act comes to deal with succession in s46, "the residuary estate of the intestate" referred to in s46(1) does include assets the succession to which is not regulated by English law.

It is on that basis that Mr Simmonds says that it is impossible to treat "the residuary estate" in s46 as confined only to the English immovable property since the words are capable of extending to movable property elsewhere. On the other hand I find it difficult to include in the words "the residuary estate of an intestate" as used in s46 assets which cannot on any basis fall to be administered under English law (eg, immovable property outside England) since such assets do not and could not fall to be administered under the trusts in s33 and therefore could not form part of the property defined as being the residuary estate of the intestate.

As I say, I find it difficult to find any rational construction which reconciles all the difficulties posed by those two sections in relation to an intestacy involving property in many different jurisdictions. However, I do not think it is necessary for me to try to resolve that problem. I will proceed on the basis that Mr Simmonds is right in saying that as a matter of construction the words in s46 "the residuary estate of an intestate" do include all the property of the deceased world-wide, including his movable property in Trinidad and Tobago. Even on that assumption, Mr Simmonds accepts that s46 can only regulate the succession to the immovable property in this country. It cannot be applied to regulate succession to the movable property of the deceased since such succession is regulated by the law of his domicile, namely Trinidad and Tobago.

On that basis, in my judgment s46 can only impose a charge for the statutory legacy on the proceeds of the English immovables. There is no way in which it can be made to impose a charge on assets not devolving under English law since such charge is part of the English law of succession. Mr Simmonds has accepted that there is no implied statutory hotchpot. In the absence of such statutory hotchpot I can see no way in which the charge on the English immovable estate can be said to have been satisfied out of the overseas assets of the deceased. The widow took the benefits out of the overseas assets in Trinidad and Tobago by virtue either of her rights in those assets under the law of intestacy of Trinidad and Tobago or under the deed of compromise. In no way that I can see can it be said that she took those benefits in satisfaction of the charge created under s46 of the English Act of 1925. Therefore in my judgment the charge on the proceeds of the English immovable property remains unsatisfied.

Mr Simmonds sought to escape this conclusion by submitting that s46 did impose a charge on the whole estate, including foreign movables. As I have said, I cannot accept that, for to give s46 that effect would be to attribute to Parliament an intention to create beneficial interests for purposes of succession in assets which do not fall for purposes of the law of succession to be regulated by English law. In my judgment s46 cannot operate to create a charge on assets the succession to which is regulated by a foreign law.

For those reasons in my judgment the widow is entitled to her statutory legacy out of the English assets. That conclusion, although turning on the words of the Act of 1925, accords with the decisions in *In re Rea, decd* [1902] IR 451 and *In re Ralston* [1906] VLR 689 in other jurisdictions.

I reach the conclusion with some regret. I think there is much force in the trenchant criticism contained in *Dicey & Morris, The Conflict of Laws*, pp613–614 as to the illogicality of requiring English immovable assets to be regulated for the purpose of succession by the lex situs rather than by the law of the domicile. However, that is the law as it stands at present. If the Law Commission choose to look at the matter, they may find factors which suggest that a rule which accords with the view in *Dicey & Morris* would be fairer and better. But my job is to administer the law as it now is.'

8 The Recognition and Enforcement of Foreign Judgments

Judgments rendered outside the EC

Adams v *Cape Industries plc and Another* [1990] 2 WLR 657 Court of Appeal (Slade, Mustill and Gibson LJJ)

• *Presence of a corporation within a jurisdiction – will a 'mere presence' suffice for international competence?*

Facts

Cape Industries was an English parent company of a number of companies involved in the marketing of products containing asbestos. These were the North American Asbestos Corporation (NAAC), an Illinois company, and Capasco Ltd, an English company responsible for the marketing of asbestos worldwide. Cape Industries and Capasco faced a number of actions with American plaintiffs for personal injuries caused by asbestos dust. In 1974 some 464 such actions were brought against Cape Industries and Capasco in the Tyler District Court (which is in Texas) (these actions will henceforth be known as the Tyler I actions). These actions were settled and Cape Industries and its subsidiaries bore $5.2 million of the damages and a consent order was made by the Tyler court in these terms.

Thereafter a further 206 plaintiffs instituted action in the Tyler court (these are known as the Tyler II actions). Cape and Capasco took no part in the Tyler II actions, and in due course default judgment was given against them. The successful plaintiffs, however, found that neither Cape Industries nor Capasco had any assets in the USA and that NAAC had been liquidated (and that a new Illinois subsidiary Continental Productions Corporation had been formed). One of these plaintiffs, J W Adams, sought to enforce in England a default judgment for $37,000 awarded by the Tyler court against Cape Industries and Capasco. But on what basis had the Tyler court international competence? The plaintiff argued that Cape Industries and Capasco were present in Illinois by virtue of their relationship with NAAC and CPC.

Held

1. The source of the jurisdiction of a foreign court to summons a defendant to appear before it was his obligation to abide by its laws and accept the jurisdiction of its courts while present in its territory; thus the voluntary presence of an individual in a foreign country is sufficient to give the courts of that country territorial jurisdiction over him enabling that court's judgment to be enforced against him in England.
2. However, a company is only present within a foreign jurisdiction if it has an established place of business there or a representative of the company has for more than a minimal period of time being carrying on the company's business there at some fixed place of business. In determining whether the presence of a representative is sufficient, a complex range of factors none of which was conclusive had to be considered.

Slade LJ:

'*The presence issue*
Under the plaintiffs' case as pleaded, the obligation of the defendants to obey the judgment of the Tyler court is said to arise because "the defendants were resident in the United States of America at the time the plaintiffs' proceedings were commenced in the Tyler court." The jurisdiction of the Tyler court is thus said to be founded on territorial factors.

Nearly 120 years ago in *Schibsby* v *Westenholz* LR 6 QB 155, the "residence" of an individual in a foreign country at time of commencement of suit was recognised by the Court of Queen's Bench as conferring jurisdiction on the court of that country to give a judgment in personam against him. In that case the court declined to enforce a judgment of a French tribunal obtained in default of appearance against defendants who at the time when the suit was brought in France were neither subjects of nor resident in France. On these facts the court decided, at p163, "there existed nothing in the present case imposing on the defendants any duty to obey the judgment of a French tribunal." However, it regarded certain points as clear on principle, at p161:

> "If the defendants had been at the time of the judgment subjects of the country whose judgment is sought to be enforced against them, we think that its laws would have bound them. Again, if the defendants had been at the time when the suit was commenced resident in the country, so as to have the benefit of its laws protecting them, or, as it is sometimes expressed, owing temporary allegiance to that country, we think that its laws would have bound them."

In *Rousillon* v *Rousillon* (1880) 14 Ch D 351, Fry J, after referring to *Schibsby* v *Westenholz* and in enumerating the cases where the courts of this country regard the judgment of a foreign court as imposing on the defendant the duty to obey it, at p371, similarly referred to one such case as being "where he was resident in the foreign country when the action began." …

Residence will much more often than not import physical presence. On the facts of the four cases last mentioned, any distinction between residence and presence would have been irrelevant. However, the brief statements of principle contained in the judgments left at least three questions unanswered. First, does the temporary presence of a defendant in a foreign country render the court of that country competent (in the private international law sense) to assume jurisdiction over him? Secondly, what is the relevant time for the purpose of ascertaining such competence? Thirdly, what is to be regarded as the "country" in the case of a political country, such as the United States of America, comprising different states which have different rules of law and legal procedure?

[This last question will not be considered here.]

Our own courts regard the temporary presence of a foreigner in England at the time of service of process as justifying the assumption of jurisdiction over him: see *Colt Industries Inc* v *Sarlie* [1966] 1 WLR 440 and *HRH Maharanee Seethadevi Gaekwar of Baroda* v *Wildenstein* [1972] 2 QB 283. However, *Cheshire & North*, 11th ed, comment, at p342:

> "… any analogy based on the jurisdiction of the English courts is not particularly convincing, since the rules on jurisdiction are operated in conjunction with a discretion to stay the proceedings, and the exercise of the discretion is likely to be an issue when jurisdiction is founded on mere presence."

We see the force of these points. They highlight the possible desirability of a further extension of reciprocal arrangements for the enforcement (or non-enforcement) of foreign judgments by convention. Nevertheless, while the use of the particular phrase "temporary allegiance" may be a misleading one in this context, we would, on the basis of the authorities referred to above, regard the source of the territorial jurisdiction of the court of a foreign country to summon a defendant to appear before it as being his obligation for the time being to abide by its laws and accept the jurisdiction of its courts while present in its territory. So long as he remains physically present in that country, he has the benefit of its laws, and must take the rough with the smooth, by accepting his amenability to the process of its courts. In the absence of authority compelling a contrary conclusion, we would conclude that the voluntary presence of an individual in a foreign country, whether permanent or temporary and whether or not accompanied by residence, is sufficient to give the courts of that country territorial jurisdiction over him under our rules of private international law. However, none of the authorities so far referred to was concerned with the question of enforcement of a foreign judgment against a corporate body. The residence or presence of a corporation is a difficult concept. A corporation is a legal person but it has no corporeal existence. It can own property. It can by its agents perform acts. It is clear that if an English corporation owns a place of business in a foreign state from which it carries on its business that English corporation is, under our law, present in that state for the purposes of in personam jurisdiction. Those clear circumstances, however, may be varied in many different ways. The corporation may not own the place of business but have only the use of it or part of it. It may, instead of carrying on its business by its own servants, cause its business to be done by an agent, or through an agent, in the foreign state. The question will then arise whether the commercial acts done are, for the purposes of our law, to be regarded as done within the jurisdiction of the foreign state (a) by the agent in the course of the agent's business or (b) by the corporation itself. Further, and this is of central importance in this case, if the English corporation causes to be formed under the law of the foreign state a separate but wholly owned corporation to carry out the business or commercial acts which it requires to be done, are those acts within the jurisdiction of the foreign state to be regarded, for the purposes of enforcement of a judgment of the courts of that state, as the acts of the English corporation within that jurisdiction merely by reason that it owns all the shares of its foreign corporation; and, if not, what degree of power of control, or of exercise of control, and/or what other factors will suffice, in our law, to cause the English corporation to be held to be "present" within the jurisdiction of the foreign state? ...

Perhaps the most helpful guidance in determining whether a foreign corporation is "here" so as to be amenable to the jurisdiction of our courts is the following passage from the judgment of Buckley LJ in the *Okura* case [1914] 1 KB 715, 718–719:

> "The point to be considered is, do the facts show that this corporation is carrying on its business in this country? In determining that question, three matters have to be considered. First, the acts relied on as showing that the corporation is carrying on business in this country must have continued for a sufficiently substantial period of time. That is the case here. Next, it is essential that these acts should have been done at some fixed place of business. If the acts relied on in this case amount to a carrying on of a business, there is no doubt that those acts were done at a fixed place of business. The third essential, and one which it is always more difficult to satisfy, is that the corporation must be 'here' by a person who carries on business for the corporation in this country. It is not enough to show that the corporation has an agent here; he must be an agent who does the corporation's business for the corporation in this country. This involves the still more difficult question, what is meant exactly by the expression 'doing business?'"

It is clear that (special statutory provision apart) a minimum requirement which must be satisfied if a foreign trading corporation is to be amenable at common law to service within the jurisdiction is that it must carry on business at a place within the jurisdiction: see *The Theodohos* [1977] 2 Lloyd's Rep 428, 430, per Brandon J.

Nevertheless, it is a striking fact that with one possible exception (*The World Harmony* [1967] P 341) in none of the many reported English decisions cited to us has it been held that a corporation has been resident in this country unless either (a) it has a fixed place of business of its own in this country from which it has carried on business through servants or agents, or (b) it has had a representative here who has had the power to bind it by contract and who has carried on business at or from a fixed place of business in this country.

We do not find this surprising as a matter of principle. Indubitably a corporation can carry on business in a foreign country by means of an agent. "It may be stated as a general proposition that whatever a person has power to do himself he may do by means of an agent": *Halsbury's Laws of England*, 4th ed vol 1 (1973), p420, para 703. However, though the terms "agency" and "agent" have in popular use a number of different meanings:

> "... in law the word 'agency' is used to connote the relation[ship] which exists where one person has an authority or capacity to create legal relations between a person occupying the position of principal and third parties": *Halsbury's Laws of England*, vol 1, p418, para 701.

Where the representative of an overseas corporation has general authority to create contractual relations between the corporation and third parties and exercises this authority, there may be little difficulty in applying the maxim "qui facit per alium facit per se". Where no such authority exists, there may be much greater difficulty. We were not persuaded by Mr Morison's submission, based primarily on a dictum of Verchere J in *Miller* v *BC Turf Ltd* 8 DLR (3d) 383, 386, that the capacity (or possible capacity) of NAAC or CPC to render Cape/Capasco vicariously liable for negligence (and thereby to create relations in tort between them and third parties) is of any weight in deciding whether Cape/Capasco were present in the United States of America. The mere authority given by Cape/Capasco to NAAC or CPC to convey a message to a third party could render Cape/Capasco potentially liable in tort to a third party if that message was carelessly transmitted. The existence of such potential liability would go no way towards establishing the presence of Cape/Capasco in the United States of America.

General principles derived from the authorities relating to the "presence" issue

In relation to trading corporations, we derive the three following propositions from consideration of the many authorities cited to us relating to the "presence" of an overseas corporation.

(1) The English courts will be likely to treat a trading corporation incorporated under the law of one country ("an overseas corporation") as present within the jurisdiction of the courts of another country only if either (i) it has established and maintained at its own expense (whether as owner or lessee) a fixed place of business of its own in the other country and for more than a minimal period of time has carried on its own business at or from such premises by its servants or agents (a "branch office" case), or (ii) a representative of the overseas corporation has for more than a minimal period of time been carrying on the overseas corporation's business in the other country at or from some fixed place of business.

(2) In either of these two cases presence can only be established if it can fairly be said that the overseas corporation's business (whether or not together with the representative's own business) has been transacted at or from the fixed place of business. In the first case, this condition is likely to present few problems. In the second, the question whether the representative has been carrying on the overseas corporation's business or has been doing no more than carry on his own business will necessitate an investigation of the functions which he has been performing and all aspects of the relationship between him and the overseas corporation.

(3) In particular, but without prejudice to the generality of the foregoing, the following questions are likely to be relevant on

such investigation: (a) whether or not the fixed place of business from which the representative operates was originally acquired for the purpose of enabling him to act on behalf of the overseas corporation; (b) whether the overseas corporation has directly reimbursed him for (i) the cost of his accommodation at the fixed place of business; (ii) the cost of his staff; (c) what other contributions, if any, the overseas corporation makes to the financing of the business carried on by the representative; (d) whether the representative is remunerated by reference to transactions, eg by commission, or by fixed regular payments or in some other way; (e) what degree of control the overseas corporation exercises over the running of the business conducted by the representative; (f) whether the representative reserves (i) part of his accommodation, (ii) part of his staff for conducting business related to the overseas corporation; (g) whether the representative displays the overseas corporation's name at his premises or on his stationery, and if so, whether he does so in such a way as to indicate that he is a representative of the overseas corporation; (h) what business, if any, the representative transacts as principal exclusively on his own behalf; (i) whether the representative makes contracts with customers or other third parties in the name of the overseas corporation, or otherwise in such manner as to bind it; (j) if so, whether the representative requires specific authority in advance before binding the overseas corporation to contractual obligations.

This list of questions is not exhaustive, and the answer to none of them is necessarily conclusive. If the judge, ante, p696G, was intending to say that in any case, other than a branch office case, the presence of the overseas company can *never* be established unless the representative has authority to contract on behalf of and binding the principal, we would regard this proposition as too widely stated. We accept Mr Morison's submission to this effect. Every case of this character is likely to involve "a nice examination of all the facts, and inferences must be drawn from a number of facts adjusted together and contrasted:" *La Bourgogne* [1899] P 1, 18 per Collins LJ.

Nevertheless, we agree with the general principle stated thus by Pearson J in *F & K Jabbour* v *Custodian of Israeli Absentee Property* [1954] 1 WLR 139, 146:

> "A corporation resides in a country if it carries on business there at a fixed place of business, and, in the case of an agency, the principal test to be applied in determining whether the corporation is carrying on business at the agency is to ascertain whether the agent has authority to enter into contracts on behalf of the corporation without submitting them to the corporation for approval ..."

On the authorities, the presence or absence of such authority is clearly regarded as being of great importance one way or the other. A fortiori the fact that a representative, whether with or without prior approval, never makes contracts in the name of the overseas corporation or otherwise in such manner as to bind it must be a powerful factor pointing against the presence of the overseas corporation.'

Black* v *Yates [1991] 3 WLR 90 Queen's Bench Division (Potter J)

• *Effect of judgment awarded by foreign court which is enforceable in England (s34 Civil Jurisdiction and Judgments Act 1982)*

Facts

Section 34 Civil Jurisdiction and Judgments Act 1982 was interpreted for the first time in the following circumstances: the plaintiff's husband had been killed in a motorcycle accident in Spain. He was a pillion passenger on the defendant's motorcycle; and it was not contested that the defendant's negligence had caused the plaintiff's husband's death. Criminal proceedings were taken against the defendant in Spain; and under Spanish law compensation claims can be dealt with in the criminal proceedings unless the right to bring a civil action was expressly reserved in the criminal proceedings. This was not done although the plaintiff (and her children on whose behalf she was also suing) was represented by a Spanish lawyer in those proceedings. In the event, the Spanish court awarded compensation of about £18,000; but the plaintiff and her children would probably have been awarded about £75,000 by an English court. The plaintiff now, on her own behalf, on behalf of her children, and on behalf of the deceased estate, brought action in England against the defendant. She was met, however, with a defence based upon s34.

Held

1. As far as the plaintiff's claims on her own behalf were concerned the English proceedings were brought on the same cause of action as that in respect of which the Spanish judgment had been given. Since the Spanish judgment was enforceable in England the requirements of s34 were complied with and thus the defence succeeded.
2. However, the claims brought by the plaintiff on the part of the children (under the Fatal Accidents Act 1976) and on behalf of the deceased estate (under the Law Reform (Miscellaneous Provisions) Act 1934) stood on a different footing. Since the plaintiff had not purported to act on behalf of the estate in the Spanish proceedings, the estate was not bound by the Spanish proceedings. And, as far as the children were concerned, the Spanish proceedings were contrary to their interests and there was no evidence that they were able to give an informed consent to the power of attorney that led to their representation in the Spanish proceedings. Section 34 was not intended to defeat the English law of infancy. Thus the court could repudiate the power of attorney; the children were therefore in law not represented in the Spanish court; and the actions brought on their behalf could proceed in England.

Potter J:

> 'Prior to 1982, a foreign judgment had been regarded at common law as only constituting a simple contract debt, no "merger" of the original cause of action in the judgment resulting. This meant that it remained open to a plaintiff to sue either on the Foreign Judgments (Reciprocal Enforcement) Act 1933, or on the original cause of action; s34 [of the CJJA 1982] abrogated that rule. From the time the section came into force, proceedings between the same parties on the original cause of action have no longer been available unless the judgment in question is not enforceable or entitled to recognition. If the foreign judgment remains unsatisfied, the proper course of action is to enforce it, either under statute or at common law, by suing on the judgment. The abrogation of the non-merger rule is achieved by making the foreign judgment a bar to further proceedings. The defendant's principal contention in this case is that the plaintiff and her two children have already received judgment in Spain in respect of the cause of action sued on in these proceedings and that the plaintiff is, therefore, debarred from pursuing proceedings by original action in the High Court in England.
>
> In order to make good that submission the defendant must show that three requirements have been satisfied: (i) the proceedings must be brought on the same cause of action as the proceedings in Spain; (ii) the proceedings must be between the same parties or their privies as the proceedings in Spain; and (iii) the judgment in the Spanish court must be enforceable or entitled to recognition in England and Wales.
>
> (i) Are the causes of action the same?
> ... I have come to the conclusion that the causes of action are the same. The words "cause of action" comprise every fact, though not every piece of evidence, which it would be necessary for the plaintiff to prove, if traversed, to support his right to judgment of the court: see *Read* v *Brown* (1888) 22 QBD 128, 131, per Lord Esher MR and authorities cited at paragraph 15/1/3 of The Supreme Court Practice 1988.

It has been elsewhere defined as: "Simply a factual situation the existence of which entitles one person to obtain from the court a remedy against another person:" see the judgment of Diplock LJ in *Letang* v *Cooper* [1965] 1 QB 232, 242. The factual situation underlying the cause of action in a fatal accident case in England appears to me to consist of: (i) the death of the deceased; (ii) the negligence of the defendant as a cause of that death; (iii) proof of dependancy on the part of the plaintiff and/or those on behalf of whom the proceedings are brought; (iv) loss resulting to the dependants by reason of that death; and (v) in the case of a claim for bereavement, proof of the appropriate relationship.

Viewed in that way, it appears to me that the plaintiff's cause of action in Spain essentially comprised the same elements. The sole or principal ground on which Mr Tyrrell, for the plaintiff, argued that that was not so was his contention that, so far as the plaintiff's action and interest were concerned, all that she had to prove, and/or all that the Spanish court investigated, was the question of causation, once the criminal offence had been established by the public prosecutor. That seems to me to ignore the fact that the plaintiff became a party to the Spanish proceedings before the criminal trial was heard and had throughout the right and opportunity to be heard on the issue of negligence, proof of which was necessary before the criminal liability, and any consequent civil right to compensation, was established. Whereas the criminal aspect of the trial was no doubt principally, and it may be (since the record is not clear) wholly conducted by the prosecutor, the plaintiff was party to the lis and present at the trial through her Spanish lawyer, whom she had empowered to act for her in both the criminal and civil aspects of the proceedings. She therefore had the opportunity to be heard on the question of negligence, even if her lawyer did not exercise it …

(ii) Are the proceedings between the same parties or their privies?
It is, of course, the case that Mr Yates is the defendant in these proceedings, just as he was in the Spanish proceedings. It seems equally clear that, in name at least, Mrs Black who is the plaintiff in these proceedings became a party to the Spanish proceedings under the provisions of arts 109 and 110 of the law of criminal procedure in order to pursue her civil remedy. Finally, it is clear that in the Spanish proceedings she purported to act also on behalf of her children, just as she acts for them, as dependents, in the present action.

It is not clear precisely how the plaintiff became party to the Spanish proceedings in the sense of any formal documentation or correspondence which may have passed between the Spanish court and the Spanish lawyer relative to the provisions of art 110 of the Code of Criminal Procedure. However, it is apparent, and Mr Tyrrell has not sought to argue to the contrary, that, through her Spanish lawyer, she was heard at the trial after which an award was made in her favour to indemnify "the successors of the deceased", which in this context was herself and her two children "as the injured heirs".

Faced with this position, Mr Tyrrell takes a series of points on behalf of the plaintiff. First, he submits that the plaintiff was not a party to the Spanish proceedings "in any real sense of the word", as he put it. He said it is clear that a Spanish court will, in hearing criminal proceedings, automatically proceed to deal also with questions of civil indemnity which the prosecutor has a duty to place before the court in so far as he has details, unless or until a party notified of the proceedings expressly waives his or her right to civil indemnity. Thus, Mr Tyrrell says, the plaintiff did not initiate the Spanish proceedings, and he submits that simply to participate in them as she did was not to render the proceedings between the same parties.

I do not consider that argument to be correct. It does not seem to me that s34 of the Act of 1982 contemplates only proceedings in which the English plaintiff was a party ab initio or indeed proceedings which were exclusively civil in character. Leaving aside any question of who may or may not be a "privy" of one or other of the parties, it appears to me that s34 contemplates proceedings of whatever character in the court of an overseas country in which the plaintiff and defendant in English proceedings have previously participated as opposing parties for the purposes of adjudicating a cause of action between them, in respect of which the English plaintiff has obtained a judgment in his favour enforceable or entitled to recognition in England and Wales or Northern Ireland. It seems to me unnecessary and inappropriate to read into the section any requirement that the English plaintiff should have been the original party in the overseas proceedings or that such proceedings be exclusively civil in character. What is aimed at by the section, in my view, is an extension of the English doctrine of merger to the judgments of all overseas courts of competent jurisdiction which are enforceable and entitled to recognition in this country.

Mr Tyrrell's second, and main, submission is to the following effect. He says that in the Spanish proceedings the plaintiff was suing on her own behalf and, in so far as she sued on behalf of the children, on their behalf as natural legal persons. By way of contrast he says that in these proceedings the plaintiff sued in a representative capacity as administratrix of her deceased husband's estate. That being so, he relies on the authority of the Court of Appeal in *Marginson* v *Blackburn Borough Council* [1939] 2 KB 426 applying *Leggott* v *Great Northern Railway Co* (1876) 1 QBD 599, both cases involving pleas of estoppel by res judicata at common law.

In *Leggott*'s case, the plaintiff, a widow, acting in her capacity of administratrix of the estate of her deceased husband, brought an action against the defendants for loss and injury to the husband's estate to the extent that his business had suffered loss and he had incurred medical and business expenses following an accident for which the plaintiff alleged that the defendant was responsible, such loss extending over a period between the time of the accident and his death some months later. That action was in the form of the ordinary executor/administrator's action. When the defendants sought to put the circumstances in the accident in issue, the plaintiff asserted that they were estopped from doing so by the reason of a finding of the court in her favour in a previous action brought by her under Lord Campbell's Act, the Fatal Accidents Act 1846 (9 & 10 Vict c93) (the precursor of the Fatal Accidents Act 1959) in which, again suing as an administratrix, she had recovered damages on her own behalf and on behalf of the children. The court held that no estoppel arose because, although the plaintiff acted as administratrix in both cases, the earlier action under Lord Campbell's Act had been brought "in an entirely different right" in order to recover damages which were in no way part of the estate but were due by way of compensation for the death of the deceased for the benefit of his dependants, whereas the later action was brought by the plaintiff on behalf of the deceased's estate only. In a well-known passage Quain J said, 1 QBD 599, 606:

> "The rule about the estoppel is very correctly, I think, laid down in the note to the *Duchess of Kingston's* case. It is this: 'It must be observed that a verdict against a man suing in one capacity will not estop him when he sues in another distinct capacity, and, in fact, is a different person in law.' In other words it is generally put in the books that the plaintiff must not be only the same person, but he must be suing in the same right." ...

Thus, the rule concerning capacity, enunciated in an unqualified form as it appears to have been in *Marginson*'s case [1939] 2 KB 426, may be a good working rule for the purposes of the law of estoppel, but should not be applied willy-nilly in the construction of s34 of the Act of 1934. I think that Mr Strachan is right in this respect. Again in the context in which s34 operates, it does not seem to me to be appropriate to jump from one jurisdiction to another, hidebound by concepts of "capacity" which may not be susceptible of accurate translation when analysing whether, in reality, the same party is suing in respect of the same cause of action. It is inevitable that as between different jurisdictions there will be different forms of action and procedure in fatal accident cases. I do not think it can have been the intention of Parliament that the English form of action in such cases, ie a claim brought by the executor or administrator of the deceased, although in fact brought for the benefit of the dependants, should limit the application of s34 to previous proceedings in those countries which have an identical form of action …

(iii) Is the judgment in the Spanish proceedings enforceable and/or entitled to recognition in England and Wales?
Broadly speaking, this question depends on whether the Spanish judgment was the judgment of a foreign court of competent jurisdiction, being for a definite sum of money and final and conclusive in character. In this respect, Mr Tyrrell takes two points. First, he submits that the Spanish court was not a court of competent jurisdiction in respect of the claims of the children. Second, based on the evidence of his expert Sr de Abando, he contends that the decision was not final and conclusive.

In relation to the second point, it was agreed between the parties that whether the judgment was final and conclusive was a matter to be decided according to Spanish law. I do not propose to recount the somewhat exiguous grounds on which Sr de Abando sought to persuade me that the judgment was not a final and conclusive one. Suffice it to say, I preferred the evidence of the defendant's expert, and I am quite satisfied that this requirement was made out.

As to the first matter, that was also the subject of conflict between the experts in relation to the significance of the power of attorney produced to the Spanish court, and whether or not the judge was justified in treating it as he did as sufficient authority for the claims of the children to be represented before him. Again, I preferred the evidence of the defendant's expert and I am satisfied that the Spanish court was competent to exercise the jurisdiction which it did. I refer to this question further below when considering the overall question of the plaintiff's powers under English law to act for the children in the Spanish proceedings and in particular to purport to empower the Spanish lawyer on their behalf to bind them in those proceedings.

Thus, so far as the plaintiff's claims under the Fatal Accidents Act 1976 on her own behalf and in respect of her dependency is concerned, I consider the defence under the Act of 1982 is made out …

The claim under the Law Reform (Miscellaneous Provisions) Act 1934
So far as the Act of 1934 is concerned, apart from any claim for the deceased's loss of expectation of life, there are two heads of claim put forward in these proceedings on behalf of the estate, namely, a claim for funeral expenses amounting to £205-odd and a claim in respect of damage to the deceased's watch to an unparticularised amount. Mr Tyrrell says that, even if his submissions in respect of the Fatal Accidents Act 1976 claim fail on the grounds that the Spanish proceedings were, in reality, made on behalf of the plaintiff herself and the children as dependants and in respect of the plaintiff's bereavement, the same could not be said of the plaintiff's claim under the Act of 1934. This, he says, is, in form and reality, under English law a claim on behalf of the estate. He says that: (i) Spanish law recognises no claim by a representative on behalf of "an estate" (ii) the plaintiff appeared in no such guise in the Spanish proceedings; and (iii) in any event, no claim was in fact made in respect of the two matters mentioned in the Spanish proceedings.

While it is true that the estate, as such, is not recognised as an entity in Spanish law, it seems to me that it has a ready equivalent in the community of heirs who may authorise or nominate one of their number to act in their name to pursue a claim on the deceased's behalf. However that may be, the plaintiff does not appear to have purported to be acting on behalf of the community of heirs for the purpose of pursuing any claim of the deceased (as opposed to a claim by herself and the children as dependants) which might be said to be equivalent to the capacity and respects in which she now sues under the Act of 1934. I therefore consider that there is no defence to the plaintiff's claims under the Act of 1934, save on the issue of quantum.

Position of the children

Lastly, it is necessary to give separate consideration to the position of the children as the infant dependants in this case.

In relation to their claims, Mr Tyrrell relies on two separate but connected propositions, arising by reason of their infancy, each of which, he says, is fatal to any contention that they are bound by the Spanish proceedings and/or are prohibited by reason of s34 of the Act of 1982 from further suit in these proceedings. First, he observes that the power of attorney, pursuant to which the plaintiff authorised the Spanish lawyer to participate in and conduct the Spanish proceedings was not under seal as required by s2 of the Powers of Attorney Act 1971, the seal being that of the notary and not the plaintiff. He further relies on the fact that it was not signed or acknowledged by either of the infants on whose behalf it was purportedly given. Second, Mr Tyrrell relies on the cases such as *Stephens* v *Dudbridge Ironworks Co Ltd* [1904] 2 KB 225 and *Arabian* v *Tufnall and Taylor Ltd* [1944] KB 685 (concerning previous awards to infants under the Workmen's Compensation Act 1897), which he says show that the courts will not hold an infant to any judgment entered in his favour as a result of any decision or agreement on the part of the infant which is said to amount to an election on his part, unless it can be shown that the decision or agreement was one in which it was in his interests to make.

Before dealing in turn with Mr Tyrrell's submissions, I can say by way of preliminary, that I am quite satisfied that the actions taken on behalf of the children in purportedly making them party to the Spanish proceedings and conducting such proceedings on their behalf, while taken with the best of intentions, were contrary to their interests in the sense that that matter falls to be considered for the purposes of the law of infancy. At the time that the power of attorney was given, the solicitor was of the opinion in these courts and was concerned only to obtain moneys on account; yet he proceeded without having taken the advice of counsel on the question of a possible election or on the applicability of the Act of 1982. Only four days before the Spanish trial, at which the Spanish lawyer could yet have reserved the civil action from the jurisdiction of the Spanish court, English counsel advised that the sum of £75,000 was an appropriate global figure in any English proceedings. It is plain that the Spanish proceedings were conducted on the basis of a misunderstanding as to their likely effect, concerning which it appears that the solicitor had never taken the advice of English counsel. This was plainly contrary to the interests of the plaintiff and her children.

Leaving aside the question of whether the absence of a seal was fatal to the power of attorney, which plainly it was not so far as the Spanish court was concerned, there was no evidence before me that the children, at the time that the power of attorney was given, were aware of any of the steps being taken on their behalf, let alone able to give them independent consideration or to give any informed consent as to the power of attorney or the authority of their mother to give it on their behalf. In these circumstances, and given the lack of benefit to the infants ... and the transaction is void on the ground that the authority was never granted ...

I turn now to Mr Tyrrell's second point. In *Stephens* v *Dudbridge Ironworks Co Ltd* [1904] 2 KB 225 an infant brought a claim against his employers under the Workmen's Compensation Act 1897 which was compromised by an agreement to accept the maximum amount payable to him under the Act during his incapacity to work. In a subsequent action for negligence to recover a greater sum, the Court of Appeal held that he was entitled to proceed on the grounds that the election provided for in s1(2) of the Act of 1897 between a claim under that Act's provisions or at common law, would not be applied in his case to prevent his repudiation of the contract of compromise on the grounds that it was not in his interests. It is clear from his judgment that Collins MR considered that the principle that the "ordinary law governing the contracts of infants" survived the Act and went not merely to enable the infant to avoid the contract of compromise, but to invalidate the infant's original decision to exercise his option, ie to elect, provided for under s1(2) …

Mr Tyrrell relied on the cases I have mentioned and said that by parity of reasoning I should not regard the provisions of s34 of the Act of 1982 as designed or intended to affect the ordinary law of infancy, so that, even if the plaintiff enjoyed the authority or ostensible authority of the infant dependants in this case to bring proceedings on their behalf in Spain, the court should retain its power to set aside such authority and avoid the effects of the Act so far as they operate to their prejudice. Mr Tyrrell says that the public policy which underlies the provisions of the Rules of the Supreme Court is a policy to protect minors from any lack of skill or experience of their legal advisers which might lead to settlement of a money claim for less than it is worth, and to provide means by which a defendant may obtain a valid discharge from a minor's claim would be defeated, or at least prejudiced, if I were to accept any contrary submission: see *The Supreme Court Practice 1988*, vol 1, pp1202–1206.

While I do not consider that the matter is quite so straightforward as Mr Tyrrell's submission would suggest, particularly in relation to a claim where the natural forum for proceedings in tort may well be thought to be the foreign country in which such tort occurred and the foreign law may itself, as in the present case, provide no impediment to parents giving a power of attorney on behalf of their children, I accept the thrust of his submissions. In this respect, Mr Strachan for the defendant has submitted that there are competing grounds of public policy in relation to the construction and application of s34 of the Act of 1982. He says: (a) the structure and intention of the Act is to recognise foreign judgments as binding in cases where a foreign court has been properly seised of the cause of action in respect of which the plaintiff subsequently sues in this country; (b) in the present case there was no reason for the Spanish court to do other than suppose that the plaintiff properly represented, and was authorised to represent, the interests of her children, as she could at Spanish law; (c) in a case of this kind the English court is not merely setting aside an agreement made or election exercised on behalf of the infants, but is withholding effect of a judgment regularly obtained in a foreign court: cf *Stephens* v *Dudbridge Ironworks Co Ltd* [1904] 2 KB 225 and *Arabian* v *Tufnall and Taylor Ltd* [1944] KB 685.

All these submissions seem to me correct so far as they go, but do they go so far as to indicate that the provisions of s34 of the Act of 1982 were designed or intended to set aside the ordinary provisions of English law in relation to infancy? I do not think so.

As to (a), it seems to me that the immediate purpose of s34 was to extend the doctrine of merger previously applicable only to English decisions to decisions of foreign courts. I have had no wider argument addressed to me by either side based on any other provisions of the Act of 1982 or wider considerations of comity or European law. As to (b), I have already indicated that the expert witnesses were agreed that, had the Spanish court in fact been apprised of the difficulties as to the authority of the mother or the interests of the children, it would have declined jurisdiction over the civil claims. As to (c), it is true that in considering the interests of the children, the court is going behind the foreign judgment to look at the position at the time of the grant of the original power of attorney; however, that is what the court should do, if necessary in order to protect the interests of an infant. If the power of attorney was no power, then there can be no injustice in permitting the children to repudiate it. Even if it was a power, the English law of infancy recognises that its benefits vis-a-vis the children should be considered, and if, as I consider, the narrower purpose under (a) is all that should be read into s34, then the defendants are in no better position than were the defendants in *Arabian* v *Tufnall and Taylor Ltd* [1944] KB 685.

Accordingly, I hold that the matters pleaded in the defence do not amount to a defence against the plaintiff's claims in so far as they relate to the dependancies of the children, although, as I have held, the plaintiff is debarred form proceeding further in respect of her own dependency and/or her personal interest.'

Comment

Although one's sympathies lie with the plaintiff, this decision is plainly right. The plaintiff's remedy, if any, must lie in negligence against her legal representatives (both in Spain and in England).

Vogel* v *R & A Kohnstamm Ltd [1973] QB 133 Queen's Bench Division (Ashworth J)

- *Residence within jurisdiction – effect of enforcement of judgment if not satisfied*

Facts

The defendants, an English company, sold leather in Israel through Kornbluth. The plaintiff was an Israeli leather merchant who was a dissatisfied customer of the defendants. He had sued them with success in Israel and now sought to enforce the Israeli judgment in England. Kornbluth never had authority to contract on behalf of the defendants, he simply solicited orders which were submitted to them.

Held

1. That as Kornbluth did not carry on business on behalf of the defendants, the defendants were not resident in Israel and thus the Israeli court had no jurisdiction over them.
2. That there could be no implied submission to the courts of another country and there had been no submission to the Israeli courts by the defendants.

Ashworth J:

'I find it more convenient to consider the question whether the defendants can be said to have been at the material time resident in the State of Israel. As has been said in many cases, residence is a question of fact and when one is dealing with human beings one can normally approach the matter on the footing that residence involved physical residence by the person in question. I keep open the possibility that even in regard to such a person he may be constructively resident in another country although his physical presence is elsewhere. But in the case of a corporation there is broadly speaking no question of physical residence. A corporation or company, if resident in another country, is resident there by way of agents.

A number of cases have been cited, all of them having some bearing on the matter, and I must refer to a number of them. I am dealing only at the moment with the question of residence. In *Littauer Glove Corporation* v *F W Millington (1920) Ltd* (1928) 44 TLR 746, the headnote reads:

> "To constitute residence by a British company in a foreign state so as to render the company subject to the jurisdiction of the courts of that state, the company must to some extent carry on business in that state at a definite and reasonably permanent place."

The main feature of that case is very different from any matter which arises in the present case because the person through whom the defendant corporation was said to have residence in the United States was not a person with any fixed or reasonably permanent place; whereas it is common ground that at all material times Mr Kornbluth had an office in Tel Aviv and could be described as having both a definite and reasonably permanent place. According ly in that case, the facts of which I need not recite, the so-called residence of the director of the defendant company was of much too fleeting a character and so lacking in permanence that the court had no difficulty in holding that the English company was not resident in the United States for the purpose of conferring jurisdiction from those courts.

The matter was also considered by Mocatta J in *Sfeir & Co* v *National Insurance Co of New Zealand Ltd* [1964] 1 Lloyd's Rep 330. In that case there was a body in Ghana which in some sense could be called an agent or agents of the defendant insurance company, who, as their name implies, were domiciled or resident in New Zealand. The entity in Ghana had a limited authority to act for the defendants. They were allowed to deal with minor claims and indeed settle them on the defendant's behalf.

In cases where the loss did not exceed £5, and the entity was reasonably satisfied that the claim was presented in all good faith, they were authorised to dispense with a survey. All claims exceeding £1,000 and all unusual claims had to be submitted to the defendants for approval. Having examined the facts in a lengthy judgment the judge came to the conclusion that this limited authority vested in the agent in Accra was not sufficient to render the defendants resident in Ghana and therfore subject to the jurisdiction of the Ghanaian courts.

Of course each case must depend on its own facts and I am only citing those to show that every effort has been made to find a case which could fairly be regarded as parallel to the present.

Dealing still only with residence I now have to examine in what sense can it be said that the defendants were resident in Israel. They had no office of their own there. All the material correspondence was conducted with them in England and their connection with the State of Israel was limited, in my view, to their dealings through Mr Kornbluth.

In examining how far the presence of a representative or agent will, so to speak, impinge on the absent company so as to render that absent company subject to the relevant jurisdiction, I find help to be obtained from cases in which the converse situation has been considered: namely, where the English courts have been invited to allow process to issue to foreign companies on the footing that such foreign companies are "here."

Much the most useful authority which has been cited to me is *Okura and Co Ltd* v *Forsbacka Jernverks Aktiebolag* [1914] 1 KB 715. It is worth reading the headnote:

> "The defendants were a foreign corporation carrying on business in Sweden as manufacturers. They employed as their sole agents in the United Kingdom a firm in London who also acted as agents for other firms and carried on business as merchants on their own account. The agents had no general authority to enter into contracts on behalf of the defendants, but they obtained orders and submitted them to the defendants for their approval. On being notified by the defendants that they accepted the orders the agents signed contracts with the purchasers as agents for the defendants. The goods were shipped direct from the defendants in Sweden to the purchasers. The agents in some cases received payment in London from the purchasers and remitted the amount to the defendants less their agreed commission:
>
> *Held* that the defendants were not carrying on their business at the agents' office in London so as to be resident at a place within the jurisdiction, and that service of a writ on the agents at their office was, therefore, not a good service on the defendants."

As Mr Boreham said, having read to me the headnote, if that was the view of the court in that case how much stronger in his favour is the present, because on the face of it there are details in the facts of that case which might have led the court to think that the corporation in question was indeed "here", whereas such features are absent in the present case. There is force in that, but the matter for which I am citing the authority is the passage from Buckley LJ's judgment where he said, at pp718–719:

> "In one sense, of course, the corporation

cannot be 'here'. The question really is whether this corporation can be said to be 'here' by a person who represents it in a sense relevant to the question which we have to decide. The point to be considered is, do the facts show that this corporation is carrying on its business in this country? In determining that question, three matters have to be considered.

First, the acts relied on as showing that the corporation is carrying on business in this country must have continued for a sufficiently substantial period of time. That is the case here. Next, it is essential that these acts should have been done at some fixed place of business. If the acts relied on in this case amount to a carrying on of a business, there is no doubt that those acts were done at a fixed place of business. The third essential, and one which it is always more difficult to satisfy, is that the corporation must be 'here' by a person who carried on business for the corporation in this country. It is not enough to show that the corporation has an agent here; he must be an agent who does the corporation's business for the corporation in this country."

Then he goes on to refer to authorities, all of them relevant and all of them in a sense interesting as showing the line of distinction which the courts have drawn in the past between the situations which were, on the face of it, somewhat similar.

At the end of the day there is a test which the courts have used as part of the material on which to reach a conclusion, namely, is the person in question doing his business or doing the absent corporation's business? Conversely, are they doing business through him or by him?

I confess I find these aphorisms, if that is what they are, apt to lead one astray; one can find the choice phrase and then fit the facts to it and so on. But they are useful and I have asked myself anxiously in this case whether in any real sense of the word the defendants can be said to have been there in Israel; and all that emerges from this case is that there was a man called Kornbluth who sought customers for them, transmitted correspondence to them and received it from them, had no authority whatever to bind the defendants in any shape or form. I have come to the conclusion really without any hesitation that the defendants were not resident in Israel at any material time.

It is fair to Mr Waldman to say that he himself accepted that if he was limited to the question of residence as the basis of this action he might find himself in difficulty. But he has another approach, overlapping, but separate. What he says is that on these facts and on the decided cases the fair conclusion to draw is that the defendants by implication agreed to submit themselves to the jurisdiction of the Tel Aviv court.

Before I examine the authorities on that issue I would start with this comment; in considering whether a term should be implied, courts have laid down over and over again that the test is not whether it would be reasonable to imply a term and I follow that guidance. But I do venture to suggest that one test which a court can at least look at is the test whether it would be unreasonable to imply such a term. And I can think of no reason in this world why the defendants should have wished to submit themselves to the jurisdiction of the Israeli courts in respect of these skins which they were selling to customers in Israel. True they might have agreed to do so but I would have thought that one can at least start with the premise that it would be surprising if by implication they had committed themselves to that result.

The problem is lamentably bedevilled by the fact that not every decided case to which I have been referred sings the same tune. If this case had been decided in 1909, after the decision in *Sirdar Gurdyal Singh* v *Rajah of Faridkote* [1894] AC 670 and of *Emanuel* v *Symon* [1908] 1 KB 302, I venture to think it would have taken a shorter time than it has taken before me. …

Those two cases in my view establish the principle that an implied agreement to assent to the jurisdiction of a foreign tribunal is not something which courts of this country have entertained as a legal possibility. Recognising that such an agreement may be made expressly they have in terms decided that implication is not to be relied upon.

There the matter might have rested but for the fact that in 1961 there came before Diplock J the case of *Blohn* v *Desser* [1962] 2 QB 116.

That was a case in which the plaintiff, an Austrian resident in Vienna, had obtained in the Commercial Court of Vienna a judgment against a partnership there. The defendant was a partner in the firm and her name was registered as such in the commercial register in Vienna. But she was only a sleeping partner receiving no income from the firm and at all material times was resident in England. The plaintiff brought an action against the defendant personally in England, on inter alia, the Austrian judgment. As counsel all agree it would have been quite possible for the judge to dispose of that claim on the short and simple ground on which he eventually did dismiss it, but in the course of giving judgment he entertained argument and gave his views upon a topic which was not necessary for his decision, and places those who come after in some difficulty when it is realised that what he there said runs completely counter to the passages which I have cited from *Sirdar* and from *Emanuel* v *Symon*. The curious thing is, if I might say so, that Diplock J then had cited to him *Emanuel* v *Symon* for the purpose of showing to him the five types of cases listed by Buckley LJ which I have already referred to. But then having set out those five cases the judge said, at p 123:

> "There may be some doubt as to whether today it would be held that the jurisdiction exists in the first category of cases, but the other four cases have never been questioned. It is also, I think, clear law that the contract referred to in the fifth case, to submit to the forum in which the judgment was obtained, may be express or implied."

I suppose that eminent as counsel were who were engaged in that case none of them directed his Lordship's attention to the intervention of Kennedy LJ or the passage in his judgment which I have cited; if they had done so I can hardly believe that he would have said that the contrary was clear law. He went on to say:

> 'It seems to me that, where a person becomes a partner within a foreign firm a place of business within the jurisdiction of a foreign court, and appoints an agent resident in that jurisdiction to conduct business on behalf of the partnership at that place of business, and causes or permits, as in the present case, these matters to be notified to persons dealing with that firm by registration in a public register, he does impliedly agree with all persons to whom such a notification is made – that is to say, the public – to submit to the jurisdiction of the court of the country in which the business is carried on in respect of transactions conducted at that place of business by that agent."

That passage has, as I am informed, and as I find in the current edition of Dicey and Morris, Conflict of Laws, 8th ed (1967), p 980, been the subject of critical comment. It would be impudent on my part to add criticism of my own; it is enough for me to say that faced with the choice between that passage and the earlier authorities I feel no hesitation in prefering the older authorities.

It is only fair to Mr Waldman to add that Mocatta J in a case already mentioned, *Sfeir & Co* v *National Insurance Co of New Zealand Ltd* [1964] 1 Lloyd's Rep 330 does seem in terms to have accepted that an agreement to submit to the jurisdiction of the foreign tribunal may be implied. Once again there were other reasons why his decision in favour of the defendants was certainly maintainable and correct and I leave it there. Leaving it there I can only say that there are clearly dicta to the contrary of what I am deciding, but at least I am fortified by having authority of high weight in favour of the view which I now take.

Of course, as Mr Waldman says, once I have reached that conclusion his claim goes. It must go because there is no express agreement here, none could be relied on, by which the defendants could be held to have agreed to submit themselves to the jurisdiction of the Israeli court.

Nonetheless because so much care has been taken in presenting this case I ought to add that if it were necessary for me to decide the point I should rule that there is no such implied agreement to be deduced in the present case. That is to say, assuming that such an agreement would give the plaintiff the relief he seeks, the facts are not enough to give rise to the implication. The facts relied on by Mr Waldman were (a) that the contract was made within the jurisdiction of that foreign tribunal; (b) by or through an agent residing there; (c) such agent was a person carrying on business residentially within that jurisdiction; and (d) the contract was to be performed within the jurisdiction. In my judgment while proposition (c) is established, namely that Mr Kornbluth was carrying on business residentially within that jurisdiction, none of the other material factors are established at all. I hold that Kornbluth was not an agent. I hold that the contract was not made within the foreign jurisdiction. And lastly I hold it was not to be performed there. On these grounds there must be judgment for the defendants.'

Defences and non-defences

House of Spring Gardens Ltd* v *Waite and Others [1990] 3 WLR 347 Court of Appeal (Fox, Stuart-Smith and McCowan LJJ)

• *Restriction of the availability of the defence of fraud*

Facts

This case concerned complicated litigation originally commenced in Ireland in which the plaintiffs claimed very large damages (about three million pounds) against the defendants for misuse of confidential information and breach of copyright. The plaintiffs were largely successful before the Irish courts: very briefly, they succeeded in establishing before Costello J that the defendants had tricked the plaintiffs into parting with valuable information about the design of certain bullet proof vests; and consequently very large damages were awarded to them.

Two of the defendants, however, sought to have Costello J's judgment set aside by the Irish courts on the ground that one of the plaintiffs 'had deceived Costello J regarding the role which he played in developing the armoured vest'. This allegation of fraud by the plaintiff was rejected by Egan J after a 21-day hearing. The plaintiffs now sought to enforce the original Irish judgment in England. (Note that this was enforcement under the common law not under the Civil Jurisdiction and Judgments Act 1982.)

The plaintiffs were met with a defence based upon the same alleged fraud as had been tried at such great length by Egan J.

Held

That the plaintiffs had had the opportunity to raise the alleged fraud as a defence to the enforcement of the Irish judgment thus the defendants were estopped from raising an issue that had been finally determined between them in the proceedings before Egan J. As an alternative to issue estoppel the court said that it would be an abuse of the process of the court to allow the same issue that was determined in the Egan proceedings in Ireland to be re-litigated in England.

Stuart-Smith LJ:

'*Were the Waites estopped by the judgment of Egan J from contending that the judgment of Costello J was obtained by fraud?*

It is common ground that in proceedings in this country to enforce a foreign judgment as a debt at common law, the defendant can set up a defence that the judgment was obtained by fraud. If, on a summons under O.14, the evidence of the defendant discloses a triable issue that the foreign judgment has been so obtained, leave to defend should be given. But a foreign judgment that is final and conclusive on its merits and is not impeachable on the ground of fraud (or other grounds that are not material) is conclusive as to any matter thereby adjudicated upon and cannot be impeached for any error of fact or law: see *Dicey & Morris, The Conflict of Laws,* 11th ed (1987), p460, rule 42. But for the judgment of Egan J, Costello J's judgment could have been impeached on the ground of fraud. But the plaintiffs contend that the judgment of Egan J is final and conclusive on the issue whether or not the prior judgment was obtained by fraud, and cannot itself be impeached. It established both cause of action estoppel and issue estoppel. Not so, argues Mr Swift, because of a rule peculiar to foreign judgments. This is because the foreign judgment can be impeached for fraud even though no newly discovered fraud is relied upon and the fraud might have been, and was, relied upon in the foreign proceedings: see *Abouloff* v *Oppenheimer & Co* (1882) 10 QBD 295 and *Vadala* v *Lawes* (1890) 25 QBD 310.

These cases have been considerably criticised over the years; they were decided at a time when our courts paid scant regard to the jurisprudence of other countries. Nevertheless, we are bound by them and they were recently followed in this court in *Jet Holdings Inc* v *Patel* [1990] QB 335. But in my judgment the scope of these decisions should not be extended, and they are clearly distinguishable. In none of these cases was the question, whether the judgment sued upon here was obtained by fraud, litigated in a separate and second action in the foreign jurisdiction. Unless Egan J's decision is itself impeached for fraud, it is conclusive of the matter thereby adjudicated upon, namely whether Costello J's judgment was obtained by fraud: see *Dicey & Morris*, rule 42. Some attempt was made before Sir Peter Pain to argue that Egan J's judgment was itself impeachable for fraud. This was not supported by any evidence, save a bare assertion in an affidavit sworn by Mr Waite on the second day of the hearing before the judge. It does not warrant consideration.

Mr Swift argued that if Mr Parish's and Mr Waldie' evidence had been tendered before Costello J and had been rejected, it would still have been open to the defendants, in enforcement proceedings in this country, to set up an allegation, based upon that evidence, to the effect that Mr Sacks had given perjured evidence and so procured his judgment by fraud. Why, then, should it make any difference that the evidence is adduced and the issue contested in a second action in Ireland? The answer is that no question of fraud on the part of Mr Sacks was in issue in the Costello action; it was in the Egan action. I have no doubt that the judge was correct to hold, on the material and argument before him, that the Waites were estopped from alleging that the judgment of Costello J was obtained by fraud, based, as that allegation was, on the evidence of Mr Parish and Mr Waldie. I propose to consider later in this judgment the effect of Colonel Piper's evidence.

The judge did not find it necessary to consider the question of abuse of process, and it is perhaps unnecessary for me to do so either. But I have no doubt whatever that, even if the judgment of Egan J did not create an estoppel, it would be an abuse of process for the Waites to re-litigate the very same issue in the English courts upon which they failed in Ireland, not least because they themselves chose that forum, which was the natural forum in which to challenge the judgment of Costello J. They could, if they had wished, merely have waited for enforcement proceedings to be taken here and then attempt to set up fraud. They did not do so. They cannot try again here to obtain a different verdict. …

Abuse of process

The judge did not find it necessary to deal with the question of abuse of process. In my opinion the same result can equally well be reached by this route, which is untrammelled by the technicalities of estoppel. The categories of abuse of process are not closed: see *Hunter* v *Chief Constable of the West Midlands Police* [1982] AC 529, 536 where Lord Diplock said:

> "My Lords, this is a case about abuse of the process of the High Court. It concerns the inherent power which any court of justice must possess to prevent misuse of

its procedure in a way which, although not inconsistent with the literal application of its procedural rules, would nevertheless be manifestly unfair to a party to litigation before it, or would otherwise bring the administration of justice into disrepute among right-thinking people. The circumstances in which abuse of process can arise are very varied; those which give rise to the instant appeal must surely be unique. It would, in my view, be most unwise if this House were to use this occasion to say anything that might be taken as limiting to fixed categories the kinds of circumstances in which the court has a duty (I disavow the word discretion) to exercise this salutary power."

That was a case where the court would not permit a collateral attack on the decision of a court of competent jurisdiction. The principle has recently been applied in this court to analogous cases, where issues of fact have been litigated exhaustively in sample cases; it is an abuse of process for a litigant, who was not one of the sample cases, to re-litigate all the issues of fact on the same or substantially the same evidence: see *Ashmore* v *British Coal Corporation* [1990] 2 WLR 1437.

The question is whether it would be in the interests of justice and public policy to allow the issue of fraud to be litigated again in this court, it having been tried and determined by Egan J in Ireland. In my judgment it would not; indeed, I think it would be a travesty of justice. Not only would the plaintiffs be required to re-litigate matters which have twice been extensively investigated and decided in their favour in the natural forum, but it would run the risk of inconsistent verdicts being reached, not only as between the English and Irish courts, but as between the defendants themselves. The Waites have not appealed Sir Peter Pain's judgment, and they were quite right not to do so. The plaintiffs will no doubt proceed to execute their judgment against them. What could be a greater source of injustice, if in years to come, when the issue is finally decided, a different decision is in Mr McLeod's case reached? Public policy requires that there should be an end of litigation and that a litigant should not be vexed more than once in the same cause.'

Owens Bank Ltd* v *Bracco and Others [1992] 2 WLR 621 House of Lords (Lords Griffith, Bridge, Ackner, Goff and Browne-Wilkinson)

• *Fraud can be raised as a defence to a foreign judgment even where it could not be raised as a defence to an English judgment*

Facts

The plaintiff bank alleged that it had lent a sum of several million Swiss francs to the defendants (an Italian company and its managing director) and that the money was due and had not been paid. It successfully established this before the St Vincent court at first instance and before the St Vincent Court of Appeal; and judgment was given for more than 10 million Swiss francs. The defence sought to be raised by the defendants before the St Vincent courts was fraud: it alleged that the documents it had signed had been altered after it had signed them; but it raised this defence at a late stage in the St Vincent proceedings and was not allowed to do so. When registration of the St Vincent judgment under the Administration of Justice Act 1920 was sought for the purposes of enforcement, the defendants raised the fraud which they had been unable to plead before the St Vincent courts.

(The point whether the defendants could raise lis alibi pendens in terms of arts 21 and 22 of the Brussels Convention (arts 27 and 28 EU Council Regulation 44/2001), since the parties were also suing each other in Italy, has been referred to the European Court whose judgment on this point is considered above (Chapter 4).)

Held

That a judgment debtor resisting registration

of a foreign judgment under the Administration of Justice Act 1920 did not, in order to raise the defence of fraud, have to prove the more stringent requirements that were necessary to resist the enforcement of an English judgment on the ground of fraud. Thus the defendants could raise their defence notwithstanding that there was no fresh evidence of the fraud that was not available at the trial.

Lord Bridge:

> 'It is not in dispute that if the loan documents were indeed forgeries and the account given by Nano in his evidence in the court in St Vincent of the transaction of 31 January 1979 at the Hotel de Rhone in Geneva was a fabrication, the St Vincent judgment was obtained by fraud. But it is submitted for the bank that the language of s9(2)(d) must be construed as qualified by the common law rule that the unsuccessful party who has been sued to judgment is not permitted to challenge that judgment on the ground that it was obtained by fraud unless he is able to prove that fraud by fresh evidence which was not available to him and could not have been discovered with reasonable diligence before the judgment was delivered. Here, it is said, there is no such fresh evidence. This is the rule to be applied in an action brought to set aside an English judgment on the ground that it was obtained by fraud. The rule rests on the principle that there must be finality in litigation which would be defeated if it were open to the unsuccessful party in one action to bring a second action to relitigate the issue determined against him simply on the ground that the opposing party had obtained judgment in the first action by perjured evidence. Your Lordships were taken, in the course of argument, through the many authorities in which this salutary English rule has been developed and applied and which demonstrate the stringency of the criterion which the fresh evidence must satisfy if it is to be admissible to impeach a judgment on the ground of fraud. I do not find it necessary to examine these authorities. The rule they establish is unquestionable and the principle on which they rest is clear. The question at issue in this appeal is whether a defendant who is seeking to resist the enforcement against him of a foreign judgment, either by an action on the foreign judgment at common law or under the statutory machinery for the enforcement of foreign judgments, is placed in the same position as if he were a plaintiff in an action seeking to set aside the judgment of an English court on the ground that it was obtained by fraud and can therefore only rely upon evidence which satisfies the English rule.
>
> A foreign judgment given by a court of competent jurisdiction over the defendant is treated by the common law as imposing a legal obligation on the judgment debtor which will be enforced in an action on the judgment of an English court in which the defendant will not be permitted to reopen issues of either fact or law which have been decided against him by the foreign court. But this is subject to the special defence that the foreign judgment was obtained by fraud. The starting-point in considering the scope of that defence is the decision of the Court of Appeal in *Abouloff* v *Oppenheimer & Co* (1882) 10 QBD 295. The plaintiff had obtained judgment against the defendant in a Russian court, the District Court of Tiflis, for the return of certain goods or payment of their value, which was affirmed on appeal by the High Court of Tiflis. She sought to enforce the judgment by action in England. To this action the defendants pleaded that the judgment had been obtained by the fraud of the plaintiff and her husband by falsely representing to the courts in Russia that the goods in question were not in their possession when in fact they were. On demurrer to this plea the Court of Appeal, affirming the Queen's Bench Division, held that the defence pleaded was good. The judgments are particularly instructive in the context of the present appeal in so far as they address and reject the very argument which your Lordships are now invited by the bank to affirm. The argument is summarised in the judgment of Lord Coleridge CJ at pp299–300:

"It has been argued that the defence is bad, mainly on the ground that upon these pleadings it must be taken that these allegations of fraud were brought before the courts at Tiflis; that the defendants did state to those courts that the goods were not in their possession but in the plaintiff's; that the courts had jurisdiction to examine this defence, and did examine it, and came to a conclusion against the defendants; and therefore that, whether this conclusion was right or wrong on the matters of fact, the question of the plaintiff's alleged fraud cannot now be tried or litigated in the courts of this country."

In the course of a lengthy judgment rejecting this argument Lord Coleridge CJ said, at pp300–301:

"... it is enough for me to say that the English courts do enforce obligations created by judgments, but that it has always been held in the courts of this country to be an answer to an action upon a judgment, that that judgment has been obtained by the fraud of the party seeking to enforce it. This principle has been laid down in the broadest terms by De Grey CJ in the answer to the two questions of the House of Lords in the *Duchess of Kingston's Case* (1776) 20 St Tr 355, 537, 544n namely, that 'fraud is an extrinsic, collateral act; which vitiates the most solemn proceedings of courts of justice. Lord Coke says, it avoids all judicial acts, ecclesiastical or temporal.' In that case one of the questions put to the judges was whether a sentence of the spiritual court against a marriage in a suit for jactitation of marriage was conclusive evidence, so as to stop the counsel for the Crown from proving the marriage in an indictment for bigamy; and speaking of this sentence De Grey CJ says: 'Like all other acts of the highest judicial authority, it is impeachable from without: although it is not permitted to show that the court was mistaken, it may be shown that they were misled.' I believe that the principle has never been either better or more tersely and neatly stated than it was in the foregoing passages; and, as it appears to me, the question for the courts of this country to consider is whether, when a foreign judgment is sought to be enforced by an action in this country, the foreign court has been misled intentionally by the fraud of the person seeking to enforce it, whether a fraud has been committed upon the foreign court with the intention to procure its judgment. From the time of the decision in the *Duchess of Kingston's Case* until the present time it has been held that fraud of that kind can be pleaded in the courts of this country to an action on a judgment, and that, if it can be proved, it vitiates the judgment and discharges the defendant from the obligation which would otherwise be thereby created."

Lord Coleridge CJ concludes his judgment by saying, at p303:

"I think, therefore, on the broad ground that no man can take advantage of his own wrong, and that it is a principle of law that no action can be maintained on the judgment of a court either in this country or in any other, which has been obtained by the fraud of the person seeking to enforce it, that the defence is good ..."

The other two members of the court addressed the plaintiff's argument more specifically and equally rejected it. Baggallay LJ said at p304:

"It has been contended on the part of the plaintiff that having regard to the terms of the defence it is fair to infer that all the facts, so far as regarded the goods being in the possession of the plaintiff, were or might have been before the Russian courts, and that although they erroneously decided in favour of the plaintiff, they were mistaken and were not misled. If all the facts from which the fraud is to be inferred had been before the foreign court, and that court did not infer fraud from them, and if an English court was called upon to give effect to the judgment obtained by the person who perpetrated the fraud, I should be prepared to hold that that foreign judgment could not be enforced in the English court."

Brett LJ said, at p306:

> "I will assume that in the suit in the Russian courts the plaintiff's fraud was alleged by the defendants, and that they gave evidence in support of the charge: I will assume even that the defendants gave the very same evidence which they propose to adduce in this action; nevertheless the defendants will not be debarred at the trial of this action from making the same charge of fraud and from adducing the same evidence in support of it; and if the High Court of Justice is satisfied that the allegations of the defendants are true, and that the fraud was committed, the defendants will be entitled to succeed in the present action."

In *Vadala* v *Lawes* (1890) 25 QBD 310 the plaintiff sued to enforce the judgment of an Italian court holding the defendant liable on certain bills of exchange. The defence pleaded, inter alia, that the bills were fraudulent. The question whether it was open to the defendant, by this plea, to invite the English court to determine the very issue which had been decided against him by the Italian court came in due course before the Court of Appeal. Delivering the leading judgment, with which Bowen LJ agreed, Lindley LJ said, at pp316–317:

> "But we now come to another and a more difficult question, and that is, whether this defence can be gone into at all. There are two rules relating to these matters which have to be borne in mind, and the joint operation of which gives rise to the difficulty. First of all, there is the rule which is perfectly well established and well known, that a party to an action can impeach the judgment in it for fraud. Whether it is the judgment of an English court or of a foreign court does not matter; using general language, that is a general proposition unconditional and undisputed. Another general proposition which, speaking in equally general language, is perfectly well settled, is, that when you bring an action on a foreign judgment, you cannot go into the merits which have been tried in the foreign court. But you have to combine those two rules and apply them in the case where you cannot go into the alleged fraud without going into the merits. Which rule is to prevail? That point appears to me to have been one of very great difficulty before the case of *Abouloff* v *Oppenheimer*, 10 QBD 295. At the time when that case was decided, namely, in 1882, there was a long line of authorities including *Bank of Australasia* v *Nias* (1851) 16 QB 717, *Ochsenbein* v *Papelier* (1873) LR 8 Ch App 695, and *Cammell* v *Sewell* (1860) 5 H & N 728, all recognising and enforcing the general proposition, that in an action on a foreign judgment you cannot retry the merits. But until *Abouloff*'s case the difficulty of combining the two rules and saying what ought to be done where you could not enter into the question of fraud to prove it without reopening the merits, had never come forward for explicit decision. That point was raised directly in the case of *Abouloff* v *Oppenheimer*, and it was decided. I cannot fritter away that judgment, and I cannot read the judgments without seeing that they amount to this: that if the fraud upon the foreign court consists in the fact that the plaintiff has induced that court by fraud to come to a wrong conclusion, you can reopen the whole case even although you will have in this court to go into the very facts which were investigated, and which were in issue in the foreign court."

After a careful examination of the judgments in *Abouloff* v *Oppenheimer & Co* Lindley LJ concluded, at pp319–320:

> "... when I come to look at the defendants' argument, and the whole judgment, I cannot conceal from myself that it has been decided to the effect I have already mentioned; and that, therefore, it is competent in point of law for the defendant in this action to raise this defence, and to satisfy the jury, if he can, that the Italian court was misled by the fraud of the plaintiff, that fraud consisting in this – that the plaintiff knowingly placed before the Italian court bills of exchange which he alleged to be commercial bills, when in truth and in fact he knew them to be nothing of the sort, but bills for gambling

> transactions. And if the jury were to find in fact, not only that the bills were for gambling transactions, but, further, that the Italian court has been imposed on by the fraud, that is a good defence according to the case of *Abouloff* v *Oppenheimer*."

These decisions have been criticised by academic writers and have not been followed in the Canadian courts: see Dicey & Morris, *The Conflict of Laws*, 11th ed (1987), p469, n66. But they have been followed and applied by the Court of Appeal in *Syal* v *Heyward* [1948] 2 KB 443 and *Jet Holdings Inc* v *Patel* [1990] 1 QB 335 and must stand as establishing the relevant English law unless and until overruled by your Lordships' House.

Mr Mann, for the bank, submits that the time has come when they should be overruled either as having been wrongly decided in the first place or, alternatively, even if the original decisions could have been justified 100 years ago, on the ground that they rest on a principle which is unacceptable today and out of accord with the approach of the courts to other issues arising in the field of private international law.

I appreciate the force of this submission and, if the issue were governed only by the common law, I would think it necessary to examine in detail both the relevant authorities prior to *Abouloff* v *Oppenheimer & Co* 10 QBD 295 and the elaborate arguments skilfully deployed by Mr Mann in support of his general thesis. But that is not the position. As I have pointed out, enforcement in the United Kingdom of the judgments of courts in the Commonwealth is governed by s9 of the Act of 1920 which is here directly in issue. The enforcement in the United Kingdom of the judgments of courts in countries with which this country has concluded reciprocal enforcement arrangements is governed by the Foreign Judgments (Reciprocal Enforcement) Act 1933. That is not here directly in issue, but it provides by s4(1)(a)(iv) that registration of a judgment, which will have been effected ex parte under s2, is to be set aside if the registering court is satisfied "that the judgment was obtained by fraud" and thus appears to raise an issue of construction which it would, I think, be difficult to differentiate from that raised here by s9(2)(d) of the Act of 1920. Subject to possible penalties in costs, it is still open to a foreign judgment creditor to resort to a common law action to enforce his foreign judgment, but such resort is now only necessary in the case of judgments delivered in countries to which, in the absence of reciprocal enforcement arrangements, the Act of 1933 has not been extended. In these circumstances it seems to me clear that before considering the possibility of overruling *Abouloff* v *Oppenheimer & Co* and *Vadala* v *Lawes* 25 QBD 310 it is necessary first to determine the scope of the fraud defence available to a judgment debtor resisting statutory enforcement in reliance on s9(2)(d) of the Act of 1920.

The Act of 1920 was preceded by the report in 1919 of a committee chaired by Lord Sumner, Report of the Committee Appointed by the Lord Chancellor to Consider the Conduct of Legal Proceedings between Parties in this Country and Parties Abroad and the Enforcement of Judgments and Awards (1919) (Cmd 251). One proposal with respect to reciprocal enforcement within the British Empire which was considered by the Sumner Committee was the adoption of a draft Bill, which had been circulated in 1916 to overseas governments within the Empire, and which followed the lines of the Judgment Extension Act 1868 (31 & 32 Vict c54). The Act of 1868 made the judgments of superior courts in England, Scotland and Ireland reciprocally registrable on satisfying purely formal requirements, whereupon they became enforceable as if they were judgments of the courts in which they were registered. The Sumner Report points out that the adoption of this principle of strict reciprocity would give to all judgments of courts within the Empire an equal status and currency in all parts of the Empire and that some overseas governments had commented adversely on this principle. The committee accepted the criticism and recommended a much more cautious approach, the reasons for which the report explains in detail. This caution leads to the specific recommendations in paragraph 35(a) and (b) which were in due course directly implemented by s9(1) and (2)(a) to (e) of the Act of 1920.

Even without reference to the Sumner Report s9(2)(d) would have to be construed with reference to the common law as understood in 1920. But the context in which the recommendations which came to be embodied in s9(2) were made leaves no room for doubt. If the Sumner Committee had embraced the strict reciprocity principle of the Act of 1868 and recommended giving to Commonwealth judgments the full status and currency of United Kingdom judgments, this would still have left such judgments open to challenge on the ground that they had been obtained by fraud in so far as the fraud could be established within the strict limits of the English rule. Having rejected that principle, the committee's recommendation that it should be one of the express bars to the enforcement of a Commonwealth judgment that it had been obtained by fraud can only have been intended to apply the much wider rule which the court had applied to foreign judgments in *Abouloff* v *Oppenheimer & Co* 10 QBD 295 and *Vadala* v *Lawes*, 25 QBD 310 and s9(2)(d) must be construed accordingly.

Confronted with this difficulty Mr Mann submitted that s9(2)(d) should nevertheless be held to do no more than embody a common law principle which was still capable of development and adaptation. The fact that Parliament had given legislative expression to the principle should not be allowed to arrest that process or to freeze the principle immutably in the form which the common law gave it in 1920. More specifically he submitted that the difference in the basis on which the court will allow a judgment to be challenged on the ground that it was obtained by fraud as between a plaintiff seeking to set aside an English judgment on the one hand and a defendant resisting enforcement of a foreign judgment on the other hand is a matter of procedure, not of substantive law, and that accordingly nothing in s9(2)(d) need inhibit the House from adapting and modernising the procedure applicable to the enforcement of judgments under s9 by confining the judgment debtor's attack on the foreign judgment within the strict limits of the English rule.

I cannot accept this submission. The difference in question is not, in my opinion, one of procedure but of substantive law and is of fundamental importance. An English judgment, subject to any available appellate procedures, is final and conclusive between the parties as to the issues which it decides. It is in order to preserve this finality that any attempt to reopen litigation, once concluded, even on the ground that judgment was obtained by fraud, has to be confined within such very restrictive limits. In the decisions in *Abouloff* v *Oppenheimer & Co* and *Vadala* v *Lawes* the common law courts declined to accord the same finality to foreign judgments, but preferred to give primacy to the principle that fraud unravels everything. In the Judgments Extension Act 1868 Parliament provided for full reciprocal enforceability as between the judgments of the superior courts in the different jurisdictions within the United Kingdom, with the effect that the judgment given in one jurisdiction and registered in another would enjoy the same finality as a judgment given in that jurisdiction, with no obstacle placed in the way of registration. By contrast, the judgment creditor seeking registration under the Act of 1920 must first surmount the obstacles which s9(2) places in his way and s9(2)(d), construed, as I think it must be, as an adoption of the common law approach to foreign judgments, specifically denies finality to the judgment if it can be shown to have been obtained by fraud.

I recognise that, as a matter of policy, there may be a very strong case to be made in the 1990s in favour of according to overseas judgments the same finality as the courts accord to English judgments. But enforcement of overseas judgments is now primarily governed by the statutory codes of 1920 and 1933. Since these cannot be altered except by further legislation, it seems to me out of the question to alter the common law rule by overruling *Abouloff* v

Oppenheimer & Co and *Vadala* v *Lawes*. To do so would produce the absurd result that an overseas judgment creditor, denied statutory enforcement on the ground that he had obtained his judgment by fraud, could succeed in a common law action to enforce his judgment because the evidence on which the judgment debtor relied did not satisfy the English rule. Accordingly the whole field is effectively governed by statute and, if the law is now in need of reform, it is for the legislature, not the judiciary, to effect it. I would dismiss the bank's appeal with costs.'

Pemberton* v *Hughes [1899] 1 Ch 781 Chancery Division (Lindley MR, Rigby and Vaughan Williams LJJ)

• *Non-defences – lack of internal competence by the foreign court appears to be no defence*

Facts

This case concerned the recognition of a divorce granted by a court in Florida dissolving the marriage of two persons domiciled in Florida. The defendants alleged, however, that because the subpoena did not give the wife ten clear days notice, as required by the law of Florida, the decree was void and should not be recognised.

Held

Provided the foreign court had international jurisdiction over the persons and subject matter in the case, an irregularity of procedure in the local law did not prevent recognition by the English courts.

Lindley MR:

'Assuming that the defendants are right, and that the decree of divorce is void by the law of Florida, it by no means follows that it ought to be so regarded in this country. It sounds paradoxical to say that a decree of a foreign Court should be regarded here as more efficacious or with more respect than it is entitled to in the country in which it was pronounced. But this paradox disappears when the principles on which English Courts act in regarding or disregarding foreign judgments are borne in mind. If a judgment is pronounced by a foreign Court over persons within its jurisdiction and in a matter with which it is competent to deal, English Courts never investigate the propriety of the proceedings in the foreign Court, unless they offend against English views of substantial justice. Where no substantial justice, according to English notions, is offended, all that English Courts look to is the finality of the judgment and the jurisdiction of the Court, in this sense and to this extent – namely, its competence to entertain the sort of case which it did deal with, and its competence to require the defendant to appear before it. If the Court had jurisdiction in this sense and to this extent, the Courts of this country never inquire whether the jurisdiction has been properly or improperly exercised, provided always that no substantial injustice, according to English notions, has been committed.

There is no doubt that the Courts of this country will not enforce the decisions of foreign Courts which had no jurisdiction in the sense above explained – ie, over the subject-matter or over the persons brought before them: *Schibsby* v *Westenholz* LR 6 QB 155; *Rousillon* v *Rousillon* (1880) 14 Ch D 351; *Price* v *Dewhurst* (1838) 4 My & Cr 76; *Buchanan* v *Rucker* 9 East, 192; *Sirdar Gurdyal Singh* v *Rajah of Faridkote* [1984] AC 670. But the jurisdiction which alone is important in these matters is the competence of the Court in an international sense – ie, its territorial competence over the subject matter and over the defendant. Its competence or jurisdiction in any other sense is not regarded as material by the Courts of this country. This is pointed out by Mr Westlake (International Law, 3rd ed 328) and by Foote (Private International Jurisprudence, 2nd ed p 547) and is illustrated by *Vanquelin* v *Bouard* (15 CB (NS) 341). That was an action on a judgment obtained in France on a bill of exchange. The Court was competent to try such actions, and the defendant was within its jurisdiction. He let judgment go by default, and and in the action in this country on the judgment he pleaded that by French law the French Court had no jurisdiction, because the defendant was not a trader and was not resident in a particular town where the cause of action arose. In other words, the defendant pleaded that the French action was brought in the wrong court (see the 13th plea). The Court of Common Pleas held the plea bad, and that the defence set up by it should have been raised in the French action. The French action in *Vanquelin* v *Bouard* 15 CB (NS) 341 was an action in personam, and the parties to the action in France were also the parties to the action brought in this country on the French judgment. The decision, therefore, does not exactly cover the present case, but it goes far to show that the defendants' contention in this case cannot be supported.

The defendants' contention entirely ignores the distinction between the jurisdiction of tribunals from an international and their jurisdiction from a purely municipal point of view. But that distinction rests on good sense, and is recognised by modern writers on private international law …

It may be safely said that, in the opinion of writers on international law, and for international purposes, the jurisdiction or the competency of a Court does not depend upon the exact observance of its own rules of procedure. The defendants' contention is based upon the assumption that an irregularity in procedure of a foreign Court of competent jurisdiction in the sense above explained is a matter which the Courts of this country are bound to recognise if such irregularity involves nullity of sentence. No authority can be found for any such proposition; and, although I am not aware of any English decision exactly to the contrary, there are many which are so inconsistent with it as to show that it cannot be accepted.

A judgment of a foreign Court having jurisdiction over the parties and subject-matter – ie having jurisdiction to summon the defendants before it and to decide such matters as it has decided – cannot be impeached in this country on its merits: *Castrique* v *Imrie* (1870) LR 4 HL 414 (in rem); *Godard* v *Gray* (1870) LR 6 QB 139 (in personam); *Messina* v *Petrococchino* (1872) LR 4 PC 144 (in personam). It is quite inconsistent with those cases, and also with *Vanquelin* v *Bouard* 15 CB (NS) 341, to hold that such a judgment can be impeached here for a mere error in procedure. And in *Castrique* v *Imrie* Lord Colonsay said that no inquiry on such a matter should be made.'

Comment

Note that Lindley MR speaks in terms of the decree being void but it was more likely that the decree was only voidable, ie it stood until set aside by the court which granted it. See the textbook.

Judgments rendered within the EC

De Wolf* v *Cox [1976] ECR 1759
European Court of Justice

• *Procedure for recognition and enforcement of a judgment granted within the EC*

Facts

De Wolf obtained a judgment against Cox in the Belgian courts. Cox did not comply with the judgment and De Wolf sought to enforce it against him in the Netherlands. He applied to the Netherlands courts for a judgment in the same terms as the Belgian courts, rather than an order for enforcement as required by art 31 of the Brussels Convention (art 38 EU Council Regulation 44/2001). This course of action was permissible under the law of the Netherlands and involved less expense to the plaintiff.

Held

Enforcement under art 31 was the only course available to the plaintiff.

Judgment of the ECJ:

'By judgment of 7 May 1976, received at

the Court Registry on the following 14 May, the Hoge Raad of the Netherlands has referred to the Court a question on the interpretation, in particular, of art 31 of the Convention on Jurisdiction and the Enforcement of Judgments in Civil and Commercial Matters of 27 September 1968, hereinafter referred to as "the Convention".

It appears from the file that the plaintiff in the main action, resident in Belgium, having obtained a judgment from the juge de paix of Turnhout (Belgium) ordering the defendant in the main action, having its head office in the Netherlands, to pay an invoice, lodged an application before the Kantonrechter (juge de paix) of Boxmeer (The Netherlands) against the same defendant and in respect of the same matter.

The Kantonrechter, having heard the defendant, held that the application was admissible and gave judgment on the substance of the case in the same terms as the Belgian court.

In so doing, the Dutch court took the view, inter alia, on the one hand, that it was required to recognise the Belgian judgment under art 26 of the Convention but that, on the other, under the legislation of the Netherlands, the procedure chosen by the applicant was less expensive for the parties than the procedure under arts 31 et seq of the Convention would have been. Under the latter procedure an application for an order for the enforcement of the judgment delivered by the Belgian court would have been brought before the President of the Arrondissementrechtbank which had jurisdiction.

The Attorney-General of the Hoge Raad brought an appeal against the judgment of the Kantonrechter before the Hoge Raad on the ground that the Kantonrechter ought to have declared the application inadmissible, because the procedure under art 31 of the Convention is the only means available to the applicant for the purpose of enforcing the judgment of the Belgian court.

The Hoge Raad is asking the Court, in substance, to rule whether the Convention prevents a plaintiff who has obtained a judgment in his favour in a Contracting State, being a judgment for which an order for enforcement under art 31 of the Convention may issue in another Contracting State, from making an application to a court in that other State for a judgment against the other party in the same terms as the judgment delivered in the first State.

The first paragraph of art 26 of the Convention provides: "A judgment given in a Contracting State shall be recognised in the other Contracting States without any special procedure being required."

Although arts 27 and 28 lay down certain exceptions to this duty of recognition, art 29 nevertheless provides that "under no circumstances may a foreign judgment be reviewed as to its substance."

When an application for a review as to substance is declared admissible, the court before which the application is heard is required to decide whether it is well founded, a situation which could lead that court to conflict with a previous foreign judgment and, therefore, to fail in its duty to recognise the latter.

To accept the admissibility of an application concerning the same subject-matter and brought between the same parties as an application upon which judgment has already been delivered by a court in another Contracting State would therefore be incompatible with the meaning of the provisions quoted. It also results from art 21 of the Convention, which covers cases in which proceedings "involving the same cause of action and between the same parties are brought in the courts of different Contracting States" and requires that a court other than the first seised shall decline jurisdiction in favour of that court, that proceedings such as those brought before the Kantonrechter of Boxmeer are incompatible with the objectives of the Convention.

That provision is evidence of the concern to prevent the courts of two Contracting States from giving judgment in the same case.

Finally, to accept the duplication of main actions such as has occurred in the present case might result in a creditor's possessing two orders for enforcement on the basis of the same debt.

The fact that there may be occasions on which, according to the national law applicable, the procedure set out in arts 31 et seq of the Convention may be found to be more expensive than bringing fresh proceedings on the substance of the case does not invalidate these considerations.

In this respect, it must be observed that the Convention, which, in the words of the preamble thereto, is intended "to secure the simplification of formalities governing the reciprocal recognition and enforcement of judgments of courts or tribunals", ought to induce the Contracting States to ensure that the costs of the procedure described in the Convention are fixed so as to accord with that concern for simplification.

The question raised by the Hoge Raad of the Netherlands should therefore be answered in the affirmative.'

Hoffmann* v *Krieg (1988) The Times 26 March European Court of Justice

• *Grounds upon which recognition or enforcement may be refused*

Facts

A wife had obtained a maintenance order from the courts in Germany and sought to enforce that order against her husband in the Netherlands in terms of art 31 of the Brussels Convention (art 38 EU Council Regulation 44/2001). However, the courts of the Netherlands had, shortly after the original maintenance order had been made, dissolved the marriage between the parties. (This dissolution of the marriage fell outside the terms of the Brussels Convention and was not recognised in Germany.)

Held

That a foreign decision ordering a husband to pay maintenance to his wife pursuant to his obligations of maintenance flowing from the marriage, was irreconcilable, for the purposes of art 27(3) of the Convention (art 34(3) EU Council Regulation 44/2001), with a national decision decreeing a divorce between the spouses concerned.

Judgment of the ECJ:

'In the present case, the decision whose enforcement was at issue ordered a husband to pay maintenance to his wife. Consequently, it was necessary to examine whether the dissolution of the marriage, declared by a court of the state in which recognition was sought, could prevent enforcement of the foreign decision, even in the case where the latter remained enforceable in its state of origin, in the absence of recognition of the divorce decree.

In that regard it was to be noted that paragraph I of the second indent of art 1 of the Convention excluded the status of natural persons from its scope and that the Convention contained no rule requiring a judge of a state in which recognition was sought to make the effect of a judgment of that state ordering a divorce subject to recognition of that judgment in the state of origin of a foreign decision on maintenance. That finding was confirmed by art 27(4) of the Convention.

It followed that the Convention did not prevent a judge of the state in which recognition was sought from drawing the consequences of a national judgment declaring a divorce in the context of the enforcement of a foreign maintenance order.

The third question sought in substance to establish whether a foreign decision ordering a husband to pay maintenance to his wife was irreconcilable, for the purposes of art 27(3), with a national decision which dissolved the marriage of the spouses or whether such a foreign decision was contrary to public policy in the state in which recognition was sought within art 27(1).

The provisions whose interpretation was requested laid down the grounds for not recognising foreign judgments. Under the second paragraph of art 34, those were the same grounds which justified refusal of enforcement.

Recourse to the public policy provision,

which was to be made only in exceptional cases, was in any event excluded where, as in the present case, the problem submitted was that of the compatibility of a foreign decision with a national decision since that problem was to be resolved on the basis of the specific provision of art 27(3), which dealt with the case where the foreign judgment was irreconcilable with a judgment given in a dispute between the same parties in the state in which recognition was sought.

In order to establish whether a judgment was irreconcilable for the purposes of that provision, it was necessary to examine whether the decisions in question led to legal consequences which were mutually exclusive.

It appeared from the file that in the present case an enforcement order had been granted in respect of the foreign maintenance order at a time when the national decision declaring a divorce had already been delivered and had become res judicata, and that the main proceedings related to the period following the divorce.

In those circumstances the decisions in question led to legal consequences which were mutually exclusive. The foreign decision which necessarily presupposed the existence of a matrimonial bond, would have to be executed although the bond had been dissolved by a decision given between the same parties in the state in which recognition was sought.

The fourth and fifth questions sought to establish whether art 36 of the Convention was to be interpreted as meaning that a party who had not brought proceedings against the order for enforcement provided for in that provision could, at the stage of enforcement of the decision, no longer raise a valid objection which he might have raised in the context of an action against the order for enforcement, and whether that rule was to be applied automatically by the courts of the state in which recognition was sought.

In order to reply to those questions, it was necessary to recall first that, in order to limit the requirements to which enforcement of judgments given in Contracting States might be subject in another Contracting State, the Convention had provided a summary procedure for granting of an enforcement order, which might only be refused for reasons set out in arts 27 and 28.

Nonetheless, the Convention merely regulated the procedure for obtaining an order for the enforcement of foreign enforceable instruments and did not deal with execution itself, which continued to be governed by the domestic law of the court in which execution was sought.

Consequently, the enforcement of a foreign decision with an enforcement order took place in accordance with the procedural rules of the national law of the judge concerned.

It followed that means of appeal available under national law were excluded where an appeal against enforcement of a foreign judgment accompanied by an enforcement order was brought by the same person who could have brought an appeal against the application for enforcement and was based upon a reason which might have been raised in the context of such an appeal.

In those circumstances to dispute the enforcement would lead to a calling in question of the enforcement order outside the strict time limit laid down by the second paragraph of art 36 of the Convention and as a result would deprive that provision of its purpose.

The imperative nature of the time limit laid down in art 36 required the national judge to ensure that it was observed. It was therefore for him, of his own motion, to declare an action inadmissible where it was based upon national law where such an action would lead to a reopening of that time limit.

That rule, which followed from the scheme of the Convention, could not however be applied where, as in the present case, it would require the national judge to ignore the effects of a national divorce decree, which was excluded from the scope of the application, on the ground that that judgment could not be recognised in the state of origin of the foreign decision whose enforcement was in question.

On those grounds the European Court rules:

1. A foreign decision recognised pursuant to art 26 of the Convention should, in principle, produce the same effects in the state in which enforcement was sought as it had in the state of origin.

2. A foreign decision which had been granted an enforcement order in one Contracting State pursuant to art 31 of the Convention and which was still enforceable in the state of origin, could not continue to be enforced in the state in which enforcement was sought where, according to the legislation of that state, enforcement could no longer take place for reasons which fell outside the scope of the Convention.

3. A foreign decision ordering a husband to pay maintenance to his wife pursuant to his obligations of maintenance following from a marriage, was irreconcilable, for the purposes of art 27(3) of the Convention, with a national decision decreeing a divorce between the spouses concerned.

4. Article 36 of the Brussels Convention was to be interpreted as meaning that a party who had not brought an action against the enforcement order provided for by that provision could, at the stage of enforcement of that decision, no longer put forward a valid objection which it could have raised in the context of an appeal against enforcement, and that rule was to be applied automatically by courts in the state in which enforcement was sought. However, that rule was not applicable where it would have the consequence of requiring a national judge to subject the effects of a national judgment which fell outside the scope of the Convention to its recognition in the state of origin of the foreign decision whose enforcement was in question.'

Comment

There was a straightforward application of the principle of *Hoffmann* v *Krieg* in *Macaulay* v *Macaulay* (1990) The Times 29 November. There an Irish maintenance decree was not enforced in England on the ground that this was irreconcilable with the divorce decree granted by the English courts.

Interdesco SA* v *Nullifire Ltd [1992] 1 Lloyd's Rep 180 Queen's Bench Division (Phillips J)

• *Raising the defence of fraud in a Brussels Convention case (art 34 EU Council Regulation 44/2001)*

Facts

This was an application to enforce in England a judgment obtained in the French courts based upon the termination of a contract for the exclusive distribution of fire resistant paint in the United Kingdom and Ireland. The English distributor (Nullifire Ltd) had terminated the contract with the French supplier (Interdesco SA). The French court, however, held that the termination was wrongful and damages were awarded against Nullifire. Nullifire had evidence that suggested that Interdesco had misled the French court in regard to whether it had had dealings with Nullifire's competitors. Nullifire sought to resist enforcement of the French judgment against it on the ground of fraud. It is clear that fraud could at common law be pleaded as a defence to the enforcement of a foreign judgment even where fraud had been argued before the foreign court and there was no new evidence of fraud. Could this common law view of the wide availability of fraud as a defence be used to resist enforcement of a foreign judgment under art 27(1) of the Brussels Convention (art 34(1) EU Council Regulation 44/2001)?

Held

In the context of the Brussels Convention different considerations applied. Generally, 'it accords with the spirit of the Convention that all issues [including fraud] should, so far as possible, be dealt with by the State enjoying the original jurisdiction. [Moreover,] the courts of that State are likely to be better able to assess whether the original judgment was procured by fraud'. In reliance upon the Schlosser Report the judge held that it would not be contrary to English public policy to enforce the judgment allegedly tainted by fraud (see art 27(1)).

Comment

1. Note that in this judgment reliance was placed upon the Court of Appeal judgments in *Owens Bank* v *Bracco*. This case went to the House of Lords and is reported ([1992] 2 All ER 193) but nothing that was said in the Lords, it is believed, would have changed the outcome of this case. An extract from *Owens Bank* v *Bracco* in the House of Lords will be found above.
2. This case makes clear that the defence of fraud is much narrower in Brussels Convention and EU Council Regulation 44/2001 cases than is the case under the common law.

Petereit* v *Babcock International Holdings Ltd [1990] 1 WLR 350 Queen's Bench Division (Anthony Diamond QC)

• *Principles governing the grant of a stay under art 38 Brussels Convention (art 45 EU Council Regulation 44/2001)*

Facts

The plaintiff (the receiver of a bankrupt German firm) had obtained a judgment against the defendant (an English company) in Germany for DM 40 million and sought to enforce this judgment in England. The judgment had been registered in terms of s4 of the Civil Jurisdiction and Judgments Act 1982 and the defendant appealed to the High Court of Justice for a stay in terms of art 38 Brussels Convention (art 45 EU Council Regulation 44/2001).

Held

That the enforcing court had a general and unfettered discretion whether to stay enforcement proceedings in such circumstances, however the judgment was to be considered as prima facie enforceable and the enforcing court should not automatically grant a stay merely because there was a pending appeal. The purpose, however, of art 38 was to protect the position of the defendant; thus care should be taken to ensure that the defendant was not deprived of the fruits of a successful appeal by the unconditional enforcement of the judgment of the first instance court. Where proceedings were stayed this should be done subject to conditions that protected the position of the plaintiff – typically by requiring the defendant to grant adequate security for the payment of the sum claimed should the appeal go against him.

Anthony Diamond QC:

> '*The court's discretion under arts 30 and 38*
>
> While it is undoubtedly the policy of the Convention that a judgment obtained in one Contracting State should be rapidly enforceable in the other Contracting States, there are two Articles of the Convention, arts 30 and 38, both of which make it clear that, as an exception to this general policy, the enforcing court has a discretion to stay enforcement proceedings where an ordinary appeal is pending in the state in which the judgment was obtained. The general principles as to the recognition of judgments, which are to be found in arts 26 to 30, demonstrate in my opinion that, subject to the very circumscribed exceptions set out in arts 27 and 28, a judgment obtained in one Contracting State is prima facie to be recognised and rapidly enforced in the other Contracting States. Article 29 sets out the important principle that under no circumstances may a foreign judgment be reviewed as to its substance. Article 30, however, expressly confers on the enforcing court a power that can be expected to militate against the rapid enforcement of judgments in Contracting States, namely, a power to stay the proceedings if an ordinary appeal against the judgment has been lodged.
>
> Similarly, the Convention when dealing with the procedure for enforcing judgments in arts 31 to 45 again demonstrates a general policy that a judgment obtained in one

Contracting State should be enforceable in other Contracting States quickly and with a minimum of formalities: see especially the ex parte procedure authorised by art 34. it is against this background, and in some ways as an exception to it, that art 38, when dealing with the powers of the court at the appeal stage (which, under English procedure is the stage at which an inter partes hearing takes place before a judge sitting in chambers pursuant to O.71 r33), provides that the court may stay the proceedings if an ordinary appeal has been lodged against the judgment or if the time for such an appeal has not yet expired.

At this stage, looking simply at the wording of the Convention, I would draw three provisional conclusions as follows: (i) that the enforcing court has a general and unfettered discretion under the Convention to stay the enforcement proceedings if an appeal is pending in the state in which the judgment was obtained; (ii) that a judgment obtained in a Contracting State is to be regarded as prima facie enforceable, and accordingly the enforcing court should not adopt a general practice of depriving a successful plaintiff of the fruits of the judgment by the imposition of a more or less automatic stay, merely on the ground that there is a pending appeal; (iii) that the purpose of arts 30 and 38 is to protect the position of the defendant in an appropriate case and to ensure that, if the appeal succeeds, then the defendant will be able to enforce the order of the appeal court and will not be deprived of the fruits of his success by reason of a previous unconditional enforcement of the judgment. It seems to me that the court's discretion to grant a stay should be exercised with this purpose in mind.

In considering this matter I have taken into account both the passages in the Jenard report which set out the general policy of the Convention and also, the judgment of the European Court in *Industrial Diamond Supplies* v *Riva* (Case 43/77) [1977] ECR 2175. I do not find that either causes me to depart from the three provisional conclusions set out above. The Jenard report discusses in a number of passages the general policy of the Convention as being "to facilitate as far as possible the free movement of judgments". It points out that the court with which the appeal is lodged may either stay the proceedings, authorise enforcement, make enforcement conditional on the provision of security or specify the time within which the defendant must lodge his appeal. The report states that art 38 originated in a previous bilateral convention between Germany and Belgium whose object was:

> "to protect the judgment debtor against any loss which would result from the enforcement of a judgment which has not yet become res judicata and may be amended."

As to *Industrial Diamond Supplies* v *Riva* it must be borne in mind that a Belgian court had invited the European Court to give a preliminary ruling on the question what appeals were to be regarded as "ordinary appeals" for the purposes of arts 30 and 38. Although the court did not have to consider the manner in which a court should exercise its discretion under these Articles, the following passage from its judgment seems to me to be helpful, at p2189:

> "Although, as a whole, the Convention is intended to ensure the rapid enforcement of judgments with a minimum of formalities when those judgments are enforceable in the state in which they were given, the specific purpose of arts 30 and 38 is to prevent the compulsory recognition or enforcement of judgments in other Contracting States when the possibility that they might be annulled or amended in the state in which they were given still exists. For this purpose arts 30 and 38 reserve to the court before which a request for recognition or an appeal against a decision authorising enforcement has been brought in particular the possibility of staying the proceedings where, in the State in which the judgment was given, the judgment is being contested or may be contested within specific periods. According to the Convention, the court before which recognition or enforcement is sought is not under a duty to stay the proceedings but merely has the power to do so."

It seems to me that in the *Industrial Diamond Supplies* case the European Court was clearly of the view that under art 38, once a judgment had become enforceable in the state in which it was given and an "ordinary appeal" had been lodged against it, the enforcing court has a general and unfettered discretion, if it thinks fit, to stay the enforcement proceedings where the possibility exists that the judgment "might be annulled or amended in the state in which [it] was given."

I conclude, therefore, that there is no reason to doubt the three provisional conclusions at which I earlier arrived as a result of considering the language and scheme of the Convention.

It is, however, important to note that art 38 sets out two alternative methods of protecting the position of the defendant in the interval between the time when the judgment becomes enforceable in the state in which it is given and the time when the appeal against that judgment is finally determined; one is to grant a stay; the other is to make enforcement conditional on the provision of security by the plaintiff. I do not think that the Convention expresses any preference as to which method is to be employed by the enforcing court. Nor do I consider that the policy of the Convention, which I have described earlier, requires the enforcing court to prefer one method as opposed to the other. In my judgment it must depend on the detailed circumstances of the particular case which method is the more appropriate. …

I turn therefore to consider in very general terms the kind of circumstances which might cause the court to prefer the mechanism of a stay, subject to the imposition of terms on the defendant, over the mechanism of enforcement, subject to an order for the provision of security by the plaintiff, or vice versa. I am very conscious of the fact that it is impossible to predict the circumstances of different cases. It seems to me, however, that it may be useful to touch briefly on two matters.

First, there is the question whether, if a stay is to be ordered, the order should be for an unconditional stay or a stay subject to terms. The disadvantages of ordering an unconditional stay in many cases can include the following: (a) that the plaintiff may have no security for payment of the judgment sum which can be readily enforced if the appeal is unsuccessful, and (b) that the effect of the stay may be that the plaintiff will sustain loss by not having the use of the sum in issue during the interval between the date when the judgment became enforceable in the country in which it was given and the date when the appeal is finally determined, and the interest recoverable on the judgment debt may not compensate him in respect of this loss. It may be possible in some cases, by imposing suitable terms as a condition for granting a stay, to overcome one or other or both these disadvantages. In many cases, therefore, if a stay is to be ordered, it may be appropriate to protect the position of the plaintiff by imposing terms on the defendant.

Second, while in many cases it will not make a great deal of difference whether the court imposes a stay subject to conditions or orders enforcement subject to conditions, there may be cases where the position of the parties can best be protected by choosing one course rather than the other. In this connection a factor to be borne in mind is that in certain situations the provision of security may not constitute an adequate remedy for the potential losses which may be sustained by the plaintiff if enforcement is refused and the appeal is subsequently dismissed, or by the defendant if enforcement is ordered and the appeal is subsequently successful. This arises because the principal effect of ordering or staying enforcement will be to determine which party is to have the use of the sum in dispute during the interval which will elapse until the result of the appeal is known. In some cases the position of the party which is not to have the use of the money can be adequately protected by a condition which compels the other party to provide security for the payment of interest. In other cases the potential losses which may be sustained by the party which is not to have the use of the money may be so serious that the payment of interest may not be an adequate remedy or may, for one reason or another, be difficult to quantify and thus be difficult to remedy by means of an order for security. These are matters which I would expect the enforcing court to take into account when deciding whether to impose a stay subject to conditions or to order enforcement subject to the provision of security.

Finally, I do not think that merely because the court of the state in which the judgment was given has considered what security should be provided by the successful plaintiff as a condition to declaring the judgment enforceable in that state is, of itself, any reason for the enforcing court not to order a stay. It is true that there may be cases where all relevant factors relating to the question whether a stay should be ordered, and if so on what terms, may have been fully debated before and considered by the court of the state in which the judgment was given. In such a case I would expect the court of the enforcing state to respect the decision of the former court and to be reluctant to reopen questions which have been determined by it unless perhaps circumstances have changed since the relevant decision was given. I do not, however, consider that the mere fact that the question of the security to be provided by the plaintiff has been considered by the court of the state in which the judgment was given is, of itself, any reason for the enforcing state to decline to exercise its responsibilities and powers under art 38.'

9 Family Law

The validity of marriage

Apt v *Apt* [1948] P 83 Court of Appeal (Tucker, Bucknill and Cohen LJJ)

• *The validity of proxy marriages is a question of form, not a question of capacity to marry*

Facts

On 15 January 1941, while the appellant was in this country, she being not only resident but domiciled here, a ceremony of marriage was celebrated at Buenos Aires between her and the respondent. She was represented by a person whom, by a power of attorney executed on 8 November 1940 in London, she had named as her representative to contract the marriage. The husband, as found by Lord Merriman P, was resident and domiciled in the Argentine at all material times. The wife gave evidence that she had at no material time any intention of revoking the power of attorney, that she was informed in due course of the performance of the ceremony, and that she was not merely ready and willing, but eager, to join her husband in Buenos Aires, but was prevented from doing so during the war. She further deposed that when, after the war, she renewed her efforts to join the husband, he took no steps to assist her and ignored her alternative suggestion of a meeting in the United States of America, and that it was this conduct on his part which decided her to present the petition in this matter.

Held

Appeal dismissed.

Cohen LJ:

'On this evidence counsel for the wife contended that in the circumstances above stated, it would be contrary to public policy for the English courts to recognise the validity of the marriage and that, accordingly, his client was entitled to the decree which she sought …

With these conclusions and with the reasons which the President gives for them we so fully agree that it is only because of the importance of the matter and out of respect to the arguments addressed to us by counsel on both sides , that we state shortly our reasons for rejecting the arguments addressed to us for the wife. These arguments may be summarised as follows – (1) It is contrary to the public policy of England to recognise any marriage by proxy; (2) it is not however necessary to reach a conclusion on the first point, since in any event it is contrary to the public policy of England to recognise a marriage by proxy if (a) the party giving the proxy is domiciled in England or (b) the power of attorney conferring authority on the proxy is executed in England or (c) the power of attorney authorises a marriage by proxy in a country where the law will recognise, as does Argentine law the validity of a marriage contracted thereunder, notwithstanding the revocation of the proxy, if the revocation has not been communicated to the other spouse or the proxy before the ceremony takes place; and (3) the granting of a power of attorney in England is governed as to essential validity by English law and it is contrary to English law to recognise powers of attorney given for the purpose of celebrating a marriage.

The first argument is, in our opinion, ill-founded. Counsel was unable to suggest any statutory provision which was relevant to it … A proxy marriage, such as we are considering, is clearly a Christian marriage within the definition given by Lord Penzance in *Hyde* v *Hyde* (1866) LR 1 P & D 130: 'the voluntary union for life of one man and one woman, to the exclusion of all others.' A proxy marriage was recognised as valid by the canon law: see *Swinburne's Treatise of Spousals or Matrimonial Contracts* where, as the President points out, the conditions of such a marriage are described. It is recognised as valid in a number of Christian countries beside the Argentine … It was argued that *R* v *Millis* (1844) 10 Cl & Fin 534 precluded us from holding that such a marriage would be recognised in England, but that case concerned only marriages celebrated in England or Ireland; it did not expressly cover the point, and is in any event no authority for the general proposition that all proxy marriages, wherever celebrated, are void.

Counsel for the wife invited us, none the less, to hold that proxy marriages were contrary to public policy since they would facilitate clandestine marriages, make easy the bestowal of British nationality on foreigners and the carrying on of the white-slave traffic, and make it possible for two minors to get married in, for example, Mexico, although they were both domiciled in England. So far as the argument is based on clandestine marriages, we have to bear in mind that the English courts have not regarded all such marriages as contrary to public policy; for example, Gretna Green marriages were held to be valid until they were prohibited by statute … In any event, a consideration of what is "public policy" in a case where the matter is not governed by statute or by clearly established principle must necessarily involve balancing advantages against disadvantages. As against the considerations advanced by counsel must be weighed the following factors: (1) The unsatisfactory position that would arise in that, if Mr Foster [counsel for the wife] is right, the parties would be married in the Argentine, the place of the intended matrimonial domicile, but not married in England; (2) the fact that, if Mr Foster is right, any children that might result from the marriage would be bastards in the eye of English law; and, above all, (3) we should in effect be holding that the law of the Argentine was contrary to essential justice and morality, a conclusion to which we should hesitate to come. …

In all the circumstances, we are satisfied that we cannot properly extend public policy to invalidate all proxy marriages . …

Finally, on this point we would repeat the citation from Lord Dunedin's speech in *Berthiaume* v *Dastous* [1930] AC 79 which was quoted by the President.'

His Lordship quoted the passage beginning 'If a marriage is good' and ending to need much quotation', and continued:

'In our opinion, the method of giving consent as distinct from the fact of consent is essentially a matter for the lex loci celebrationis, and does not raise a question of capacity, or, as Mr Foster preferred to call it, essential validity …

We return to the second point. In our opinion, this also fails. As regards sub-division (a) thereof, we are unable to see any reason in public policy which would require the English courts, if they recognise the validity of proxy marriages celebrated outside the United Kingdom, to deny to a person domiciled in this country the right of so celebrating a marriage provided, of course, that he or she has in other respects capacity to marry and does not infringe any provision of English law. (b) is really another way of stating the third argument presented for the wife. We think it impossible to hold that, in the absence of some statutory prohibition, it is contrary to public policy to execute in England a power of attorney which the same person could validly execute in the Argentine, the power of attorney being intended to authorise an act in the Argentine which is lawful by the law of that country. As regards (c), we agree with the President that this point does not arise. If a case occurs where the proxy is revoked before the ceremony takes place but the other spouse and the proxy are unaware of the revocation, it may be that the courts of this country would hold that the purported marriage was void; but that would not be because of any general objection to proxy marriages, but because, on the facts of the particular case the court was satisfied that the marriage was not a voluntary union.'

Berthiaume* v *Dastous [1930] AC 79 Privy Council (Viscount Dunedin, Lord Warrington of Clyffe, Duff J and Sir Lancelot Sanderson)

• *The formalities of marriage are governed (in general) by the lex loci celebrationis*

Facts

In 1913 the respondent, a 17-year-old French Canadian of the Roman Catholic faith, went on a trip to Europe with her father. She there met the appellant, a member of a Quebec family and also of the Roman Catholic faith, who had been living in Paris for several years. He proposed to her, and she accepted. The appellant asked the respondent to make the necessary arrangements. The curé of the parish informed her that there were certain civil formalities to be gone through and that he would celebrate the marriage. She asked her fiancé to attend to the civil formalities, and he took her to the British consulate where certain papers were signed and a certificate issued which was given to her fiancé. After that the parties proceeded to the church, the certificate was handed to the curé, who then proceeded to celebrate the marriage according to the form of the Roman Catholic Church.

The parties lived together as husband and wife until the year 1926, when on returning from an absence from home the respondent discovered that the appellant had been guilty of infidelity and had introduced a mistress into their home. The respondent then applied to the court in Paris for a divorce. The court demanded the exhibition of a civil certificate of marriage. She then discovered that the certificate which her fiancé had procured at the British consulate was only a notice of intended marriage, and that the officiating curé had carelessly omitted to notice that it was not a certificate of marriage.The court declined to proceed with the case for divorce. The respondent raised the present action in the Superior Court of the Montreal district seeking a declaration of marriage, decree of separation, a dissolution of the communaute des biens – the marriage having been without a marriage contract, communaute des biens would ensue – and a judgment for alimony.

Held

Appeal allowed. The court disagreed with the decision of the Court of King's Bench, which by a majority, upheld the judgment of Loranger J who held the marriage valid, pronounced a decree of separation, dissolved the community of goods and granted a decree against the appellant for an alimoney allowance of $1,500 a month.

Viscount Dunedin:

'Their Lordships are unable to agree with the judgment under appeal. If there is one question better settled than any other in international law, it is that as regards marriage—putting aside the question of capacity – locus regit actum. If a marriage is good by the laws of the country where it is effected, it is good all the world over, no matter whether the proceeding or ceremony which constituted marriage according to the law of the place would or would not constitute marriage in the country of the domicile of one or other of the spouses. If the so-called marriage is no marriage in the place where it is celebrated, there is no marriage anywhere, although the ceremony or proceeding if conducted in the place of the parties' domicile would be considered a good marriage. These propositions are too well fixed to need much quotation. They were laid down long ago in England in the well known case of *Dalrymple* v *Dalrymple* (1871) 2 Hag Con 54 and in *Scrimshire* v *Scrimshire* (1752) 2 Hag Con 395, approved by Lord Stowell in *Ruding* v *Smith* (1821) Hag Con 371. ...

Now in the face of the facts set forth in the narrative above given, and these facts were found by all the judges of the courts below and are amply borne out by the evidence, it is clear that under international law there was no marriage in this case. The law of France is peremptory. There must be a civil ceremony of marriage, and if that has not taken place any religious ceremony is an idle performance so far as the law is concerned …'

Brook v *Brook* (1861) 9 HL Cas 193 House of Lords (Lord Campbell LC, Lords Cranworth, St Leonards and Wensleydale)

• *Capacity to marry is governed (in general) by the lex domicilii of each party immediately before the marriage*

Facts

William Charles Brook had married twice. First he married Charlotte Armitage in England; he had two children by her and then she died. Then he married, in Denmark, Emily Armitage his deceased wife's sister, and had a further three children by her. Then both Emily Armitage and William Brook died of cholera within a few days of each other.

At all times Brook (as well as the Armitage sisters) were British subjects domiciled in England. The second marriage had taken place in Denmark during a temporary visit. Such a marriage would have been void if celebrated in England because of the relationship between the sisters, but was valid under the law of Denmark.

William Brook's will left the residue of his property to his children mentioning them all by name. But one of them (Charles Armitage Brook a child of the second marriage) died soon after his father without making a will. And the question arose who was entitled to Charles Brook's share of William Brook's estate; and that depended upon whether the second marriage was valid or void.

Held

Although the formalities of marriage were governed by the lex loci celebrationis, the essentials of the marriage depended upon the law of the country in which the parties are domiciled at the time of their marriage (and in which the matrimonial residence is contemplated).

Lord Campbell LC:

'My Lords, the question which your Lordships are called upon to consider in the present appeal is, whether the marriage celebrated on 9 June 1850 in the duchy of Holstein, in the kingdom of Denmark, between William Leigh Brook, a widower, and Emily Armitage, the sister of his deceased wife, they being British subjects then domiciled in England, and contemplating England as their place of matrimonial residence, is to be considered valid in England, marriage between a widower and the sister of his deceased wife being permitted by the law of Denmark?

I am of opinion that this depends upon the question whether such a marriage would have been held illegal, and might have been set aside in a suit commenced in England in the lifetime of the parties before the passing of the Marriage Act 1835, commonly called Lord Lyndhurst's Act.

There can be no doubt that before Lord Lyndhurst's Act was passed, a marriage between a widower and the sister of his deceased wife, if celebrated in England, was unlawful, and in the lifetime of the parties could have been annulled. Such a marriage was expressly prohibited by the legislature of this country, and was prohibited expressly on the ground that it was 'contrary to God's law'. Sitting here, judicially, we are not at liberty to consider whether such a marriage is or is not 'contrary to God's law', nor whether it is expedient or inexpedient. …

Indeed, this is not denied on the part of the appellants. They rest their case entirely upon the fact that the marriage was celebrated in a foreign country, where the marriage of a man with the sister of his deceased wife is permitted.

There can be no doubt of the general rule, that 'a foreign marriage, valid according to the law of a country where it is celebrated, is good everywhere'. But while the forms of entering into the contract of marriage are to be regulated by the lex loci contractus, the law of the country in which it is celebrated, the essentials of the contract depend upon the lex domicilii, the law of the country in which the parties are domiciled at the time of marriage, and in which the matrimonial residence is contemplated. Although the forms of celebrating the foreign marriage may be different from those required by the law of the country of domicile, the marriage may be good everywhere. But if the contract of marriage is such, in essentials, as to be contrary to the law of the country of domicile, and it is declared void by that law, it is to be regarded as void in the country of domicile, though not contrary to the law of the country in which it was celebrated. ...

It is quite obvious that no civilised state can allow its domiciled subjects or citizens, by making a temporary visit to a foreign country, to enter into a contract to be performed in the place of domicile, if the contract is forbidden by the law of the place of domicile as contrary to religion, or morality, or to any of its fundamental institutions.

A marriage between a man and the sister of his deceased wife, being Danish subjects domiciled in Denmark, may be good all over the world, and this might likewise be so, even if they were native born English subjects, who had abandoned their English domicile, and were domiciled in Denmark. But I am by no means prepared to say that the marriage now in question ought to be, or would be, held valid in the Danish courts, proof being given that the parties were British subjects domiciled in England at the time of the marriage, that England was to be their matrimonial residence, and that by the law of England such a marriage is prohibited as being contrary to the law of God. The doctrine being established that the incidents of the contract of marriage celebrated in a foreign country are to be determined according to the law of the country in which the parties are domiciled and mean to reside, the consequence seems to follow that by this law must its validity or invalidity be determined.

Sir FitzRoy Kelly argued that we could not hold this marriage to be invalid without being prepared to nullify the marriages of Danish subjects who contracted such a marriage in Denmark while domiciled in their native country, if they should come to reside in England. But on the principles which I have laid down, such marriages, if examined, would be held valid in all English courts, as they are according to the law of the country in which the parties were domiciled when the marriages were celebrated.'

Kochanski* v *Kochanska [1958] P 147 Probate, Divorce and Admiralty Division (Sachs J)

• *Marriage – where the parties do not subject themselves to the law of the country in question (the lex loci celebrationis)*

Facts

The parties were born and domiciled in Poland. In 1939 the husband was an officer in the Polish army and was captured by the Germans and sent to a prisoner of war camp, where he met the wife. In 1945 the parties were liberated by the Russians, crossed into the British Zone, and were placed in a displaced persons camp at Nordheim. There the Poles lived the life of a separate community and refused to fraternise with the Germans. In June 1945 the parties were married in the Roman Catholic parish church by a Polish priest. The marriage did not conform to German law. The husband petitioned for divorce on the ground of desertion.

Held

On the evidence the parties had not subjected themselves to the lex loci celebrationis and therefore it was open to the court to apply the common law of this country; applying that law there had been a valid marriage between the parties and, desertion having been proved, the husband was entitled to a decree.

Sachs J:

'Hitherto the decisions of the courts as to the circumstances in which an exception to the above general rule has been established appear, broadly speaking, to have been confined to two categories of circumstances. The first, of which *Taczanowska* v *Taczanowski* [1957] P 301 is itself an example, relates to members of armies operating in the field and of occupying forces. The second relates to persons who are, in effect, so marooned that there is no set of formalities in the relevant area with which they can reasonably comply. This category covers, for instance, areas in which no such set of formalities has ever existed, areas where chaos has so supervened that conformityis a matter of insuperable difficulty (*Savenis* v *Savenis* [1950] 5 ASR 309), and areas where conformity would go contrary to the conscience.

The present case, however, is not one in which it can be said, in *Taczanowska* v *Taczanowski*, that one of the parties to the marriage was a member of an occupying force: indeed, it cannot be safely said, despite the nature of the form of organisation adopted in the displaced persons camp, that they were members of any force. Nor is the present case one in which, as in *Savenis* v *Savenis* [1950] SASR 309, any insuperable difficulties existed precluding the celebration of a marriage conforming to the laws of Germany. So the present marriage does not seem to fall into either of the above categories.

Once, however, it is appreciated that, in the case of such a marriage an issue of fact can arise as to whether, in the particular circumstances, the presumption of subjection to local law has been rebutted, it ceases to matter whether the set of circumstances before the court does not happen to fall into a particular category that has already been the subject of a decision ... Suffice it, accordingly, to say that in the present case I am simply concerned with an organised community that found itself in an unusual position, and to add that nothing in this judgment is intended to decide whether or in what circumstances an individual who does not fall within one of the above two categories and who is acting in isolation can assert that he has not subjected himself to the law of the locality in which he goes through a form of marriage.

The community in the present case consisted of Poles who had just been liberated from prisoner of war or similar camps and had thus escaped from a much hated form of subjection. The whole basis of their life in the displaced persons camp – no matter whether technically military or civilian – was one of having nothing to do with those who had now ceased to hold them in that subjection.

Any presumption that the recently liberated members of this community had, at the material time, subjected themselves to the laws of a country which they then hated fervently and at whose violent hands they had suffered severely is, to my mind, clearly rebutted. Indeed, to hold that they had, at that time, so subjected themselves would be an odd conclusion.

The presumption of subjection to German law having been rebutted, it is open to this court to apply the common law, and as the celebration, by a Roman Catholic priest in a Roman Catholic church, was of the same type as that which was the subject of the decision in *Taczanowska* v *Taczanowski*, it follows that the marriage was valid at common law ...

Turning now to the petition in the present case, once it has been established that the marriage between the two parties to this cause was a valid one, it only remains to consider whether the husband has proved desertion by his wife for upwards of three years before the date of presentation of the petition. The evidence on that issue is clear, and desertion as from 1946 has been established. The husband is accordingly entitled to his decree as prayed.'

Ogden* v *Ogden [1908] P 46 Court of Appeal (Sir Gorell Barnes P, Cozens-Hardy MR and Kennedy LJ)

• *Characterisation as formal or essential validity*

Facts

The appellant, an Englishwoman domiciled in England, married in England Léon Philip, a 19-year-old Frenchman domiciled in France. This marriage took place without the consent of Léon Philip's parents as required by the French Civil Code. When his parents found out about the marriage they brought him back to France and had the marriage annulled before the French courts.

Thereafter the appellant married William Ogden. This relationship, however, also failed; and William Ogden petitioned the English courts for a decree of nullity based on the applicant's prior marriage to Léon Philip. At first instance the court granted the decree of nullity and the appellant now appealed.

The crucial question was whether the marriage to Léon Philip was valid or not; and the only ground (ignoring for the present the French decree of nullity) on which it could be argued that it was invalid was that Léon Philip lacked capacity to marry under his domiciliary law because of the absence of parental consent.

Held

The absence of parental consent was a matter of form which was governed by the lex loci celebrationis, viz, English law.

Sir Garrell Barnes:

> 'The simple question for determination in the present case upon the first point is whether or not a marriage taking place in England between an English person domiciled in England with a foreigner temporarily residing in this country, which it was not disputed would be held in England to be a valid marriage if celebrated between two inhabitants of this country, ought to be held invalid on the ground that the foreigner was by the statute law of his country subjected to the necessity of complying with certain formalities in order to be at liberty to enter into the marriage. It is desirable to state this limited proposition very clearly, because, with regard to questions which may be raised as to the validity of marriages in England between persons domiciled abroad, certain cases have been decided (to which reference will be made further on in this judgment) which do not necessarily involve the consideration of the particular point already indicated, or any decision thereupon; and it is desirable, therefore, to avoid the confusion which appears to have arisen sometimes between the consideration of the principles which have been laid down for determining the validity of a marriage where the ceremony alone was in question, and of those which have been considered, in determining whether it was lawful for the parties to intermarry at all. ...
>
> ... We are concerned in this case only with the question of a disability imposed by foreign law upon one of the parties to the marriage in respect only of want of parental consent, and compliance with certain formalities required by such foreign law.
>
> There appears to be no case in this country (certainly no case was cited to us in argument on this appeal) in which in such a case at last mentioned the view has been expressed that such a marriage would be held invalid in this country. We know of no principle recognised by English law which would justify the court in coming to the conclusion that such a marriage ought to be held invalid; for, although to a certain extent the lex domicilii is recognised in this country, for instance, in the familiar case where it is held that mobilia sequuntur personam, yet such recognition appears never to have been extended to the case of a matrimonial engagement entered into in this country between an inhabitant of another country and an inhabitant of this country. In such a case, where there are two different systems of law, one may well ask, which is to prevail? Why should it be recognised that a person who comes over to this country and validly enters into a marriage with one of

its inhabitants according to English law should be held unable to do so here because of the regulations of a foreign system of jurisprudence which places upon him a personal incapacity to contract unless he complies with formalities required by the foreign law? It may be observed here that the 3rd section of art I of the French Civil Code ordains that the French laws relating to the conditions and privileges of persons are to govern Frenchmen although residing in a foreign country, so that it would seem from this provision that the French rule as to competency by reason of minority is not based upon domicile, but upon nationality, and therefore that even in the case of a Frenchman domiciled in England celebrating a marriage with a domiciled Englishwoman the French courts would be at liberty, if the question arose before them, to declare such a marriage null and void, on the ground that it was governed by the laws of France, although celebrated in this country; but it could hardly be contended in England, if both persons parties to a marriage were domiciled in this country, that our courts ought to hold such a marriage invalid because one of the parties by the laws of his or her nationality may not have adequate competency to enter into the contract ...

The case principally relied on by the appellant was the case of *Sottomayor* v *De Barros* (1877) 3 PD 1; 47 LJP 23. Now this court hearing this appeal is bound by the decision of the Court of Appeal in the case of *Sottomayor* v *De Barros*. It is not necessary, even if we were at liberty to do so, to consider whether that case was rightly decided, but it is permissible to point out that the commencement of the paragraph above set out could scarcely be considered correct in stating that "it is a well-recognised principle of law that the question of personal capacity to enter into any contract is to be decided by the law of domicile", for, if so, it would logically seem to follow that that part of the judgment which indicates that the opinion of the court was confined to cases where both the contracting parties were, at the time of their marriage, domiciled in a country, the laws of which prohibited their marriage, should not have expressed that limitation, and that the case of *Simonin* v *Mallac* (1860) 2 Sw & Tr 67 should have been overruled, and yet that case, according to our reading of the judgment, is approved. The probability is that that sentence should be read with the context and be confined to the case present to the minds of the court in relation to marriages which could not be contracted at all by the laws of the country of domicile. Even then it may be questioned whether that sentence is correct, and whether the question of capacity is really raised at all in such a case; that is to say, where both the parties are capable of entering into a marriage but may not marry each other because such a marriage would be illegal in their own country. That is rather a question of illegality than of capacity, and it may, perhaps, not be unreasonable for one country to refuse to recognise a marriage contracted in it between two persons by the laws of whose domicile a marriage between them is illegal, and yet it may be quite proper and reasonable for a country, in which a marriage takes place between persons domiciled in another country, to recognise it as a valid marriage when it would be legal in such other country if contracted after compliance with all formalities required in such other country, and, further, to protect its citizens in all cases of marriages where one of the contracting parties is domiciled in the country first referred to – that is to say, where the marriage takes place – and the other is domiciled in a foreign country, and there is a conflict between the laws of the two countries as to the validity of the marriage.

... After very careful consideration of the present case we have come to the conclusion that the first point must be decided against the appellant, and that the marriage between her and Léon Philip must be declared valid in England.'

Comment

Note how unenviable Mrs Odgen's position was. She could not divorce Léon Philip in

France (because under French law she was not married to him at all); and she could not divorce him in England since (at that time) the English courts had no jurisdiction to grant a divorce because Philip was domiciled in France. There was really nothing that she could do to get rid of the husband she had married in a fit of youthful indiscretion!

Paine, Re [1940] Ch 46 Chancery Division (Bennett J)

• *Marriage abroad in 1875 by German subject with deceased wife's sister – English domicile of wife – validity of marriage contract – effect on bequest to child of marriage*

Facts

A testatrix, who died in May 1884, bequeathed £250 on trust for her daughter for life and, in the event of her dying leaving any child or children her surviving, in trust for her absolutely. In the event of her death without leaving any child or children her surviving, the testatrix directed that the money should be held on the trusts therein mentioned. In June 1875 the testatrix's daughter Ada Paine Toepfer (while domiciled in England) married Frantz Robert Toepfer at Frankfurt on Main in Germany, in accordance with the laws of Germany, by which such marriage was valid. Frantz Robert Toepfer had before his marriage with Ada Paine Toepfer been married to her sister Mary Ann Paine Williams. That marriage took place on 18 July 1871, and she died in August 1872. Frantz Robert Toepfer was born in Germany and, according to the evidence, he remained a German subject until his death on 22 October 1919. He and his second wife both lived in England until their respective deaths. They had three children, one of whom, Maud Ada Mary Waterhouse, survived her parents. A summons was taken out for the determination of the question whether the above-mentioned sum of £250 was held on trust for the legal personal representatives of Ada Paine Pownall Toepfer on the footing that the expression 'child or children' included a child or children of her marriage with Frantz Robert Toepfer.

Held

At the time of the marriage the testatrix's daughter had not the capacity to contract the marriage – the marriage being, at that time, a contract of marriage which could not be made by English law – the absolute gift failed and the gift over took effect.

Bennett J:

> 'I think that, on the evidence, I must hold that the husband never lost his domicile of origin, but it is plain that, at the time of the marriage, Mrs Ada Paine Toepfer was a domiciled English woman. There were three children of the marriage, of whom one survived Ada Paine Toepfer, and the question to be determined is whether Ada Paine Toepfer had a child or children living at her decease, in which case the sum of £250 is to be held by the trustees of the testatrix's will for her absolutely, or whether she died without leaving any child or children her surviving, in which case the sum of £250 would devolve as under an intestacy.
>
> The first question is whether the English law will regard the marriage between Ada Paine Toepfer and Franz Robert Toepfer as a valid marriage.
>
> In my judgment, according to English law, the marriage was invalid, because by English law the lady had not the capacity to contract it. In my view that point is settled by the decision of Sir Cresswell Cresswell in *Mette* v *Mette* (1859) 28 LJP & M 117. That was a case in which the husband was domiciled in England and he was without the capacity to contract the marriage in question. The learned judge says in the course of his judgment:
>
> > "If Bernard Mette was incapacitated from contracting such a marriage, this latter distinction cannot have any effect. There could be no valid contract unless each was competent to contract with the other. The question rests upon the effect of domicile and naturalisation."

That statement of the law has been recognized by text book writers. In particular I refer to *Dicey's Conflict of Laws*, 5th ed, p732, where the following statement appears:

> "Rule 182. Subject to the exceptions hereinafter mentioned, a marriage is valid when (1) each of the parties has, according to the law of his or her respective domicile, the capacity to marry the other."

In *Westlake's Private International Law*, 7th ed, p57, r21, this statement is to be found:

> "A marriage is invalid ... if either party is by his personal law under an incapacity to contract it, whether absolute, in respect of age, or relative in respect of the prohibited degrees of consanguinity or affinity."

In *Halsbury's Laws of England*, 2nd ed, vol vi, p286, it is stated:

> "The marriage must be a good and legal marriage according to the law of the domicile of both contracting parties at the time of the marriage."

On the authority of *Mette* v *Mette*, supported as it seems to be by the textbook writers, in view of the fact that the domicile of the lady was English, I come to the conclusion that her marriage, in the year 1875 to a domiciled German, at Frankfurt on Main in Germany was invalid, because the husband had been the husband of the lady's deceased sister. The marriage was, therefore, a contract of marriage which, at that time he was prohibited from making by English law.

It follows that the gift over takes effect, unless it can be said that the testatrix intended to refer to the children of the union of the lady with Mr Toepfer as the children who survived the lady.

That depends upon whether there is a context in the will, which enables me to say that the testatrix had in mind the child or children of Ada Paine Toepfer by Frantz Robert Toepfer.

In my judgment there is nothing in the language of the will of the testatrix which enables me to arrive at that conclusion.

The gift over takes effect and the absolute gift to the lady in question fails.'

Penhas (Isaac)* v *Tan Soo Eng
[1953] AC 304 Privy Council (Singapore) (Lords Merriman, Normand, Oaksey, Reid and Asquith)

- *Marriage and the common law*

Facts

The case raised the question whether a marriage celebrated in Singapore in 1937, between A, a Jew, and the respondent, a non-Christian Chinese, in a modified Chinese form constituted a valid marriage. A and the respondent were British subjects domiciled in Singapore. The marriage was solemnised at the respondent's house by a Chinese priest who asked A and the respondent whether they were willing to be man and wife to which they replied 'Yes'. Both prayed in accordance with the customs of their own religion. Neither party had been married before that ceremony and after it they lived together as man and wife until 1942 when A was murdered by the Japanese. The Court of Appeal of Singapore, held that the respondent had been lawfully married to A.

Held

There was nothing in the religion or customs of Jews or Chinese domiciled in Singapore which prevented them from contracting a common law monogamous marriage. The common law of England was in force in Singapore in 1937. As no form of marriage ceremony was applicable to both parties they had adopted a composite ceremony which was intended by them to constitute a valid common law monogamous marriage; therefore, the appeal must be dismissed

Lord Oaksey:

> 'The principal question to be decided is, therefore, whether there was in 1937 anything in the religions, manners or customs of Jews or Chinese domiciled in Singapore

which prevented them from contracting a common law monogamous marriage. No case has been cited which suggests that mixed marriages between domiciled inhabitants of different religions or races cannot validly be contracted. On the contrary, *Carolis De Silva* v *Tim Kim* (1902) 9 SSLR Appdx 8 is authority that they can, and, indeed, the appellant's counsel did not contend that such marriages were impossible.

In accordance with these decisions their Lordships hold that the common law of England was in force in Singapore in 1937 except in so far as it was inapplicable and except in so far as it was necessary to modify it to prevent hardships upon the inhabitants who were entitled by the terms of the Charter to the exercise of their religions, manners and customs.

Their Lordships agree with the view expressed by Evans J in the Court of Appeal in the present case that in a country such as Singapore, where priests are few and there is no true parochial system, where the vast majority are not Christians, it is neither convenient nor necessary that two persons such as the respondent and the deceased should be required to call in an episcopally ordained priest to effect a marriage. The case of *Wolfenden* v *Wolfenden* [1946] P 61 and the cases there cited are in point and were in their Lordships' opinion rightly decided.

There was no form of a ceremony of marriage in the present case which was applicable to both parties to the marriage, and accordingly they seem to have adopted a composite ceremony, the wife worshipping according to her Chinese custom and the husband according to his Jewish custom. Such a ceremony performed in the circumstances already stated was indubitably intended by the parties to constitute a valid marriage. The only question which in their Lordships' view admits of any doubt is the question whether the marriage intended by the parties to be constituted by the ceremony was a common law monogamous marriage or a Chinese polygamous marriage.

This question was not raised in the courts below and no questions were put to the respondent in cross-examination on the subject. Abraham Penhas was dead, and in such circumstances it would, in their Lordships' opinion, be altogether wrong to invalidate a marriage so solemnised, followed as it was by years of cohabitation as man and wife, and to bastardise the two children of the marriage, even if the other evidence were equivocal as to the status intended. But it is not necessary to decide the case on this narrow ground, for their Lordships hold that the evidence as it stands sufficiently proves a common law monogamous marriage. The wishes expressed by the respondent and her mother for a Church marriage, the reason why a modified Chinese ceremony was substituted, the presence of Jewish friends at the ceremony, the words spoken by the Chinese gentleman who performed the ceremony as to a lifelong union, the cohabitation as man and wife which followed and continued till the husband's death, and the introduction by the deceased to a Christian pastor of the respondent as his wife, and last, but not least, the baptism of their children as Christians with the approval of their father, all indicate that the spouses intended to contract a common law monogamous marriage.

Their Lordships will therefore humbly advise Her Majesty that this appeal ought to be dismissed. The appellant must pay the costs of the appeal.'

Preston (Otherwise Putynski)* v *Preston (Otherwise Putynska) (Otherwise Basinska) [1963] P 411 Court of Appeal (Ormerod, Donovan and Russell LJJ)

• *Marriage of two Poles in Germany celebrated by episcopally ordained clergyman – formalities not in compliance with lex loci celebrationis*

Facts

In June 1945 the parties, then domiciled in

Poland, went through a ceremony of marriage at a military camp at Nordheim in Germany. The ceremony, which was performed by an episcopally ordained priest, was void by German law, not having been performed in the presence of a civil registrar. The husband was not a member of the forces in belligerent occupation of that part of Germany where the marriage took place, but was a member of the Polish armed forces associated with the Allies, who were in belligerent occupation of that part of Germany. In 1960, when the parties were domiciled and resident in England, the question of the validity of the marriage arose as an issue in a matrimonial suit between them; the wife claimed, that the marriage was valid as an English common law marriage.

Held

That all the members of a group of Allied soldiers organised under military command (as members of a belligerent army occupying conquered territory) were in the same privileged position, so far as concerned the lex loci of marriage formalities. Namely, that their peculiar position excepted them from complying with the local law. Therefore, the husband came within the exception referred to and accordingly the marriage was valid as an English common law marriage.

Ormerod LJ:

> 'The nature of the camp and the status of the husband at the time of the marriage are relevant questions …
>
> The judge came to the conclusion that the purpose of the camp was to train men and women who had served in the Polish forces to fit them for service in Germany or Italy or elsewhere. He concluded that it was a military camp and not a camp for displaced persons, as had been the conclusion of Sachs J in *Kochanski* v *Kochanska* [1958] P 147 (a conclusion arrived at on different evidence). It may not be important to be able to describe the camp exactly. There is little evidence to show what discipline, if any, was exercised over the inmates of the camp. There is, however, in my judgment, enough evidence to show that the camp was at least a part of the organisation of the Allied Armed Forces, that its inmates were associated with, if not members of, those forces, and that preparations were being made to integrate them more closely with one or another of the Allied armies.
>
> A further question to be decided is the status of the husband at the time of the marriage. The judge concluded that he was a member of the Polish Armed Forces. He said this:
>
> > "In my view, the husband was at the material time a member of the Polish forces. I base this conclusion on three factors: (1) the evidence of General Pelczynski, former Chief of Staff to the Polish Commander-in-Chief, as to his technical status; (2) the evidence of Miss Osuchowska, commandant of a women's block at the camp, that it was always a military camp; (3) the husband's unquestioned wearing of uniform with badges of rank in the camp."…
>
> The second reason given by the judge for his conclusion that the husband was at the material time a member of the Polish forces, ie, that the camp was a military camp, supported the General's evidence in that it seemed unlikely that the husband (and consequently the wife) would have been admitted to the camp if he had not been regarded as a member of the Polish Army.
>
> The judge relied further on the wearing by the husband of uniform with badges of his rank as a cadet-corporal. To my mind, that is not a strong reason.
>
> It is not easy to extract from the authorities the correct principle to be applied. …
>
> The canons of international comity demand that, on questions of form, one country should recognise the marriage laws of another, and in consequence it is now well established that persons choosing to marry in a foreign country shall be deemed to have submitted themselves to the marriage laws of that country. This rule does not apply in all circumstances, but it is not enough for the parties to say or to show by their actions that they do not intend to

submit to those laws ... In this case, the parties were in a camp where the husband could receive military training or else be directed to a place appropriate to the duties required of him. The camp existed as part of the organisation set up for the purposes of the hostile occupation of Germany, and the inmates of it were there for the purposes of such occupation. In those circumstances, there was, in my judgment, no obligation on the parties to observe the lex loci, and the judge was right in holding that this was an English common law marriage and therefore valid.

I would dismiss the appeal.'

Donovan LJ:

'There are no merits in the husband's petition – he is simply tired of his wife – and he revealed himself before the judge as an unscrupulous witness. As a witness the wife, apparently, was not much better.

The judge, if I may say so, considered this case with obvious care and impartiality. I agree with his findings of fact and with his conclusion of law. And, lest by adding something to his judgment I may prejudice some future and more deserving case, I say no more. I think the appeal should be dismissed.'

Pugh* v *Pugh [1951] P 482 Probate, Admiralty and Divorce Division (Pearce J)

• *No marriage is valid if either party is domiciled in England and one party (not necessarily the party domiciled in England) is under the age of sixteen*

Facts

The wife was born in Hungary with a Hungarian domicile of origin. In 1945 she left Hungary with her parents to escape from the Russian advance and went to Austria. There she met the husband, who was a serving British officer domiciled in England. They were married in Austria in October 1946 when the wife was 15 years of age. They lived together in Austria and Germany at places where the husband was stationed. It was the husband's intention to return to England with his wife after his service abroad. The parties came to England in October 1950 but parted soon afterwards. The wife petitioned the High Court for a decree of nullity on the ground that at the time of the marriage she was under age.

By Hungarian law the marriage was voidable until the wife's seventeenth birthday when it became valid. By Austrian law the marriage was valid. By s1 of the Age of Marriage Act 1929 (now s2 of the Marriage Act 1949) 'a marriage between persons either of whom is under the age of sixteen shall be void.'

Held

Pearce J:

'Mr Simon, for the wife, makes two submissions. The first is this: The Age of Marriage Act 1929 applies to the husband as a British subject with an English domicile, wherever he may marry. Its effect is extra-territorial and is not merely confined to marriages in the United Kingdom. Therefore it makes this marriage void. His second submission is this: The validity of such a marriage as this has to be tested as to its essentials by the law of the country of the husband's domicile, or alternatively (see *De Reneville* v *De Reneville* [1948] P 100), by the law of the country of the proposed matrimonial home. On either alternative that is English law, and by English law the Age of Marriage Act 1929 makes such a marriage void. If either of those submissions is correct the wife is entitled to a decree of nullity ...

It is urged on me that the statute is ambiguous and also (rightly in my opinion) that if I am in doubt as to its meaning the marriage is to be deemed valid and the wife has failed to make out her case.

But is the statute ambiguous? The words are clear and general. It must be remembered that personal status and capacity to marry are considered to be the concern of the country of domicile. It is right and reasonable that the country of domicile should (as it did by Lord Lyndhurst's Act) from time to time vary and affect the personal status of its subjects and their capacity to marry as changing religious, moral, and social conditions may demand.

I see no reason to put upon the words any other limitation than the obvious one that they are not intended to apply to marriages abroad of persons who are not domiciled here and who are not the concern of or subject to the laws of Parliament. …

The common law before the Age of Marriage Act 1929 was this: By canon law which continued after and in spite of the Reformation a boy of fourteen years could marry a girl of twelve. The "mischief and defect for which the common law did not provide" was this: According to modern thought it is considered socially and morally wrong that persons of an age, at which we now believe them to be immature and provide for their education, should have the stresses, responsibilities and sexual freedom of marriage and the physical strain of childbirth. Child marriages are by common consent believed to be bad for the participants and bad for the institution of marriage. Acts making carnal knowledge of young girls an offence are an indication of modern views on this subject. The remedy that "the Parliament has resolved" for this mischief and defect is to make marriages void where either of the parties is under sixteen years of age.

To curtail the general words of the Act so that a person can evade its provisions by merely going abroad and entering into a marriage where one of the parties is under sixteen in some country like Northern Ireland where canon law still prevails, and then returning to live in this country after the marriage, seems to me to be encouraging rather than suppressing "subtle inventions and evasions for the continuance of the mischief."

Parliament must be deemed to have known the effect of *Brook* v *Brook* (1861) 9 HL Cas 193. In my view it was by the Age of Marriage Act 1929 deliberately legislating on a matter that is its own peculiar concern, namely, the personal status of its subjects and their capacity to contract marriage. This Act was intended, as was Lord Lyndhurst's Act, to affect that capacity in all persons domiciled in the United Kingdom wherever the marriage might be celebrated.

I come now to the second submission. So far as the form of marriage is concerned it is clearly established that the law of the place of the marriage is the effective law; but so far as concerns the essential validity of a marriage the position is different …

In view of those authorities it is clear that this marriage was not valid since by the law of the husband's domicile it was a marriage into which he could not lawfully enter.

On both submissions put forward by counsel for the wife she is entitled to succeed. There will be a decree of nullity on the wife's petition.'

Simonin* v *Mallac (1860) 2 Sw & Tr 67 Ecclesiastical, Admiralty, Probate and Divorce (Channell B and Seating J)

- *Petition for nullity of marriage*

Facts

C and D, being native subjects of France, and then domiciled in that country, came over to London in June 1854, and were married by licence according to the law of England, but without the observance of certain formalities and consents required by the law of France in respect of the marriage of its own subjects in foreign countries. C and D returned to France, where D, the man, refused to celebrate the marriage according to the French law, and C. instituted a suit for nullity in the French courts, which D did not defend. In December 1854 C obtained a decree of nullity. C subsequently came to reside in England and petitioned for a decree of nullity; personal service of the citation was effected on D in Naples, who did not appear.

Held

That D having entered into a contract in this

country was subject to the jurisdiction of the courts of this country in respect of the personal status resulting from such contract. Secondly, that the personal status resulting from such contract is to be ascertained by the law of this country in which the contract was made, and not any special law of the country of the domicile of the parties to the contract.

Channell B:

'The question is this – whether a marriage duly solemnised in England in the manner prescribed by the law of England, between parties of full age and capable of contracting according to that law, is to be held null and void because the parties to that marriage, being foreigners, contracted it in England in order to evade the laws of the country to which they belonged and in which they were domiciled. ... It was contended that, the parties being French, the law of that country affixed to them an incapacity to contract marriage without attending to the formalities prescribed, and that such incapacity was a personal status which travelled with them everywhere, and rendered them incapable of making a valid contract in any other country. ...

Every nation has a right to impose on its own subjects restrictions and prohibitions as to entering into marriage contracts, either within or without its own territories; and if its subjects sustain hardships in consequence of those restrictions, their own nation only must bear the blame; but what right has one independent nation to call upon any other nation equally independent to surrender its own laws in order to give effect to such restrictions and prohibitions! ...

Would it not then be more just, and therefore more for the interest of all, that the law of that country should prevail which both are presumed to know and to agree to be bound by? Again, assume that one of the parties is English: would not an English subject have as strong a claim to the benefit of English law as a foreigner to the benefit of foreign law? But it may be said that in the case now before the Court both parties are French, and therefore no such difficulty can arise. That is true; but if once the principle of surrendering our own law to that of a foreign country is recognised, it must be followed out to all its consequences; the cases put are, therefore, a fair test as to the possibility of maintaining that by an comitas or jus gentium this Court is bound to adopt the law of France as its guide. ...

The great importance of having some one certain rule applicable to all cases the difficulty, not to say impossibility, of having any rule applicable to all cases, save that the law of the country where a marriage is solemnised shall in that country at least decide whether it is valid or invalid; the absence of any judicial decision or dictum, or of even any opposite opinion of any writer of authority on the law of nations, have led us to the conclusion that we ought not to found our judgement in this case on any other rule than the law of England as prevailing amongst English subjects.

France may make laws for her own subjects, and impose on them all the consequences, good or evil, that result from those laws; but England also may make laws for the regulation of all matters within her own territory. Either nation may refuse to surrender its own laws to those of the other, and if either is guilty of any breach of the comitas or jus gentium, that reproach should attach to the nation whose laws are least calculated to ensure the common benefit and advantage of all. For these reasons we feel bound to dismiss this petition.'

Sottomayor v *De Barros (No 1)* (1877) 3 PD 1 Court of Appeal (James, Baggallay and Cotton LJJ)

- *Essential validity of the marriage*

Facts

Here two first cousins married in England. But they were both believed to be domiciled in Portugal and nationals of Portugal at all material times. Under the law of Portugal first cousins lack capacity to marry each other in the absence of a papal dispensation.

Held

Personal capacity to enter into any contract, including marriage, is to be decided by the law of domicile, viz, Portuguese law.

Cotton LJ:

'Under these circumstances the petitioner, in November 1874, presented her petition for the object above mentioned, and Sir R Phillimore, before whom the case was heard, declined to declare the marriage invalid and dismissed the petition, but did so, as we understand, rather because he felt himself bound by the decision in the case of *Simonin* v *Mallac* ((1860) 2 Sw & Tr 67; 29 LJPM & A 97) than because he considered that on principle the marriage ought to be held good. If the parties had been subjects of Her Majesty domiciled in England, the marriage would undoubtedly have been valid. But it is a well-recognised principle of law that the question of personal capacity to enter into any contract is to be decided by the law of domicile. It is, however, urged that this does not apply to the contract of marriage, and that a marriage valid according to the law of the country where it is solemnised is valid everywhere. This, in our opinion, is not a correct statement of the law. The law of a country where a marriage is solemnised must alone decide all questions relating to the validity of the ceremony by which the marriage is alleged to have been constituted; but, as in other contracts, so in that of marriage, personal capacity must depend on the law of the domicile; and if the laws of any country prohibit its subjects within certain degrees of consanguinity from contracting marriage, and stamp a marriage between persons within the prohibited degrees as incestuous, this, in our opinion, imposes on the subjects of that country a personal incapacity, which continues to affect them so long as they are domiciled in the country where this law prevails, and renders invalid a marriage between persons both at the time of their marriage subjects of and domiciled in the country which imposes this restriction, wherever such marriage may have been solemnised.

But it is said that the impediment imposed by the law of Portugal can be removed by a Papal dispensation, and, therefore, that it cannot be said there is a personal incapacity of the petitioner and respondent to contract marriage. The evidence is clear that by the law of Portugal the impediment to the marriage between the parties is such that, in the absence of papal dispensation, the marriage would be by the law of that country void as incestuous. The statutes of the English parliament contain a declaration that no Papal dispensation can sanction a marriage otherwise incestuous; but the law of Portugal does recognise the validity of such a dispensation, and it cannot in our opinion be held that such a dispensation is a matter of form affecting only the sufficiency of the ceremony by which the marriage is effected, or that the law of Portugal, which prohibits and declares incestuous, unless with such a dispensation, a marriage between the petitioner and respondent, does not impose on them a personal incapacity to contract marriage. It is proved that the courts of Portugal, where the petitioner and respondent are domiciled and resident, would hold the marriage void, as solemnised between parties incapable of marrying, and incestuous. How can the courts of this country hold the contrary, and, if appealed to say the marriage is valid? It was pressed upon us in argument that a decision in favour of the petitioner would lead to many difficulties, if questions should arise as to the validity of a marriage between an English subject and a foreigner, in consequence of prohibitions imposed by the law of the domicile of the latter. Our opinion on this appeal is confined to the case where both the contracting parties are, at the time of their marriage, domiciled in a country the laws of which prohibit their marriage. All persons are legally bound to take notice of the laws of the country where they are domiciled. No country is bound to recognise the laws of a foreign state when they work injustice to its own subjects, and this principle would prevent the judgment in the present case being relied on as an authority for setting aside a marriage between a foreigner and an English subject domiciled in England, on the ground of any personal incapacity not recognised by the law of this country.

The counsel for the petitioner relied on the case of *Brook* v *Brook* ((1861) 9 HL Cas 193; 4 LT 93) as a decision in his favour. If, in our opinion, that case had been a decision on the question arising on this petition, we should have thought it sufficient without more to refer to that case as decisive. The judgment in that case, however, only decided that the English courts must hold invalid a marriage between two English subjects domiciled in this country, who were prohibited from intermarrying by an English statute, even though the marriage was solemnised during a temporary sojourn in a foreign country. It is, therefore, not decisive of the present case; but the reasons given by the Lords who delivered their opinions in that case strongly support the principle on which this judgment is based.

It only remains to consider the case of *Simonin* v *Mallac*. The objection to the validity of the marriage in that case, which was solemnised in England, was the want of the consent of parents required by the law of France, but not under the circumstances by that of this country. In our opinion, this consent must considered a part of the ceremony of marriage, and not a matter affecting the personal capacity of the parties to contract marriage; and the decision in *Simonin* v *Mallac* does not, we think, govern the present case. We are of opinion that the judgment appealed from must be reversed, and a decree made declaring the marriage null and void.'

Starkowski v *Attorney-General* [1954] AC 155 House of Lords (Lords Reid, Morton, Tucker, Asquith and Cohen)

• *Retrospective legislation in the locus celebrationis validating a formally invalid marriage will be given effect to, even though the parties are domiciled in England at the date when it takes place*

Facts

Henryka Juszczkiewicz and Richard Urbanski were born in Poland with a Polish domicile of origin. In 1944 they moved to Kitzbuhel in Austria but remained domiciled in Poland. They were both Roman Catholics and anxious to be married in a church by a priest. Owing to the German occupation of Austria there were difficulties in their way and the priest at Kizbuhel at first refused to marry them, but when the Germans were driven out there was much confusion and he eventually agreed to do so on 19 May 1945, when they went through a ceremony of marriage according to the rites of their Church in the parish church at Kitzbuhel. In June 1945 a daughter Barbara was born to them. Henryka and Richard arrived in England in the autumn of 1946 and became domiciled here. In 1947 they separated. By the German marriage law in force in Austria on 19 May 1945 a religious ceremony did not constitute a valid marriage since a civil ceremony was required. On 26 June 1945 the Austrian government promulgated an Order (No 31) enacting that religious marriages celebrated between 1 April 1945 and the date of the decree should be valid as soon as they were registered in the Family Book kept by the registry office. By some oversight the religious ceremony between Henryka and Richard was not registered until 18 July 1949. Before that date the law of Austria would not have regarded the parties as married, but after that date it would have regarded them as having been validly married on 19 May 1945.

Held

The Lords held that the balance of justice and convenience was clearly in favour of recognising the validity of such retrospective legislation and the objections to doing so were neither substantial nor founded on any compelling principle.

Lord Reid:

'It has long been settled that the formal validity of a marriage must be determined by the law of the place where the marriage was celebrated. But if there has been retrospective legislation there, then a further question arises: are we to take the law of that place as it was when the marriage was celebrated, or are we to inquire what the law of that place now is with regard to the formal validity of that marriage? This question does not appear to have arisen for decision in England. …

Persons domiciled in England may have been married in another country by ceremonies apparently valid but later discovered to be invalid, and retrospective legislation may then have been passed in that country. If people have lived and acted and brought up families in the reasonable belief that they were married, it is highly desirable that the law should recognise some practical way of neutralising a belated and fortuitous discovery that their marriage was formally invalid. But if retrospective legislation in the country where the marriage was celebrated is to be of no avail to persons domiciled outside that country, it will seldom be possible for the country of their domicile to afford any remedy. If validating legislation is passed soon after the cause of the invalidity has been discovered, it is not easy to see how any practical difficulties or hardships can result from it.

But serious difficulties could arise if there were a long interval between the discovery of the invalidity and the remedial legislation. If the spouses are still living together when the invalidity is discovered, they can avoid most of the difficulties by remarrying. But if they have separated they would be in the position of knowing that they are for the moment unmarried but are liable at any time to become married against their wishes by retrospective legislation. It was argued that we should only recognise foreign retrospective legislation if the spouses in some way consented to its operation, but that argument is based on a misapprehension of what such retrospective legislation sets out to do. It has no concern with the state of affairs at the time when it is enacted: its purpose is to validate the original ceremony, and if there was then the necessary consent to marry, that is all that matters. Then it was argued that no valid consent was given in this case at the ceremony in 1945 because the wife Henryka knew that the ceremony was insufficent to constitute a legal marriage; but it is not proved that the husband Urbanski also knew that, and the wife cannot be heard to say that her consent freely given in church was not a consent to marry. I need not consider what the position would be if both parties knew at the time that the ceremony was insufficient in law.

It was suggested in argument that the law of England might recognise foreign retrospective legislation subject to certain qualifications or exceptions. For example, it was said that if one of the parties had entered into another marriage before the retrospective legislation took effect, then a different rule should apply; and it was suggested that if an English court of competent jurisdiction had decided that either party was unmarried, then subsequent retrospective foreign legislation should not affect that decision. It would not be proper to attempt to decide such questions in advance, but I shall assume for the purpose of the present argument that such exceptions would not be made and that a person who knew that his marriage abroad was invalid for want of form might be left in complete uncertainty if the circumstances were such as to make it at all reasonable to suppose that validating legislation might be passed. If that is so, there is at first sight compelling force in the appellant's argument that a person ought at any time to be able to find out with certainty whether he or she is married or not, and that the law of England ought not to recognise a principle which may result in a person being for the moment unmarried in law but knowing that he is liable to become married retrospectively. If there were any substantial likelihood of this happening I would be inclined to agree, but one must look at realities. I find it difficult to suppose that in any country there would be substantial delay in deciding whether to legislate retrospectively once the reason for the invalidity had come to light, and I cannot think that anyone who had discovered that his marriage was formally invalid would for long be in any real doubt whether there was to be remedial legislation. In the present case remedial leglislation was promptly enacted, and this could have been discovered and, indeed, may have been known to the parties: it was only by a mischance that the necessary executive action in Austria was delayed for four years.

Accordingly, in my opinion the balance of justice and convenience is clearly in favour of recognising the validity of such retrospective legislation (subject, it may be, to some exceptions), and the objections to doing so are not substantial and are not founded on any compelling principle. Once it is settled that the formal validity of a marriage is to be determined by reference to the law of the place of celebration, there is no compelling reason why the reference should not be to that law as it is when the question arises for decision. I therefore agree that this appeal should be dismissed.'

Szechter v *Szechter* [1970] 3 All ER 905 Probate, Divorce and Admiralty Division (Sir Jocelyn Simon P)

• *No marriage is valid if by the law of either party's domicile he or she does not consent to marry the other*

Facts

Nina was born in Poland on 10 June 1940 and was of Jewish parentage. When she was very young she was despatched by the Germans with her mother to an extermination camp. On the way there her mother threw her out of the railway train into the snow, hoping thereby to save her life. Nina was rescued and brought up in Warsaw by a Mrs Karsov, whom she thought to be her real mother. Mrs Karsov was a Roman Catholic and brought Nina up in that faith. Later in life Nina worked as a journalist and in the course of this she met the respondent and his wife Lydia. Nina became the respondent's secretary and by 1966 she was being treated like a daughter of the family by the respondent and Lydia and their children. On 12 August 1966, the respondent, Lydia and Nina were all arrested by the security police. Nina was imprisoned for ten months. During this time, the respondent attempted to get Nina freed and into hospital. After being ten months in prison she was for the first time allowed to receive a lawyer. This was the first news Nina had of the Szechters since her arrest. The lawyer put to Nina the plan that Lydia and the respondent should obtain a divorce and that the respondent should then go through a ceremony of marriage with Nina and take her to Israel as his wife. Once there the respondent would remarry Lydia. On 2 February 1968 Nina and the respondent went through a ceremony of marriage in Mokotow Prison. On 5 September 1968 Nina was released – in other words, after serving less than one year of her three-year sentence – and in early November 1968 they both went to Austria as stateless persons, where they were looked after and then brought to England. Nina then petitioned the court for a declaration of nullity, alleging that a ceremony of marriage performed (according to the certificate of registration) in the Mokotow prison in Warsaw, between herself and Szymon Szechter was inoperative to give rise to the status of marriage by reason of the fact that she went through the ceremony as a result of duress.

Held

A decree nisi of nullity was granted.

Sir Jocelyn Simon P:

'There are two preliminary questions to be considered. The first is whether an English court has jurisdiction to make the decree which Nina seeks. [His Lordship reviewed the authorities, which are obsolete since the Domicile and Matrimonial Proceedings Act 197, and continued] ... I am therefore satisfied that I have jurisdiction to entertain this petition on the grounds of both common residence and common domicile in England.

The second preliminary question is what is the proper law to apply in order to determine whether an ostensible marriage is defective by reason of duress. There is little direct authority on this matter. But the effect of duress goes to reality of consent and I respectfully agree with the suggestion in rule 32 of Dicey and Morris *The Conflict of Laws* that no marriage is valid if by the law of either party's domicile one party does not consent to marry the other. This accords with the old distinction between, on the one hand, "forms and ceremonies", the validity of which is referable to the lex loci contractus, and, on the other hand, "essential validity", by which is meant (even though by, as the editors of *Rayden on Divorce* remark, "not a happy terminology") all requirements for a valid marriage other than those relating to forms and ceremonies, for the validity of which reference is made to the lex domicilii of the parties: *Rayden on Divorce; De Reneville* v *De Reneville* [1948] P 100 by Lord Greene MR. So far as capacity (also a matter of "essential validity") is concerned, there can be no doubt that no marriage is valid if by the law of either party's domicile one of the parties is incapable of marrying the other: *Re Paine* [1940] Ch 46; *Pugh* v *Pugh* [1951] P 482.

Moreover, in *Way* v *Way* [1950] P 71 Hodson J said:

> 'Questions of consent are to be dealt with by reference to the personal law of the parties rather than by reference to the law of the place where the contract was made. This view is not covered by direct authority, but it is, I think, supported by the judgment of Lord Merriman P in *Apt* v *Apt* [1947] P 127. …
>
> When giving the judgment of the Court of Appeal dismissing the petitioner's appeal in this [*Apt*'s] case, Cohen LJ said: 'In our opinion the method of giving consent as distinct from the fact of consent is essentially a matter of lex loci celebrationis and does not raise the question of capacity.' Marriage is essentially a voluntary union and as Dr Idelson put it (and I cannot improve on the phrase) 'consent is an emanation of personality'. It is therefore, I think, justifiable and consistent with authority to apply the matrimonial law of each of the parties."

When that case went to the Court of Appeal, under the name of *Kenward* v *Kenward* [1951] P 124, Sir Raymond Evershed MR at 133 assumed that what Hodson J had said about the relevant law to be applied was correct.

Both Nina and the respondent were domiciled in Poland at the time of the ceremony of marriage on 2 February 1968. It is therefore for Polish law to answer whether, on the facts as I have found them, the marriage was invalid by reason of duress … [His Lordship considered the evidence of Mr Jaxa, the expert witness on Polish law, and continued]:

Mr Jaxa sums up his opinion as follows:

> "I am of the firm opinion that if the agreement of the parties to enter into matrimony was given under constraint, that marriage is void in Polish law, I am well aware of the facts of the 'marriage' which is the subject of this suit, and in my opinion, if such a case were to come before the Polish courts, it would be held to be void, and would have been void at the date of the marriage, that is, 2 February 1968."

So far as English law is concerned, private reservations or motives are not in general matters cognisable to vitiate an ostensibly valid marriage. [But] as the American writer Bishop states in his *Commentaries on the Law of Marriage and Divorce*: "Where a formal consent is brought about by force, menace, or duress – a yielding of the lips, not of the mind – it is of no legal effect. This rule, applicable to all contracts, finds no exception in marriage."…

It is, in my view, insufficient to invalidate an otherwise good marriage that a party has entered into it in order to escape from a disagreeable situation, such as penury or social degradation. In order for the impediment of duress to vitiate an otherwise valid marriage, it must, in my judgment, be proved that the will of one of the parties thereto has been overborne by genuine and reasonably held fear caused by threat of immediate danger (for which the party is not himself responsible) to life, limb or liberty, so that the constraint destroys the reality of consent to ordinary wedlock. I think that in the instant case that test is satisfied. In my view, English law returns the same answer to the juridical situation as the Polish law as deposed to by Mr Jaxa.

In those circumstances I made a decree nisi of nullity at the conclusion of the argument, reserving my reasons, which I have now delivered.'

Taczanowska v *Taczanowski* [1957] P 301 Court of Appeal (Hodson, Parker and Ormerod LJJ)

• *Marriages celebrated in conditions in which compliance with the local form is impossible*

Facts

Two Polish Nationals, domiciled in Poland, had been married in Italy by a Polish Army Chaplain who was an ordained Roman Catholic priest. The marriage did not comply with the formalities required by Italian domestic law. Italian rules of private international law would have upheld the marriage if it were valid by the parties' national law but the marriage was also void under Polish law. The husband was serving in the Polish 2nd Corps, part of the army of occupation of Italy at that time.

The couple settled in England, then they separated, and in 1955 the wife petitioned for a nullity decree on the ground that the marriage was void because it did not comply with the local formalities.

Held

The parties were presumed not to have submitted themselves to the local law. Thus the local law would not be applied; instead the English common law would determine the validity of the marriage.

Hodson LJ:

> 'There remains the argument put forward by the Queen's Proctor, and supported by counsel for the appellant husband, that the ceremony was valid at common law, and the requirements of the lex loci as to form did not apply. At the material date the Polish land forces in Italy were forces in belligerent occupation of Italian territory and therefore, it is said, exempt from the requirements of the lex loci. Karminski J pointed out that the position of such persons has always been recognised by English law as requiring special consideration with regard to formalities. It is true that they may, in fact, submit to the lex loci, but there is no evidence that the parties did so. The ceremony was indeed performed in an Italian church, but by a Polish Army chaplain acting as a member of the Polish Forces, and no attempt was made to comply with the local law. ...
>
> The principle in *Scrimshire's case* (2 Hag Con 395) that parties by entering into a marriage contract in a foreign country subject themselves to have the validity of it determined by the laws of that country, does not apply in the case of a contract performed in an occupied country by a member of the occupying forces. Sir Edward Simpson said (ibid 408):
>
> > "There can be no doubt, then, but that both the parties in this case, though they were English subjects, obtained a forum, by virtue of the contract, in France. By entering into the marriage contract there, they subjected themselves to have the validity of it determined by the laws of that country."
>
> Later he said (ibid 412):
>
> > "As both the parties, by celebrating the marriage in France, have subjected themselves to the law of that country relating to marriage; and as their mutual intention must be presumed to be that it should be a marriage or not, according to the laws of France, I apprehend it is not in the power of one of the parties, by leaving the place, to draw the question of the marriage or contract, 'ad aliud examen' to be tried by different laws than those of the place where the parties contracted. They may change the forum, but they must be tried by the laws of the country which they left. This doctrine of trying contracts, especially those of marriage, according to the

> laws of the country where they were made, is conformable to what is laid down in our books, and what is practised in all civilised countries, and what is agreeable to the law of nations, which is the law of every particular country, and taken notice of as such."

This reasoning has no application when one is considering the position of a conquering army in a conquered country. This case is not complicated by any terms of capitulation and there was no evidence that in 1946 the Allied Forces in Italy were in any way subject to the laws of that country. I see no reason, therefore, why the validity of the ceremony in form should be governed by the lex loci in the case we are now considering. If it be said that since the parties are not British subjects, the common law of England does not apply to them, my answer is that such is the law prima facie to be administered in the courts of this country. There is no question here of personal incapacity to marry or any other consideration apart from form for which one would look to the law of the domicile, and there would be a grave difficulty in applying the law of the domicile or nationality, amounting to an impossibility in some cases, where a marriage had been celebrated between persons of different nations or different domiciles.

In dealing with form this obstacle to applying the law of the domicile was pointed out by Sir Edward Simpson in *Scrimshire* v *Scrimshire* (2 Hag Con 395, 417):

> "If that principle is not to govern such cases, what is to be the rule, where one party is domiciled, and the other not? The jus gentium is the law of every country, and is obligatory on the subjects of every country. Every country takes notice of it; and this court observing that law, in determining upon this case, cannot be said to determine English rights by the laws of France, but by the law of England, of which the jus gentium is part."

The common law conception of marriage knows no distinction of race or nationality. The effect of the decision in *Reg* v *Millis* ((1844) 10 Cl & Fin 534) is that such a marriage to be valid must be celebrated before an episcopally ordained clergyman. A priest of the Church of Rome is in the same position as an Anglican clergyman: see *Reg* v *Inhabitants of Brampton* ((1808) 10 East 282).

The common law conception of marriage is thus stated in the speech of Lord Brougham in *Reg* v *Millis* (1844) 10 Cl & Fin 719:

> "Now, by the civil law, and by the earlier ecclesiastical law – indeed by that law until the sixteenth century – marriage was a mere consensual contract, only differing from other contracts of this class in being indissoluble even by the consent of the contracting parties. It was always deemed to be a contract executed without any part performance; so that the maxim was undisputed, and it was peremptory, 'Consensus, non concubitus, facit nuptias vel matrimonium.'"

The ceremony of marriage here fulfils all the essentials of a common law marriage, and in my opinion should be recognised as such notwithstanding the foreign nationality and domicile of the parties at the date of the ceremony.'

Wolfenden* v *Wolfenden [1946] P 61 Probate, Divorce and Admiralty Division (Lord Merriman P)

• *A valid common law marriage may be celebrated abroad if there is a significant difficulty in using the local form*

Facts

This concerned a petition for nullity of marriage on the ground of lack of form. The parties, both Canadian, went through a ceremony of marriage in October 1938 at a Church of Scotland mission church in a remote part of China. It was performed by the minister of the mission, without banns or licence. He was not episcopally ordained or authorised to perform a marriage under the Foreign Marriage Act 1892.

Held

The marriage was valid.

Lord Merriman P:

> 'The question in this case is whether, in order to effect a valid common law marriage in the District of Ichang, in the Province of Hupeh, in China, in the year 1938, it was or was not necessary that the ceremony should be performed by an episcopally ordained priest. …
>
> [T]he matter was dealt with in what I regard as conclusive fashion by Sir Erskine Perry C J, delivering the judgment of the full Court of the Supreme Court of Judicature of Bombay in *Maclean* v *Crislall* (1849) Perry's Oriental Cases 75. In that case the matter arose because the husband was suing an adulterer in an action for criminal conversation … The matter was fully considered and the Chief Justice delivered a considered judgment in the course of which, after setting out the full effect of *R* v *Millis* (1844) 10 Cl & Fin 534, he discussed the question whether that judgment applied in India with all its full effect. In the course of so doing he said:
>
>> "But the next step of the reasoning, as to the extent to which the English law has been introduced into India, is the point on which the judgment in the present case must depend. The rule on this subject is afforded by the doctrine of the common law with respect to colonies, which, though not strictly analogous, is more in point than any of the other rules in our law books. The rule in such case is, that although colonists take the law of England with them to their new home, they only take so much of it as is applicable to their situation and condition. In many cases no question will arise as to the inapplicability of several provisions of English law which are clearly seen to be merely municipal; but whenever a question does spring up it must be decided, like other disputed points of law in the Law Courts of the country. Blackstone lays down the rule very authoritatively on this subject: 'What shall be admitted and what rejected, at what times, and under what restrictions, must, in case of dispute, be decided in the first instance by their (the colonists') own provincial judicature, subject to the revision and control of the King and Council.'"…
>
> It was suggested that there was a distinction, inasmuch as we are here dealing with a place to which the Foreign Marriage Act applies, and a place in which, at the time in question, British citizens had extra-territorial rights. It is common ground in this case that the Chinese Order in Council of 1925 applied to the Province of Hupeh. The Order recites that "Whereas by treaty grant, usage, sufferance, and other lawful means, His Majesty the King has jurisdiction within the Dominion of the Republic of China His Majesty by virtue of and in exercise of the powers in this behalf was pleased to pass an Order in Council" setting out a system of judicature in that province, to the details of which it is unnecessary to refer. It was suggested therefore, that that raised a different situation; that in such a situation at any rate, the principles available to the first entry of colonists into a new territory and the like could not apply, and if the theory is that this particular province (or any other place to which extra-territoriality applies) is British then the whole law of England, without any exception, must apply also – in other words, that the decision in *R* v *Millis* would apply with full force and effect. 1 do not think that that can be so for two reasons. First of all I do not see any distinction in principle between applying in a colony, as New South Wales was at the time of Dr Lushington's judgment, only so much of the English law as suited the situation (but applying it notwithstanding the fact that there was a local Act of Parliament) and applying only so much of the English law as is suited to the situation of a British subject in this Province of Hupeh, notwithstanding that by Order in Council having the effect of leglslation the courts of law are set up there to administer British justice. Unless there is something in either case which excludes anything but that which is laid down in the legislation it seems to me that precisely the same principles apply in the one case as in the other.

In fact, there is nothing in the legislation which is inconsistent with that view, for I find in s104 of the Chinese Order in Council this provision: "Subject to the provisions of this Order the civil jurisdiction of every court acting under this Order shall, as far as circumstances admit, be exercised on the principles of and in conformity with English law for the time being in force." That certainly cannot possibly be said to be exclusive. It seems to me that whether one puts it on this basis that one of the circumstances which must be taken into account is that the English law is being imported into a foreign country which in all material respects is indistinguishable from a colony, so far as access to priests of the Established Church and the like is concerned, or whether one puts it on the other basis, that when it is indicated that the jurisdiction of the court shall "be exercised on the principles of and in conformity with the English law for the time being in force", the English law for the time being in force consists not only of the decision in *R* v *Millis* but of the decision in *R* v *Millis* as interpreted, as far as such a situation is concerned, by the decisions in *Catterall* v *Catterall* (1847) 1 Rob Eccl 580 and *Maclean* v *Cristall*, one comes to the same result. In such a territory as this there is, so far as the requirements of English law are concerned in relation to a common law marriage, no obligation that the ceremony shall be performed in the presence of an episcopally ordained priest.

In my opinion, therefore, so far as the first point is concerned, it seems to me that the petition on the ground of nullity must fail, and that it is my duty to say that this marriage was a valid marriage.'

Polygamy

Baindail v *Baindail* [1946] 1 All ER 342 Court of Appeal (Lord Greene MR, Morton and Bucknill LJJ)

• *A polygamous marriage will be recognised as valid in England unless there is some strong reason to the contrary – thus it constitutes a bar to a subsequent monogamous marriage by one of the parties*

Facts

In 1928 the respondent, a Hindu domiciled in India, married an Indian woman in India according to Hindu rites. This marriage was a polygamous marriage by the customs and laws of the Hindu race and was valid in India. In 1939, while his Indian wife was still living, the respondent went through a ceremony of marriage with the petitioner, an English woman domiciled in England, at a registry office in London. In 1944 the petitioner, having discovered an invitation to the respondent's former Hindu marriage, presented a petition for nullity on the ground of bigamy. Barnard J granted a decree. The respondent appealed.

Held

Appeal dismissed.

Lord Greene MR:

> 'The problem, as it seems to me, requires to be approached de novo and from quite a different angle; that was the view which the learned judge took and, if I may respectfully say so, I entirely agree with the decision to which he came. The question as it presents itself to my mind is simply this: On 5 May 1939, when the respondent took the petitioner to the registry office, was he, or was he not, a married man so as to be incapable of entering' into another legitimate union? The proposition I think would not be disputed that in general the status of a person depends on his personal law, which is the

law of his domicile. By the law of the respondent's domicile at the time of his Hindu marriage he unquestionably acquired the status of a married man according to Hindu law; he was married for all the purposes of Hindu law, and he had imposed upon him the rights and obligations which that status confers under that law. That status he never lost …

The practical question in this case appears to be: Will the courts of this country, in deciding upon the validity of this English marriage, give effect to the status possessed by the respondent? That question we have to decide with due regard to common sense and some attention to reasonable policy. We are not fettered by any concluded decision on the matter. The learned judge set out in a striking manner some of the consequences which would flow from disregarding the Hindu marriage for present purposes. I think it is certainly a matter to bear in mind that the prospect of an English court saying that it will not regard the status of marriage conferred by a Hindu ceremony would be a curious one when very little more than a mile away the Privy Council might be sitting and coming to a precisely opposite conclusion as to the validity of such a marriage on an Indian appeal. I do not think we can disregard that circumstance. We have to apply the law in a state of affairs in which this question of the validity of Hindu marriages is necessarily of very great practical importance in the everyday running of our Commonwealth and Empire.

If the marriage with the petitioner was a valid marriage it would have this consequence: that she is entitled to the consortium of her husband to the exclusion of any other woman, that he is entitled to the consortium of his wife, and that she is bound according to our notions of law to live with him provided he gives her a suitable home. If he decided to go back to India it would be her duty as a wife to follow him to the home that he would provide. Assume that this takes place. Directly they land in India by the law of India he is a man married to the Indian lady, and assuming as I think we are bound to assume that Hindu law would be the same in this respect as English law, that Hindu lady is his lawful wife in India and as such would be entitled to his consortium, he would be entitled to insist that she should live with him and she would be entitled to insist that he should provide a home for her. The position therefore would be that this English lady would find herself compelled in India either to leave her husband or to share him with his Indian wife. What the position would be with regard to divorce in India I do not know, but if he had an Indian domicile she apparently could not divorce him in England. Whether or not she could divorce him in India because in India he was associating with a woman who under Indian law was his lawful wife I do not know and I do not stop to inquire. Is it right that the courts of this country should give effect to a ceremony of marriage, the result of which would be to put the petitioner into such a position? It seems to me that effect must be given to common sense and decency and that on a question which is not covered by authority considerations of that kind must carry very great weight. On principle it seems to me that the courts are for this purpose bound to recognise the Indian marriage as a valid marriage and an effective bar to any subsequent marriage in this country.

Those are the short grounds on which I think this appeal should be decided. If we have not thought it necessary to reserve judgment in order to study more fully the cases which have been cited it is not that we have failed to appreciate them, but because at any rate so far as I am concerned I do not find it necessary to examine them very closely. The opinion which I have formed relates and relates solely to the facts of the present case which are connected with the validity of the English marriage in the circumstances of this case. I must not be taken as suggesting that for every purpose and in every context an Indian marriage such as this would be regarded as a valid marriage in this country. … I think it right therefore to say that so far as I am concerned nothing that I have said must be taken as having the slightest bearing on the law of bigamy. On the question of whether a person is "married" within the meaning of the statute (which is a criminal statute) when he has entered into a Hindu marriage in India I am not going to express any opinion whatever. It seems to me a different question in which other considerations may well come into play. I hope sincerely that nobody will endeavour to spell out of what I have said anything to cover such a question.'

Chaudhry* v *Chaudhry [1976] Fam 148 Family Division (Dunn J)

• *The summary remedy provided by s17 of the Married Women's Property Act 1882 applies to the parties to a valid polygamous marriage*

Facts

In 1959 the parties were married under Islamic law in Pakistan, where they were domiciled. The marriage was potentially polygamous. In 1963 they came to England without acquiring a domicile here. In July 1972 the husband divorced the wife by talaq in the Pakistani Embassy in London. This divorce became final in October 1972. At that date the talaq would have been recognised by the English courts as validly dissolving the marriage, because it was pronounced before s16 of the Domicile and Matrimonial Proceedings Act 1973 came into force on 1 January 1974. Under s39 of the Matrimonial Proceedings and Property Act 1970 the wife had three years from the date of dissolution of the marriage in which to issue a summons under s17 of the Married Women's Property Act 1882. That section provides that in any question between husband and wife as to the title to or possession of property, either party may apply to a judge by summons and the judge may make such order with respect to the property in dispute as he thinks fit. In February 1974, well within the time limit, the wife issued a summons asking for a declaration that she was entitled to an interest in the former matrimonial home in London. The registrar transferred the application to the High Court for the determination of a preliminary question of law.

Held

Dunn J:

'Counsel for the husband submits that at common law, as it was stated in the leading case of *Hyde* v *Hyde and Woodmansee* (1866) LR 1 P & D 130, the parties would not have been recognised as husband and wife, and that the words "husband and wife" in s17 of the Act of 1882 did not apply to the parties to polygamous marriages ... Counsel for the husband went so far as to submit that all that the Matrimonial Proceedings (Polygamous Marriages) Act 1972 had done was to enable the court to grant decrees of divorce, nullity, and judicial separation, and make orders for wilful neglect to maintain and alterations of maintenance agreements, and that it was significant that there was nothing in s1 which referred to property; and he submitted that if Parliament had intended that the rights of parties to polygamous marriages in property should be altered, then it could easily have said so.

I cannot accept that particular submission. Section 47(2)(d) of the Matrimonial Causes Act 1973 gives the court power, notwithstanding that the marriage was a polygamous one, to make "an order under any provision of this Act which confers a power exercisable in connection with, or in connection with proceedings for, any such decree or order as is mentioned in paragraphs (a) to (c) above; ..." In my judgment, that provision gives the court power not only to grant relief under Part I of the Act of 1973 but also to make orders for financial relief under Part II, and orders for the protection and custody of children under Part III notwithstanding that the marriage was a polygamous marriage.

But the matter does not rest there, because counsel's submission is that, whatever changes in the law have been made or not made by the Act of 1972, there is no express or implied reference in that Act to s17 of the Married Women's Property Act 1882 and that the common law position with regard to s17 still is that the English court would not recognise a polygamous marriage when deciding property rights between the parties.

He referred me to a number of cases, *Ali* v *Ali* [1968] P 564; *Imam Din* v *National Assistance Board* [1967] 2 QB 213; *Baindail* v *Baindail* [1946] 1 All ER 342 and *Sowa* v *Sowa* [1961] P 70 and he submitted finally that all that the Act of 1972 had done was to change the law in regard to the granting of matrimonial relief, but that so far as s17 of the Act of 1882 was concerned, the English courts would not regard these two people as husband and wife.

Counsel for the wife suggested that, as the law has developed, at common law a polygamous marriage would be recognised for the purpose of an application under s17 of the Married Women's Property Act 1882 just as it has been recognised when considering what is meant by a husband and wife in other legislation, noticeably the Supplementary Benefit Act 1966, and he submitted that for the purpose of this application the wife was entitled as a wife. …

I accept that submission of counsel for the wife. It is, I think, important to remember what was decided in *Hyde* v *Hyde and Woodmansee* and what was not decided. Lord Penzance said, at 138:

> "This court does not profess to decide upon the rights of succession or legitimacy which it might be proper to accord to the issue of the polygamous unions, nor upon the rights or obligations in relation to third persons which people living under the sanction of such unions may have created for themselves. All that is intended to be here decided is that as between each other they are not entitled to the remedies, the adjudication, or the relief of the matrimonial law of England."

It is that authoritative statement of the law which was finally changed by the Matrimonial Proceedings (Polygamous Marriages) Act 1972 as a result of the Report on Polygamous Marriages. But before that change was made there were a number of cases, which have been cited to me, referring to different statutes in which the words 'husband and wife' fell to be construed in which the courts held that the parties were husband and wife for the purpose of the statute, notwithstanding that the marriage was a polygamous one. …

In my judgment, the parties having been married according to the law of their domicile, the English court would regard them as husband and wife for the purpose of deciding any application by either of them under s17 of the Married Women's Property Act 1882. Any other conclusion would, in my judgment, be most impractical and an affront to common sense, because one would have the highly inconvenient situation that parties to a polygamous marriage could apply for transfers and settlement of property under the Matrimonial Causes Act 1973 but could not apply for their rights to be determined or for sale under s17 of the Married Women's Property Act 1882. For those reasons, my view of the preliminary issue is that the wife in this case is entitled to proceed under the section.'

Hussain* v *Hussain [1983] Fam 26 Court of Appeal (Ormrod, Griffiths and Slade LJJ)

• *A marriage is not polygamous if neither party can take another spouse during the subsistence of the marriage*

Facts

Mr and Mrs Hussain had married in Pakistan in accordance with the Muslim Family Laws Ordinance 1961 which allowed the husband to take a second wife but denied the wife the opportunity to take a second husband. At the time of the marriage the husband was domiciled in England (although the wife was domiciled in Pakistan). Was this marriage polygamous and, therefore, void in accordance with s11(d)?

Held

The husband lacked capacity to enter a polygamous marriage since he was domiciled in

England and the wife even under the Family Laws Ordinance could not take a second husband; thus the marriage was not polygamous and not void in terms of s11(d).

Ormrod LJ:

'Miss Bracewell, for the husband, contends that "a polygamous marriage" refers to the character and incidents of marriage under the relevant régime. If the régime permits polygamy in any form, she submits that such marriage is void if either party to it is domiciled in England or Wales at the date on which it was entered into. Mr Jackson, for the wife, contends that it refers, not to marriages which may be categorised as polygamous in general terms, but to the particular marriage which is in question. He submits that a marriage which is not actually polygamous at its inception, and incapable of becoming actually polygamous, by reason of the personal laws of the parties at the time it was entered into, is not void under this paragraph. On the facts of this case the husband, by England law, is incapable of contracting a valid marriage when he is already lawfully married (s11(b)), and the wife, by Pakistani law, cannot marry another man so long as she is married to the husband, so this marriage can never become polygamous. Consequently, the marriage was not polygamous at its inception and cannot become polygamous at any time in the future. It is, therefore, not avoided by s11(d). ...

Section 11(d) of the Matrimonial Causes Act 1973 is not very happily phrased and does not fit in at all well with the rest of the section, and in the process of consolidation, it has become widely separated from its proper context. It was originally s4 of the Matrimonial Proceedings (Polygamous Marriages) Act 1972, and was passed to deal with the new situation created by s1 of that Act (now s47 of the Act of 1973). Section 11(d) must be read, therefore, with s47.

When these two provisions are read together a significant difference can be seen between the language used in s47 and in s11(d). Section 47 refers to "a marriage entered into under a law which permits polygamy". This is the exact equivalent in English law of the proposition in the textbooks; it clearly refers to the lex loci celebrationis and not the law of either party's domicile. But s11(d) refers simply to "a polygamous marriage" and goes on to provide that a marriage may be polygamous although at its inception neither party has an additional spouse.

Miss Bracewell's argument has to overcome the difficulty that if her construction of s11(d) is right, the draftsman, originally, in the Matrimonial Proceedings (Polygamous Marriages) Act 1972 used two very different formulations to express the same idea in a short Act containing only two relevant sections (sections 1 and 4). Had the intention of Parliament been to prevent persons domiciled in England and Wales from entering into marriages under the Muslim Family Laws Ordinance, or under other similar laws which "permit polygamy", it would have been easy to say so in so many words. On the other hand, once the position of *Hyde* v *Hyde and Woodmansee* (1866) LR 1 P & D 130 had been abandoned, the question of the capacity of persons domiciled in England and Wales to enter into polygamous or potentially polygamous marriages had to be considered. Actually polygamous marriages were already covered by what is now s11(b) of the Act of 1973, but potentially polygamous marriages were not completely covered by the existing law. The spouse domiciled in England and Wales is, of course, incapable of marrying a second spouse, but if one of the spouses in the first marriage retains a domicile, the law of which permits polygamy, a situation could arise in which the spouse domiciled in this country becomes a party to a polygamous union. Mr Jackson submits that s4 of the Matrimonial Proceedings (Polygamous Marriages) Act 1972 (now s11(d) of the Matrimonial Causes Act 1973) was passed to prevent this situation from arising. The effect would be that a marriage between a woman domiciled in England and Wales, and a man domiciled in Pakistan, would be a polygamous marriage because the husband has the capacity, by his personal law, to take a second wife, but not vice versa.

The language used by the draftsman is, at least, consistent with this construction. The insertion of the qualifying words at the end of s11(d) suggests that without them the phrase "polygamous marriage" would, or might be, confined to a marriage which was actually polygamous at its inception, that is, one in which one of the spouses was already married to another spouse. The use of the word "may" in the qualifying words suggests that the draftsman had some contingency in mind, the happening of which would make a marriage between two unmarried persons polygamous, within the meaning of the provision, that is, as it is called, a potentially polygamous marriage. A marriage can only be potentially polygamous if at least one of the spouses had the capacity to marry a second spouse.

On a broader view, it is difficult to conceive any reason why Parliament, in an increasingly pluralistic society, should have thought it necessary to prohibit persons, whose religious or cultural traditions accept polygamy, from marrying in their own manner abroad, simply because they are domiciled in England and Wales. On the other hand, it is obvious that Parliament, having decided to recognise polygamous marriages as marriages for the purposes of our matrimonial legislation, would think it right to preserve the principle of monogamy for persons domiciled here.

Finally, the consequences of accepting Miss Bracewell's submission in this case would be far reaching and very serious. It would mean that all marriages contracted abroad by people domiciled in this country, in accordance with the local law, would be void if that law permitted polygamy in any form. The repercussions on the Muslim community alone in this country would be widespread and profound.

For these reasons the narrower construction of s11(d) of the Matrimonial Causes Act 1973 is to be preferred. On the facts, the marriage in this case is monogamous and should be held to be a valid marriage. The husband's contention, therefore, fails and his appeal should be dismissed. The petition should be restored to the list as soon as possible for the pronouncement of the decree of judicial separation.'

Comment

Note that had the wife been domiciled in England and the husband domiciled in Pakistan the result of the case would have been the exact reverse.

Hyde v *Hyde and Woodmansee* (1866) LR 1 P & D 130 Court of Probate and Divorce (Lord Penzance)

• *Marriage as understood in Christendom is the voluntary union for life of one man and one woman, to the exclusion of all others*

Facts

The petitioner was an Englishman, and in 1847, when he was about 16 years of age, he joined a congregation of Mormons in London, and was soon afterwards ordained a priest of that faith. He made the acquaintance of the respondent, then Miss Hawkins, who was a Mormon, and they became engaged to each other. Their marriage took place at Salt Lake City in April 1853, and it was celebrated by Brigham Young, the president of the Mormon church, and the governor of the territory, according to the rites and ceremonies of the Mormons. They cohabited as man and wife at Salt Lake City until 1856, and had children. In 1856, the petitioner went on a mission to the Sandwich Islands, and on his arrival he renounced the Mormon faith and preached against it. A sentence of excommunication was pronounced against him and his wife was declared free to marry again. In 1857 he resumed his domicile in England. In 1859 or 1860, the respondent contracted a marriage according to the Mormon form at Salt Lake City with the co-respondent, and subsequently she cohabited with him as his wife, and had children by him. At the time when the marriage between the petitioner and the respondent was celebrated, polygamy was a part of the Mormon doctrine, and was the common custom in Utah. The petitioner and the respondent were both single, and the petitioner had never taken a second wife.

A counsellor of the Supreme Court of the United States proved that a marriage by Brigham Young in Utah, if valid in Utah, would be recognised as valid by the Supreme Court of the United States, provided that the parties were both unmarried at the time when it was contracted, and that they were both capable of contracting marriage.

Lord Penzance:

> 'The petitioner in this case claims a dissolution of his marriage on the ground of the adultery of his wife. The alleged marriage was contracted at Utah, in the territories of the United States of America, and the petitioner and the respondent both professed the faith of the Mormons at the time. The petitioner has since quitted Utah, and abandoned the faith, but the respondent has not. After the petitioner had left Utah, the respondent was divorced from him, apparently in accordance with the law obtaining among the Mormons, and has since taken another husband. This is the adultery complained of …
>
> Marriage has been well said to be something more than a contract, either religious or civil – to be an Institution. It creates mutual rights and obligations, as all contracts do, but beyond that it confers a status. The position or status of "husband" and "wife" is a recognised one throughout Christendom: the laws of all Christian nations throw about that status a variety of legal incidents during the lives of the parties, and induce definite lights upon their offspring. What, then, is the nature of this institution as understood in Christendom? Its incidents vary in different countries, but what are its essential elements and invariable features? If it be of common acceptance and existence, it must needs (however varied in different countries in its minor incidents) have some pervading identity and universal basis. I conceive that marriage, as understood in Christendom, may for this purpose be defined as the voluntary union for life of one man and one woman, to the exclusion of all others.
>
> There are no doubt countries peopled by a large section of the human race in which men and women do not live or cohabit together upon these terms – countries in which this Institution and status are not known. In such parts the men take to themselves several women, whom they jealously guard from the rest of the world, and whose number is limited only by considerations of material means. But the status of these women in no way resembles that of the Christian "wife." In some parts they are slaves, in others perhaps not; in none do they stand, as in Christendom, upon the same level with the man under whose protection they live. There are, no doubt, in these countries laws adapted to this state of things – laws which regulate the duties and define the obligations of men and women standing to each other in these relations …
>
> Now, it is obvious that the matrimonial law of this country is adapted to the Christian marriage, and it is wholly inapplicable to polygamy. The matrimonial law is correspondent to the rights and obligations which the contract of marriage has, by the common understanding of the parties, created. Thus conjugal treatment may be enforced by a decree for restitution of conjugal rights. Adultery by either party gives a right to the other of judicial separation; that of the wife gives a right to a divorce; and that of the husband, if coupled with bigamy, is followed by the same penalty… If these and the like provisions and remedies were applied to polygamous unions, the Court would be creating conjugal duties, not enforcing them, and furnishing remedies when there was no offence. For it would be quite unjust and almost absurd to visit a man who, among a polygamous community, had married two women, with divorce from the first woman, on the ground that, in our view of marriage, his conduct amounted to adultery coupled with bigamy. Nor would it be much more just or wise to attempt to enforce

upon him that he should treat those with whom he had contracted marriages, in the polygamous sense of that term, with the consideration and according to the status which Christian marriage confers.

If, then, the provisions adapted to our matrimonial system are not applicable to such a union as the present, is there any other to which the Court can resort? We have in England no law framed on the scale of polygamy, or adjusted to its requirements. And it may be well doubted whether it would become the tribunals of this country to enforce the duties (even if we knew them) which belong to a system so utterly at variance with the Christian conception of marriage, and so revolting to the ideas we entertain of the social position to be accorded to the weaker sex.'

Radwan* v *Radwan (No 2) [1973] Fam 35; [1972] 3 All ER 1026 Family Division (Cumming-Bruce J)

• *Capacity to contract a polygamous marriage may be governed by the law of the intended matrimonial home*

Facts

The husband, a Muslim domiciled in Egypt, and the wife, then domiciled in England, were married before the Egyptian Consul-General in Paris in 1951 in polygamous form. At that time the husband had a wife living in Egypt whom he divorced by talaq in 1952. The parties lived together in Egypt in accordance with their ante-nuptial intentions until 1956. Owing to the Suez affair they moved to England where the husband acquired a domicile of choice by 1959. They had eight children. The wife petitioned for divorce on the ground of cruelty. The husband cross-petitioned on the same ground.

Held

The court held that by contract she became the wife of the respondent. (It should be noted though that virtually all academics agree that this was wrongly decided.)

Cumming-Bruce J:

'Though much has been written, and many observations made in English cases, this is the first time an English court has had to decide whether the wife's capacity to enter into a polygamous marriage abroad is governed by the law other domicile at the time of marriage, or by the law of the country of intended matrimonial residence, which often, as in this case, is the same as the law of the husband's domicile. I have, with proper humility, to grasp the nettle and decide whether to award the accolade of this court to Dr J H C Morris, the editor of *Dicey & Morris, Conflict of Laws* for his statement of rule 35 in his chapter on marriage, or to Professor Cheshire who has for many years advanced the contrary view. To pose the problem a little differently, in *De Reneville* v *De Reneville* [1948] P 100 Lord Greene MR and Bucknill LJ with both of whom Somervell LJ agreed, held that the law of the matrimonial domicile governs essential validity in relation to nullity on the ground of incapacity or wilful refusal to consummate. And in *Kenward* v *Kenward* [1951] P 124, Denning LJ said obiter and without argument, that capacity to enter into polygamous marriage depends upon the law of the matrimonial domicile. Yet in a number of cases extending over the last 100 years judges of first instance have stated that the law of prenuptial domicile govern capacity to marry. Who is right? What is the law? Many are confident that the question is already settled, and that the rule of dual domicile is settled English law governing all questions of capacity save for the one exception given as exception no 3 to rule 31 in *Dicey & Morris*, based on *Sottomayor* v *De Barros (No 2)* (1879) 5 PD 94 and exceptions founded on the penal or oppressive characteristics of foreign law. So the Law Commission in their Report on Polygamous Marriage stated: "Thus, if a person domiciled in England goes through a polygamous form of marriage abroad, that marriage will, under English law, be void, even if it was only potentially polygamous". And at para 89, "The marriage is also regarded as void if either party lacks capacity to marry under the law of the domicile of that party"; though there is a footnote to that proposition which gives *Brook* v *Brook* (1861) 9 HL Cas 193 as the authority and states: "There is another line of authority which has been interpreted as implying that it is the law of the matrimonial domicile which is decisive." It is to be observed that in *Ponticelli* v *Ponticelli* [1958] P 204 where counsel for the husband had argued in favour of choice of law of matrimonial residence Sachs LJ expressly left the point open as it was unnecessary to his decision. Against that background I examine the authorities ...

The three most important modern cases appear to be *Re Paine* [1940] Ch 46; *Pugh* v *Pugh* [1951] P 482 and *Padolecchia* v *Padolecchia* [1968] P 314...

And so the question that I have to decide is really this. It is clear that at the time of *Brook* v *Brook* (1861) 9 HL Cas 193 and *Warrender* v *Warrender* (1835) 2 Cl & Fin 488, the factor of the intended matrimonial home played a part in the formulation of the concept of domicile. But that since then the factor of intended matrimonial home appears long to have been disregarded as relevant to choice of law in relation to capacity to marry, certainly in relation to polygamous marriage. Hence, Mr Ewbank rightly drew my attention to the confidence and the unqualified character of the dicta in the cases to which he referred, and the rationes decidendi, and reminded me there is no vestige in any of those cases of a continuing appreciation on the part of judges of the courts that matrimonial residence is relevant. But that may well be because the matter has never been argued until today, and I have to consider whether the assumption that has been made as a result of the expressions of view in the cases to which I have referred is solidly founded upon the common law foundations that are supposed to lie beneath them, and I have come to the conclusion that Mr Michael Davies [counsel for the wife] is right in his submission that it is my duty to return to examine the foundations in *Brook* v *Brook* and *Warrender* v *Warrender* of the propositions that have since been founded upon them. And my conclusion is that Miss Magson had the capacity to enter into a polygamous union by virtue of her prenuptial decision to separate herself from the land of her domicile and to make her life with her husband in his country, where the Mohammedan law of polygamous marriage was the normal institution of marriage. I recognise that this decision may make it necessary for Parliament to consider a further amendment to the Nullity of Marriage Act 1971, if it is indeed the policy of Parliament to prevent such unions on the part of domiciled Englishmen and women, and to require a change of domicile before there is capacity to enter into them. But this court is only concerned with the common law rights of Miss Magson, as she was in 1951, and with the status, if any, that she acquired as a result of her decision to enter into a polygamous union with a domiciled Egyptian. My decision is that by that contract she became the wife of the respondent. Nothing in this judgment bears upon the capacity of minors, the law of affinity, or the effect of bigamy upon capacity to enter into a monogamous union. Having had the benefit of argument, I do not think that this branch of the law relating to capacity for marriage is quite as tidy as some very learned authors would have me believe, and I must face their displeasure with such fortitude as I can command.'

Divorce and the nullity of marriage

Holmes* v *Holmes [1989] 3 All ER 786 Court of Appeal (Purchas, Dillon and Russell LJJ)

• *Matrimonial and Family Proceedings Act 1984 Part III – appropriate test regarding 'substantial ground' for granting leave to apply for financial relief*

Facts

The parties married in 1968, settled in New York in 1978. They purchased an apartment there and a cottage in joint names in Wiltshire. Consequent upon both parties being granted a divorce the Supreme Court of New York ordered that both properties be sold and the proceeds divided equally between the parties. After the New York court confirmed the order for sale the wife applied in England for financial relief under s13 of the 1984 Act. The judge dismissed the application on the grounds that her financial provision was a matter for the American court.

Held

Refused leave to appeal. The court, under s13(1), could only grant leave to make an application for financial relief in England or Wales if there was a substantial ground for so doing; that the test was a stringent one and essentially a matter for the judge at first instance to consider the relevant matters, including being satisfied that the criteria for entertaining an application in s16 had been met; and that, since the New York court had examined the issue between the parties in the natural forum for the resolution of their dispute, the judge had properly refused leave under s13(1) of the Act to apply for financial relief .

Purchas LJ:

> 'There is no direct authority that the diligence of counsel was able to find dealing with the manner in which these powers should be exercised... The phrase "substantial ground for the making of an application for such an order" is clearly central to the issues in this application. Looking at that expression in the immediate context of the Act, I have formed the view that what is required is that the applicant should demonstrate to the court that there is in all the circumstances surrounding the application for financial relief – the orders that may or may not have been made, the presence or absence of powers to grant financial relief in the foreign forum – reasons for saying that there is a substantial ground for making an application; that is a substantial ground upon which the court could be invited to exercise its powers under s12 within the jurisdiction of s15. In particular, when the court comes to consider such an application, it will have to take into account under s16(1) whether in all the circumstances of the case it will be appropriate for such an order to be made by a court in England and Wales. If it is not satisfied that it would be appropriate (and that is a positive onus), the court shall, as a matter of mandatory instruction, dismiss the application.
>
> In my judgment that section reflects the fundamental rule of comity as between competent courts dealing with matters of this kind. Of course s16 is to be considered on the application itself. [Counsel] very properly drew the distinction between the criteria which the court should take into account if it decides to entertain the application and those which the court has to consider on the application for leave to make the application. Nevertheless, if on the application for leave to apply it is clear that if leave were given the application must founder at the first hurdle of s16(1), then it would clearly be wrong for the court to grant leave to apply in the first instance. So it is not possible to isolate the considerations which arise under this group of sections ...
>
> To decide whether or not there is a substantial ground – which imports in itself a detailed consideration of all the subsections of s16 – is a matter essentially for the consideration of the judge at first instance. This court would be very slow to interfere with a judge, who has the opportunity of considering all the features of the case. Perhaps this case is not one of the more complicated ones or one in which the judge has had a large area of ground to traverse in his consideration of whether or not a substantial ground for making an application is established or to consider the features which arise under s16. Nevertheless, the principle must be the same, that this court will be very slow to intervene.
>
> If analogies are of any assistance at all, perhaps assistance can be obtained from the

approach by Lord Templeman in his speech in *Spiliada Maritime Corporation* v *Cansulex Ltd* [1987] AC 460, 465:

> "The factors which the court is entitled to take into account in considering whether one forum is more appropriate are legion. The authorities do not, perhaps cannot, give any clear guidance as to how these factors are to be weighed in any particular case. Any dispute over the appropriate forum is complicated by the fact that each party is seeking an advantage and may be influenced by considerations which are not apparent to the judge or considerations which are not relevant for his purpose. … In the result, it seems to me that the solution of disputes about the relative merits of trial in England and trial abroad is pre-eminently a matter for the trial judge."

I would gratefully adopt those expressions to the features of this case which are, of course, different in their facts and nature but in principle not too dissimilar. The problem here is whether or not, on the application of one of the parties, the courts in this country should interfere with the resolution of matrimonial difficulties and disputes, particularly in the field of financial relief where there is in place a competent forum in a foreign jurisdiction seized of the matter, where the parties at the material time were domiciled or otherwise within the jurisdiction of that court, have submitted to the jurisdiction of that court, and, apart from one aspect, had been content to abide by the judgment of that court. …

As I have said, the court must always be slow to interfere with a competent court seized of the matter, as was the Supreme Court of the State of New York, which has made orders which are clearly enforceable, which is capable of enforcing them, and has dealt with the matter on a reasonably careful assessment of all the features. I understand the attraction of the course proposedby the wife in this case. But, from the point of view of jurisdiction, the application, had leave been granted, was doomed to failure. Therefore leave should not be granted. In the same way, that goes for the application for leave to appeal to this court. On the same consideration, that leave must be refused.

I would therefore refuse the application for leave to appeal.'

Comment

The purpose of the Matrimonial and Family Proceedings Act 1984 Part III was to give the courts jurisdiction to grant a spouse financial relief where the marriage had been terminated abroad, but leave to make an application for financial relief would only be granted if there was a substantial ground for doing so. In this instance Purchas LJ favoured the approach by Lord Templeman in his speech in *Spiliada Maritime Corporation* v *Cansulex Ltd.*

Lawrence* v *Lawrence [1985] 3 WLR 125 Court of Appeal (Ackner and Purchas LJJ, Sir David Cairns)

• *Validity of divorce – capacity to remarry*

Facts

A Brazilian domiciled woman had divorced her first husband in Nevada (and almost immediately married her second husband (a domiciled American) there). The law of Brazil did not recognise divorce but under the then rules of English law (as well as the current rules: s46(1) of the Family Law Act 1986) the Nevada divorce had to be recognised in England. Was the second marriage valid notwithstanding her lack of capacity to marry under her domiciliary law.

Held

The marriage was valid.

Ackner LJ:

> 'In my judgment, this appeal does not raise the general question of what law governs capacity to marry. With considerable diffidence, and all proper deference to Anthony Lincoln J, and indeed to Purchas LJ, who does not share my view, I am entirely satisfied that the solution which it is recognised

would appeal to the "plain man" is the right one. It has the added advantages of being short, simple and provides that which Mr Johnson, for the wife, urged us to strive for, namely, a test that produced some certainty in this uncertain field.

We are concerned with one – and only one – species of alleged incapacity to re-marry. That incapacity is said to arise, notwithstanding the Nevada divorce, out of the continued existence of the marriage contracted by the wife in Brazil in 1944. It is alleged that since that marriage was at all material times – that is to say up to and including 12 September 1970 – indissoluble by Brazilian law, then when the wife purported to marry her husband in Nevada she was, by the law of her domicile, incapable of so doing because she was then still married to Mr Harley. Accordingly, the marriage in Nevada was a nullity.

To my mind, this submission totally ignores the Nevada decree of divorce granted the day before the Nevadan marriage, the validity of which the English courts are required to recognise. The essential function of a decree of divorce is to dissolve the marriage hitherto existing between the parties. I consider that it is plainly inconsistent with recognising a divorce to say in the same breath that the marriage which it purported to dissolve still continues in existence. Such a recognition would be a hollow and empty gesture.

In *Perrini* v *Perrini* [1979] Fam 84 (which concerned the recognition of a foreign decree of nullity and to which the Act had no relevance) Sir George Baker P, having held that the foreign decree should be recognised, had no hesitation in saying, at p92: "Once recognised it must be taken to have declared the pretended marriage a nullity, with each party free to marry." That fact that one of the parties could not marry in Italy, the country of his domicile, was no bar to his re-marriage in England where, by the foreign decree, he was free to marry. "No incapacity existed in English law."

It would, of course, have been open to Parliament to provide in s3 that the validity of the divorce should only be recognised if, and only if, the marriage to which it related was dissoluble according to the law of the domicile of the parties seeking such a divorce. It could have provided – although this would have appeared somewhat startling, since a decree of divorce would be expected to assert expressly or by necessary implication – that the relationship between the parties was no longer such as to prevent re-marriage and that nothing in the Act of 1971 should affect the person's capacity to re-marry. Parliament has, however, provided in s8 of the Act for specific exceptions from recognition and indeed the section is thus headed. It makes no provision for excepting from recognition a divorce obtained by a party whose marriage, according to the law of his or her domicile, was indissoluble.

Mr Johnson submits that a highly significant limitation is placed upon s3 by the terms of s7, despite the fact that no reference is to be found in either section to the other. Section 7, as amended by sections 2(3) and 15(2) of the Domicile and Matrimonial Proceedings Act 1973, provides:

> "Where the validity of a divorce obtained in any country is entitled to recognition by virtue of ss1 to 5 or s6(2) of this Act … neither spouse shall be precluded from re-marrying in the United Kingdom on the ground that the validity of the divorce would not be recognised in any other country."

It is common ground that s7 is intended to implement art 11 of the Hague Convention on the Recognition of Divorces and Legal Separations (1970) (Cmnd 6248). That article provides:

> "A state which is obliged to recognise a divorce under this Convention may not preclude either spouse from remarrying on the ground that the law of another state does not recognise that divorce."

I cannot accept Mr Johnson's submission that it is only in the case of remarriages that take place in the United Kingdom following upon an overseas divorce recognised by the Act of 1971 that we are obliged to accept that the earlier marriage was dissolved by the overseas decree of divorce. Section 3 provides for the recognition of the validity of an overseas divorce. It does not expressly impose any further obligation upon our courts. In particular, it does not impose the obligation to permit the remarriage of a spouse involved in that divorce, where its validity would not be recognised in another country.

Article 11 and this section were, in my judgment, designed to make assurance doubly sure and to prevent the sort of situation arising which arose some three years earlier in the well-known case of *Reg* v *Brentwood Superintendent Registrar of Marriages, ex parte Arias* [1968] 2 QB 956. In that case it was held that as a normal rule, a "lawful impediment" within s32(2)(a) of the Marriage Act 1949 existed to the marriage in England of parties who could not be married according to the law of the country in which they were domiciled.

Section 7 of the Act does not, in my view, detract from, or diminish the extent of the recognition to be accorded by virtue of s3 to an overseas divorce. As regards the reference to the section to the "United Kingdom", this is wholly explicable by the fact that that is the forum over which Parliament has jurisdiction and any attempt to have legislated further afield would have been without effect. The amendments to the section made by the Domicile and Matrimonial Proceedings Act 1973 are, in the context of this case, of no relevance.

I, accordingly, conclude that any incapacity said to be due to a pre-existing marriage cannot be relevant where the validity of the divorce dissolving such a marriage has to be recognised under the Act. Of course, if there are other alleged incapacities, not based upon an alleged subsisting marriage but arising out of, for example, age or consanguinity or affinity, that will raise an entirely different and distinct problem.

Thus, in cases where the entitlement to remarry is based exclusively upon an overseas divorce, we are required only to consider whether the circumstances of that divorce are such as to oblige us (pursuant to the provisions of the Act) to recognise its validity. We are not concerned to decide which of the two conflicting theories – the dual domicile doctrine or that of the intended matrimonial domicile – is to be preferred. If I am right in the views which I have expressed, then it would seem that Parliament will have satisfied, in this respect, the legitimate expectations of the plain man and we have taken a further step towards reducing the tyranny of the rule of domicile which Lord Wilberforce in *Indyka* v *Indyka* [1969] 1 AC 33, 105 considered was both justified and long overdue.

I would accordingly dismiss this appeal, but not by applying the doctrine of the law of the intended matrimonial domicile, in the sense used by Anthony Lincoln J but on this quite simple ground. The inevitable consequence of our recognising the Nevada divorce – as we are obliged to do under the Act – is to recognise that it dissolved the Brazilian marriage. Thereafter, that dissolved marriage could no longer be a bar to the wife's remarriage and no other incapacity is alleged.'

Comment

The same result would be reached under s50 of the Family Law Act 1986. The case is included here not because of the result reached but because of the discussion of the various approaches to the validity of marriage in the judgments.

Le Mesurier v *Le Mesurier and Others* [1895] AC 517 Privy Council (The Lord Chancellor, Lords Watson, Hobhouse, Macnaghten and Morris, Sir Richard Couch)

- *Foreign domicile – divorce jurisdiction – matrimonial domicile*

Facts

In February 1883 the appellant, who was a member of the Ceylon Civil Service, was married in England to a French lady, the leading respondent in this appeal. From the date of their marriage the spouses had their principal residence in Ceylon, due to the appellant's official duties there. In July 1892, he commenced an action against his wife and three other defendants, praying for a divorce based on the allegation that she had committed adultery with one of these defendants in the year 1887, with another of them in the year 1889, and with the third of them at various times between May 1891 and April 1892. Except on the last of these occasions, when the adultery was alleged to have taken place at Kandy, none of these matrimonial offences was said to have been committed within the jurisdiction of the courts of Ceylon. The loci assigned for these acts on the two other occasions were, on the first, the steamship Ghoorkha, during a voyage from England to Colombo; and, on the second, the steamship Ravenna, during a voyage from Colombo to Marseilles, and two hotels, one at Marseilles and the other in Paris. The respondent pleaded that the District Court had no jurisdiction to entertain the suit. She denied all three charges of adultery, and with respect to the first charge, pleaded alternatively that it had been condoned by the appellant. Two of the other defendants, who were alleged to have been participant in her adulterous acts on the first and third occasions, denied the charges and pleaded that they were not subject to the jurisdiction of the Court.

Held

The matrimonial law applicable to British and European residents in Ceylon was the Roman-Dutch law, and that law did not contain any rule specially conferring on the local courts divorce jurisdiction over spouses where marriage and domicile were in England. Further, the permanent domicile of the spouses within the territory is necessary to give to its courts jurisdiction so to divorce a vinculo as that its decree to that effect shall by the general law of nations possess extra-territorial authority. A so-called 'matrimonial domicile', said to be created by a bona fide residence of the spouses within the territory of a less degree of permanence than is required to fix their true domicile, cannot be recognised as creating such jurisdiction.

Lord Watson:

> 'Their Lordships, in deciding this appeal, must observe the limits which the law of Ceylon imposes upon the matrimonial jurisdiction exercisable by the tribunal before which the action was originally brought. It therefore becomes necessary to consider whether the District Court of Matara was competent to entertain the action and to pronounce a decree of divorce a vinculo. To that point, which is one of some importance to British and other European residents in the island, the arguments of counsel on both sides of the Bar were exclusively directed. …
>
> In order to sustain the competency of the present suit it is necessary for the appellant to shew that the jurisdiction assumed by the district judge of Matara was derived, either from some recognised principle of the general law of nations, or from some domestic rule of the Roman-Dutch law. If either of these points were established, the jurisdiction of the District Court would be placed beyond question; but the effect of its decree divorcing the spouses would not in each case be the same. When the jurisdiction of the Court is exercised according to the rules of international law, as in the case where the parties have their domicile within its forum, its decree dissolving their marriage ought to be respected by the tribunals of every civilised country. The opinions expressed by the English common law judges in Lolley's Case gave rise to a doubt whether that principle was in consistency with the law of England, which at that time did not allow a marriage to be judicially dissolved. That doubt has since been dispelled; and the law of England was, in their Lordships' opinion, correctly stated by Lord Westbury in *Shaw* v *Gould* (1868) LR 3 HL 55 in these terms:
>
> > "The position that the tribunal of a foreign country having jurisdiction to dissolve the

marriages of its own subjects, is competent to pronounce a similar decree between English subjects who were married in England, but who before and at the time of the suit are permanently domiciled within the jurisdiction of such foreign tribunal, such decree being made in a bonâ fide suit without collusion or concert, is a position consistent with all the English decisions, although is may not be consistent with the resolution commonly cited at the resolution of the judges in *Lolley's Case*."

On the other hand, a decree of divorce a vinculo, pronounced by a Court whose jurisdiction is solely derived from some rule of municipal law peculiar to its forum, cannot, when it trenches upon the interests of any other country to whose tribunals the spouses were amenable, claim extra-territorial authority…

When carefully examined, neither the English nor the Scottish decisions are, in their Lordships' opinion, sufficient to establish the proposition that, in either of these countries, there exists a recognised rule of general law to the effect that a so-called matrimonial domicile gives jurisdiction to dissolve marriage. …

Their Lordships attach great weight to the consideration that the theory of matrimonial domicile for which the appellant contends has never been accepted in the Court of last resort for England and Scotland. The matter does not rest there; because the theory is not only in direct opposition to the clear opinion expressed by Lord Westbury in *Pitt* v *Pitt* (1864) 10 Jur NS 735, but appears to their Lordships to be at variance with the principles recognised by noble and learned Lords in *Dolphin* v *Robins* (1859) 7 HL Cas 390 and in *Shaw* v *Gould*. …

Their Lordships have in these circumstances, and upon these considerations, come to the conclusion that, according to international law, the domicile for the time being of the married pair affords the only true test of jurisdiction to dissolve their marriage. They concur, without reservation, in the views expressed by Lord Penzance in *Wilson* v *Wilson* [1903] P 157 which were obviously meant to refer, not to questions arising in regard to the mutual rights of married persons, but to jurisdiction in the matter of divorce:

"It is the strong inclination of my own opinion that the only fair and satisfactory rule to adopt on this matter of jurisdiction is to insist upon the parties in all cases referring their matrimonial differences to the Courts of the country in which they are domiciled. Different communities have different views and laws respecting matrimonial obligations, and a different estimate of the causes which should justify divorce. It is both just and reasonable, therefore, that the differences of married people should be adjusted in accordance with the laws of the community to which they belong, and dealt with by the tribunals which alone can administer those laws. An honest adherence to this principle, moreover, will preclude the scandal which arises when a man and woman are held to be man and wife in one country and strangers in another."

Their Lordships will, therefore, humbly advise Her Majesty to affirm the order appealed from. The appellant must pay to the first and fourth respondents their costs of this appeal.'

R* v *Immigration Appeal Tribunal, ex parte Jan (Asfar) [1995] Imm AR 440 Queen's Bench Division (Tucker J)

• *Recognition of talaq divorce pronounced in the UK – husband of subsequent marriage domiciled in the UK – validity of marriage under s11 Matrimonial Causes Act 1973*

Facts

J, a citizen of Pakistan, applied for leave to enter the UK as the spouse of K, her sponsor. There had been a marriage ceremony in Pakistan between them on 14 February 1993. J had been married twice before. Her first husband had died when she was only 16 or 17.

She married M, her second husband in 1973 in Pakistan. J had been M's second wife. M had come to live in the UK with his first wife and children. On 18 March 1981 M divorced J by talaq pronounced in the UK. The entry clearance officer had refused clearance on the basis that she was not satisfied as to the validity of the marriage under English law. She had also not been satisfied that the applicant, if admitted, could be maintained without recourse to public funds. The adjudicator refused the appeal on 27 July 1993. The Immigration Appeal Tribunal refused leave to appeal on 28 October 1993, stating that it would not grant leave because the findings as to maintenance could not be disturbed. Applying for judicial review of the decision J argued that she had been validly married to her sponsor and the tribunal had been wrong not to interfere with the adjudicator's findings as to maintenance.

Held

1. Since the talaq had been pronounced in the UK it could not be said that there had been divorce proceedings in Pakistan.
2. Since M had been resident in the UK in the year before the talaq was pronounced, J could not satisfy ss46(2) and 54 Family Law Act 1986 recognising the validity of overseas divorce proceedings.
3. M was not domiciled in England and Wales so that the marriage between J and M was not invalid within the meaning of s11 Matrimonial Causes Act 1973.
4. M could not demonstrate that at the time of her application she was validly married to her sponsor.
5. There had been no flaw in the adjudicator's approach as to maintenance.
6. The tribunal was correct to refuse leave on this ground alone: *R* v *Immigration Appeal Tribunal, ex parte Khan (Majid)* [1995] Imm AR 19; *R* v *Immigration Appeal Tribunal, ex parte Kathiravelu* (unreported, 1984); and *R* v *Immigration Appeal Tribunal, ex parte Ali (Tohur)* [1988] Imm AR 237; [1988] CLY 1872 considered.

Legitimacy, adoption, custody and guardianship

Motala and Others* v *Attorney-General and Others [1990] 2 FLR 261 Family Division (Sir Stephen Brown P)

• *Domicile of origin – determines whether legitimate or illegitimate*

Facts

This case concerned whether the children of Mr and Mrs Ismail Motala were citizens of the United Kingdom and Colonies or not. However, it is not necessary for us to enter the maze of nationality law. Suffice it to say that the nationality status of some of the children depended upon whether they were legitimate or not. The circumstances surrounding the marriage of the parents were the following: the marriage took place according to Sunni Muslim rites in 1950 in what is now Zambia but was then Northern Rhodesia. Apparently this would have been an invalid marriage under the lex loci celebrationis but under the law of India the marriage would have been valid and the children legitimate. Throughout the parents retained their domicile of origin in India. The crucial question was whether two children, Safiya and Faruq, born in Northern Rhodesia before independence, were legitimate (in which case they were citizens of the United Kingdom and Colonies) or illegitimate (in which case they had no such entitlement?)

Held

That *Shaw* v *Gould* (1868) LR 3 HL 55 must be considered as limited to its own facts and thus the court followed instead dicta from *Re Bischoffsheim* [1948] Ch 79 and *Re Goodman's Trust* (1881) 17 Ch D 266 and held a person's status was determined by the law of their domicile; and since the domicile of origin of the children was plainly Indian and Indian law considered them legitimate, they were legitimate under English law; and entitled to British nationality. (An appeal against Brown J's judgment on grounds other than the legitimacy point was dismissed by the Court of Appeal on 30 January 1981.)

Sir Stephen Brown P:

> 'It is accepted at this hearing that Ismail retained his Indian domicile throughout. Indian law does not recognise legitimatio per subsequens matrimonium. Accordingly, the four children concerned in these proceedings are unable to rely upon the civil marriage of their parents in 1968 as having achieved their legitimation. The petitioners have put before the court an affidavit sworn by Mr Mohammed Wahid Khan, a barrister practising at 9 Kings Bench Walk in the Temple. He is an expert in the law of India and in particular in Muslim law as it is applied in India. His evidence is not challenged. In his affidavit he says that he has perused the documents relating to the Islamic marriage of Ismail Motala and Ayshabibi celebrated on 27 July 1950. He states:
>
> > "That a court of competent jurisdiction in India will accept the said documents as evidence of a valid Islamic marriage between the said Motalas and the children born to the parties out of the said marriage will be recognised as the legitimate children of the said Motalas ... I say that under Islamic law the children are the legitimate children of Ismail Mohammad Motala and Ayshabibi Motala born out of a valid Islamic marriage and that a court of competent jurisdiction in India would accept the said children as such."
>
> The petitioners contended that a person's status is to be determined by the law of his domicile. If that law treats him or her as legitimate then it is submitted English law will recognise that legitimacy for all purposes concerned with status. The authorities show that there is a reservation in cases which concern the succession to real property or to titles. The contention of the petitioners is that since by the law of India which was the law of Ismail's domicile the children are recognised as legitimate pursuant to the marriage of 1950, their status should be so recognised by English law.
>
> Accordingly, their right to be considered as citizens of the United Kingdom and Colonies would be established. In support of this proposition Mr Collins has referred to a number of authorities commencing with *Birtwhistle* v *Vardill* (1835) 2 Cl & Fin 571, and (1840) 7 Cl & Fin 895. More particularly he relies upon certain passages in the judgments delivered on appeal in the case of *Re Goodman's Trusts* (1881) 17 Ch D 266. That appeal concerned the right of the appellant to share in a portion of the personal estate of one Rachel Goodman who had died intestate. The issue was whether the appellant, who had been born before the wedding of her parents who were domiciled in Holland at the time of her birth, was entitled to a share in the personal estate of the deceased who had died intestate. According to the law of Holland, she was legitimated by the subsequent marriage of her parents. At that date English law did not recognise the legitimation of issue by the subsequent marriage of the parents. At p292 of the report, Cotton LJ, after referring to a number of authorities, said:
>
> > "If, as in my opinion is the case, the question whether a person is legitimate depends on the law of the place where his parents were domiciled at his birth, that is, on his domicile of origin, I cannot understand on what principle, if he be by that law legitimate, he is not legitimate everywhere, and I am of the opinion that if a child is legitimate by the law of the country where at the time of its birth its parents were domiciled, the law of England, except in the case of succession to real estate in England, recognises and acts on the status thus declared by the law of the domicile." ...
>
> Mr Holman summarised his submissions by stating the following propositions:
>
> > "Where, in the view of English law, the marriage propounded and relied upon as conferring legitimacy is void (a fortiori when no marriage at all) then the child is not legitimate in England, even if regarded as legitimate by the law of his

> domicile of origin and place of birth (this latter feature absent from the present case)."

I find myself unable to accept that proposition as a valid statement of the present law. In my judgment, the authorities of *Re Goodman* (above) and *Re Bischoffsheim* (above) correctly state the law. Accordingly, I am satisfied on the basis of the undisputed factual and professional expert evidence in this case that the petitioners Safiya and Faruq, and the two further children Abubaker and Osman are all the legitimate children of their parents and should be so regarded for the purpose of their status as citizens of the United Kingdom and Colonies. I, therefore, propose to make the declaration sought in the petition of *Safiya* v *Motala*. In the case of Abubaker and Osman my decision with regard to their status as the legitimate children of their father necessarily involves the conclusion that they are entitled to the status of citizens of the United Kingdom and Colonies and I shall so declare.'

Shaw* v *Gould (1868) LR 3 HL 55 House of Lords (Lords Cranworth, Chelmsford, Westbury and Colonsay)

• *Legitimacy of children – capacity to remarry – recognition of divorce*

Facts

Much of the estate of John Wilson had been left on various trusts to the lawfully begotten children of his great-niece, Elizabeth Hickson. Although Elizabeth Hickson had given birth to three children following her marriage to John Shaw, were those children legitimate?

The difficulty over the legitimacy arose because Elizabeth Hickson, then domiciled in England, had while very young married one Buxton (also a domiciled Englishman). She had subsequently obtained a divorce from Buxton but only by inducing Buxton for a pecuniary consideration to come to Scotland and to stay in Scotland long enough for her to divorce him there. Such a divorce obtained by collusion would not generally be recognised by English courts.

None the less, Elizabeth Hickson thereafter married in Scotland John Shaw a domiciled Scotsman and the three children were born. Were the children legitimate?

Held

The collusion prevented the recognition of the Scottish divorce; and until the first marriage was dissolved there was no capacity to contract a second marriage; thus the children were illegitimate.

Lord Cranworth:

> 'Adopting, however, the more reasonable views on this subject by which the courts of this country are now guided, we may safely act on the hypothesis adopted by all parties in the argument case, that the children of Elizabeth are either her lawful children by John Shaw, or are illegitimate. That they are illegitimate, if we are to look only to the laws of England, is certain; for ex hypothesi they are not the children of Buxton, who was the husband of Elizabeth when they were born. This, therefore, brings us to consider whether, in order to help us in deciding this question, we are warranted in looking at any other law than that of England – whether we may to any extent be guided by the law of Scotland.
>
> If the parties in this case had been Scotch, and not English, and if all which occurred had occurred not in England but in Scotland, there would, I presume, have been no question on the subject. If Thomas Buxton, being a domiciled Scotchman, had married in Edinburgh, Elizabeth Hickson, being a domiciled Scotchwoman, and afterwards, while their Scotch domicile continued, she had obtained a decree of divorce in the Court of Session, and then had married John Shaw, the issue of that marriage would certainly have been legitimate. The argument of the appellants is, that the consequence must be the same, though the parties were at the time of the first marriage domiciled in England, and were married there. The

question, it is contended, is whether, when the second marriage was contracted, the parties to it had the capacity to contract marriage; in other words, whether the effect of the divorce was to enable them to enter into a valid contract of marriage, which, but for the divorce, they certainly could not have entered into. The whole, therefore, turns on the validity of the divorce. Now, the law of Scotland seems clear that a residence in Scotland for forty days makes that country the domicilium fori of any person so residing in the country, in which, for the purposes of litigation, he is to be treated as being domiciled. And it is assumed that this is true whatever be the nature of the litigation; that it holds equally in cases the decision in which may involve the personal status of those who may claim through the litigant parties; as also where it is a mere dispute between the litigant parties themselves. Taking this, however, to be the undoubted law of Scotland, the question is, whether that principle is one which this country is bound to recognise. I think it is not.

The facts of this case do not raise the question as to what would have been the status of these children if Buxton and Elizabeth Hickson, though married at Manchester, had always been Scotch persons, and had always lived in Scotland; or even what it would have been if, before the proceedings for the divorce, Buxton had actually bona fide quitted England permanently, and established himself in Scotland, so as to have acquired a Scotch domicile for all intents and purposes. It may be that in these circumstances the courts of this country would recognise the status of these children, so as to entitle them, after the death of their mother, to the fund given to her children; which, no doubt, must be construed as meaning her legitimate children. But on that point I express no opinion. The decision in *Doe* v *Vardill (Birtwhistle* v *Vardill* (1840) 7 Cl & Fin 895, 6 Bing NC 385), though the case did not turn on any question depending on the validity of a divorce, yet rests on principles hardly, to my mind, distinguishable from it; and it may certainly be assumed that these children could not, in any circumstances, claim real estate in England by descent. But the opinions of the judges in that case, and of the noble Lords who spoke in the House, left untouched the question of legitimacy, except so far as it was connected with succession to real estate. I think they inclined to the opinion that for purposes other than succession to real estate, for purposes unaffected by the Statute of Merton, the law of the domicile would decide the question of status. No such decision was come to, for no question arose except in relation to heirship to real estate. But the opinions given in the case seem to me to shew a strong bias towards the doctrine that the question of status must, for all purposes unaffected by the feudal law, as adopted and acted on in this country, be decided by the law of the domicile. Even, however, if that had been expressly so decided, it would not affect this case. The domicile to produce that result must be a bona fide domicile for all purposes, not, that which alone existed in this case, a mere residence of forty days, so as to give jurisdiction to the Scotch courts.

The important differences on the subject of marriage and divorce which exist in the different parts of the United Kingdom often give rise to perplexing difficulties, and exhibit a state of our law little creditable to us. But these difficulties make it more than usually incumbent on those who have to administer the law to take care that wherever a clear line has been drawn by judicial decision the course which it has marked out should be rigidly followed. Now, whatever be the difficulties in such cases as the present, I think the doctrine that no divorce in Scotland resting merely on a forum domicilii had, at all events before the passing of our English Divorce Act in 1857, any effect in England on the validity of an English marriage, is established on the highest authority.

It is impossible to have a strong authority for this than the case of *Lolley* (*R* v *Lolley* (1812) 2 Cl & Fin 567), for it was decided there by the twelve judges that by the second marriage he was guilty of bigamy, though on general principles every leaning in a criminal case would be in favour of the party accused.

That case was followed by Dr Lushington in *Conway* v *Beazley* ((1831) 3 Hag Ecc 639). There, as in the present case, the second marriage was had in Scotland, not, as in *Lolley*'s case, in England; and it was attempted on that ground to distinguish the two cases. But Dr Lushington held that the principle was the same wherever the second marriage was solemnised, for that as neither of the parties to the first marriage had been, at any time, bona fide domiciled in Scotland the principle of *Lolley*'s case must prevail.

The same question arose in this House in *Dolphin* v *Robins* ((1859) 7 HL Cas 390; 29 LJP & M 11). The case was very fully considered, and the conclusion at which your Lordships arrived unanimously was, that the Scotch courts have no power to dissolve an English marriage where the parties are not really domiciled in Scotland, but have only gone there for such a time as, according to the doctrine of the Scotch courts, gives them jurisdiction in the matter.

These cases clearly decide the one now before the House, for if the first marriage here was not dissolved there could not have been a second marriage. Till the first was dissolved there was no capacity to contract a second. If after the second marriage Buxton and Elizabeth had again cohabited, and there had been an issue, that issue would certainly have been legitimate by the law of England, and it cannot be argued that the issue of both unions could share together.

The view which I take of this case relieves me from the necessity of considering whether the resort to Scotland for the purpose of the divorce, and the arrangements made among the parties for bringing about that object, were or were not of such a character as to taint the whole of the proceedings with fraud; I am not at all satisfied that they were, but I am glad to be relieved from the necessity of deciding on such a ground.

There is only one further observation which I desire to make; it is this: In saying that the Scotch courts have no power to dissolve an English marriage where the parties have only gone to Scotland for the purpose of obtaining there a domicilium fori, I do not mean to express any opinion as to what might be the effect of a divorce so obtained considered merely as a Scotch question. In the anomalous state of our laws relating to marriage and divorce, it may be that such a proceeding may be valid to the north of the Tweed, but invalid to the south. And I am painfully sensible of the inconveniences which may result from such a state of the law. But it must be for the legislature to set it right. The authorities seem to me to shew clearly that whatever may be the just decision of the Scotch courts in such a case as the present, on this subject of divorce according to Scotch law, it is one in which this country cannot admit any right in them to interfere with the inviolability of an English marriage, or with any of its incidents. To do so would be to allow a prejudice to English law to be created by the decisions of what, for this purpose, we must call a foreign law, thus going beyond what any country is called on to do.'

To complete your order, please fill in the form below:

Module	Books required	Quantity	Price	Cost
		Postage		
		TOTAL		

For Europe, add 15% postage and packing (£20 maximum).
For the rest of the world, add 40% for airmail.

ORDERING

By telephone to Mail Order at 020 8317 6039, with your credit card to hand.

By fax to 020 8317 6004 (giving your credit card details).

Website: www.oldbaileypress.co.uk

By post to: Mail Order, Old Bailey Press at Holborn College, Woolwich Road, Charlton, London, SE7 8LN.

When ordering by post, please enclose full payment by cheque or banker's draft, or complete the credit card details below. You may also order a free catalogue of our complete range of titles from this address.

We aim to despatch your books within 3 working days of receiving your order.

Name

Address

Postcode Telephone

Total value of order, including postage: £

I enclose a cheque/banker's draft for the above sum, or

---

charge my ☐ Access/Mastercard ☐ Visa ☐ American Express

Card number

☐☐☐☐ ☐☐☐☐ ☐☐☐☐ ☐☐☐☐

Expiry date ☐☐☐☐

Signature: .... Date: ....